THE SCOTTISH MOUNTAINEERING CLUB JOURNAL

| Vol. XXXVIII | 2002 | No. 193 |

SMITH'S ROUTES – A SHORT HISTORY

By John Inglis

CLUB member John Inglis was killed in a fall from near the top of the Tough-Brown Traverse, Lochnagar on February 19, 1994. His obituary in the 1995 Journal includes the fact that he "was in the midst of preparing an article on Robin Smith when he died". Eight years on, and on the 40th anniversary of Robin's own death in the Pamirs, that article now sees the light of day. I am indebted to Jimmy Cruikshank, a contemporary and climbing partner of Robin Smith, and also his biographer, for the work he has done on the manuscript. (Ed.)

THE enduring appeal of Robin Smith's brief brilliant career owes much to his legacy of fine Scottish first ascents, in both summer and winter. Any ambitious modern climber who may know nothing of the man, his articles, or escapades, just cannot avoid the striking quality of his many fine climbs. Stated simply, most major Scottish climbing grounds explored during the late 1950s boast a 'Robin Smith Route', usually following a compelling, often inescapable, central feature, and frequently giving the best climb on the cliff.

The most famous rock climbs, such as Shibboleth (E2 5c), Yo-Yo (E1 5b), The Bat (E2 5a) and The Needle (E1 5a) all fit this description, and were recognised as classics the moment they were recorded. All four were included in the climbing anthology *Hard Rock,* with Smith responsible for almost a third of the Scottish climbs in this highly influential book. Paul Nunn and Martin Boysen, both fine English climbers, accord the climbs (and Robin) considerable praise in their accounts of The Bat and Shibboleth. Robin would have appreciated this since, despite a joyfully professed disdain for English climbs and climbers, his respect for ability scorned nationality and he greatly admired the legendary 'climbing plumbers' from Manchester, Joe Brown and Don Whillans.

Smith's best winter climbs are of a different order. In common with the rock climbs they are hard, clean (well-defined), lines, but they are unlikely

Robin Smith at Gunpowder Green, Glen Coe. Photo: Jimmy Marshall.

to be repeated in the manner in which they were originally climbed. The huge technical advances in winter climbing equipment have made the sport faster, safer, and far less strenuous than in the days when overcoming a steep ice pitch might involve hours of agonising step-cutting with a single straight-pick axe, and primitive ice piton protection. Despite impressive advances in winter standards, lines like Orion Face Direct (Grade V) and Smith's Route, Gardyloo Buttress (IV), both climbed with Jimmy Marshall in February 1960, were so far ahead of their time that they still remain two of the most sought-after hard winter routes on Ben Nevis.

A recurring feature of Smith's routes is that of 'the line', pure and logical, the ideal of the serious mountaineer. Committed climbers of all standards habitually (obsessively) trace all possible easy, hard, finest, most direct lines up any large steep obstacle. Preferably, this will be a mountain or rock face, although quarries, viaducts, and even ornate public monuments can substitute. A good natural line on a cliff taking an obvious corner, arête, or steep slab may compensate to a surprising degree for vegetatious pitches, poor protection and loose rock. These natural features are usually the most aesthetically appealing way to the top, and while standards may improve sufficiently for a particular crag to be scaled from any direction, the best climbs will tend to be the most obvious, regardless of difficulty. A balance must be struck here, since the leading climbers of each generation tend to outdo the efforts of the previous elite. Lines previously thought unjustifiable, or simply impossible, succumb to higher technical standards, improved equipment, and a diminishing sense of awe at overhanging holdless rock walls or (in winter) impending verglassed grooves. Successive waves of experts prowl the same arenas for ever harder challenges, with an ever dwindling range of options. In a sense, Robin Smith was lucky that his technical ability, intense drive, and eye for a natural line matured when they did. He was presented with, and gleefully accepted, repeated opportunities to carve out his personality with dazzling climbs on Scotland's steepest, bleakest cliffs. There were other Scots climbers at the time like John Cunningham, John McLean, and Jimmy Marshall capable of performing at Smith's standards, though few were as hungry for the direct intimidating line he so often chose. Frequently, they had their own ideas for exploration anyway. But the spur of real or imagined competition, apparent even in his earliest accounts and articles, drove Robin Smith particularly hard and must have played a part in the leap he took into new standards of climbing. His best rock routes were often quickly repeated by his immediate peers, followed by long intervals while the rest of the climbing world caught up. In winter the margin was much wider and there were virtually no takers for the Smith and Marshall Nevis routes for more than a decade.

At this stage, it may be worth considering the major changes that have taken place in climbing in the 30 years since his death. Firstly, equipment, and the associated concept of protection, have improved beyond recognition. Smith was wearing the tight-fitting rubber-soled PAs by 1958, soon after they appeared over the Channel from France. This footwear permitted a dramatic leap in technical standards, by allowing the exploitation of tiny ripples on rock as friction footholds. [Even so, according to Jimmy Marshall in 1994, Smith "regularly wore much-battered, lightweight walking boots even on some of his most significant new routes".] Today, high-friction sticky rubber boots are impregnated with resins which allow purchase on steep rock totally devoid of holds. Specialist footwear now exists for smearing, edging, limestone, gritstone, and competition climbing, always with the added allure of the season's chosen colours.

The science of rock-climbing protection has advanced substantially. Running belays in the 1950s consisted mainly of short lengths of rope or nylon threaded around rock spikes and chockstones as they were encountered on the pitch. Pitons were sparingly used for belays, even on new ground, and always with a definite reluctance – at least in the mountains. A rapid gear evolution has occurred in the last few decades, with abundant protection now provided by sophisticated wired-wedges of all shapes and sizes, and intricately engineered alloy camming devices – Friends – which adjust to fit any available crack or slot in the rock face. Ropes, karabiners and slings are all now stronger, lighter and better designed. Sit-harnesses and safety helmets have removed much of the bite from the twin hazards of falling off and of rock-fall.

As previously mentioned, winter climbing has also seen a fundamental change since Smith's day, with the advent of the dropped pick ice-tool, and the universal adoption of front-pointing technique on steep ice. Almost at a stroke this dispensed with the prodigious effort required to hack holds out of ice, allowing the exploration of longer steeper pitches than was previously possible. (It is a measure of Smith's and Marshall's achievements that their harder winter routes will remain out of reach for many modern climbers.) Improvements in clothing – lightweight waterproof 'breathable' fabric, plastic-shelled boots, and in protection – high-tech titanium ice-screws, have further cushioned winter climbing for the masses

A standardised open-ended technical grading system has been developed for rock climbing, and very recently for winter climbing, whereby the gymnastic demands of individual pitches on a climb can be precisely defined by a numerical grade, currently 4a to 7c, with the overall ferocity, or otherwise, of a route conveyed by a single adjectival grade – Difficult to Extremely Severe 9 or E9). This is very different from the situation in the 1950s and 1960s when the highest Scottish grade, Very Severe (VS), covered everything from present-day VS (now considered entirely straightforward) to horrors now belatedly graded at E3. Climbers tackling VS routes then were dependent upon the climb's word-of-mouth reputation, what they could see of it from the foot of the cliff, and from the identity of the first ascent team.

The cumulative effect of the changes outlined above has been to alter profoundly the rock-climbing experience for the ordinary climber today. Setting off up a climb armed with precise details of the barriers ahead, and with modern gear, is far less of a leap into the unknown than the equivalent trip in Smith's era. Perhaps to compensate for this, average climbing standards have rocketed, not because of increased ability but because to maintain the thrill of climbing, the boundaries must be pushed out, safety margins squeezed. Today's best climbers, gymnasium-honed, perform feats that Smith could barely have imagined, but with far less risk (the gear again) than he faced as he set off up the crux pitch of Shibboleth for the first time. Many of the routes mentioned here will remain among the finest in the country, but the real Smith legacy to Scottish climbing, the daring, brimming talent, the joyful acceptance of challenge, and the wild delight in steep places is a finer one still.

* * *

SMITH served a traditional, although rapid, rock climber's apprenticeship beginning in late 1954 with an initiation on Salisbury Crags and, shortly afterwards, at the climber's altar – Buachaille Etive Mor in Glencoe. His early efforts were overseen by Archie Hendry, a schoolmaster and a past president of the SMC and responsible for several new routes in the previous decades. Within two years, Smith had climbed most of the easier routes, and several harder ones, on the Buachaille and on the Cobbler in Arrochar, with productive visits to Skye, Ben Nevis and the Lake District. These trips were made during school holidays with Jimmy Cruickshank, although Smith also joined the Edinburgh section of the JMCS. During the winters he climbed a few easy snow gullies, but found these disconcerting compared to equivalent summer climbs. This was perhaps due to a combination of inexperience and deficient winter equipment, but there is no doubt that almost from the beginning he was aware of his natural ease on rock, while his confidence on snow and ice developed more slowly.

By the summer of 1956 he had acquired the confidence and experience to tackle VS climbs, at that time the hardest grade, and was beginning to exceed the capabilities of his regular climbing partners. This was to lead to exciting manoeuvres on occasion. In September 1956 he persuaded an inexperienced JMCS party to join him in an attempt on The Crack (HVS 5a), an infrequently attempted Nevis climb with a sinister reputation. The ensuing drama saw Smith stranded alone on the cliff, above the crux, attempting in vain to solo an overhanging chimney in the dark and almost failing to regain the sloping ledge below. After a chilly night, the dawn light revealed an escape route to easier ground just in time to avoid ignominious rescue. This instructive experience was to be related as *Twenty-four Hours,* Smith's first published article and an original, vivid piece of writing for an 18-year-old.

His first new routes were short technical test pieces on Salisbury Crags and other outcrops in the Queen's Park, where his rock technique was developed and sharpened. These steep striking cliffs dominate the city skyline, and despite a prohibition on climbing there for more than 70 years, have attracted successive generations of Edinburgh climbers [legalised for members of climbing clubs in 1994]. Harold Raeburn, one of the city's earliest climbing heroes, pioneered several short routes in the park at the turn of the century, several of which are still climbed. The rock, a rough basalt, can be loose in places, but gives good climbing over a wide range of difficulty. The Great Quarry boasts what was probably Scotland's hardest rock climb of its time, the steep, technical, and unprotected groove of Steeplejack's Staircase (now E2 5b), first led by Derek Haworth shortly after the Second World War. Smith was to make the third ascent (after Jimmy Marshall) by late 1957, as well as adding several new climbs and variations to climbs around the park. Few of these receive regular traffic, being difficult and dangerous, and with the ever-present risk of arrest by the Park Police. Names like Vertical Sand, Hell's Wall and Scuttle (all HVS grades) convey some of the flavour, if not the fear factor, of these early creations.

His first recorded mountain routes began to appear in early 1957 with Blockhead on Garbh Bheinn and Glueless Groove on the Cobbler, both now graded E1 5b. From the beginning, Smith produced routes of a high technical standard, often with little secure protection. A divergence of attitudes starts to become apparent here, as the Smith description of Blockhead, "a fine steep climb, with several small running belays", contrasts somewhat in tone with the consensus "a difficult and serious climb" in the SMC guide. In fact, Smith had been dreaming of this line for a year, first spotting (and attempting!) it during the Easter holiday in April 1956 with Jimmy Cruickshank. On his next visit to Garbh Bheinn, with EUMC novice member Victor Burton, he was already much more experienced, and the route duly conquered. Less is known about Glueless Groove (E1 5b), with no second recorded even though the climb has three pitches. It is likely that the second failed to complete the top crux pitch ("A good route, the higher the harder:" R.S.) up a steep, quartz-spattered wall. During the same Cobbler trip it is significant that Smith did two difficult existing climbs on the same face as Glueless, presumably reconnoitring the testing finish of his own route. On the University Arran meet in May, he soloed the Rosetta Stone, "a fine little mouthful to follow the South Ridge". This 30ft. HVS boulder problem had first been top-roped 63 years previously, but apparently never led before.

The summer of 1957 saw several noteworthy developments in Smith's rock-climbing. An EUMC trip to Wales resulted in the completion of more than 20 classic routes in a week, with "a rich haul in pitons, slings and karabiners...garnered". More importantly, virtually all of the then hardest VS routes on the Buachaille were hammered in May and June, in a campaign which was to yield significant returns the following year. In July, Smith travelled to the Alps for the first time with Jim Clarkson, secretary of the Edinburgh JMCS. The weather was poor that summer, but Smith completed several classics both with Clarkson and other climbers he encountered. One of these was Gunn Clark who was to partner Smith on the first British ascent of the Walker Spur two years later. Robin rounded off a good first Alpine season with a solo ascent of the NNE ridge of Aiguille de l'M.

A September trip to Skye with the University club produced two first ascents, both VS, on Sgurr nan Eag. Chasm Left Edge and Ladders ("very good pitches doubtfully connected") were noteworthy for being the first routes on this face, and for the fact that, despite three long pitches, no second was recorded for the ascent of Ladders. The final climbing flourish of the year came in Glencoe with a first winter ascent of The Long Chimney on Cuneiform Buttress, Buachaille Etive Mor in December 1957. Robin climbed with Derek Leaver, a fine mountaineer from the Edinburgh JMCS, who was to make significant later ascents with both Smith and Jimmy Marshall. On the same day as Long Chimney was climbed, Marshall, Donald Mill and George Ritchie were on the same cliff recording Cuneiform Buttress, Ordinary Route, also a Grade IV.

By now Robin had become EUMC secretary and was climbing almost every weekend. Despite apparently effortless progress in philosophy, mountains had become an obsession, and much of his time in Edinburgh was spent plotting the summer's ploys. He had become widely known in Scottish climbing circles, and from this point onwards was increasingly mentioned in the accounts and articles of others. He was also developing his own writing style, producing a string of memorable, intricately crafted pieces around his major routes and adventures. More than any other source, these articles epitomise the atmosphere of the time and are worth reading in their entirety.

Activities in 1958 began with several very hard winter ascents including Crowberry Ridge Direct IV/V and ("most of") Eagle Ridge (V) on Lochnagar. The apprehension felt on the earlier winter climbs had obviously been exorcised, although he had not yet reached the standards of the remarkable Jimmy Marshall who poached the first winter ascent of Parallel B Gully (V) from under Aberdonian noses as Smith toiled up and down Eagle Ridge. The rock climbing year began with a second trip to Wales, where Smith made an early lead of Joe Brown's Cenotaph Corner (E1 5c), perhaps the most famous hard rock climb in Britain. This was completed at a leisurely pace, Smith claiming that he didn't want to "embarrass the natives". In common with Joe Brown, Smith was never renowned for his speed of climbing. Slow steady climbing on difficult rock often indicates great ability, combining the stamina and poise required to rest in strenuous positions with a fierce controlled drive to decipher and execute hard moves overhead. A meet in the Lake District in May resulted in on-sight first ascents of Chartreuse (E1 5a) and Leverage (E1 5a) on Scafell's fierce East Buttress. Both climbs are now graded Extreme, reflecting the paucity of protection rather than technical severity. The current Scafell guide mentions "a superb day's work by one of Britain's best climbers". Derek Leaver seconded Chartreuse but, oddly, was not mentioned in the original description of Leverage; once again the crux pitch may have been unseconded or rope assisted.

Back in Scotland, and pausing only for a new route on Edinburgh Castle Rock during Students' Charities' Week, Smith settled down for a concentrated spell of exploration in Glencoe. He had already settled on his major summer project – a central line up the awesomely steep and intimidating Slime Wall on the Buachaille. This cliff had received increasing attention in the preceding two years, most notably from Pat Walsh, a prominent member of the Glasgow-based Creagh Dhu. Walsh had put up no less than five routes here in the summer of 1956, and despite the addition of the elegant Link Pitch by Marshall the following year, there was a widely held Glaswegian view that the Slime Wall was Creagh Dhu property. Smith had repeated some of the Walsh routes in summer 1957, and now conceived of a grand scheme to register his arrival at the forefront of Scottish climbing (in time for the forthcoming Glencoe guidebook), and simultaneously to restore Edinburgh prestige in a friendly inter-city rivalry. While the rock dried out, and between preliminary sorties to monitor the state of the weeping crux groove, various other new lines in the vicinity were snapped up.

Much of this climbing was done with Andrew Fraser, a fellow student who had seconded the Edinburgh Castle Closet Climb (HS). Together they recorded two more Buachaille first ascents with Dwindle Wall (HVS) and the strenuous July Crack (HVS), which the pair had mistaken for the much easier August Crack! There was time for a trip down the glen to the North Face of Aonach Dubh and the route that was to become Yo-Yo (E1 5b). Smith and David Hughes, also EUMC, forced the first section. Halfway up a monolithic corner fault it was with delight, "some trophy", that Smith recovered Don Whillans's peg hammer from below the climb, tangible evidence of success where the master had retreated. But better was to come…

The following day, Smith and Andrew Fraser breached the Slime Wall with the first three pitches, and crux, of 'the big line'. Shibboleth (E2 5c) is considered by many to be Robin Smith's finest piece of work, taking a great central groove up through desperately sustained, steep, almost featureless rock. The pair then escaped up the easier finish (still VS) of Revelation, returning the next day to add the finishing pitches, after an approach avoiding the crux groove. The following weekend was set aside for the first all-in-a-day ascent, including a new and difficult fourth pitch to give a completely independent line. This was almost achieved as planned, although it was to be the events surrounding the climb that made banner headlines in the *Daily Record* two days later. This front-page scoop featured the dramatic all-night rescue of Fraser, who had fallen, exhausted, while leading the penultimate 'easy' pitch (still 5a), breaking his leg. The accident played its part in the notoriety that Shibboleth quickly acquired, while Smith's heroics during the rescue only underlined the fact that he had charged into the front rank of British rock climbing in less than four years.

The 1958 Alpine season saw Robin completing two hard routes with two well-known English climbers. With Trevor Jones, he made what was only the second complete ascent of the Voie Britannique on the Aiguille de Blaitiere West Face. This had first been climbed by Joe Brown and Don Whillans in 1954, and was one of the routes which had heralded a resurgence of the best British climbers to top post-war European standards. Teaming up with Joe 'Mortimer' Smith, Robin then climbed the West Face of the Petit Dru, finding it "more magnificent and serious", despite a "vast excess of pegs". Morty Smith played a central role in the saga of the legendary Rock and Ice Club (the dominant force in 1950s' English rock climbing), and had the impressive reputation of being physically stronger than either Brown or Whillans.

The remainder of Robin's year was without recorded climbing incident. In August, John Cunningham and Mick Noon had produced Carnivore (E2 5c), a futuristic wall climb on the Buachaille, to maintain a high Creagh Dhu profile in the area. The following month, Jimmy Marshall and Derek Leaver climbed Trapeze (E1 5a), a striking corner line on E Buttress, Aonach Dubh to complete a golden summer of Glencoe exploration. Also in September Smith submitted his SMC application, proposed by Archie Hendry and seconded by Jimmy Marshall. He was duly admitted in October along with Derek Leaver, Ronnie Marshall, and the Aberdonians Ronnie Sellars and Graeme Nicol.

Smith immediately exercised his right to use of the CIC Hut below the cliffs of Ben Nevis on a visit with Dick Holt, an EUMC member. On New

Year's Day, 1959 they recorded Tower Face of the Comb (now Grade V), and soon afterwards Orion Face (V), described as "a great route" in a current guide. The latter climb was the first in winter to directly tackle the huge west face of North East Buttress, the highest continuous cliff in Britain, and one shortly to receive further attention from Smith. A second winter contingent including Jimmy Marshall and Dougal Haston chose to spend the New Year in Glencoe, at the Lagangarbh hut. No climbing was done here until the third of January, although it is not clear whether this was due to adverse weather conditions or the comforts of nearby Kingshouse Hotel. Marshall had already acquired the reputation he retains today as one of Scotland's best winter climbers, perhaps only rivalled at that time by the great Tom Patey. In the following few weeks, Marshall was to add the superb Smith's Gully (Grade V) and 1959 Face Route (IV) to Creag Meaghaidh, and Minus Two Gully (V) and Hadrian's Wall (IV) to his list of fine winter routes on Ben Nevis. Smith spent the early summer in Glencoe adding the finishing touches to Yo-Yo with David Hughes, and a 'true finish' to Shibboleth, up an impressive overhanging crack, with John McLean of the Creagh Dhu. This characteristic tendency to edit and improve was a hallmark of Smith's attitude to his climbing, and he clearly valued the long-term aesthetic impact of his best lines as well as the transient pleasure of their execution. "A conscious and disciplined artist in all things essential" was Geoff Dutton's considered judgement in the 1962 SMCJ. He found time to prospect a new project on the Great Buttress of Carn Dearg, Ben Nevis, where he had spotted a steep corner between the Brown/Whillans/Downes classics Sassenach (E1 5a) and Centurion (HVS 5a). These fine English lines on a superb Scottish cliff were seen as an affront to national pride, almost an international version of the Edinburgh/Glasgow Slime Wall rivalry from the year before. In the company of Dick Holt a devious but determined approach pitch was established, with a rightwards traverse from Centurion weaving across an impressive sweep of undercut and overhanging slabs. Bad weather intervened, and it was time for the Alps again.

Two days after arriving in Chamonix, Robin and Gunn Clark scored a notable success as the first British climbers to overcome the 4000ft. Walker Spur on the North Face of the Grand Jorasses. Equalled in fame only by the North Face of the Eiger, it was at the time considered one of the hardest classic Alpine routes and is perhaps still the finest. A day behind Smith and Clark, a party comprising Chris Bonington, Don Whillans, Hamish MacInnes, Les Brown and John Streetly repeated the climb, under the impression that they would be the first to achieve this coup. The discovery of jammed rope slings (peculiar to British climbers) and Smartie packets *en route* aroused the suspicions of MacInnes, confirmed by the appearance of the dishevelled but exultant Smith and Clark as the second party came off the mountain. For Robin, several weeks of 'misadventures' (no big routes) followed, with three hard climbs in the Dolomites, one a Grade 6 solo, right at the end of the trip. Sweeping straight back to Ben Nevis, The Bat was completed with Dougal Haston, "the only climber I could find", filling in for Dick Holt who had exam re-sits. If Shibboleth is Smith's greatest rock climb, then *The Bat and the Wicked,* which related the tortuous development of this latest triumph in the 1960 SMCJ may well be his most accomplished written piece. It captures Smith, Haston and the whole spirit of late 1950s climbing as nothing before it; a rip-roaring rock epic, with cultural and philosophical asides. To appreciate Robin Smith's rich talent, his intellect, his tenacity, and his sardonic glee in life, it has to be read. Countless articles in club journals have been modelled on it ever since, and in 1979 the mountaineering film-maker Jim Curran was inspired to film the story using real climbers and the original location.

Back to dry fact. In September John McLean enlisted Smith's help for the final assembly of The Long Wait (E2 5b) on the Etive Slabs. The route had been gradually pieced together by McLean in the company of Cunningham, Noon and Whillans, and now Smith led the completed pitches leaving the finish to McLean; presumably in a neat reversal of the Shibboleth True Finish climb earlier in the year.

The winter arrived, and Smith teamed up with Jimmy Marshall for a week on Ben Nevis in February 1960. What followed was to be the most written about and analysed goldrush in Scottish winter climbing. Conditions were superb, both men at their physical and psychological peak, and well aware that they were creating history. The CIC logbook entry is a model of dry, crafted wit; laconic in the route descriptions, and detailing their mid-week marathon winter hike and pub crawl in a few crisp phrases. Both Smith and Marshall wrote articles on the climbs for the following year's SMC, and these too have become part of the legend. Ken Crocket devotes almost a chapter, *The Pinnacle,* to the events of this period in his definitive history of climbing on Ben Nevis, and it seems superfluous to discuss them in detail here. A welter of routes, The Great Chimney (Grade IV), Minus Three Gully (IV), the superb Smith's Route (Gardyloo Buttress) (IV), and Observatory Buttress (Ordinary Route) (V), all new and all hard, were climbed on consecutive days. There followed the second ascent of Point Five Gully (V), a seven-hour romp achieved in far better style than the original, multi-bolted, five-day siege conducted by Ian Clough the previous winter. A well-earned rest day was next for Smith and Marshall, featuring a marathon 20-mile hill walk, pub crawl, arrest ("21.15 Police Station: Interrogation, Confession, Humiliation, Dismissal") and return to the hut by midnight. The final two days saw a return to exploration with Piggot's Route (The Comb) (V), and the gem of the week, Orion Face Direct (V), "one of the finest winter lines in

Scotland". This climb more than any other by Smith and Marshall captured the spirit of the week, and the imagination of Scottish climbers for decades. Orion Direct ventures through similar terrain to Smith and Holt's Orion Face, and may be no harder, but more than any other winter route of the time it was Alpine in both scale and conception. Marshall was to be married a month later, and as befitted what might have been his last big new route, he got most of the good (hardest) leading to do. Smith was later to complain in print that this had happened all week.

Towards the end of March Dougal Haston and Andy Wightman (both EUMC) made a half-hearted attempt at only the second ascent of Zero Gully (V), to be joined by Smith at the CIC hut late that evening. Starting at 2pm next day the three returned to the assault, Smith leading, using Haston's axe and a rope 'borrowed' from the hut. Haston's choice of *Nightshift in Zero* to title his later account of the climb seems almost understated; they did not reach the hut again till dawn. The CIC logbook entry for 23.3.60 merely reads "Zero Gully, quite hard conditions, n hours, D. Haston, R. Smith, A. Wightman".

By this stage, Robin was confidently climbing new lines on any cliff he visited. April saw the fall of the impressive Thunder Rib (HVS 5a) on Sgurr a'Mhadaidh in Skye, a much-eyed but persistently virgin 1000 ft. of loose rock. On Carnmore Crag in Wester Ross, he produced Gob (HVS 5a) with Haston, another of the five Smith routes in the *Hard Rock* anthology ("Gob' is good Gaelic...beak of a bird", but the more abrasive Haston edge is becoming apparent). It was the adventure of climbing, not new routes, that was important though. The Lagangarbh log for April mentions an ascent of Raven's Gully on the Buachaille: "Snow, boulders, etc., very wet" by a Smith-led EUMC party comprising Howard Andrew, John Lever, Jim Rorke, and a mended Andrew Fraser. With James 'Big Elly' Moriarty, two less spectacular Glencoe routes Yo-Yo (continued) and Dan (E1) on the Upper Etive Slabs were made in May, and with John Hawkshaw (EUMC), a last rock climb on Ben Nevis, Central Route (HVS 5a) on Minus Two Buttress.

The summer was enlivened by the Russian visit, a group of Soviet climbers (and assumed political theorists) invited over by the SMC and Alpine Club to further international relations. As a leading Scots climber, Robin was selected to entertain the harder Russian climbers, and also commissioned to report upon events for the SMCJ. *A Week on the Hills* is a short, complex, scathing masterpiece, poking fun at several establishment figures, although altogether free of malice. Together with George Ritchie, there was time after the day's guiding duties to make a first ascent of Marshall's Wall (E1 5b) in the Lost Valley, an ahead-of-its-time steep wall climb earlier 'investigated' by Jimmy Marshall. The name neatly repaid the ironic debt of Smith's Gully, climbed the previous winter by Marshall and Tiso, after a rare Smith defeat.

That summer, the weather in the Alps was poor, with a first British ascent of the Fiescherhorn Norpfeiler by Smith and Brian Wakefield (EUMC) the only real achievement, featuring "unpremeditated bivouacs before, during, and after". Smith joined Haston for a sojourn under the North Face of the Eiger, then, frustrated by conditions, moved on to Chamonix where desultory attempts on the unclimbed South-east Face of the Fou in the company of Joe Brown and Dennis Gray were rained off.

The next Smith encounter with the aristocracy of English rock climbing occurred only a month later at Lagangarbh in Glencoe. Allan Austin, who was up for a week's climbing with the equally talented Eric 'Matey' Metcalf, later wryly described the incident in *A Guided Tour*. Smith and Moriarty persuaded the English pair that Clachaig Gully (Severe) was a good wet weather climb, and proceeded to steer them up a series of increasingly sheer waterfalls ("regrettable misdirections by Mr Smith"). Robin would derive some good-humoured pleasure from his victims' discomfiture; Austin, an outstanding 1960s Lake District climber, had produced (with Metcalf) the superb slab climb Astra (E2 5b) on Pavey Ark in Langdale earlier in the year, and both were fair game for a sandbagging.

The winters which began the 1960s were remarkable for their lack of exploratory climbing in Scotland, due mainly to indifferent conditions, but also perhaps a hangover from the momentous events of February and March 1960 – Vanishing Gully (V) by Graham Tiso and Ronnie Marshall being a fine exception. Only one Smith route is recorded for the winter of 1961, a comparative stroll, in the company of Dougal Haston, up the gentle summer line of Jubilee Climb (II), on the Central Trident Buttress, Ben Nevis. Similarly, just one new route emerged from the pre-Alps summer on a trip to Garbh Bheinn, scene of Robin's first big route Blockhead. The Peeler (HVS 5b) was climbed with Elly Moriarty, who had become a regular summer partner since before the Russian visit. The main event of the early summer belonged to Jimmy Marshall who found an unlikely rising traverse across the steep front of Carn Dearg Buttress, featuring a crux descent move on the fourth pitch. Climbed with Jimmy Stenhouse, The Bullroar (HVS 5a) may be Marshall's best of many Nevis rock climbs, and it remains highly regarded today. Two weeks later, Smith and Moriarty conducted their own more whimsical tour of the buttress, climbing a hybrid of The Bat and Centurion incorporating most of the hard pitches from each.

Smith, Haston and two other EUMC members, Sheila Samuelson and Rosemary Brindle, drove out to the Alps where they "abortively and disjointedly assaulted the North Face and Hornli Ridge of the Matterhorn". Moving on to the Dolomites, Smith and Haston made an agonising first Scottish ascent of the Swiss Direttissima on the North Face of the Cima

Ovest de Lavaredo. This wall is largely overhanging, with the occasional monster roof, and both climbers found the almost uninterrupted aid climbing arduous and brutally abrasive to fingers and knuckles. Their "cunning plan" to ferry supplies from the support party at the foot of the climb went hilariously wrong, due to navigational mishap, horrendous rope snarl, and sheer exhaustion. Smith's bitterly funny version of events in *Snakes and Ladders* was his last published article, *Nocturnal* (1960-61 EUMC Journal – *Nocturnal*), and has to be read to be believed.

It is difficult to avoid viewing the remainder of 1961 in the light of the following year, and what appears now as a last rush to record new routes across the whole country was presumably just Robin Smith operating at normal intensity after a frustrating summer. By August, his recovery from the Cima Ovest ordeal was sufficient to pioneer yet another Glencoe classic, The Big Top (E1 5a), with Jimmy Gardner on Aonach Dubh's West Face. The route is bold rather than unduly technical, and fatal leader falls have occurred on the poorly protected top pitch; the current SMC guide describes it as one of the 10 best climbs in the area.

Trips to Hell's Lum Crag in the Cairngorms – The Clean Sweep (VS 4a), the best route on the cliff, and Coire Mhic Fearchair of Bheinn Eighe – Boggle (E1 5b), which set an entirely new standard for rock climbing in Torridon) stand out from the autumn's list of new climbs. The Clean Sweep probably receives more ascents than any other Smith mountain route, due to its good protection, and comparative lack of severity as much as its undoubted quality. Although originally graded Severe by Smith and Tiso, it is now considered to be a full-weight Very Severe (4a).

A Lakes expedition to Gimmer Crag in Langdale with Moriarty resulted in two climbs, neither of which have survived to the present guidebook. Gee-Gee, a slightly contrived line "to the right of 'F'-route…blinkers were worn to conceal escape routes" is unmourned, but Variant to Variant to Kipling's Groove was a steep bold wall pitch which was later incorporated into Allan Austin's classic assembly Gimmer String (E1 5b). Revenge for a soaking perhaps.

There are few recorded details of Smith's activities in his last winter season, although the CIC logbook records a solo ascent of Tower Ridge on Ben Nevis in November. He was editor of the EUMC *Nocturnal* that year (a nod to the benightments that had become routine where he and Haston were concerned) and produced a notably literary issue, including two of his own articles, and Haston's *Nightshift in Zero*. In January 1962, he visited Chamonix, becoming an early British exponent of winter alpinism. This was a very recent development in the early 1960s, although later to be pursued with great success by Dougal Haston. Smith's mountaineering ambitions were certainly turning towards the greater ranges by this time, with the accessibility of the Alps a key factor in his choice of London as the venue for intended Ph.D. studies.

Things go quiet again until the EUMC 'Easter Parade' at Lagangarbh in Glencoe. By now a rowdy, hard-climbing splinter group had emerged from the EUMC, featuring Haston, Neil Macniven, Wightman, and a young Robin Campbell, with Ronnie Marshall and Elly Moriarty as SMC support. Smith missed that chaotic April weekend which featured such interesting in-hut activities as 'The Sitting-Room Traverse'; Lagangarbh was left in some disarray, after the Parade "had gone through it like a bomb". (Entry in the Lagangarbh log by the next hut occupiers). However, the group also did a considerable amount of high standard climbing including the often-attempted North Face Girdle of Aonach Dubh (E2 5b) by Campbell, Haston, Macniven, and Smith. This 1000-foot *tour-de-force,* later described in Campbell's SMCJ article *The Ugly Sister* ended in darkness, but despite their exertions, Smith and Macniven found the energy to assault Cunningham's Carnivore the next day.

On June 8, 1962, Robin Smith recorded his last new route in Scotland. The Needle (E1 5a) on the Shelter Stone Crag in the Cairngorms directly attacks the "manifestly impossible…great vertical bastion" mentioned in the 1961 guidebook, tracing a sustained line through the lower slabs and walls to thread the (easier!) overhanging chimney-crack on the final pitch. Before the arrival of Smith and Davie Agnew, ventures onto the Shelter Stone face had been few, and unsuccessful. The closest approach had been Citadel (VS, 1958), some way off to the left. Presumably, some reconnaissance had been carried out the previous September, when The Clean Sweep was climbed just across the corrie. Today, The Needle remains one of the Northern Cairngorms' most popular Extreme climbs and, as Smith's final contribution to Scottish rock climbing, is a fitting monument to the brilliance of his route-finding abilities and climbing technique. He left for the Pamirs three weeks later.

CLIMBING IN THE COLD

By Mick Fowler

THE appeal of Scottish winter climbing is not something readily understood by the average person. I have to admit that I too struggled to come to terms with it. Perhaps though, that is one of the attractions. Successes that are won too easily are inevitably those that are the least rewarding.

My first attempts to savour the pleasures were back in the mid-1970s. At that time I was based in London, pennies were tight and I depended on the cheapest possible reliable form of transport – in those days an Austin Mini-van. I got through 13 in all before moving on to other vehicles. By buying them second-hand from small businesses, running up perhaps 25,000 miles on weekend climbing trips and then selling them six months later as a 'private' owner, I usually broke even or made a small profit. There were two engine sizes, 850cc and 1000cc. The 1000cc engines were much better but somehow I tended to end up with 850cc ones. Either way, the drive to Scotland seemed to be a long way, although we were spurred on by stories we had been told about glorious, crisp, clear days and fantastic climbing.

The usual form was to keep the driver awake through the night by quizzes based on climbing guidebooks. For some reason this has left me with an encyclopaedic knowledge of the Crew/Harris 1970 guidebook to Tremadoc. Why this should be so, when so many more hours were spent testing each other on the Scottish guides, I do not know – but if anyone is interested I can still, to this day, reel off the graded list of Tremadoc extremes in the 1970 guide. (Best steer clear of me at parties, when too much alcohol tends to prompt recitals whether asked for or not!)

My regular climbing partners in those early days were Mike Morrison and John Stevenson, both south Londoners who, like me, had an urge to escape the smoke whenever possible. One of my earliest Scottish memories is of arriving in Glencoe intent on spending a week front-pointing up crisply frozen classics. The rain poured incessantly and the water by the Clachaig Inn was ankle deep. In the then harshly cold confines of the public bar (up to then the only place I had ever worn my down jacket), we were just in time to hear the well known guide Terry Taylor say how good Zero Gully on Ben Nevis had been the day before. We were gutted. Were we too late? Had we missed the 'conditions'? "What do you think about tomorrow?" we inquired naively. "Only one way to find out," came the calm and practical reply.

But we hadn't learned the game by then. We equated wind and rain in Glencoe to wind and rain on the Ben, (bad mistake this!) and spent a whole week drinking in the Clachaig and splashing our way up wet snow slopes. I remember John being particularly excited when he was able to find a section of ice substantial enough to get four or five consecutive placements in. Looking back, Ben Nevis was probably in excellent condition or, as Gordon Smith – a keen activist of the time – once entered into the CIC Hut log book: "Ground conditions excellent, air conditions disgusting."

I liked that comment; to me it summed up the unique flavour of Scottish winter climbing.

One week in particular sticks in my mind as the turning point in my attitude to the Scottish winter. In 1978 there had been magnificent conditions in North Wales, and Mike Morrison and I had spent a superb week ticking off unclimbed, or rarely repeated, ice streaks throughout Snowdonia. It wasn't that we were particularly talented, it was simply that, after a series of lean years, winter climbing was nowhere near as popular as it is today. We couldn't help but conclude that, if Snowdonia plums like the 300ft. Craig Rhaeddr waterfalls in the Llanberis Pass were unclimbed, then the scope for adventurous action in Scotland must be unlimited. So in 1979, Victor Saunders and I got together to take advantage of two unfilled places, booked by the Croydon Mountaineering Club, in the CIC Hut on Ben Nevis.

It was the first time that I remember climbing with Victor. True to form, he had introduced some uncertainty into the proceedings by arranging that we would give a lift to a friend of his. I never did work out quite who this chap was, but on the drive up it became clear that, while we had decided to climb in Glencoe on the Saturday, this chap wanted to be dropped off in Fort-William, 30 miles or so farther on. For some reason I refused to let anyone else drive, with the result that, by the time the trusty mini-van had rumbled its way from London up to Fort-William and back to Glencoe, I was falling asleep badly and not feeling at my perkiest. I can still vividly recall hallucinating and swerving sharply to avoid imaginary (well I think they were!) animals on the road. In contrast, the Saunders body had snoozed gently all the way up and was nauseatingly enthusiastic. Somehow we struggled up Raven's Direct before returning to Fort-William and taking up our places at the hut late that night.

Times had moved on in the years since our early week splashing about in Glencoe, and I had made a couple more attempts to get into winter climbing on the Ben. Success had been very limited. Once, Mike Morrison and I camped about an hour short of the hut. We managed to climb Zero Gully, but my main memory is of our much-prized tent freezing to the ground and the bottom parting company with the rest when we tried to prise it away.

On another occasion, Phil Thomas and I tried to camp outside the hut

Mick Fowler on the first ascent of 'Ice Bomb' (Fowler Grade V/VI) Coire Ghranda, Beinn Dearg. Photo: Dave Wilkinson.

itself. Arriving in the dark, we discovered that we had somehow forgotten the poles, and so tried to use the fabric to construct a bivouac of sorts against the wall of the hut. It was a foul night, and at about 9pm a very refined sounding gentleman ventured out to complain that, firstly, we were breaking rules by using the hut wall as a shelter, and secondly, we were irresponsible in not treating the Highland weather with the respect it deserved. The tone of his voice was such that we felt inclined to take up semi-permanent residence. But as the night progressed, the cold seeped in and discomfort grew, to the extent that a foray down to Fort-William to pick up the poles was deemed in order. Come the morning, there was much unhappiness when our plans to be the first away were thwarted by he who had upset us the previous night stepping briskly from the cosy interior and striding purposefully up ahead of us.

But I digress. This time I was inside the hut for the first time. It all seemed so unethically easy. The Ben was there on our doorstep, and Victor was his usual, irrepressible self with a long tick list of routes to do. Success on new winter routes in Wales had led me to view the Ben differently than on previous visits and I couldn't help but notice a thin ice streak dribbling down the right hand side of Carn Dearg buttress. The classic routes attracted us more to begin with, but by late in the week we decided to give it a go and managed Shield Direct, our first new winter line in Scotland. I remember clearly feeling that, if obvious ice streaks were unclimbed on popular crags like the Ben, then the possibilities elsewhere in the Highlands must be immense. I also remember the route being heralded as the first Scottish Grade VI. Victor and I had graded it V, and never did quite understand how it came to be rated VI before anyone had repeated it. Not to worry; it was good for the ego!

By the end of the week the Fowler body was knackered. It was tough going to climb big routes every day, even from the luxury of the CIC Hut. Also, the hut was only convenient for the Ben, and looked like being a one-off experience anyway. A different approach was clearly necessary if we were to make any impact on the more remote crags up in the North West.

For some years, a group of us from London spent a week or so roaming Scotland at Christmas and New Year. The weather was invariably poor, and most of the time was spent checking out various (very fine) drinking spots in the North West. But, in between the sheets of rain, we did manage to explore some of the areas that we were interested in. Applecross, Torridon, Achnashellach – all names that I had heard of, read about and longed to visit. And all of them appeared to have unclimbed ice streaks adorning rarely visited corries. We managed a few routes, things like Sheet Whitening in Applecross, on these early ventures, but they tended to be one-offs from the road or outings from damp bivouacs under boulders. It

Jamie Andrew back in winter action, climbing 'Left Twin' (Grade III) Aonach Mor. Photo: Chris Pasteur.

wasn't until we had pinpointed venues and weekend trips started in earnest that we really got to grips with the almost unlimited severity on offer in the North West.

Partly, I suppose, it was better roads that allowed the introduction of the weekly dash from London – but it was also a matter of learning from experience. I have never been the world's best walker (many would put it stronger than that), and experience was beginning to show that more than a couple of consecutive days on the Scottish hills led to increasing lethargy and unproductive time away from the desk. Weekends were much better. Even I could keep going for two days with five at the sedentary office desk in between. In driving terms, 650 miles had to be looked at as just over 150 each. Then it somehow all seemed a bit more manageable.

Fellow weekenders were not difficult to come across. I have always thought that one of the best things about London is that, whatever perverse urge one has for the weekend, like-minded characters always seem to materialize. In climbing terms this meant that there was always a full car, whether the venue was chalk cliffs on the south coast or ice streaks in the north of Scotland.

In the 1980s and early 1990s there were some real characters on the scene. Strange nicknames came their way: Phil 'Lobby' Butler (after being memorably buried alive by an avalanche of lobster pots); Jon 'Carless' Lincoln after his reluctance to buy a car; Chris 'One Pint' Watts after an infamous Chinese drinking occasion; Dave 'Willie' Wills named after I don't know what; and Phil 'Ode' Thornhill named for reasons I won't go into. And there were others too – Simon Fenwick, Danuska Rycerz, Peta Watts, Henry Todd…wild and interesting characters; the list was long and easily drawn upon.

A full pool of willing activists meant regular visits – 11 weekends in a row being my personal record – and an ability to keep abreast of the conditions. If it was pretty good in, say, Applecross one weekend, close monitoring of the temperature reports during the week meant that we had a very good idea of what things were likely to be like in, say, Skye the following weekend. Of course, the more we climbed, the more objectives we spotted. The list of 'possibilities' grew distressingly long, so long that I am glad to say that many still remain today.

The North West became a firm favourite, its relative remoteness and lack of people being particular attractions. It is interesting to note the increasing popularity of this area over the last 20 years. When I first started venturing this way in the late 1970s, a strong group of people wanted not to record climbs and keep the place a wilderness area. The guidebooks that did exist were hopelessly out of date, and it is fair to say that I cannot recall ever meeting another climber on the hills in winter. It was fantastic. By the mid to late 1980s we would meet the odd enthusiast, but these were virtually always people we knew. The 1990s saw a sea change, with glossy guidebooks sporting photos of instantly attractive climbs, the number of activists increased sharply and, shock horror, we began to come across other climbing parties that we didn't know.

But the North West is a long way from the centres of population, and competition for the plethora of new lines was limited. Andy Nisbet, as ever, was in action on a broad front, as were people like Rab Anderson and Martin Moran. Martin in particular tended to have a similar eye for a line to me. On at least two occasions we ended up competing for the same route.

Once we were a bit uncertain about the conditions, and so I telephoned him on a Friday night before leaving London. We chatted for a bit, confirmed that it sounded worth going, and headed up to Achnashellach, just a few miles from his home in Lochcarron. Parking by the station at 5am or so, we set off immediately (experience having shown that trying to catch a quick snooze in the car is a bad idea) and, even at my pace, managed to arrive at Fuar Tholl's main cliff by 8am or so. This is an excellent, rarely-visited venue, which streaks up well in the right conditions. I remembered that when climbing the central streak, Tholl Gate, (in the conditions an outrageous lead by the normally reserved Phil Butler) there was another streak adorning the wall to the right. This was what we were heading for. Amazingly, Martin was too. Out of all the unclimbed lines throughout the North West, we had somehow chosen to head for the same objective on the same day.

They followed us up one pitch behind. Even I felt a bit guilty – after all it was Martin who had been good enough to admit that conditions were pretty good. Without his advice we might easily have gone elsewhere.

A similar situation, though not quite so close, arose on Skye. Here, Deep Gash Gully, on Sgurr a'Mhadaidh was, for those in the know, an obvious winter challenge. Frankly, I was not completely 'in the know', but I was very aware of the guidebook description which referred to the summer climb as being deeply cut, normally damp, greasy and, at HVS, challenging.

From previous jaunts in the area, particularly Waterpipe Gully where Doug Scott beat Victor and myself to the first winter ascent by one day, I was vaguely aware that there was a gully of sorts up there, but I had no real idea about how good it might be. Jon Lincoln and I just about managed it in time to spend a relaxing evening in the Sligachan lounge – a special Skye attraction complete with roasting log fire and snoozing *in situ* Labrador. We didn't get round to recording it for a few weeks, in which time Martin had repeated the climb, thinking he was doing the first winter ascent – sorry Martin.

In line with the increasing popularity we had noticed elsewhere, other climbers were visible (in the distance admittedly) when we finished Deep Gash Gully in 1991. Even so the sight of an unattended car parked after dark on the Glenbrittle road was so unusual as to be brought to the attention of the police.

Other areas too produced their fair share of memorable action. Applecross became a favourite, and I well remember doing Gully-of-the-Gods on Bheinn Bhan with the classic East End character Simon Fenwick. This, we knew, had been attempted way back, around 1960, by the intrepid duo of Chris Bonington and Tom Patey. We had sniffed around at the base during one of our Christmas/New Year forays, and so knew it to be an intimidating parallel-sided wet gully, which might ice up well.

At our walking speed it was near on five hours to get to the foot of the crag, but it was worth it. We were rewarded with orgasmic conditions. Ice smeared the sides of the weeping fault line and it was one of those 'now or never' days.

Simon announced that he felt ill. He looked distinctly pale. Clearly, he wasn't joking. But turning back now, when faced with such perfect conditions, was out of the question. We must have made an unusual first ascent team. At one point Simon stopped seconding and I spent some time pulling as hard as I've ever pulled, only to discover that he had clipped into a peg to be sick. But regular blasts of wind-whipped snow in the face were clearly what the doctor ordered – or perhaps good Scottish winter days are a tonic in themselves. Either way, the Fenwick body was clearly in better condition at the top than it had been at the bottom. Probably a first.

Andy Nisbet has long been one of the most prolific and respected activists on the Scottish winter scene. I first remember meeting him on the North Face of the Eiger way back in 1980, but it was some time later, at the roadside below Creag Meaghaidh, that I first recall coming across him in his native environment.

Victor Saunders and I had just completed a rather faltering drive from London. What, with a miraculously disconnecting distributor cap and spells of challengingly slippery roads, we eventually arrived just in time to see a torch click on in a small roadside tent. A head poked out and the unmistakable outline of the Nisbet beard glistened in the moonlight. We regarded each other blearily, and spoke only enough to confirm that both teams were heading for the Pinnacle area. I didn't really need to know any more. I had already driven literally thousands of miles in an effort to nab the first full ascent of an obvious direct winter line based on the semi-sieged line of 'The Fly'. The chances that Andy would be he heading for the same line were distinctly high.

But the Nisbet body was bound to be a speedy walker. Victor looked distressed but knew that, with me present, we would inevitably lose any walking race. In any event, by the time we were ready to leave the Nisbet team was surging forth. I tried ineffectually to run after Victor – but it was clearly hopeless. The snow underfoot was crisp and frozen; there was one slim possibility that sprang to mind – the river bed. The end result was a first (and probably a last) in Fowler walking history. Victor and I crunched crisply along the smooth snow of the river bed while the Nisbet team followed the longer route along the path. We arrived perhaps five minutes before them, and stepped briskly on to the perfect ice streaks of Fly Direct.

All those miles of driving had been worthwhile; the conditions were the best I had ever seen on Creag Meaghaidh. White ice drooled down the lower slabs and choked the 600ft. corner line which formed the meat of the route. We twanged our way upwards while Andy contented himself with yet another Nisbet first, The Midge, just to our right. It was one of those rare days when everything goes exactly according to plan. Lying in the sun on top of Creag Meaghaidh was a moment to be savoured. Victor was bouncing uncontrollably as he does when excited.

So, on the Sunday, we found ourselves in Glencoe peering up at a hanging ice streak up and to the left of the well known column of Elliott's Downfall. Our approach had been interestingly unconventional, and at one point involved overcoming a particularly steep rock wall by clambering up a handy, if fragile, tree. It wasn't until we were roping up beneath the line that Victor realized that he had left his axes behind.

"You lead and slide yours down the rope." He suggested. And so I set off on disturbingly steep and brittle ice, clipping in just one of our two ropes.

The pitch was insecure and unnerving, to the extent that I felt increasingly uncomfortable with this arrangement. Eventually, I pulled on to a ledge and belayed. Looking up, it was clear that we were above the main difficulties, and without a further thought I clipped both axes into the free rope and let them zoom off out of sight. The pitch was vertical for some distance, and the axes descended most efficiently. Regrettably, I was unable to see Victor's strenuous efforts to run away from a couple of kilos of sharpened steel homing in on him. Being tied onto the other end of the rope there was no escape and after fruitless exertions he bore the full force of two axes from 50m. A muffled cry reached me, and it was a not very pleased Mr Saunders who arrived at the stance some time later. As he led off, I made very sure that the Fowler body was protected by an early runner in both ropes.

To me these recollections sum up a lot about Scottish winter climbing. Conditions are fickle, early starts wearing and success comes only to those that persevere. But the memories bite deeply, the friendships are warm and the pleasures long lasting. These are the important things. I remain hooked.

THE CROW

By Nic Bullivant

THE crow. It must have been the crow. I woke involuntarily, sweating, despite the cold. It was pitch dark in the snow hole. Why had I decided to bother snow holing? It was one of those rare windless winter nights. A tent would have been so much more comfortable. Holes are a terrible trouble to dig, too. Tents are heavier, though. Ah, well, can never be sure. My mind went back to Hogmanay in the tent. Up all night trying to hold it up. That was some blow! What was I doing backpacking in January? Time I grew up. There was a warm bed back home. And a lovely girl. And four kids. (Four! I ask you!) I wondered which of them was getting up in the middle of the night and padding in to our bedroom to snuggle under the duvet.

Huh. Here in this filthy black hole I couldn't even be bothered to light the night light. Strange about the crow. It had really got under my skin. It was like the old black hen I was supposed to have put down before I came away. Black. Covered in black feathers. With a beady eye that looks at you in that knowing way. It knows you have got murderous intentions. It knows you have got food for it. If it unnerves you enough from your murderous intentions, you will give it food. I gave it food. I certainly didn't deliberately feed the crow. It just appeared. I had only just sat down and opened my rucksack and there it was on the snow, 10ft. away. I had some tea from my flask and some biscuits. I packed everything up and carried on. I had only just stood up when it was in there, pecking up the crumbs.

It was a brilliant period of weather. The sort of time when you say hang it all and go off irresponsibly breaking your own trail. There was lots to look at. The valley mist was just superb. Isolated hills were rising out of it. It was too low to produce Brocken Spectres, but I didn't mind. I walked right round into the next coire, and stopped at the foot of the crags. A couple of guys were having a tough time on one of the routes. The leader was doing a good job, though, and made it up to the stance. The second followed. I took off my sack again, and got out my camera. The light cloud round the summit was gathering again, and I missed the shot. I looked up from putting away my camera and there it was again. The crow. I'm sure it was the same bird. It just waited till I'd finished and packed up, then it flew in to where I had been standing, hardly waiting for me to vacate my footprints. Up the back of the coire is a big snow slope leading to the plateau above.

The cloud cleared again in front of me. I went slowly, trying to reduce the perspiration. I was well ready for refuelling at the top and sat to have another bite to eat. Out came the food. Drat that crow! It was still following me. It flew over me and something light floated down and landed nearby. Black feathers. It's moulting, I thought. It turned and fixed a beady eye on me. The sun caught its black feathers. Gleaming black, iridescent, slightly blueish. No sign of moulting. It watched me eat – very closely.

I'm not usually mean. I'll throw crusts to the gulls on the beach or to the ducks at the pond, when we go with the children. But somehow, I didn't want to encourage the crow. It seemed to have adopted me, and I didn't want it around. In any case, hadn't we all read warnings about feeding alien scavengers who then turn their attention to the native birdlife, stealing eggs and taking chicks. Not that there'd be any eggs or chicks around in this snow, but the principle's the same.

The light mist drifted back, making the navigation across the plateau more interesting. I didn't see the bird again all day, so why was it waking me up in the snow hole? What if it was trying to tell me something? What was that about the black feather? Did it know I was going to kill the old black hen and trying to make me feel bad about it? What else was I supposed to be doing that I've not got round to?

Jen's birthday! I forgot her birthday! Hang on. No – I didn't forget her birthday. We went out for a meal. Hah! Panic attacks! I remember having them for months after I appeared in the school play. It was always the same. I hadn't remembered my lines. I had let everyone else down. I hadn't kept up the pretence that we were Shakespearean actors with talent and knew what we were doing.

Damn! The alarm. It can't be, already, oh! It is. You get no idea of the time in the pitch black. Well, what's the hurry? I'll just sneak a few more minutes in my pit. Make up for all the hours tossing and turning worrying about that dratted bird. Funny how it's always easier to fall asleep after the alarm's gone. Should set it to go off at midnight…

No, must get up. Hell, is that the time? I must have nodded off again. What a midden this is. Can't wait to get out. Out at last. What the...? I reckon something got it in the night and blew it to pieces. Good. Saved me the job. I trudge off, leaving my snow hole empty behind. Someone else might have the pleasure of finding it, enlarging it and using it for the night. I am on an upward trajectory. On, up, out of the cloud sea, right on to Ben MacDhui's generous summit. It is not as early as it might have been if I hadn't been skulking so long. There are several people at the summit – and a crow.

It can't have been yesterday's crow. That one fell to pieces hanging around my snow hole. The day is going to be a short one. Early lunch, I think. What the hell's that bird doing? It's hopping around with something small and round in its beak, but drops it when it sees me looking and flies off a little way. I go over to see what the small round thing is. Eeargh! It's an eye, a bird's eye. Cannibals! I knew crows pick out eyes, but this is a bit too gory for comfort. The eye looks at me, unblinking, reproachfully. It's the bird I didn't feed yesterday. The bird I didn't put out of its misery yesterday. The family I left behind to indulge myself. The guilt comes rolling in like the cold clammy hand of reproach and the mist bank from the plateau, now moving across the summit, cutting out the sun.

It's suddenly bitterly cold in the cloud. I've become careless in my lack of attention. I had already been cooling down, but now I'm chittering. Three more layers of clothes to put on. Much better, again, fortified against the outside world.

It gets warmer again on the descent, but the mist stays thick. It's quite a tricky job, concentrating on the navigation in the whiteout. At last the slope begins to dip downwards. I'm coming to the end of my high. At a big block overlooking an invisible abyss, I stop for a last time. I haven't seen anyone since I left the summit, and there are no footprints near this rock, but the soft snow seems patterned by pockmarks over a wide area.

There it is again. The crow. All right! You black-cassocked gloom merchant. I've had my panic attack and you've managed to make me feel really guilty about going off for my own pleasure. You should be working for the church. Get lost. Go on.

Why is it taking no notice? Of course, I can't tell whether it's the same one. It's had no way of following me here in the whiteout. What's it up to now? It's beaking about in the pockmarks in the snow. What's it finding? Food?

I tell you, I didn't stay to find out. I fleetingly saw what it pulled out of one of those pock marks, I thought at first it was a worm - a thin strip of pink meat, before it disappeared into that bird's beak. I ran. I have only run off a mountain once before, in the face of an approaching thunderstorm, and I tell you, I ran as fast this time as for any approaching bolt of lightning. I was down the hill, into the car and back home in an hour. The family was surprised to see me home so soon, but they were all fine.

"Thanks for doing the hen before you left," Jen was saying "but you might have buried it, the other hens have been going mad, there's been a terrible pile of crows round its corpse. Look. They've completely picked it clean."

THE NORTHERN PINNACLES OF LIATHACH AND THE KINLOCHEWE MEETS OF 1899 AND 1900

By Robin N. Campbell

THE possibility of a route to Mullach an Rathain by way of the series of pinnacles between it and its northern outlier Meall Dearg was first noted by Lionel Hinxman in 1891.[1] Then William Douglas traversed Liathach with William W. King in April 1893 and observed that "we were charmed with the view of the unclimbed ridge of Meall Dearg...with its seven pinnacles'.[2] Douglas returned to investigate on June 11, 1894, accompanied by Hinxman and John Rennie and guided by William Macdonald, head keeper at Torridon House where the party had stayed on the previous night. Macdonald's orders were simply to direct the party to the start of the Pinnacles, but he was "delighted at being asked to join the expedition". The party reached the ridge at the lowest col from the north side and proceeded roped to the summit. Douglas remarked that "were it not for the unstable condition of the whole structure, the climb would have been a very simple affair". Keeper Macdonald put it rather differently: "For all the world like climbing over an old tooth-comb, and a —— old tooth-comb at that." (Expletive not recorded).[3]

In the ensuing years, members showed little interest in the Torridon hills until the Kinlochewe Easter Meets of 1899 and 1900. They were occupied in tidying up after Collie in Glencoe, Ben Nevis and Skye. Unsurprisingly, it was Collie again who delivered the reminder with an obscurely-reported ascent/descent of the Central Buttress of Coire Mhic Fhearchair in 1898 or earlier.[4] It had also became apparent to Hugh Munro and others that the mountains between Loch Maree and An Teallach were very poorly mapped. So the Club was not short of reasons to visit Kinlochewe.

The 1899 Meet was attended by 14 members and visited by uniformly bad weather. The recorder, Hinxman, noted that the evenings were "enlivened by Rennie at the piano and the sweet tones of [Munro's] flute". The photographers consoled themselves with staging graceful group photographs, two of which have survived.[5] Some climbing was managed by the rope of Harry Lawson, William Ling and George Glover – a route on the east end of Liathach from Coire Dubh Mor and a gully on Sail Mhor, and by Glover, William Inglis Clark and an unidentified other – the Waterfall Climb on Beinn a' Mhuinidh.[6] The Club, in much the same company, immediately returned to Kinlochewe at Easter 1900, where they found weather even worse than the previous year. The Meet, which was reported by Sandy Mackay in a deplorably sketchy and facetious manner, "lasted from Thursday evening to Tuesday morning (April 12 to 17), Munro forming a fringe at either end. (He was found in his slippers and left in bed)".[7] Although little detail is provided, Mackay allowed that those attending were President Maylard, Hinxman, Rennie, Wm. Naismith, Douglas, Munro, Harold Raeburn, Lawson, Ling, James Parker, Mackenzie, Gall Inglis, Herbert Boyd, Squance, Mackay and Cookson (Guest).[8] Much of the party of 16 left on Monday morning, but those seven or eight who remained enjoyed a magnificent day on Liathach. "A party of six" made what we would now call the first winter ascent of the Northern Pinnacles, then traversed Liathach eastwards to Glen Torridon, returning in the very late evening to Kinlochewe. Only five took part in the actual ascent of the Pinnacles, one of the party making his way independently to Mullach an Rathain and rejoining the five on the summit. Mackay mentions in his Meet report that "Mackenzie performed excellent service by scouting around the hither end of the mountain, sighting the enemy, himself unseen", while "Inglis made splendid practice as a snapshooter", but he fails to specify the five who ascended the Pinnacles. In the following number of the Journal, Mackay contributed a short article – albeit in the same cryptic undergraduate style – which gave some more detail.[9] The successful party consisted of two ropes: Naismith and Mackay led the way, and the second rope was led by Raeburn.

But who were the other two climbers? Mackay does not say. However, Munro is a candidate, since he was evidently still around on the Monday, and his "being left in bed" on Tuesday implies activity on the previous day. And 50 years later Ling, reminiscing about Club Meets, recalled his attendance at Kinlochewe and "a fine climb over the Northern Pinnacles of Liathach in icy conditions, a party of six, from which we got back to Kinlochewe at 10.50 p.m."[10] So Raeburn's rope consisted of Ling and one other, possibly Munro. The photograph facing page 33 seems to provide confirmation of this suggestion. It shows the five concerned perched on a snowslope on what may very well be Mullach an Rathain. It was was found in a box of negative glass plates belonging to James Gall Inglis and passed to me for safe keeping by his son, Robin, in the 1970s.[11] We know from Mackay that Inglis was on the mountain taking photographs: indeed, one of them illustrates Mackay's article. And we know that a photograph was taken of the successful party. After the successful ascent, "presently, all foregathered for a photograph in marching disorder". However, Mackay fails to make clear whether Inglis (who must have taken the summit photograph) was the sixth member of the Pinnacles party or whether we have an eighth climber to identify on Liathach that day.

So it is certain that the first winter ascent party contained Naismith, Mackay, Raeburn and Ling, and extremely probable that the fifth member was Munro. I say 'extremely probable' since there is no doubt that the photograph was taken by Inglis and that it was taken at the 1900 Kinlochewe Meet: the coincidences of clothing, personal appearance (age) and personnel exclude other possibilities. These five and Inglis might have been together on Friday, on the Black Men or on Slioch. This is rather unlikely, since Mackay reports: "Through the day party after party (so my recollection goes) kept arriving at the Hotel." But on Saturday Lawson and Ling went to Coire Mhic Fhearchair, and on Sunday Lawson, Ling and Munro went to A'Mhaighdean.

The preceding paragraph (complete with its errors of reasoning, soon to be revealed) appeared in a draft of this note which I sent to Bob Aitken. Bob suggested consulting Ling's diaries, held by the Alpine Club Library – documents not known to me. I did this with the help of Archivist Susan Scott and discovered the following entry for Monday, April 16, 1900: "Ben Leagach. With H. T. Munro, W. W. Naismith, H. Raeburn, J. G. Inglis, A. M. Mackay & H. G. S. Lawson (Lawson was dropped off before lunch to go walking, and Munro went his own way after part of the initial climb. The two ropes then consisted of (i) Naismith & Mackay; (ii) Raeburn, Inglis and Ling. Later in the day, when rejoined by Munro, the ropes were (i) Raeburn, Munro, Mackay; (ii) Ling, Inglis, Naismith)." So the mysterious fifth member of the climbing party was Inglis, whom I had foolishly excluded from consideration except as photographer, and the sixth "independent member" was Munro. However, my inferences regarding the splendid historical photograph are strongly supported.[12] I can now stop worrying about the missing rope: it is around photographer Inglis's neck!

NOTES:

[1] *Beinn Eighe and the Torridon Hills,* SMCJ, 1891, I, 187-94.

[2] *Leagach, Torridon,* SMCJ, 1893, II, 320. Douglas's count of seven pinnacles included Meall Dearg and Mullach an Rathain, but Meall Dearg is normally omitted by climbing to the lowest col from the north side, and later descriptions have not counted the Mullach as one of the Pinnacles. So the traditional numbering proceeds from 1 the pinnacle above the lowest col to 5 – the last pinnacle before the Mullach itself.

[3] *The Northern Pinnacles of Leagach,* SMCJ, 1894, III, 131-5

[4] *A Reverie,* SMCJ, September 1898, V, 93-102. Collie referred to this ascent in a letter to Douglas dated 26-4-98, which began: "We had a great time at Kinlochewe, and I think I have discovered the finest rock climb in the British Isles." So it seems likely that this alluded to a recent (thus 1898) visit, although the photographs illustrating Collie's article show that the condition of the crags was not at all wintry. One of the other members of Collie's party was W. Cecil Slingsby. He read a paper to the Yorkshire Ramblers Club on 14-4-96 entitled *An Easter Holiday in the Scottish Highlands* and this was eventually published in YRCJ, 1900, I, 173-87. Slingsby's paper was a report of the activities of an Alpine Club group organised by Collie and friends who were present at Fort William during our own Easter Meet on April 3-7, 1896, an event completed only a week before his address! In a footnote to the printed article he noted that "since I wrote the above paragraph I have had several other little campaigns in the Highlands, and have spent three days upon that most remarkable mountain, Ben Eighe in the Torridons. The crags of Coire Mhic Fhearchair on this mountain are steeper, and in some respects wider, than those of Ben Nevis".

[5] See illustrations facing p. 32.

[6] For the Meet Report see SMCJ, 1899, V, 253-6, and for Glover's account of the Waterfall Climb see ibid. 257-60. Apart from those mentioned, the other members present were President R. A. Robertson, D. S. Campbell, W. Douglas, T. Gibson, J. Gall Inglis, D. Mackenzie and F. C. Squance. Glover, when complaining about the absurd bulk of cameras on the route, identifies the unidentified member of the Waterfall Climb party as a photographer. Since the only other known climbers, Lawson and Ling, were active elsewhere that day (Slioch) it is very likely that the unidentified third man was – given his zeal for photography – the self-effacing Douglas.

[7] See SMCJ, 1900, VI, 59-60. Alexander Morrice Mackay is an unsung but interesting early member. A son of Aberdeen, he went to Trinity College, Cambridge and there fell under the influence of Geoffrey Young. He formed an Alpine partnership with Young which ended with the bad and stupid accident to Mackay on the North Face of Cir Mhor described in Young's book *Mountains with a Difference*. This brought a promising mountaineering and tennis career to an abrupt conclusion. Mackay went on to become a Court of Session judge. He is best known for the audacious ascent of the Barrel Buttress of Quinag with Raeburn and Ling in 1907 (see the belated account in SMCJ, 1928, XVIII, 207-13) and for his biographical sketches of early members, and of Young, in SMCJ, 1950, XXIV, 169-80.

[8] The gathering is shown in the splendid photograph facing page 33. Identification of the climbers in this and the 1899 photographs was helped by the considerable overlap in those attending. A poor photograph published in SMCJ, 1927, XVIII, 8 shows Squance in 1897; Susanna Kerr of the National Portrait Gallery supplied a photograph of Mackay; Mackenzie and Lawson were identified by inference based on knowledge of their ages and the fact that they attended both meets; the 1899 Campbell is the same man as one of those in the Yacht Meet photograph, and is therefore taken to be D. S. – he being the only Campbell recorded as present there; Gibson, although also present at the Yacht Meet is distinguishable from Campbell by age. In the captions, identifications based on positive evidence are in roman type; those that depend on inference are shown in italics. The figure positively identified as W. Lamond Howie, (cf. 1906 Meet photograph) has moved his head and so this is offered rather tentatively. In addition, Howie was not recorded as attending the 1900 Meet, but Naismith (not in the photograph) was definitely there. It has been suggested that 'Howie' is Naismith. However, he seems much older than Naismith. If it is Naismith, then he has been patronising Howie's bonnet-maker.

[9] *The Northern Pinnacles of Liathach*, SMCJ, 1900, VI, 87-90.

[10] *Meets, 1897-1950*, SMCJ, 1950, XXIV, 190-93.

[11] *Safe keeping*, I am ashamed to say, has meant languishing forgotten in a cupboard for almost 30 years!

[12] Ling's diary places him and Lawson on Beinn Eighe on Friday, so Monday was the only day of the Meet when the five in the photograph were together on the hill.

BEER AND ROCKING IN LAS VEGAS

By Allan Scott

The Rannoch Club eating, drinking and climbing at Red Rocks, Nevada.
November 2001 (though not necessarily in that order).

THE Rannoch Club dates back to around the 1960s and boasts among its
early activists such great luminaries as Ted Maden, Colin Stead, Dave
Jenkins, Morton Shaw and Ed Jackson. The Great Meteor Catastrophe in
the 1970s caused the mass extinction of climbing activity and in the early
1980s a Renaissance began with the addition of a group of non-luminous
new members mostly ex-Glasgow and Strathclyde University climbers.

With the current decline in weather standards (probably due to that
meteor) the club have regular trips to Spain in the quest for warm dry rock
and cold wet beer. This was the second Rannoch trip in 2001. We had
already been to Majorca in May, and after another typically poor Scottish
summer we opted for a 'once in a lifetime' trip to the US to end the year
with some good weather and good rock.

The flight from Heathrow was L-O-N-G, but was helped by an endless
supply of free swally. Travel was spoiled only by an irritatingly loud,
alcoholic, tattie-howking caricature of an Irishman whose rowdy
protestations (sic) caused me to be banned from the drinks trolley, I guess
I shouldn't have said I was a 'Bluenose' from Glasgow, but thankfully, it
was near the end of the flight. However, the worrying thing was that he
said he was also going to Las Vegas, on the same flight as us from San
Francisco…but he died of a liver failure induced heart attack when they
announced there would be no drinks served on the flight. His body was
jettisoned at 34,000ft. As they say: "It's the luck of the Oirish."

Our arrival in Las Vegas was more or less on time and we picked up a
hire-car, a Chevrolet Redrocker and moseyed-on-down to the apartments
on the east side. Not a bad hut, with a big fridge for the beer and a telly for
the Afghanistan War updates. There was a pool with jaccuzzi round the
front. In Hut One were Stefan Kass, with John Dunn, Colin Grant and
myself. Hut Two had Alan Shand and his girlfriend Carol, with Tim
Whittaker, Iain White and Bish McAra. An interesting combo, but at least
they had someone to do the housework.

There were four climbing teams, each with at least one SMC member.
This would ensure sound mountaineering practice and good hill-sense at
all times. Naismith's Rule would apply to all walk-ins and there would be
no retro-bolting on mountain crags.

First Night: We went out looking for food, and drove just down the road
to a place called the Long Horn Casino, it looked promising. There were

wall-to-wall slots, and wall-to-wall sluts. Elvis was in the corner trying to make himself heard over the cacophony of fruit-machines. Some trailer-trash rednecks in check shirts and stetsons were slugging it out over a pool table. Then unbelievably, an elderly, long-haired, grey-bearded dude walked in and *he had breasts*. Honest! Yee-ha! This was Las Vegas alright.

An enormously fat, sweating waitress approached. I said: "Gonnygeezalookatamenu," in my finest Glesga accent, she visibly wobbled all over and stared with a (fat) blank expression: "D'uh...Excuse me?"

"May we possibly peruse one of your menus perchance?" I enunciated in my best Invernesian BBC accent.

"Yes-sirree-bob! Have-nice-day-you're-welcome-sir," she drawled in her best Texan.

We ordered good wholesome American fare…Mexican food and French Fries!…portions were enormous but cheap, e.g. my starter, the Taco Salad consisted of a pound of chilli in a bucket-sized taco with piles of salad and a quart of guacamole, and only $3…hmm, a sign of things to come I thought. After the meal we went back to the hut for some much needed jetlag-induced slumber.

Day 1: We had no food at the hut so we went out for breakfast and found the Blueberry Hill Pancake House. On the menu was something called the Double 2-Double 2, consisting of 2 eggs, 2 bacon, 2 sausages, and 2 pancakes…2 much!

Crag: It is around a half-an-hour drive to Red Rocks from Las Vegas. Access to the climbing areas is from a one-way loop road. We decided on some sport climbing for the first day at the Black Corridor and Magic Bus crags from the Second Pull Out (car park). The routes – 5.9, 5.9+, 5.10d, 5.10a, 5.8, 5.9+, 5.8. Great climbing, and it would be good to see if it would improve performance on the Glasgow Climbing Wall when we got home. The Black Corridor was a bit like the Whangie with a short walk-in to a narrow rock gash with superb rock and well-bolted routes…hmmm…nothing like the Whangie really, but anyway it was a good introduction to Red Rocks, although it did get a little busy later on.

Evening: Back to the hut for a beer and scrub-up, then along the road to the Boulder Station Hotel. Slot-machines as far as the eye can see, wall-to-wall-craps etc, etc, the usual Vegas thing. For eats we tried El Diablo Mexican Cantina. Tons of tacos, tortillas, burritos, fajitas, dips, guacamoles and buckets of Corona beer. Well, we were on holiday after all!

Day 2: Breakfast – Blueberry Mountain of Pancakes. It just had to be the Double 2-Double 2…2222 calories.

Crag: Some more sport-climbing at Dog Wall, First Pull Out, 5.10a, 5.10b, The Gallery, Second Pull-out, 5.8, 5.9, 5.10a, Wall of Confusion, 5.10b. Superb routes again. Perfect rock and warm and sunny. Marvellous.

Evening: Boulder Station Hotel, American Steakhouse. All-you-can-eat soup and salad starter followed by all-you-can-find-room-for meat, cow, buffalo, bison, steer, heifer, moose…and all-you-can-drink beers, of course.

Day 3: Mega-early start – an improvised Double 2-Double 2 at the hut, (Double coffee, 2 toast, 2 cereal)

Crag: Black Velvet Canyon – Prince of Darkness*** (5.6, 5.10b, 5.10a, 5.9, 5.9, 5.10c.) A fantastic route, face climbing of the highest order on a stunning wall with all belays hanging. It was unusual in that the climb was really a six-pitch sport route on a predominantly traditional crag. We got started ahead of three French climbers. I met the leader on the first hanging belay and he seemed *tres* friendly…"Grimpeurs Ecossaise? Ooh-la-la! Haw-hee-haw! C'est magnifique! Mon amis!!".

However, the tone quickly changed at the end of the route, as first Stef and I, then Colin and JD (on the same descent after doing Dream of Wild Turkeys***) had to abseil over, under and around them, totally tying them in knots and scuppering the *Entente Cordiale*.

"Sacre bleu! Zut alors! Vous etez merdes bastardes d'Ecosse." Alas the Auld Alliance is no more.

Shandboy and Tim enjoyed their route (Fiddler on the Roof***), and the crag so much they decided to spend a very cold night out, on a hanging belay halfway up the wall after an abseil-rope jammed. Bad show lads…even the rappel-rope-ravaged frogs managed to get down…but shit happens I suppose. Anyway *we* got down safely but starving, imagine my horror to find an empty foodbag…gofers ate my snickers! Wee furry bassas!

Evening: Couldn't face another Tex-Mex pork-out so it was an American-style phone-up pizza pork-out instead. Three satellite-sized pizzas were duly delivered and scoffed with mucho beers while watching American Football on the TV. We were really getting the hang of this American stuff. The evening was, however, fraught with worry about the lads stuck back at Black Velvet Canyon: "Pass another slice of pepperami and a beer"?…"Sure, cheers buddy"!…hic!

Day 4: International Rescue is go go go. We were up at the climbing area at first light to assist Tim and Al off the crag. After a few worrying moments, (i.e. we could only see one of them at first), everything turned out OK. Shandboy, after all, is an old hand at this benightment lark.

After a late breakfast at IHOP (International House of Pancakes, or more accurately, Indescribably Huge Order of Pancakes)…Double 2-Double 2…a double fry-up, 2 many pancakes, and 2 visits to the john. The team adjourned to the hut for a spot of R&R. Even in late November temperatures were in the mid-70s, just nice for a couple of hours by the pool. Then it was off to the Crag – Sandstone Quarry Area, Mass Production

Wall, sport routes – 5.8, 5.9, 5.10a. A-hootin-and-a-hollerin! So much good rocking!

Evening: Boulder Station Italiano Ristorante…mucho vino collapso at the JD and Colin end of the table, and mucho birra italiano at every other end of the table. With the drinks I had antipasta, midpasta and postpasta. (No wonder I'm a fatbasta). On the way back to the hut we made a major discovery. The Dew Drop Inn, just a few hundred yards from the hut and perfect for the lads…Cheap beer ($5 for a three-pint pitcher), pool table (25c a game), great Jukebox, and a barmaid with nice buns…it was the American Dream…God Bless America. We met some interesting characters, mostly construction workers, including Loopy Lou from Arkansas, sporting an American Civil War Confederate cap and very chatty and laid back. Indeed, he was totally unflappable in the face of a slightly inebriated and aggressive member of the party who shall remain nameless, with his one-liner self-introduction: "How come so many Americans are fat bastards?"

I'm just glad it wasn't Big Detroit Dave he confronted, he was like a Yankee version of Giant Haystacks.

Later, Lou started cracking 'Religious' jokes (must be a Southern Thing, The Bible-Belt and all that). Hilarious! Here was I, a 'Teddy Bear' from Glasgow listening to an American telling me sectarian jokes. Bizarre indeed.

Day 5: Breakfast – Double 2-Double 2…Double helpings, 2 barfs, 2 paracetamol.

Crag: Willow Spring – off the loop road. One pitch sport and trad routes. 5.10, 5.9, 5.11-, 5.10, 5.8. Hot-diggety-dawg! This climbing lark just gets better and better.

Evening: A trip to the Strip, the Neon-Nightmare in the centre of Las Vegas. We went to Caesar's Palace for the buffet meal. WOW! MEGUM HOTELUM! What a size of a place! What a size of a plate of food! After several visits to Caesar's vomitorium, we took a cab back to the Dew Drop to meet some more American nutters. Tonight's characters included, The Hustler – a dude playing pool with personal cue, cue-glove and chalk-clip…he was shite – I gubbed him, and Air-Guitar man who stopped mid-shot several times to perform whenever a guitar-solo was on the juke-box. Also Juan Kerr a Hispanic pool shark – I was shite – he gubbed me.

Day 6: Breakfast – Double 2-Double 2…getting 2 fat, 2 rounds of toast; 2 little; 2 late.

Crag: Pine Creek Canyon, The Mescalito – Dark Shadows*** (5.6, 5.7, 5.7, 5.8+), superb bridging up a big 'varnished' corner at a very amenable standard. Total enjoyment even though it was the first time on the holiday to have been cold. The route being on a north-facing crag with a howling wind. It was just like being 'up the Ben' (without the English hordes and

Kinlochewe, Easter Meet, 1899

...ng: D. S. Campbell, G. T. Glover (sitting in window), W. N. Ling, R. A. Robertson, F. C. Squance, J. G. Inglis, W. Douglas.
Sitting: D. Mackenzie, L. Hinxman, W. I. Clark, J. Rennie, T. Gibson, H. G. S. Lawson.
Photo: J. Gall Inglis, SMC Collection.

Kinlochewe, Easter Meet, 1899.

Standing: H. T. Munro, R. A. Robertson, H. G. S. Lawson, G. T. Glover, F. C. Squance.
...ing: D. S. Campbell, J. Rennie, L. Hinxman (on window), D. Mackenzie, W. Douglas (on window), W. I. Clark,
T. Gibson, W. N. Ling.   Photo: William N Ling, SMC Collection.

Kinlochewe, Easter Meet, 1900.

Standing: W. N. Ling, Cookson, W. L. Howie, H. Raeburn, J. G. Inglis, H. G. S. Lawson, H. T. Munro, L. Hinxman, H. C. Boyd, F. C. Squance, A. M. Mackay (in window). Sitting: A. E. Maylard (Pres.), W. Douglas, J. Rennie (on ground), J. A. Parker, D. Mackenzie.

Photo: J Gall Inglis, SMC Collection.

After the Northern Pinnacles.

(Left to right) H. Raeburn, W. N. Ling, W Naismith, A. M. Mackay, H. T. Munro

Photo: J Gall Inglis, SMC Collection

midges.) Also visited Brass Wall (surely a misnomer), on the sunny side, 5.9+ trad route. Superb and hot-hot-hot.

Evening: Pizza phone-in. Mini-Dish size this time...still couldn't finish them. Then we dropped in to the Dew Drop Inn. Tonight's entertainment...Steve, The One-armed Bandit, astonishingly able to play pool using only one hand. In one game he slammed the cue-ball so hard he potted the black, just the black!...an incredible and rare shot, (indeed, only the second time Steve had done it in 20 years!) and under American Rules an automatic win. Imagine his chagrin when we told him we were playing Scottish Rules and he had just lost! Oh how we laughed, and drank, and laughed some more.

Day 7: Breakfast – Double 2-Double 2...2 late I'm blobbed-out now, 2 of everything, with double maple-syrup. Not even any room left for a wafer-thin mint.

Crag : I went to Pine Creek Canyon with Tim. Stefan had gone home to the gym and Shandboy was away shopping with Carol on the Strip. (I guess that's one of the drawbacks of bringing your girlfriend). We went to Straight Shooter Wall and Brass Wall on the sunny side. Routes 5.9+, 5.10, 5.8+.

Evening: Another Boulder Station Mexican trough-session with bucketed-Corona overload. The Dew Drop Inn seemed to be holding some kind of Ironworkers Union Convention. Big Lew (an American Arthur Scargill), was handing out car bumper stickers, badges etc. He even hinted at offering us some work...I was sorely tempted, with rates of pay at $60 an hour! One of the union guys, Septic Hank, (so called after he likened living in Scotland to being in a septic tank...cheeky yankee sod), told us his life story (zzzzzzzzzzz) and about his three beautiful daughters. This was all very doubtful, since he was a short, fat, grizzled, stinking, one-eyed, bow-legged, halitosis-suffering hobo. It all led to another beer-fuelled frenzy, with some raucous badinage with our American hosts.

Day 8: Rest day. So I thought I'd take a wee walk down the road to the Toys'R'Us I'd spied on Flamingo Road...2 hours and 3 litres of Gatorade later I arrived rather footsore. Got a sack load of Harry Potter stuff for my kids and got the bus back to the hut.

Brunch: Double 2-Double 2...2 stomach pumps an enema and a double colonic irrigation. I was knackered and spent the rest of day by the pool.

Evening: A plethora of pizza, pitchers and pool.

Day 9: Last day. Breakfast – Double 2-Double 2...It's Lardsville, Nevada-drastic measures called for – 2 stomach staples, 2 liposuctions and a double jaw-clamp.

Crag: It was those old 'last-day blues' when you know it's nearly all over and you're going home soon. We went to Pine Creek Canyon, and rather fittingly to Flight Path Wall, 5.9, 5.9, 5.9. Then finished off at Calico Basin, 5.9+

Evening: A team trip to the Strip. We did the Rollercoaster ride at NewYork, New York. Brilliant! Then on to the buffet at Bellagios'...and I thought Caesars was big! You could fit the whole of Byres Road into the foyer of this place. They had top-quality food in exquisite surroundings. Incredibly, with superb *haute cuisine* on offer (braised red snapper, roast wild hog, duck a l'orange etc etc) most of the Yanks were porking-out on PIZZA for chrissakes!

No wonder they're all so fat. Yes, Colin, you were right all along. Afterwards, we shoe-horned ourselves into a cab back to the hut. A couple of us went for a final fling at the Dew Drop. We soon became barfast, chatting to the locals with a few pitchers and swapping addresses with a few folk. Truly a terrific bar. Magic and unforgettable.

Days 10-11: It was with heads heavy with hangovers we dropped the cars off – then it was a blur of airport lounges, trolley-dollies, double vodkas, cans of Bud, airport sushi-bars and last-minute gift shops all the way to a dull, damp, Glasgow.

The Routes: bonaire–bone2–crudeboys–dancinwithagod–neonsunset–electrickoolaid–technicoloursunrise–catwalk–itsabitch–sportsclimbingisneither–bucksmuscleworld–gelatinpooch–therunaway–princeofdarkness–partsisparts–batterypowered–trigerhappy–bigfoot–blacktrack–unknowntoprope–planf–raggededges–darkshadows–toplesstwins–straightshooter–simpatico–varnishingpoint–asimpleexpedition–cartalk–dointhegooddrive–pendingdisaster.

The Future Tick-list Too many routes, too little time, too many big breakfasts, too fat. (Catch Double 2-Double 2).

I can't wait for the next 'once in a lifetime trip'.

(Apologies to Hunters. S. Thompson and Joseph Heller).

GRADE I GULLIES CAN BE FUN
(or the perils of guidebooks)

By Nigel Suess

LEVEL 4 avalanche risk, especially in North-facing gullies, winds up to 50mph and wet snow lying down to Loch Leven. The hut was not troubled by early breakfasting. Some chose to walk in the woods; others opted for a Corbett or a low ridge walk.

John came over. "Have you a car?"

"Why?"

"Because I don't."

We paired up, then debated hills. "What about this one?" He pointed to the most boring Corbett in the West of Scotland.

"Done it." To the next suggestion. "Did that a couple of years ago."

Well, we both have more years mountain experience behind us than ahead of us (as the reader may conclude after reading on).

"What about Sgor na h'Ulaidh and perhaps we could have a look at Vixen Gully? Of course, if that is not in condition we could take the walkers' route. The point is that the gully will give us some shelter from the wind; and the book says: 'Grade I...a straight-forward snow climb.' MacInnes gives the same grade and says: 'An easy route to the summit, can sometimes be used for descent.' We can check out the conditions when we get to the corrie."

"Got any gear?"

"An axe."

"Well, I've 90ft. of rope, four krabs and three hexes."

The hexes proved to be all about the same size. No rocks, no friends, no slings, no pegs, no ice screws, no deadman, no second ice tool, no harnesses.

"My last bowline tie on was in 1973."

By the time we parked the car, patches of blue sky evidenced the swift passage of the clouds, but there was no rain, sleet or snow. We enjoyed our walk up Gleann leac na Muidhe. We had not been out on the hill together before and chatted about the Alps. John had been on a first British ascent on the Alphubel in 1956 and had climbed most of the 4000m peaks. Well, that inspired confidence.

In recent years we had both pootered about on the Ben classics. Spirits rose further. But the overnight snow was soft and deep up into the corrie. We chose to dismiss its windslab-like texture when we got to around 600m. The hill was clear and we could see right into the gully. Here the volume seemed fairly minimal, probably blown out by the wind which was strong and northerly. We agreed that there was no serious cornice to plop off and that the gully, though continuous, had several rocky outcrops. These suggested a closer look was not entirely imprudent. But first, hot coffee and some food.

We gingerly moved up into the jaws of the gully and soloed to below a short ice pitch. Here, we geared up, a somewhat grand name for tying on to each end of the rope and getting out the three hexes. I made a good bucket seat. John reckoned that the short ice pitch should be followed by a simple snow couloir to the top (after all the SMC guidebook and the MacInnes book are clear in their description of the route and definition of Grade I).

"With a short rope we should not have any problem keeping in touch."

No sooner was he over the 5m ice pitch than he looked for a belay. Yes, a good placement for two of our hexes. I trotted up and took the residual rack. The next section was soft snow on névé and I ran out the rope to a wee bay; no gear here, so I excavated another bucket seat. John had a similar third pitch, but found a placement for a sound belay anchor. My next pitch was probably the most worrying. For about a dozen metres there was deep slabby snow over the névé. We had both agreed to keep near to the gully walls where it would be marginally less deep. The technique was to jam in the single axe and use the other hand to snow plough the gully ahead (depositing most of it onto the unfortunate belayer). The rope length stopped the pleasure and a hex belay was found below a névé groove (presumably where the soft stuff had blown away). Above, we saw the next short ice pitch leading to a rock bollard centre stage. John moved up, commenting on the excellent hand holds on the bollard, above which he planted himself. As we climbed higher, the wind blew more and spindrift was now a nuisance.

The character of the gully began to change, less defined and twisting left to a steeper section with more ice. I set to work. As the ice steepened, I used my adze to cut nicks for the other hand and progressed with tradition on my side. The pitch seemed rather lengthy in relation to our rope. I decided that I would need to belay on the 55° ice. Miraculously, a crack appeared in the rock overhead on the left – yes hex-sized. I kicked nicks in the ice and hung there. By now spindrift was becoming a real concern (as was confidence in the route descriptions in the guidebooks). I faced inwards with the shoulder belay somewhat inadequate. John motored up, took over the second part of the ice-pitch, here more than 60° for a few metres, and found a good block where the ice ended. We had now completed seven pitches and knew that the top must be close. Three more pitches, notable for spindrift not ice, left me 5m below the negligible cornice on névé, but without adequate belay. My partner came up quickly, over the rim and tied on to a fence post.

Amazingly, here at 990m on an exposed ridge we were sheltered somehow and loosened our bowlines. Just below, on the South Face vortices of spindrift played. To the west the entire summit ridge of Meall Lighiche was silhouetted by spindrift, back-lit by the mid-afternoon sun. A few steps took us to the summit cairn and we agreed that it had been a great day, when careful assessment of the conditions on the ground and experience of more serious routes had seen us through. John noted that as a descent route it could be lethal. The variability of Scottish winter conditions emphasised that one should use a guidebook as a guide and not as an instruction manual. Or, perhaps guide book editors do not get many reports back on Grade I gullies?

LOOKING WEST

I dream we are two Viking jarls
today, with simple action plans
and strategies – along the lines
of take life by the throat;
travelling in thrall into high places
spying out these wide Hesperides

from Skye's blue jagged Cuillin
to Jura's rounded paps, Kintyre
and even far-off Arran's hazy peaks
and all the lateral wonders
of a world adjacent and in between
the blest islands of the west:
Iona, Colonsay,
Coll and Tiree,
the Uists,Barra, Mingulay,
stretching into the blue,
with Staffa,Ulva,Eorsa nearer to
our vantage point of Mull's big hill.

This summit is among the high points
of two lives. Mind how you go,
you two. Evade descent.
Postpone the parting handclasp.
Consider another golden moment
and reflect. Beyond this pinnacle
a setting sun declines
into the anecdotage of Valhalla
and the sea, for everything
that rises has to ebb.

Gordon Jarvie.

TWO DAYS IN THE CAIRNGORMS

By John Irving

CONDITIONS change quickly. On Friday afternoon I had arranged an early exit from work, to continue the struggle with that summer's new toy and stumbled and rolled in the Pease Bay surf. On Saturday morning the alarm kicked in to California Dreams, and dragged me onto the A9 for the familiar sweeping curves and fast straights that lead to the frozen Northern Corries of Cairngorm. I met Finlay trying on hats in Clive Rowland's, unable to settle on that season's colour. I passed on the universal fashion rule: "Black is the new black," and that seemed to help. We headed through Rothiemurches to the car park.

The walk in was a pleasant one. Shallow snow lay on soft peat, we left chocolate footprints in sugar icing, and chatted along the few miles to Coire an Lochain. Visibility was restricted by the low clouds, but we hoped for good conditions on the crags as cold damp weather had been present all week. The back corner of the Lochain was the best bet in Scotland for thick riming and Savage Slit was a long-standing ambition.

Contouring below No. 6 Buttress felt exposed. The steep slopes dropping a long way to the lochan had sufficient snow cover to feel slippy but not enough to provide support. I edged nervously along to the base of the route, clutching at the rocks above as my feet felt all the rigid limitations of the unfamiliar plastic boots. Then freezing fingers and threatened hot-aches hustled me into the harness and onto the first pitch before I could settle properly. Rounded granite blocks rise to the base of the crack. These are obviously moderate in summer, and pangs of longing for warm dry rocks, and sticky rubber filled me as anxiety refused to dissipate.

This was very different from the last winter outing which had featured reassuring hooks and clamping torques on blocky Quinaig quartzite. Fin was tied onto a single, and far-from-perfect Friend, belaying with an air of impatience contained with deliberate effort, and an implied intolerance of faffing that verged on disgust. Hexes refused to settle in flared cracks and I continued to make insecure lurches upwards, fighting the growing conviction that this was a big mistake, and asking myself; had I not properly learned the folly of belays on single camming devices from the run-out below Point Five those eight years before?

I grovelled onto the ledge below the start of the actual crack, fixed a runner and immediately felt better. One move up with good hooks on flat edges and this brought up another ledge and another good runner – I was in the swing of things again. Long-standing ambition had led to detailed inspection of numerous magazine articles, and I knew the precise distance out from the wide corner crack to sweep clear the hoar, and excavate a second crack that took solid, large wire runners at two-metre intervals.

Neat knee locks for the left leg provided a solid base to clear hand holds and axe placements from the horizontal striations that seam across the corner. I made steady progress to immediately below the next ledge, perhaps the last runner had been fitted with slightly too much haste, considering the one before had been lacking true bombproof credentials, but safety lies in a confident state of mind. I moved onto small crampon edges and stretched slightly precariously for the ledge, hunting for the turf to bang home the axes and get really secure again.

There is none on such a popular route, and in my digging, I pulled off a face-full of snow. This lodged behind my glasses and I was effectively blinded. I shook my head but failed to restore vision. This was serious. I did not have a spare hand to clean the glasses. I could not see the footholds to step back down to. The early neurotic panics did not return but were not far away. Peering through the gap cleared by a hurried index finger showed the location of a flat hold opposite my right hip. Twisting quickly on my left toes I planted the right knee and thrutched all my weight up and onto it. Supported by a single point of contact I was entirely committed, but I could now reach blocks at the back of the ledge and haul myself off the vertical and catch my breath.

The glasses were secure in a pocket, I had another proper runner, and the next section of crack lead steeply to the halfway ledge and belay. I had heard of people climbing this section inside the crack. Certainly, it was wider than body width, but not by much. I found the verglassed depths repellent. I could imagine a horrible rattling fall, axes clattering off the walls on wrist fracturing leashes, and wedging beyond reach as a grisly warning to over-ambitious winter climbers. Perhaps I might survive the season, maintaining a fragile existence, advising passing leaders on the lower section of the pitch and surviving on Mars Bars tossed in by bored belayers. I would crawl out ready for summer with a rock star's thin frame. Actually, the climbing up the jaws of the crack is easier than it looks. More leg jams and precise crampon work, and a combination of hooks and cold crimps took me up to the belay on a wedged chokestone.

This had been a very satisfying pitch, and my enjoyment of it was to be augmented. Fin was obviously out of form and was struggling hard. Every move was accompanied by an unintelligible commentary. His breathing was loud. My helpful suggestions were not acknowledged. He approached the belay in a slow series of painful spasms. In the top crack his increasing fatigue led to unorthodox technique. With a muttered: "Hope this works," he slotted the pick of his hammer through the slotted adze of his piranhas, then wedged the composite creation across the crack. He slithered his body up behind, wedged and quickly advanced the tools to another precarious jam. As he tried, and failed, to hook the rounded top of the chokestone I took pity on him and stood on his axes, which landed him on the belay. After two minutes he had sufficiently recovered his breath to blame it all on the sack. I was a bit dubious as it only held the other empty sack, a duvet jacket and a two-litre bottle of Irn-bru.

I enjoyed the contents as he readied himself for the second pitch. There is nothing quite as enjoyable as a climb that is in the bag, I had a solid belay at the top of a hard-fought lead, and could look forward to enjoying a top rope up the last difficult pitch. Warmth and rehydration were my sweet companions as Fin's form improved and he accelerated up the corner to a belay on the edge of the buttress. I was looking forward to the next bit.

The sack still seemed light swinging it round onto my back as the ropes tightened above me. I stretched for the first hooks and had to step down again. The straps needed adjusting as they impeded the free reach of the arms. I tried several arrangements but none seemed to help. As I set off on the climbing my arms seemed unusually exhausted. The careful, calculating technique I had enjoyed on the lower pitch was immediately replaced by fumbled lodging of axes, and tired thrutches between inadequate footholds. My initial discomfort crumbled rapidly into anger, I was too knackered to unclip runners from the ropes and the frozen quickdraws added to the awkward encumbrance. My language deteriorated until I was left shouting a single repeated obscenity at every object that blocked my way. Fin was giggling quietly to himself, which transmitted down the rope in infuriating shakes. I understood that I was making a spectacle of myself but lacked inspiration to lift myself from grim frustration. I slowly gained height, and polluted the pristine hills with my moronic litany. A final ledge allowed me to suspend the sack from the harness, which made the climbing easier, but it jammed fast on the final chokestone, requiring some uncomfortable guddling before I could be released.

Humour was restored by an easy pitch, and the sight of a lost vole falling in my footprints and taking an inordinate time to climb out again. We wandered along the plateau to the Goat Track and easily made Tescos in time for steak and Roquefort.

A few weeks later we were back at Feshie Bridge. This time things were more serious. We were climbing for the first time with Mark Robson, who would be on the next summer's trip to Pakistan. Some prestige was at stake. The alarm went off seriously early and we were away at an unprecedented hour.

Snow had been falling all night and though there was no more than a couple of inches, it was possible that the snow gates would be closed at Glenmore. The ski fences had yet to fill up so ploughs would not be clearing the road before tourist hours. However, we had risen before the gates could be closed and followed a single set of tracks up the hill. Our celebrations were premature as we slithered to a halt below the Sugar Bowl car park. The previous car was stuck halfway up the slope. Mark and I were ordered out and onto the bonnet over the wheels, to add traction.

No joy. The wheels spun and blue fumes filled the sharp morning air. I was ready to grab the pack and start walking but Fin had other ideas. He turned the car and slipped it into reverse. The wheels only spun faster, and the unburned petrol spewed from the exhaust. Instead of moving upwards the car started pivoting across the road towards me. I stepped back smartly and as the wheel spun towards me it caught on the verge and briefly regained traction. The Nissan Sunny moved six inches up the hill. Fin was spinning the steering wheel back the other way and the car slewed back towards Mark. He jumped clear, the near side wheel caught on the verge, and the car gained another six inches. Mark caught my eye.

As the car swung onto my verge I reached out and shoved. The car gained two feet of altitude, It spun back over the road and Mark did the same. Fin kept spinning the wheel back and forth and swinging the car from verge to verge and with the aid of our well-timed shoves, briefly jolted upwards at every turn. The upwards progress was slower than glaciers in retreat, but loads more fun than walking. The smell of petrol was overwhelming. The Nissan engine squealed in protest. Around us rare lichen curled up their fronds and died, ptarmigan fell choking from the sky.

We gradually drew towards the perched Vauxhall Astra, and its occupants emerged. Geoff and Graham had beaten us out of the cottage, but were flabbergasted by the Bennet solution to the hill. They meekly backed down the hill to let us pass. We quickly regained lost momentum and disappeared from their view. As we rounded the left-hand corner the gradient eased, and by sitting over the wheels, the car made progress in a more conventional fashion. Facing forward again, Mark and I passed the time of day as the scenery rolled by. We were by now attaining speeds of five, even six miles-an-hour but the day was windless. We were very comfortable perched on the bonnet, rolling cigarettes and swapping stories.

We passed the empty Coire na Ciste car park and swung round onto the level traverse towards Coire Cas. Traction improved and gradually, the car began to pick up speed. The acceleration was minimal but constant. Mark and I were ready to quit our positions as external ballast and knocked on the windscreen but Fin ignored us. With fingers hooked under the bonnet, we stayed in place, now not enjoying the ride so much. The rush of winter air blew away the earlier convivial warmth. Then the junction with the direct Coire Cas road appeared. A two-foot mound of drifted snow blocked our way. We belted towards it.

"Fin…! Stop!"

"No!…"

The car hurtled into the drift and stopped. Mark and I were catapulted forward, cleared the drift and landed on the tarmac. We somersaulted into the crash barrier, which blocked a long drop to a distant burn. Fin got out looking slightly sheepish. I picked myself up and seemed to have escaped major trauma.

"There's often a drift there from the snow ploughs, said Fin. "We'll make it next time."

Like lambs walking obliviously into the slaughterhouse we settled back over the wheels, and retreated for another run up. Sure enough we made it through the drift and onto the car park, whooping like cowboys going to town after months on the trail.

(We later learned that the snowgates were subsequently closed, reopening at I0am Everyone else went to S'neachda.)

After an approach of this kind the walk over to Loch Avon should have been a piece of cake. The guys had invested in Salomon 9s which seemed as light as carpet slippers. They disappeared into the mist. I was massively burned off. As I sweated up to the cairn at the top of the Fiacail, they shivered theatrically and set off down Coire Raibert.

The Loch Avon basin is a special place for Scottish mountaineers, the romantic heart of the Cairngorms is guarded by many steep granite crags. The outlook over the loch to the remote mountains at the head of Glen Avon is truly wild in the romantic tradition. Unfortunately, it is very well publicised. In summer large crowds of Duke of Edinburgh Awardees and German Uberbackpackers erode further the many paths that follow each contour in rings above the loch. I once found a plastic bag of rubbish with that Saturday's *Times* shoved between two rocks. The readership is going down market faster than the paper these days.

Anyway, we had it all to ourselves. We emerged from the clouds and rounded Loch Avon to the boulders below the Sticil. The towers and buttresses of Cairn Etchachan loomed above us out of the murk. We followed the entry ledge along to the base of Crevasse Route. Fin set off up the first pitch. Mark and I settled into the pleasure of a shared belay, conversational gambits were initially wide-ranging, but were increasingly dominated by negative assessments of the leaders skill, as warmth drained from both body and spirit. This was again an imposter, appearing moderate in gradient and decorated with helpful features, but on closer inspection, rounded and bleak. I find seconding on a single 9mm rope unsettling. It emphasises the exposure, the consequences of a slip seem more serious. Mark and I were climbing simultaneously and generally getting in each other's way. I misjudged a move but lacked space to reconsider it. Spreadeagled on poor holds, with the ropes twisting through runners and pulling sideways, I was close to falling off. Incipient hot aches added to my woes, but with company my usual morale-boosting strategy of foul swearing was suppressed. I stayed on, but only just, hiding my pull on the runner with the last dregs of cunning.

At the belay we debated the lead of the crux. I declined to offer to lead it. Mark raised his eyebrows, but did the honourable thing. Steep flakes lead up the corner. He cammed both axes in and laybacked up, crampon points on ripples, poised cat-like below the ledge. Then a curious change:

his left knee flexed up gracefully, hooked the ledge and initiated a scuttling sideways thrutch, three metres along the ledge to another crack that he used to stand up with. "Interesting," he said, placing one of my wires in the crack and wellying it home with some heavy blows from his hammer. He disappeared into the chimney above and kept the ropes moving at a good pace to the next belay.

Fin followed first, leaving me to dwell on my fragile climbing psyche, and the third pitch which was unavoidably mine. Described as a steep crack, I was gloomily imagining hanging over my head. This distracted me from the matter in hand, which was a shame. It's a great pitch, technical torquing up the corner, then a vertical chimney that twists up to a fine ledge, perched below the unavoidable crack. My companions were well settled on the ledge, resting on their laurels and their packs. Savage Slit's wee brother split the headwall of the buttress. No parallel cracks offered reassurance of intermediate security. The crack was much bigger than any protection we carried. Feeling like a condemned man I assembled our rack. No pleading was going to get me out of it, and I set off. Once again appearances were deceptive: this was a very civilised slit. Flat ledges provided big holds, and a remarkable number of runners. As I wrapped the ropes around the boulder at the edge of the plateau, I was once again enjoying myself, and feeling satisfied that I had contributed a decent lead to the expedition. The guys joined me and we shook hands.

Dusk was gathering as we decided to avoid the long walk around the plateau, and headed down a shallow gully on the east side of Carn Etchachan. This had been in the lee for the day and I was concerned about the potential for avalanches. I hung back as Fin stepped off the rocks onto the snow slope. I had never before believed that it was possible to fall up to one's neck in snow, but seeing is believing. Fin dug himself down the slope, and into the boulder field, and I followed carefully.

I wondered if they had maybe tired each other out with the mornings efforts, and would be walking out at a slower pace. I was wrong. Mark was so concerned by the effort with which I mantel-shelved off the steep bouldery steps at the top of Coire Raibert he handed over his last Mars Bar in a clear understanding of whose need was greater. They outpaced me again on the slopes up to the cairn at the top of the Fiacail, and I was left in my own pool of headtorch light. The night was calm but visibility was minimal in the cloud. Without my glasses my perception of the trail was difficult. I followed my nose, trying not to worry about the lack of ability to fix accurately on my bearing, peering anxiously for steep ground at the top of the Mess of Pottage or the Coire Cas headwall. The wide path off Cairngorm was a reassuring landmark and I found my companions again in the lee of the cairn. We headed down into Speyside together, out of the wilderness and into the ski fields.

'THE BOYS' FROM EDINBURGH

By Douglas Wood

THE diaries and photograph album of my father George Wood give an interesting insight to this group of climbers from the early 1930s. The group was based around four young bankers at the head office of the Bank of Scotland at the Mound in Edinburgh – Ian Charleson, Ian Macdonald, Charlie Ruxton and George Wood, who referred to themselves as 'the Boys'.

At times they were joined by others, with Alan Lennox and Ted Forde featuring frequently. Charleson later became President of the SMC, and he along with Forde are credited with having accomplished the first Greater Traverse of the Cuillin in a single day in June 1939 – the main Cuillin Ridge with Clach Glas and Blaven. Opportunities for regular serious climbing at that time were limited considerably by a six-day working week, and a highlight was the expedition during the two-week summer holiday. Descriptions of these expeditions by the Boys are given in some detail in the diaries and can also be followed through a series of photographs.

It was the time of nailed boots, the Bergen rucksack, Primus stove, Tinker tent, aneroid to support map and compass for navigation, and when kilts were worn for walking in the hills. Postcards were sent home to report progress, and mail collected from Post Offices *en route* brought letters and parcels of baking from home. In fact, the journey was as much a part of the expedition as the climbs. In June 1932 the Boys headed for the Cairngorms and had a two-week trek that started at Kirriemuir and eventually finished at Pitlochry via Braemar and Kingussie. This took them over the Tolmount hills, all the high tops of the Cairngorms, as well as Beinn a' Ghlo in Glen Tilt.

A routine that features throughout was to rise in the morning and then go for a swim in the nearest river or loch. They would then go looking for milk and eggs at any habitation nearby, and quite often this was provided without payment – indeed the offer of payment could sometimes cause offence. Typical breakfast menu was porridge and milk, bacon, sausages and eggs, bread and marmalade, and lashings of hot cocoa. It could be over three hours before starting.

An expedition to Skye followed in the summer of 1933, the first night being spent with the lighthouse keeper at Corran, Mr McKechran. It was a long approach on foot taking three days to reach Mallaig by Loch Sunart, Acharacle, Moidart, the hill track to Glen Uig, and finally the train from Lochailort. At Mallaig the Boys negotiated a crossing to Skye and were taken the following morning in a small open boat to Camasunary for eight shillings a head, ascending Blaven in the late afternoon. Poor weather dogged them for the next week enforcing some unscheduled rest days that used up precious supplies. A six-and-a-half hour trek in the rain was required for the walk round the coast to Glen Brittle, via Loch Coruisk "rather disappointing compared with Loch Avon", followed by endless rock and bog. Gaps in the rain gave opportunities for at least two worthwhile days. On one of these days the Boys ascended the stone shoot to Sgurr Alasdair, then continued on to Sgurr Sgumain. They then proceeded to Sgurr Dubh na Da Bheinn, Sgurr Dubh Mor, Sgurr nan Eag and Garsbheinn, then back over the boggy moor to Glen Brittle.

The following day, in brilliant weather, they climbed Sgurr Dearg by the west ridge, bypassed the Inaccessible Pinnacle (which they returned to another year), then on to An Stac and Sgurr Mhic Choinnich, back to Sgurr Dearg and on to Sgurr na Banachdich, Sgurr Thormaid, Sgurr a' Ghreadaidh, Sgurr a' Mhadaidh, and down over Sgurr Thuilm – 11 hours. These two days were not without some tricky moments but the Boys were clearly inspired by their first experience of the Cuillin. Continuing poor weather forced the group to make an early departure from Skye and they headed over to Sligachan, from where they got the bus to Broadford and then a boat back to Mallaig.

Of course, as soon as they left Broadford the good weather returned! After a swim at the Silver Sands they made their way along the north side of Loch Morar. Arriving at the lodge at South Tarbert, Mr Caldwell, "a crusty old boy", refused to ferry them across the loch and insisted they would have to go up the loch for a farther nine miles of rough ground and bracken. However, a little farther on, in the glen to Loch Nevis, they pitched camp and had better luck later in the evening, meeting Sandy Macdonald who arranged to ferry them over to Meoble in the morning. So the journey continued by Meoble, Loch Beoraid and over to Loch Eilt to camp the night in the station waiting room at Glenfinnan, courtesy of the Station Master.

The penultimate day saw them catch the eight o'clock train to Fort William, then a 12-hour day on the Mamores before returning to camp in Glen Nevis at 11.45pm. In fact, it was six years later and after two further visits to the Cuillin that Charleson and Forde did their pioneering Greater Traverse which is described by Charleson in the Journal (Vol. xxii, p 127-132). In the article he refers to his companion rather grandly as Woodhurst E. Forde.

It records setting out from camp at the base of Gars-bheinn at 1.30am on Monday, June 12, 1939 reaching the summit at 3.05am. They had left caches of food and drink at the base of the Inaccessible Pinnacle and on the summit of Bidein Druim nan Ramh and a tent stocked with food and spare clothing near the mouth of Harta Corrie. In a strong blustery wind the two of them completed the traverse of the main ridge to Sgurr nan Gillean by 3.35pm and had a rest at the tent in Harta Corrie before continuing over Clach Glas to reach the summit of Blaven at 11.05pm.

By 1934 two of the Boys had cars. That summer they had two days in Glen Coe (Aonach Eagach, and Ossian's cave/Aonach Dubh/Bidean), then continued on to Dundonnell, Torridon and Glen Affric. The diary records a day on Beinn Alligin and Liathach.

"Our camp is situated at Glen Grudie where a path leads up the glen between the Beinn Eighe range and the Liathach group. As bread is scarce bake scones which, surprising though it may seem, appear to be enjoyed. Have breakfast of shredded wheat and prunes, boiled eggs and marmalade. As this is to be a big day we try to get away early. By 10.30 we are off in Ian Mac's car for Torridon. Leave car above Torridon House at Coire Mhic Nobuil and at 12.30 set out in blazing heat for Beinn Alligin. See huge dragon flies. Head up ridge of Gruagaich (2904ft.). Reach summit at 2.30pm and then easier going to Sgurr Mhor (3232ft.).

"Descend over broken ground and stop for lunch at 3.30pm. Here we sunbathe and waste precious time until 5.30pm. Ian finds a young fawn nearby. Drop down to about 1000ft. and then commence long climb over broken ground to gain ridge of Liathach. Commence the climb by 5.45 and after hot pull up and scramble over steep ground gain summit of Meall Dearg (3150ft.) by 7.30pm. From here to Mullach an Rathain (3358ft.) we have difficult climb over and round pinnacles of loose stone. Rock gives way in huge chunks and earthy scree gives poor foothold. Charlie successfully makes traverse round grassy ledges on the east side of second last pinnacle while we others go round west side dropping some height before clambering up stone gully. This takes fully 1 hour 30 miutes but we consider this the worst part so far.

"On the way round the pinnacles I come across a magnificent specimen of fossil vegetation in sandstone. We continue along ridge with pinnacles to Am Fasarinen with low incoming clouds below us. Then by 11pm we have reached Spidean a' Choire Leith and finally complete the ridge at 11.45pm at Stuc a' Choire Dhuibh Bhig (3000ft). Then commence difficult descent over broken and very steep ground at midnight. Taking care, we accomplish this successfully and by 12.45am have returned. The two Ians return to Torridon to collect the car arriving back at 2am. After hot Oxo, chocolate and cake we are soon fast asleep. We have probably climbed 7000ft. over the day."

Elsewhere on this trip, there is a comment: "Proceeding to Coinneach Mhor (3130ft.) we come upon a ptarmigan sitting on young and she lets us stroke her gently."

On another day: "Milk not obtainable owing to cows calving so we return and have breakfast of porridge and buttercup cream, boiled eggs and fruit salad."

It is fascinating to appreciate the different context of self-sufficiency and physical stamina that emanates from these accounts, and to hear about some of the characters the Boys met on their travels. Nearly all the people they met were those who lived there. While the hills and the routes may have changed little, developments in communications, equipment and transport have without doubt altered the element of adventure.

WEIRD SCENES INSIDE THE GOLD MINE

By Bish McAra

TUESDAY. It was a Tuesday. I think it was a Tuesday. Does it matter? In any case Project-X had loomed for some time. This was a private project. A project not to be shared. Not even when it was complete. It was to be a non-recorded adventure that left no trace. Just an adventure to be reclaimed by those who follow. Project X was to be a recyclable project. A project still preserved for the satisfying of the egos of those yet to come.

A Tuesday was a good day. Let's say it was a Tuesday. I'm not one for recording dates. My photo album and diary is my mind. But a Tuesday was good. The hill would be quiet with no witness to record the project. A quick raid. Done and dusted. A gem of high-risk self-indulgence left unrecorded and free to satisfy the vanity of future explorers.

The line was obvious. In point of fact it was nothing new, being clearly visible from road and rail for all to view.

The nature of the plan had dictated a night of worry. An early departure was assured. Northward progress up the loch side was rapid on this March morning. Flexitime had clearly failed the masses and my plan for an empty hill was assured.

Park up, pump-up. Make sure these bike tyres will take the load. No timely walk-in to Project X. Approach on foot might result in more time to rationalise the risk and abandon the plan. No, a fast and committed approach by bike was called for.

The project looked feasible. The weather was excellent with just a little frost overnight. Progress was rapid with Eas Annie slipping past within 35 minutes. Not much ice on that today. A smile crept over my face and the tension lifted for a moment recalling past adventures in these environs. On being unable to tolerate waiting our turn for Eas Annie I recalled a retreat into the gold mine for an afternoon of alternative adventure. Capstan full-strength perhaps aided the weird scenes inside the gold mine.

But today was different. Years of inactivity and life commitments dictated a drop in grade. But for Project X this mattered little.

With bike abandoned, upward progress was swift. Perfect névé. Not best for Project X but what the hell, I was there now. All this high-tech gear makes it easy. And music softens the feeling of risk. The narrows approach and my scheme to emulate the early pioneers via a crampon-free ascent came to an end. With crampons on and rope out I now at least had a companion. With 60ft. between us we climbed upwards though the narrows and on towards the summit. On topping out it's confirmed. I have the hill to myself. The route had demanded respect and it was some time since I'd ventured upwards on a Grade 1 gully. The line was strong and the summit snowfield worryingly steep but it was a classic by any account, with a great summit finish. With crystal clarity past projects were in view. The Y-Gully on Cruach Ardrain to the east, Ben Ime to the south and Stob Ghabhar to the north-west.

Considerable time was then spent in assessment of the feasibility of Project X. In the event it lived up to expectations, the narrows flashing past in a flurry of adrenaline and the exit onto the lower run-out marking the point of assured survival. The return to the bike was over within minutes.

Back at the car the bike and kit was flung into the boot and consideration of Project-Y commenced. On this trip, my companion was manufactured by Buff, a maker of snowboards.

An account of the descent of the Central Gully of Ben Lui on a snowboard by Bish McAra (March 1999).

Footnote: I record this event with some misgivings as my preference is to share my good fortune with those adventurers still to come via a policy of non-recording. To view some on-line resources with a different view of Scottish climbing please take a moment to view www.climbrannoch.co.uk

TOWARDS THE BEN, SPEAN BRIDGE   JOHN MITCHELL

Alan Shand on the Red Rocks classic 'Running Man' (5.11), Las Vegas, Nevada. Photo: Iain White.

From the new series guide to Glen Coe and Ardgour. Emma Williams climbing 'Lady Jane' (E2 5b), Aonach Dubh. Photo: Mark Glaister.

SURVIVAL TECHNIQUES FOR USE IN COMMITTEE MEETINGS

By Iain Smart

I know from conversations that many members of the Club use their mountaineering experiences to relieve the excruciating boredom of long committee meetings, particularly those in which they are powerless participants. Cases of brain damage from unprotected exposure to such meetings are common. In this context the recycling of mountaineering experiences is a useful technique with many successes to its credit. I know someone who claims to be the first person to have mentally climbed all the Munros during a single committee meeting (Munrosis psychorepetans or, I suppose, in some cases, Munrosis waltermittiensis). According to him, he survived unharmed while everyone else suffered severe psychological collapse. These notes describe a fairly pedestrian, run of the mill application of the technique. I remember it because of its ending which showed me I was not a lone skywalker. I am sure others have more exciting accounts that could be added to the literature on this commonly used but little written about form of committee survivormanship.

I was almost at the top of Integrity a climb just within my ability. I seemed to be climbing solo and yet enjoying it immensely, moving skilfully on the sun-warmed rock, relishing the exposure. I stopped for a breather before finishing the last few moves, sensing the vast emptiness of Coire Lagan behind. I looked between my feet down the cleavage of the east face to see the Cioch with some aspirant climbing on to it. I topped out from the crack with a few more confident moves, walked over to the skyline and beheld Rum and Canna and let my eye roam over the silvery sea cats-pawed with little breaths of wind to the low profile of the Long Island. Just then a voice sounded somewhere to my left. It was saying, "And what conclusion has your sub-committee come to on this matter, Dr Smart?". I had been waiting for it and knew what to do. I mentally abseiled down from Sron na Ciche . . . .
. . . . *into a committee room in the University in the middle of a meeting planning yet another curriculum reform. As I was re-entering my body I heard my preprogrammed voice saying, "Our sub-committee agrees with the conclusions of the main committee on this matter and has nothing to add." I sensed all round me the general approval of the good sense of our sub-committee. Originally we had been enthusiastic and creative but this only caused trouble. We were now more mature and had given up wasting the time of our betters by having a mind of our own. The next item I would be required to agree with was much further down the agenda so I*

Getting to grips with the 'Incredible Hand Crack' (5.10c), Supercrack Buttress, Indian Creek, Canyonlands, Utah. Photo: Tom Prentice.

*was free for at least another half hour. To endure the intervening tedium
while remaining fully conscious of the present would be dangerous.
Preservation of sanity required another journey into the astral plane. So
setting part of my mind listening on the emergency channel I teleported
the rest of it back to the Cuillins* . . . .
. . . . This time I found myself walking up
to the Coire Tairnealar on a hot summer's day. I stopped for a dive into
each be-water-falled rock pool as it passed by, enjoying the tingle of cool,
clear water against skin and seeing the sun-dappled surface from
underneath as I rose up from the pebbled bottom where the shadows played
in jumbled colours, then the pleasure of drying off luxuriously on a warm
rock slab while watching the breeze ruffling the feathers of the little poplar
trees. Eventually I reached the inner Coire and started up the vast
intimidating boiler plates of Mallory's climb. This time I wasn't in such
good form as on Sron na Ciche; the old familiar fear radiated from the pit
of the stomach. I definitely needed a companion. Tom Weir appeared from
somewhere. We had an exhilarating time particularly when a warm wind
got up and tried to pluck us off the slabs. We then went up Bidein Druim
nan Ramh, my favourite peak and had lunch on its platform summit. It
was a clear day and the view was great. 'A real magic moment', I heard
Tom saying as clearly as if he had really been there. . . . .
. . . . By way of
contrast I then changed channels to the top of Sgurr na Lapaich on a winter's
day of some sunlight and a lot of moving shadow. The glen bottoms were
filled with glooms of navy blue and black; lonely patches of sunshine
wandered around the upper snows sometimes keeping up with the gaps in
the clouds and sometimes getting lost and dying. It was a day of high
drama – I was so grateful to be there. Five other people were also present:
two Snaddens, a couple of Slessers and our national hero, William Wallace
- all good company on the hill. When I arrived they were about to ski back
down again towards Glen Strathfarrar. A brilliant rainbow now appeared
spanning the glen in front of us. The others took off. They spread over the
slopes of the curving corrie, turning gracefully like autumn leaves floating
down in the wind until coming together again as black dots a few hundred
feet below under the enchanted arch of many colours. I enjoyed the
loneliness for a moment savouring the ambience. Before following on I
sharpened up the focus of the landscape to reveal more detail, adjusted
the contrast between light and shade to add to the drama and modulated
the colours of the rainbow to the maximum glory consistent with retaining
the aesthetic balance of the whole. On occasions like this you might as
well take advantage of all the facilities available. I could hardly believe
my good fortune to be skiing down after the others amid so much space
and colour. It was good Spring snow, the turning was easy, I could hear
the skis biting in at each turn. The rainbow and the autumn leaf effect of

the skiers must have cross-referenced in my mind for suddenly I found myself . . . . miles to the Westward on the shoulder of Beinn Dearg Mor, looking North across Strath na Seallag on a luminously gloomy day with little wind. It was indeed autumn because the birch trees were yellow in the bottom of the glen. A half rainbow with its open side directed to the west arched over the head of the Loch, brilliant against the blue-black raincloud with trailing silver showers veiling the brooding bulk of An Teallach. Just then a skein of about a dozen geese (barnacles I think) flew honking down the glen. They entered from the darkness on the right into the brightness within the arc of the rainbow and as they caught the sunlight, the voice again obtruded . . . . *and I was back in the Committee room. My voice was saying: "Yes my committee would gladly consider the changes that had just been proposed and I would bring back their agreement at the next meeting". I would of course have to find out from someone what the required changes were. My answer phone had failed to record the details. I spent the next ten minutes hanging around in the meeting. Those who had power were manoeuvring around trying to use it, most of them (to be just) with the best intentions. Once I was sure there was no way I could usefully contribute I left and found . . .* . . . . myself at Loch Scavaig enjoying an evening beer in the cockpit of the yacht "Goodbye Girl' which was riding at anchor there on a calm summer's evening. My friend Phil was on the foredeck playing his pipes and the vale profound was overflowing with the sound of 'Farewell to the Creeks'. We were pleasantly tired after traversing Sgurr Dhu na Da Bheinn and, as we sipped our beer, felt some detached sorrow for the campers on the nearby shore being driven crazy by the midges. . .
. . . . The scene then changed of its own accord to another time and place. I found myself on Ladhar Bheinn on a sunset evening. It must have been a clip from the time in the late forties when I dossed there on a fine night of high summer with Hamish Nicol. He was a student friend who, after graduation, vanished somewhere down south and nevermore was heard of again in the land of the living, a pity because I seem to remember he was an amusing character. . . . . I then fast forwarded memory 40 years on to another time on Ladhar Bheinn on an equally fine evening. We had ascended directly from Loch Hourn and could see our yacht anchored below our feet in the shadows of the coming night. . . . . Then I hopped a few miles south into the rough bounds of Knoydart and

wandered about on Sron na Criche for a while watching the glens fill with midnight blue before descending . . . . *to the meeting again in response to bad vibes arriving on the emergency channel. There was a stushie of some kind going on . It didn't seem to concern our sub-committee but was, nevertheless deserving of attention as it was developing into good theatre with some accomplished ham acting. The plot as far as I could gather was that some of the people who had power had ganged up against one of their own number. It looked pre-arranged to me, a clever ambush. The ambushed party was eventually forced to submit but not without some considerable recititivo and a plangent terminal aria before the curtain fell. For those who had ears to hear there was some silent but enthusiastic one-handed, zen-type hand clapping. It had really been quite a creditable performance. Things were going to be quiet for a bit as each side regrouped, so I hopped into the teleporter and beamed up again to the astral plane.. . . . .*
. . . . .This time I landed up on the top of Blaven and took control of events. I started with a clear fresh dawn with one star still awake and made the sun come up over the mainland until the world was filled with light. As the morning wore on the shadows shortened until the glare of noon flattened the landscape, the profiles of the world becoming blurred in heat-haze. As the torpid afternoon progressed shadows gradually returned and the trembling land regained relief. The mellow evening progressed. A full moon rose exactly opposite a setting full sun which is, of course, how it should be in real life at high latitudes at the summer solstice. The panorama of sea and mountain changed to silver and shadow; the stars came up and a mild summer's night gradually entered into another dawn. . . . .
. . . . *a quick nip back to the committee - all seemed well - so I returned to the astral plane* . . . .
. . . . I adjusted the position of the moon until it kept a geostationary due south on the plane of the ecliptic. This resulted in a full moon every night and a solar eclipse every day at noon. This must have done something terrible to the tides but I couldn't work out what even on paper. Easter and other lunar dependant events would have had problems too . . . .
. . . . Then transporting the scene to the equator, I brought the sun straight up from the horizon, overhead at noon and straight down again so that night fell with a bang somewhere behind Benbecula. It made a noise a bit like the one o'clock gun in Edinburgh. The southern constellations then blazed in a black velvet sky. Skye itself had already shrivelled under the noonday heat into something resembling the Sinai peninsula. I don't know what the good people of Skye were thinking while this was going on but no doubt it has all been

recorded in the West Highland Free Press. Certainly it must have thrown astrologers into confusion. Being fairly confused myself by now . . . .
. . . .
. . . .*I returned briefly to the meeting where the top predators were repressing an attempt to come back from the dead by the disaffected victim who seemed unable to accept the brilliant success of the original ambush. He thought he had been misunderstood. They were trying to get through to him that he had been understood (that was the major part of his problem) and that he should shut up and settle the matter later in private with his fellow carnivores rather than embarrass his peers by carrying on in such an unsophisticated manner in front of the herbivores forming the rest of the committee. We herbivores sat there with eyes averted placidly munching away at the low-calorie intellectual diet that was our lot. For a little respite from life at the bottom of the pyramid I . . . .*
. . . . . .teleported
to Greenland to a fine day on a granite ridge on a peak at the head of the Roslin Glacier in the awe-inspiring Stauning Alps. It was one of those overwhelming Greenland days of windless silence. Frost and granite crystals were a-twinkle in the morning sun and the clear air brought the structural features of distant peaks into sharp focus. I was just beginning to enjoy the fabulous panorama. In fact Malcolm and I had started to inspect a knot of spectacular rock spires to the north. We were discussing possible routes when I had to leave Malcolm there alone as I sensed the meeting was about to end. (He must have got back alright because I saw him again recently.) . . . .
. . . . The Chairman was saying, "Before we adjourn could I ask Dr Eccles if he has done anything about the accommodation required for the new course we have been discussing ?" There was dead silence. The Dr Eccles referred to, a herbivorous nonentity like myself, was sitting next to me and his eyes were fixed on the horizon. He vouchsafed no answer. The chairman repeated the question. It was obvious to all that Dr Eccles was not with us, so I gave him a gentle prod. He jumped a foot and started to talk incoherently; he was obviously under considerable stress. I knew he was a fellow space traveller and recognised that he was having a malfunction of his teleporter. I threw him a lifeline , "Say , 'The matter is receiving urgent consideration'" , I hissed at him. "The matter is receiving urgent consideration", he dutifully intoned. "Do you think it will be satisfactory?". Prolonged silence. Charles was still somewhere else. I think his teleporter had got fankled up in the coordinates of space-time. (Easily done, I have often had that trouble myself). I could hear him broadcasting an SOS on the psychological equivalent of the international distress frequency, namely 121.5 kilopsychles. "Say 'Yes' I broadcast. "Yes, Mr Chairman," announced Charles, "It should be all right." The emergency was over. He had returned and was coherent again.

After the meeting he said: "Thanks for your help. You got me out of a tight corner. I really was in great danger. I had been sailing alone around the world. I was off Cape Horn; I could see it through the rain less than a mile away. The boat was being driven before a wind of gale-force, maybe more, gusting, I'd say to Force 12 at times; even the storm jib had been carried away and I was running under bare poles trying to keep her from broaching. I had one hand on the helm and was struggling to get some warps out of the rope locker to trail behind to slow her up. That was when you poked me in the ribs; I thought the tiller had broken off. No wonder I jumped; I thought I'd had it."

BEGINNINGS

The holds were there
somewhere
asking to be caressed
into a route of sorts
Extremities
(finger tips and toes
not yet frozen) –
were made aware
– tinglings
        – tensions
                – tremblings
– and laughter

Rock rasped the core
of a pumping heart,
pulling in my sack
and belayed me
with cobweb delicacy
to the hard rock
of a daft game
I thought was reality.

The first frost found us out
Gaping at a lit moon.
Honed by the knife edge of cold,
Salt-sharp star-shivery,
We took refuge under the pines
And pulled on a pullover of past years
To face the winter ahead.
But the ice and the moon and the roaring
Zeroed our reality. Cold, moon, stags
Were all present, our NOW –
Which is all the place
We can ever be.

Hamish M. Brown.

PETER B. AYSCOUGH AND THE NAISMITH HUT

By Bill McKerrow

WHEN the Club was informed in February 1993 that it was to be the recipient of the sum of almost £74,000 in an astonishingly generous legacy, the natural assumption was that this was as a result of the foresight and thoughtfulness of one of our own august late senior members. It turned out, much to the surprise and curiosity of the Club hierarchy, that the benefactor was not only not a Club member, but was not even known to any Club members, as far as they were willing to admit! The man who had the best interests of Scottish mountaineering at heart was one Professor Peter Brian Ayscough, late of Leeds University and otherwise man of some mystery, of whom more anon.

As befits an organisation renowned for its thrift and prudence, the legacy was quickly stashed away in the Club coffers and, if not quite forgotten about, at least ignored for the next year or so. Discussions followed among the great and the good of the Club with even the members being tentatively canvassed for ideas as to how to put this smiling of good fortune upon us to best use. A consensus slowly emerged according to the best traditions of obfuscation and mysticism, which are hallmarks of the conduct of the Club's affairs, and on this occasion, the debate was largely uninfluenced by the hard core of the 'awkward squad' within the membership! The solution of how to unload our bounty with the least embarrassment and the maximum potential benefit for the majority of the members was obvious. The near mythical concept of 'a hut in the North West' was born and by the time of the AGM in December 1994, the Club was happy to accept the recommendations of the Committee and put the plan into action

The next challenge was to decide where the hut would be situated. Nearly three years elapsed without very much happening until the Committee took the decision that 'something would have to be done'. Never known to shrink from a joust with the near impossible, a small team of completely unqualified non-experts consisting of Gerry Peet, John MacKenzie and myself were charged by the then President Bob Richardson to scour the country north of Ullapool with the brief to identify either a suitable property or possibly a site where a hut could be located. Several trips north and various discussions with landowners and the planning department followed. Numerous properties and several sites were prospected, discussed, considered and rejected on various grounds until finally, what seemed like a possible viable hut was identified in Elphin. The property in question was known as Hillside, birthplace and, at the time, still residence of 78-year-old 'Murdo the Joiner' fittingly, one of the MacKenzie clan (but uninfluenced by any pressure from the clan chief) who had finally given in to the unequal struggle involved in keeping his birthplace wind and watertight and had decided to opt for a council house in Ullapool.

At first sight it didn't seem ideal. It wasn't exactly how most of us envisaged a mountain hut, in that it was part of a small hamlet of several houses, some of them relatively modern and it was right next door to a modern house owned by Murdo's son. Nonetheless, it did fulfil the brief set by the Committee to find a traditional property north of Braemore and south of Kylesku which was reasonably close to the main road. The house itself was really on its last legs. The tin roof was leaking and the interior damp, cramped and in poor condition. The view, however, was stupendous, with Suilven in pole position and set up to the westering sun. The price, too, if not quite so breathtaking (we had already become used to the concept that the price of a few square feet of bog amid countless thousands of similar acres commanded around £25,000) was reasonable, so it seemed almost a bargain to consider paying a few thousand more to have four walls and an electricity and water supply thrown in. The Committee agreed and, after sterling attention to the legal side by Peter Macdonald, the house was purchased in the early summer of 1997. Within a few months I was, by some mysterious process, which had something to do with the force of personality of the then President of the Club, nominated to be Custodian.

The next decision was what to do with it. The choice seemed to be between patching it up in the short-term and just using it as a glorified bothy or going for the full monte and converting the building into a proper mountain hut. It shouldn't have been too difficult a decision. After all, we had the money thanks to the generosity of Peter Ayscough. Nonetheless, once again, prudence and thrift reared its head and considerable effort, primarily by Bob Reid, was put into ascertaining that we were not eligible for grant assistance for converting the building, at least not without major potential strings attached.

Meanwhile, that unsung hero of the Club, Dougie Niven, relatively recently retired but still an architectural consultant and fresh from triumphs at the Raeburn Hut and Lagangarbh, happily (or perhaps not) took on the substantial task of designing the conversion. The primary remit was for simplicity together with functionality, with systems as failsafe as possible, bearing in mind that the building would be unoccupied for several days or even weeks at a time. The 'idiot factor', exhibited not only by those visitors who are not members of the Club, had also to be incorporated into the design. Tenders then had to be sought for the work. This turned out to be a far more difficult task than we had forseen, builders being in relatively short supply in the area. The original favoured contractor, a local Ullapool joiner, after initially giving the impression of enthusiasm, withdrew at the last moment and several other tenders turned out to be dauntingly high. Comparative figures were obtained from two central belt contractors that confirmed that these tenders were not unreasonable at around £75,000.

The fact that some of the possible contractors were based 40 or more miles away did nothing to increase their enthusiasm to take on the contract or to price for it competitively. Finally, we hit what turned out to be the jackpot. John Smith, well known in the area as a skilled tradesman indicated that he would be keen to take on the contract. However, he had pursued a somewhat unorthodox and fairly relaxed lifestyle over the years which had included building fibreglass boats, smoking mackerel (and possibly other things), assisting in running a caravan site, being a nature warden on Coigach estate and general 'good lifer', as well as doing jobbing joinery work. I had known John for more than 20 years but I was reluctant to push his name forward to the Committee for fear of having to field the flak if things did not go as planned! Nonetheless, John tendered by far the lowest price at £51,200 and with much of his contracted work being VAT exempt, he was the obvious man for the job.

In the event, he turned out to be an extremely happy choice for, apart from a rather 'west coast' timescale lasting for the best part of a year and partly weather related, John has delivered superb workmanship, excellent aesthetics and overall a first-class job at a very reasonable cost to the Club. I strongly suspect (without being in any way partisan) that this is in no small measure related to the fact that his roots are in the North-east, and his work ethic is accordingly strong! He had the additional advantage of living relatively close by at Ardmair and was willing to deal with any problems at short notice and at times when it may have been difficult for me to deal with them. He even managed to impress Dougie with the standard of his workmanship and several helpful hints on how to avoid problems with the planning regulations. This was especially beneficial as direct architectural supervision was very difficult in view of the distances involved. Dougie and John seemed to earn each other's mutual, possibly grudging respect, in that John's standards remained high throughout the whole contract while Dougie's attention to detail was exemplary with more than 40 architectural drawings for every fine detail of the building.

And so, with a little gentle encouragement and a following wind, John finally completed the works to a level which made the building habitable. Furniture and fittings were purchased and the hut was officially inaugurated on the occasion of the annual dinner in Strathpeffer on the first weekend of December 1999. Full furnishing and commissioning took another few weeks and by early January, the first use of the hut by members was possible. Since then, with a few minor hiccups, the hut has been universally acclaimed by both members and visiting guests. It has hosted the great and the good of the Club, old and young, Tigers and Salvationists, and the worst that the climbing clubs of the UK could throw at it – so far – with really very little in the way of problems, and hopefully, this will continue for many years to come. Its convenience for the unique hills of the far North-west offering some of the most remote Munros and Corbetts in the country, idyllic coastal outcrop and mountain rock climbing and demanding winter routes, has contributed to its popularity but, whatever the prime interest of the visitor, there is no doubt that the ambience of the hut appeals to virtually all who spend time there and will ensure its lasting popularity.

So much for the hut, what do we know of the man? Who was Peter Ayscough, our mysterious benefactor? As far as we can tell, no one in the Club knew him personally and attempts to get more information from the solicitors administering his will by our Secretary John Fowler were unfruitful. It appeared that he was a very private individual, unmarried, who nonetheless achieved academic prominence as Professor of Physical Chemistry at Leeds University. He died in January 1993 and it appears from the terms of his will that he intended, provided she survived him, that his mother would be his sole beneficiary. In the event, she predeceased him and in the terms of the will, his estate was to be divided into five equal parts between the Masters and Fellows of St. Catherine's College, Cambridge (his old alma mater), The National Trust, The Spastics Society, the Mountaineering Association of Great Britain and 'The Scottish Mountaineering Club of Glasgow'. It turned out that the Mountaineering Association of Great Britain had been absorbed into the Youth Hostels Association and after legal discussion, this part of the legacy lapsed, and eventually, went to the late professor's distant relatives. No such detailed debate was required about 'The Scottish Mountaineering Club of Glasgow'. Fortunately, it appeared that at the time the will was made, the club secretary and hence the address for correspondence was indeed in Glasgow and so the good Professor's executors and solicitors were quite happy that his intentions were that part of his estate should go to our Club.

In the absence of any information about his recreational activities, likes and dislikes and any affinity he might have with mountaineering and with Scottish mountaineering in particular, the reasons for this beneficence remained obscure to us. It did, however, seem likely that one of his main interests was in the hills, bearing in mind that two of his beneficiaries were mountaineering organisations,

In the spring of 2001 I received a booking for the hut from John Farrow, a member of the Rucksack Club and a few of his club colleagues. In the course of conversation it turned out that Peter Ayscough was also a member of the Rucksack Club and was reasonably well known within that club, although he was also known there as a very 'private' man. John asked a fellow Rucksack Club member and former colleague of Ayscough's at Leeds University, Don Smithies, to write a brief biographical note from his admittedly limited knowledge of his colleague.

This reads as follows:

"Peter Ayscough was born in Lincoln in 1927 and educated at City School, Lincoln and St. Catherine's College, Cambridge. From 1953-55

Peter worked in research in Ottawa and then moved as a lecturer to Leeds University. In 1975, he became Professor of Physical Chemistry there, retiring from that post in 1989.

In his younger days he was a keen cyclist, touring Europe, and in his 50s took up motor-cycling. His introduction to the hills came through the Cambridge University Mountaineering Club and from his Leeds base he was particularly fond of walking in the Lake District and the Yorkshire Dales. Peter joined the Rucksack Club in 1990 and until his untimely death was an active member, climbing some of the easier Alpine peaks and setting out to complete a round of the Munros.

He died in 1993 at the age of 66 years of a heart attack while on a solo walk in the Pennines."

This sums up all we know of our Club's benefactor but from these brief details it seems probable that he would be highly satisfied with the Club's stewardship of his legacy. It seems likely that he would have relished spending days among the hills of Wester Ross and Sutherland at what we now know as the Naismith Hut. I suspect also that he would approve of the name selected for the hut by the Club commemorating one of the founding fathers of Scottish Mountaineering and would have found 'The Ayscough Hut' somewhat pretentious and not at all to his liking.

We, as a Club, and many other clubs who have used the hut and will do so in future, owe him a debt of gratitude for his generosity and, judging by the testimonials so far to the quality of the hut, the money has been well spent.

REINCARNATION ON THE BEN

By M. G. Anderson

I ANNOUNCED to the ice-coated rock in front of me: "Sod this for a game of soldiers."

Why did I bother? The only person remotely within earshot was my second, 80ft. below and he didn't give a monkey's as long as we were out of here before chucking-out time. 'Here' was a vertical groove smothered in slushy ice, two-thirds the way up Ben Nevis, a blizzard blowing inside my anorak and night about to fall. A dodgy move lay in waiting on iffy snow with crampons scratching about on something or nothing, and throbbing forearms overdosed on lactic acid to the point where I was about to lose contact with the mountain. The alternatives were proceed and perhaps fall, or stay put and certainly fall. I took a peek at the lonely ring peg 30ft. below, my only point of attachment to the mountain besides Dudley. Its rusty crust did not inspire confidence. My heart was going like a jack-hammer on overdrive, flushing my system with adrenaline.

"C'mon you idle sod, stop posing, and get a bloody move on, or do you want us benighted?" That was the thing with Dudley, he was so there for me. Even without his encouragement, I had to move. What was I doing stuck up here so late, in these crummy conditions I kept asking myself, frutching about on tenuous whiskers of ice? There was nowt I could do about it, so the question was academic. The bed-and-breakfast caper hadn't helped for a start. "Did you say Earl Grey?"

"No, thankee, Lapsong Souchon with a touch of lemon and a sprinkle of sugar, please.

Dudley had to have his little comforts. "Just a sprinkle, mind," and the landlady who had taken a fancy to him went off to fuss.

"Just a sprinkle," said she half-mocking half-admiring to her husband hovering uselessly on the fringe of the breakfast room.

"Such a particular gentleman," she murmured loving every minute of it. With every little fuddy-duddy fastidiousness my stomach churned like a doomsday clock. B & B landladies don't do Alpine starts, and with each passing minute, I could see a bivouac on the Ben looming larger.

"A full Scottish Breakfast, you'll be having?"

The diction was precise, naice almost, with none of the explosive glottal stops beloved of the tartan proletariat. And why not, we've paid for it. So we got our money's worth, wading through a multi-course extravaganza of porridge, bacon, eggs, tomatoes, mushrooms, beans, black pudding and the requisite supporting items. What with that, paying the bill, complimenting our hostess on her Wedgwood china, we were late on the hill. Now the conditions. I have always been a believer in 'if it don't feel right it ain't right'.

Today the ambient moisture content was that of a tepid Turkish bath. Now, as we turned the corner into the great cirque of the Allt a'Mhuillin there was the proof of the pudding. "Look at it, Dudley. You can see it's a bag of shite." He looked. The warmish temperature had melted the Ben into a soggy Baked Alaska, with great sickly grey sheets of ice dribbling down into lumps of black sludge, gobs of soggy ice making little splash bombs on the path. The other two, Dave and Jim, stopped, took stock and waited for us to make up their minds for them. Odd, I thought, as all of us were familiar with the Ben and it's wintry moods, and today it was at its most malignant, dark dangerous and dismally off-putting. Maybe they were being subtle. Deferring the decision to someone else is an old climber's game.

"If you think I've driven all the way from Manchester, just to put my arse down in some bloody Scotch pub...

Neatly put, Dudley. That was that then. Never mind the weather, when you're out on the heather. Dudley had the car and therefore the casting vote. On we went bashing our way upwards in execrable wind-slab snow. The others soon sped ahead, and I could hear them above thumping the snow with their ice-axes, sounding as if they were assaulting cardboard boxes. So here we were stuck on Observatory Ridge, rime-covered breeches crackling in the gale, way past our bedtime, on snow that you wouldn't wish on your worst enemy. The climbing up to this point had been not much more perilous than your average winter outing, but I had lingered longer on my leads than Dudley who had been dashing and efficient, thus making us late.

If I had been properly assertive this morning the only thing cold would be the pint I was nursing. "Get a move on." This was me talking to myself. "There's bugger all you can do about it now." My forearms turned to rubber, while farther down a knee trembler started revving up. After a few nervous false starts I managed to howk my boot onto a thinly-iced slab, which held me grudgingly. My left axe planted into névé, was tested with a slight tug. It would hold, maybe. The right axe sunk in soft snow, was pulled gingerly. The reply was not reassuring.

Meanwhile, my right foot was straying inexorably down the slab wrapped in a cellophane layer of broken ice. I had to move very soon. Catching sight of the shards of ice glinting underfoot, I hesitated. Would the axes hold? Just then. "For Pete's sake get a jildi on, you lazy pillock." I remembered he had been on one of those sensitivity courses. OK, holding my breath I pulled myself up. Immediately, the right axe pulled like a knife through hot butter. The ice under my crampon shattered into a thousand sparklers as my foot shot down the slab. I was off! I jack-knifed backwards through the dark air, thinking: "Christ that piton has to hold me." There came a resounding ping, and the ring peg was whipped out. Jesus Christ! But Dudley must catch me on his belay. Out of the corner of my eye I saw a grey shape as he was yanked off his stance, hurtling down beside me. The information was passed onto my brain and so quite objectively, I knew I was going to die. Oh well, this is the way it goes. I put my hands in front for protection, thinking why am I bothering, Andy was chopped on Lochnagar in similar circumstances.

These thoughts came to me calmly despite my increasing velocity as the ground 1000ft. below came speeding up to meet me. Whoops! I was jerked to a halt, bouncing up and down at the rope's end like a demented bungy jumper. Something had grabbed the rope. The Hand of God perhaps or another supernatural entity. It was a bloody miracle, a one-in-a-million chance, for, as far as the eye could see through the mist, the wall we had dropped over was plumb vertical, without a bump or projection ruffling its surface. The second I came to rest at the end of the rope, serene detachment went out the window, and panic took over. Whatever was holding my lifeline could easily let it go, like Eurydice snatched from the brink of Hades only to be casually dropped back again into the maws of death. I must have shouted: "Help!" because out of the mist a surprising number of voices shouted back: "Where are you?"

"Hanging off the side of Observatory Ridge."

"You OK for now?"

"Yea, I suppose."

"OK Hang on. We'll fetch the rescue."

A ragged fracture just right for a large hex was staring right at me within arm's length. Thank Christ! I whipped a moac stopper off my rack, stuffed it into the crack, pulled this way and that till it lodged, and clipped in. It would do the trick for the time being. Frantically, I fumbled through my harness for a bomb-proof anchor. There, I found it. A shiny ice peg with the price tag still sticking to it. I hesitated. It had cost me all of nine quid that week, a pretty penny. Scots miserliness battled briefly with self-preservation. What the bollocks am I thinking? It took about a second for me to work my instinctive parsimony through my mental processing unit. Casting £9 to the winds, I frantically hammered the piton hard into the crack, tied on, and immediately the tension surged from my body. I was safe for the moment. A cry came from above: "Are you all-right?" This was Jim. Dave had vomited on the spot when he saw us peel.

"Yea, like bollocks I am," I thought, but confined myself to saying "Yea, but drop me a rope fast, like."

"Will do. Wait a sec till we get a belay."

Then followed the ring of a hammer bashing a peg in. Swinging gently in the breeze, there was nothing else to do but take stock. As my mitt had fallen off in the fall, my right hand would soon be out of commission, while below me Dudley hanging upside down with the rope caught round his ankle was twirling round in little circles. "I'm in the shit," he said. Right, I thought, and there's sod all I can do to help you. Far below the icy terrain of Observatory Gully beckoned uninvitingly. Not much cause for optimism anywhere I looked. The wind spun me round to face the rock again. The peg I had hammered in so lustily as a lifeline had shattered the frost-riven crack, leaving peg and nut clasped together by what was not much more than a mosaic of tottering biscuit crumbs. "Oh God!" Peering through the gloom at my disintegrating lifeline, I prayed for the first time in my adult life.

"I promise if I ever get out of this bleeding jam, I'll never mess around with other people's wives, never steal Biros from the kids, and look at their mums as bonking fodder. And I'll never ever, never use people, if You will save me, God."

I knew that was a major road block to salvation and if I could get it past the front office I could be home and dry. "I'll make my own cups of tea and not blackmail my girlfriend into brewing up," offering up a specific sample of the previous. Promises, promises. I would have promised the Earth if I'd had it. Only this time I meant to keep them, honest! Fear cleaned out the mind's Augean Stables, purging life's petty squabbles out of my system. Even people I cordially hated came up for re-evaluation. Trying not to breathe on the fragile piton, I made a mental note to make a tick list of the above, seek them out and in the unlikely event of them getting over the initial surprise re-befriend them.

Jim called from up above. "Still alright, Gavin?"

"Am I buggery! Send down a bleeding rope, pronto, mate."

"OK, won't be a minute with the belay."

I heard the dull banging of a piton hammer. He sounded calm and deliberate like it was Monday morning and he was back in the classroom, handing out papers to his pupils.

Meanwhile, was I imagining things or did the peg really twitch in the crack? "Hurry, for Christ's sake!"

"Don't worry, Gavin." More banging as another peg was bashed home.

"C'mon, Jim!" It came out high pitched, pure counter tenor-who said castrati were extinct – as my situation came home to me. If the rope rolled it would pull nut, peg, and me, back onto the original flight plan.

"Would it be too much to ask if you could possibly expedite sending down the bloody rope?"

"Just a mo." No exasperation at all, the assured teacher facing a difficult pupil. Another peg sank home. Slowly, out of the fog a rope poked and prodded its way down, slithering like an Arctic snake. I tied on and started to breathe. Another rope was dropped, to which I attached two prussik slings. This was tricky as the hand without the glove was as useful as a lump of frozen wood. I began slowly jumaring up the rope, with every step giving me grief. Experimenting with prussiks in the comfort of your own home in front of an admiring audience, whose idea of adventure is a stroll to the pub, is a lot different from Saturday night on the big, bad Ben swinging back and forth on a frozen cable, snow pouring in at all the surprising gaps in your clothing. At every step, the reluctant knot froze and had to be untied with one hand and teeth, all which frigging about not aided by the temperature dropping and the blizzard seriously picking up momentum. There's a lot to be said for sticking to the movies on a Saturday night.

I looked down and saw Dudley safely ensconced on a snowy ledge, a bit forlorn, but not too much the worse for wear. When I rolled onto the ledge, for no apparent reason Jim said: "You're a great guy, Gavin." No one had ever called me that before and it was doubly odd coming after my cock-up. I was touched. He tied me on. "What about Dudley?" I asked, for the first time thinking about someone apart from myself. "Too late. He'll have to stick it out till morning," and he leaned over the cliff to pass the bad news on to poor Dudley. No dithering about making that unpleasant decision. I had to admire his powers of leadership. Two weeks ago I had been on an all-night bus from Andorra, and thought it the longest night of my life. Now shuffling about on a tiny ledge on the Ben I recalled it's hedonistic luxury with nostalgia.

There were other things I was finding out that night. For instance, I never believed it possible to fall asleep standing up. It is. But it has the serious drawback of getting jerked awake whenever I slumped onto the belay. Bin bags over our heads protected us from the worst of the blizzard, but the insistent drubbing of little avalanches were a constant reminder of our unpleasant situation. It was a bitter night, but I didn't care. For some reason I was as full of beans as a kid on Christmas Morning revelling in a euphoria, that would take weeks to shake off. I was going to live. To pass the time, we concocted little divertissements, which held out the promise of reward, coming in the shape of a chocolate biscuit. The law of supply and demand inflated this commodity's exchange rate to such an extent that the prize could only be won by telling a successful joke. A gale of hearty laughter was optimistically judged as the standard to be aimed at; mere chuckles would leave you hungry.

For a while the icy flanks of the Ben were the unlikely setting for Saturday Night Comedy Theatre. Old ones were dredged up from dusty drawers of memory. Stories about vicars at tea parties, vicars drunk in the pulpit, vicars and choirboys, bishops and actresses, bounced from buttress to gully making the round of the crag making it a bad night for prelates all round. I am here to tell you that not a biscuit crumb was awarded after the first round. No one laughed; not even a titter emerged from that ledge. Each rib-tickler was met by a stony silence. It wasn't the way we told them, but humour requires a modicum of bodily comfort and warmth for the funny bone to function. Our currency became so devalued we ended up giving the prize to anyone just having a go. By the way the biscuits turned out to be very salty, something you don't notice under normal non dry-mouthed conditions.

Peter Ayscough above Loch Monar. Photo: John Farrow.

'The Boys', June 1934. Left to right – Ted Forde, Charlie Ruxton, George Wood, Ian Macdonald and Ian Charleson.

Dawn came seeping in grudging and grey, mist blanking out every feature. At cock crow, the buzzing of rotors heralded our rescue, then the helicopter appeared, circling above the hut, firing off green smoke bombs like it was Apocalypse Now. The chopper hung in the sky above us, the rotors birling only feet away from the cliff. Out popped our Redeeming Angel in the shape of an RAF corporal at the end of what seemed like a fishing line, hands clasped in front of him as if praying. Here was a joker who could get a real laugh. I had first go, irritating our rescuer, him bouncing to and fro from the ledge like Peter Pan, while cack-handed me couldn't untie my knot, what with one hand a frozen lump and the rest of me not much better. "Haven't you got a bloody knife?" He shouted unangelically. No a bloody knife was something I had omitted to bring along. Jim sorted out this one, hacking the Gordian Knot apart with his axe, and the next moment I was flying skywards hugging my rescuer. When level with the chopper, someone grabbed me by the seat of my pants, threw me into the cabin – so this is how they do it – and then checked me for damage.

The others followed tossed in like potatoes bouncing about in a hopper, and without further ado we were whisked off to Fort William for our brief encounter with media stardom. Flashbulbs popped, mikes and cameras thrust in our faces, as we were served up for our 15 minutes of fame. Jim the real hero of the affair rendered himself ineligible for celebrity by refusing to play up for the cameras, answering each stupid question in an abrupt: 'How can you ask such a stupid question?' manner. Unsatisfied, the battery of cameras, mikes assorted electronic gizmos swung round to face me. Sensing he was not giving them the goods, I put on my 'I am seriously thinking about this', act, when they asked me: "What were you thinking about when you were falling?" I pondered, looked straight into the camera lens and replied gravely that all I could think of were the generations of schoolchildren who would now be deprived of the full riches of their education.

On a lighter note I regretted all the exercise books I had failed to mark. I was asked that daft question so many times I began to believe my daft answer. Getting into my stride I described with much gesticulation, the drama on the mountain so that I, the screw-up, emerged as a charismatic TV personality, holding the nation enthralled for all of the two and a half minutes allotted to me, while Jim the real man of the moment found himself relegated to a minor footnote. Funnily enough my mates did not seem to resent me hogging the limelight, so maybe they were all camera shy. The linesman was wheeled out and we were made to shake hands, no hardship in that, but it made me wonder how many similar gestures are merely setups. I was asked to say something. I must have dried up for all I could think of to say to him was: "Thanks." Then he was asked to say a few words. Oh dear! Here we go. I'll be exposed as a wally expecting other

The CIC Hut and Carn Dearg Buttress, Ben Nevis. Photo: Donald Bennet.

people to risk their lives. But all he said was: "Next time take a knife." He was a professional after all.

That night we were on every TV channel; after the usual litany of disasters, the upbeat finale to the Sunday night bulletin, so we could all go cheerfully to work on Monday. At school I had the novel experience of being stared at as an interesting phenomenon with an aura, nothing to do with my miraculous escape, but because I had been on the box, and for a moment walked with such gods as Terry Wogan, and Simon Dee. For the next week we were fodder for the Press, receiving all sorts of unwarranted attention, and at its end we were tossed aside, last week's news, our only use, wrapping for fish suppers. We were of interest as a freak phenomenon, during that weekend eight people had died in the Central Highlands and Ben Nevis. Somebody up there had liked us. The episode had a weird postscript. Instead of being chastened, I went around in a state of intoxication, thinking I had been granted the gift of invulnerability, like Achilles without his foot problem. I insulted bigger folk than myself in pubs, put lighted cigarettes in mates' pints, and went barging up to women, who wouldn't have touched me with a barge pole.

Fortunately, this notion of immortality wore off before they locked me up, but my odd behaviour caused not a few friendships to be put on hold. Nowadays, of course, I would have gone into therapy, then they just kept me at arms length in the bar, till I had passed a satisfactory period of probation. Twenty years on I seldom think of the incident, involving as it does dwelling on the awful consequences if the rope had twitched a millimetre or so to the side. When I do think on it, I ask, why me? Life since has done me few favours, nor have I reciprocated. I have not been set aside for some special destiny. My country has never called me in her hour of need. No cure for cancer has been discovered in my laboratory. I have no cello concertos to my name. I haven't even found a new way to cook chicken. Life goes on. The four of us drifted apart, as is the way of things. An occasional Christmas card and an even more occasional sighting has to do for the camaraderie of the rope. Last summer, I bumped into Jim in the Lakes. An indifferent damp week had ended in a glorious weekend. We were sitting outside the New Dungeon Gyll enjoying the Lakeland summer evening, contented with our outing on the hill and relishing our pints. He had had a great day, he said, and now seeing me had topped it all off for him. The complement as unexpected as it was undeserved reminded me of the nice thing he had said as I rolled onto the belay. Perhaps, just for that it was all worth it. I did go back to the Ben, once.

The incident had shattered what little confidence I had on ice, so when confronted with this medium I climbed with timid skittering steps, tentative surges followed by scurrying retreats, and as a consequence I went back to relearning the basics. When I completed my repeated apprenticeship, I sought out a climb suitable for my swan song. Green Gully, it had to be.

Rod and I climbed it late in the season, so fortunately, we had plenty daylight. The four major ice pitches were tackled successfully and we arrived below the cornice just as the sun was dropping behind the Ben. I climbed a rope's length on very steep unconsolidated snow. No falling here; Rod had only a fragile ice-axe belay. The cornice overhung by about four feet. I crept up to nestle beneath it like a sparrow under the eaves of a house. Tapping the ice I realised it was as solid as concrete. My axe couldn't even scratch it. It would need a pneumatic drill to break through this lot. My familiar icy companion, fear, seized me.

Our position was unenviable, for we were virtually sealed in the gully. Over to the left I could make out faintly in the gloaming, beyond the swirling snow devils, a steep arête where the cornice had fallen away. It had to be the way out. Reversing the steep unstable snow was something I would rather not linger over. After an anxious half-hour I reached the exit, clamped my axes over the edge, and performed a neat Western Roll to end up sprawling flat on the summit plateau. Beneath the icy crusts of the mountains, the whole world was as black as Hell's Night, except the great sea lochs, which the echo of the sunset had plunged into molten fingers probing into Scotland's dark heart. We trudged down the hill, crampons making that satisfactory creaking noise, when you know all is well with the snow. The wind cutting across the plateau made us suddenly aware of the cold.

MOONLIGHTING

By Jamie Thin

"Oh it's a wond-er-ful ni-ght for a moon-dance..."

IT WAS Saturday night and I'd been working all day, but for once Van the man was right. And as I drove north, the moon was full and bright, throwing silver shadows across Fife. The end of the financial year, stock-checks ... life is too short for all this accounting... I picked up John and Serena in Ladybank, and then by a devious route we made for Braemar. Now John (or Coylie as we know him) is still a youth – and as a youth is prone to sudden enthusiasms.

"Time for a wee adventure, Mr Thin?" Not with a dodgy character like you, I thought – but at least Serena might keep him in line.

Chips and curry in Blairgowrie and I was beginning to shake off the weariness of the day. We got to Braemar at 11pm, just as the Gypsy Kings were breaking into the Salsa, and John and Serena spilled out onto the empty street to dance.

The advance party were ensconced in the pub. The day had been fine and they were happily supping their beer. "But lads, you can't sit in here, its a beautiful night – who's on for a midnight foray to the hills?"

Not even Serena could be persuaded, so I found myself alone with Coylie at the Linn o' Dee, talking in the hushed voices of conspirators. There was a dusting of crisp snow, and we opted for the fell-shoes to make the run-in more enjoyable. The rest of the kit, plastic boots, axes and crampons were hurriedly shoved into bulging sacks.

The snow covered path led us through the dark of the woods, and out towards Derry Lodge. The deer moved sleepily, as we ran past, lifting their heads and pausing. While behind them, the moon broke through the clouds to show the glen in sharp contrast.

Barely a breath of wind, the only sounds were our own. We turned up Luibeg and made for Coire Sputan Dearg. As the snow got deeper our progress slowed, and we switched back to big boots. We climbed higher and we could just begin to see the tops of Cairn Toul and Braeriach, silvery and bright, before we plunged back into the gloom of the coire. The moon cast a broad shadow across the crags.

Axes and crampons were out now and the névé was perfect. Slab chimney was in the dark shadow, but when we paused in the neck of the gully, we looked back to see a ghostly Derry Cairngorm framed by the gully walls. We hardly dared speak lest the spell was broken – magic.

We topped out and headed across the plateau, the moon casting our long shadows on Ben Macdui. Down below, the winking lighthouses on the north coast seemed strangely near. A faraway glimpse into another world of boats and the sea

Back over Derry Cairngorm, it got dark again at 5am as the clouds swept in and the moon disappeared. But not for long, and the first light of dawn saw us running back to Derry Lodge in our stiff and frozen fell-shoes.

Now it was a race. We winked at each other, it would be great to get back to Braemar before the others were out of their beds!

* * *

The Grand Traverse:
Winter had come again, and conditions were perfect for the much discussed alpine tour. We had planned and waited and planned again. Purist style, no messing – ski to the west face, climb the route with skis and then ski off the slopes to the east. The approach would be long and hard, the route would be committing and we would need the strongest team possible. First, I had to persuade the boys. But that wasn't hard – the trap had already been set – for the last few months I had been regaling them with tales of perfect verglas and solid névé from the previous year, and they were just waiting for the call.

"Right. Early start. See you at 5am."

Mick and I stepped into our skis in the gloom of the half-night. Just as we were setting off on ski, Garry caught up with us, just down from Inverness. He preferred to keep to his feet, still carrying the Highlander's inbred suspicion of the ski. We laboured up the slopes, sweat pouring through the layers of fleece. Thoughts of success and failure loomed large in our minds as the dark crags looked on at us coldly. It always looks steeper from below I told myself half-heartedly. At last as the steely grey of dawn began to pick out the features, we reached the foot of the gully. Steep snow lead to the first rock step, and then the route disappeared into the depths of the gully.

Mick and I took off our skis and fixed them to our sacks. Garry caught us up and for speed, we all tied into one rope. I set off up the first pitch, sparks flying as the crampon points skittered off barely covered rocks and the axes sought out uncertain placements. Onto the first steepening – balance difficult with the skis pulling me backwards – nothing for it but a big lunge up, hoping axes would gain purchase on some edge. Some undignified scrabbling followed and I was up into the gully proper, the others followed. Now ensconced between the narrow walls, I felt a bit more secure and while the others followed up, I turned round to admire the magnificent skyline – grey clouds, the pink hint of dawn and the jagged peaks of Allermuir, Craiglockhart and St. Giles!

Aye, it was Edinburgh, and we were on the wee gem of a route that is the Cat's Nick. An innocuous moderate in the warm light of a summer's day, but in mid-winter it has the situation and atmosphere of the pipes on Meagaidh. Perched high above the city, it feels like you're on the big mountain, even if you're only five minutes from your kitchen.

Neither Garry nor Mick wanted to fight their way past my skis, so I was left to lead up the rest of the route. The conditions were perfect – I mean there wasn't any ice, but it was winter and it was cold, and if you looked down it almost looked like there was lots of snow.

Like all classic routes the crux is the last step, bridging out past a prow of rock, to reach the only good placements on the whole route, in the turf at the top. That was the crux, but the highlight was watching Mick follow up, as he tried a direttissima and got his skis stuck under the prow – there was much cursing and growling before he finally emerged. We were now in great danger of being be-lighted, so Gary disappeared at the run to get to work, while Mick and I got back on the skis to finish the last leg of our grand traverse – or at the very least to finish off our last legs as we charged into great tussocks of grass and were catapulted headfirst into Hunter's Bog.

They say you have to travel the world, so that you can arrive back home and see it for the first time. And they're right. The best adventures are on your own doorstep.

EDINBURGH CASTLE ROCK

THE following account of climbs on the Castle Rock of Edinburgh and other public buildings has been sent in by an, understandably, anonymous correspondent. No law-abiding citizen would think of climbing on the Castle Rock of Edinburgh today. About 50 years ago it was otherwise. At one time you could even do it in public on special occasions with minimal interference from the authorities.

Our correspondent writes:– In the late Forties there was a thing called Charities Day when the student population went around extracting money from the public. As far as I remember it took place on a Saturday in May. Students dressed in whatever fancy dress they could and went round the town in the morning shaking collecting cans at the dismayed citizens and doing various stunts to entertain or amaze the good people of the town. Among the exercises to impress the public the EUMC staged an assault on the castle, climbing up the rock facing Princes Street starting from the region of St. Cuthbert's Chapel. There were several routes up to the base of the wall, all of about Diff. standard.

Although good enough climbs, as far as I know, they never achieved guidebook listings. The crux of the ascent of the Princes Street Face was the final wall of the castle itself. There is a recessed corner which can be straddled. I remember a certain Derek Haworth climbed this free. The rest of us clambered up an old wooden ladder used during the war for firewardens to get onto roofs to put out incendiary bombs. (Each block of flats had one between the doors of the top flat.) I also seem to remember we had a bugle which sent inexpert calls across the gardens to the watching crowds who shook their heads sadly.

There was also a certain amount of night climbing during the dark winter nights. Edinburgh in the late Forties of last century was not the bustling, cosmopolitan, over-ripe metropolis it is now. On a winter's night after, say seven o'clock, the streets were empty, even Princes Street was quiet and the darkness was lit by circles of brown gaslight. On such nights it was possible to enter the castle by a pair of pipes on the Synod Hall Face that led up the wall to just below the overhang of the parapet. From there a stretch and heave brought you inside the wall. Once over the wall you had the freedom of the dark castle – no flood lights in those days. The windy battlements and moon-shadowed courtyards were all your own. The farthest we penetrated was into the dungeons below the half-moon battery.

These were not the first climbs done on the rock. I remember reading in a pre-war Journal that ascents were made from the Johnstone Terrace side. As so often happens I cannot find the reference again. It may be that there are other unrecorded explorations of this massive piece of volcanic crag. It is also a fact that one night the final spire of the Scott Monument was climbed, not from the ground but from the topmost balcony. Admission to the staircase within the tower was gained when it was found that the key to someone's backgreen door also fitted the door at the bottom of the monument.

Another ascent, or strictly speaking partial ascent, was of the Mercat Cross in the High Street. A strenuous move took you above the overhang and over the parapet onto the platform from where announcements are made to the public. On this occasion I seem to remember that Scotland was declared to be a free and autonomous nation. (Could this be a clue to authorship and the grouping responsible? *Ed.*) The ascent of the final pinnacle was abandoned at the request of the police who arrived from the adjacent station. The force was a benevolent institution in those days. The admonition, "come doun oot o there, laddies. Awa hame tae your beds and dinna gie us onie trouble", was sufficient to restore law and order – 'autres temps, autres moeurs'.

It is said that the participants in these ascents were later admitted to the Club, even rising to high office. This is unlikely but the tale should be kept alive as an entertaining myth. Nevertheless, it might be interesting to look at the application forms of Edinburgh people who joined in the Fifties to see if any of these pioneer efforts were recorded as qualifications. Without such evidence no credit should be given to these folk tales. Nevertheless, if there is any truth in them it might be wise to consider retrospective action to protect the name of the Club.

Anon.

NOTE: SMCJ, 1959, XXVI. 150, p419 gives the following: Robin Smith and A. Frazer send a belated report of the ascent in May 1958 of the Closet Climb on the Princes Street Face of Edinburgh Castle Rock about, 350ft. (S).
(1) 80ft. Up broken rocks and short steep column to start of obvious white shelf left of great central overhang.
(2) 70ft. Up shelf and left to belay.
(3) 50ft. Right by zig-zags past tree to stance above overhang.
(4) 120ft. Up overhanging corner 15ft., then by steep grass to foot of Castle wall (no belay).
(5) Up wall.
I have no doubt that the committee will be sympathetic to a request to meet bail should a re-enactment attract the attentions of the law, provided, of course, that the Journal is given an exclusive. The implication by the writer that the present guardians of the city, Lothian and Borders Police, may no longer be 'a benevolent institution' as in days of old is borne out by the fact that the only recorded ice climb on the Castle Rock, again on the Princes Street Face is called Breach of the Peace.

TWENTY-NINE HOURS IN THE CUILLIN

BY ADAM KASSYK

THERE was no moon, and the peaks were shadows in the night, their presence sensed rather than seen against the star-studded sky as I climbed the path from upper Glen Brittle towards the north ridge of Bruach na Frithe. Underfoot, fat slicks of ice gleamed dully among the dry grass. After a couple of hours I gained the lower part of the ridge and sought a place to stop. It was well after midnight, and since I had spent a day at work and had a long drive, I felt very much in need of sleep. There was a brisk breeze and I cast around for some shelter, but the few boulders nearby were disappointingly small. A few minutes later I was settled into a slight hollow, looking out over the dark rolling moors beyond Sligachan, a velvet landscape quiet under the blanket of night. A distant car headlight waxed and waned, briefly lighting the horizon as a late-night traveller returned home. The light served as a reminder of a different world that I was briefly leaving behind.

It was mid-January and the hills had already been under snow for more than two months. I had envisaged in my mind the perfect solo day, a long narrow ridge on a sharp, snowy peak, leading eventually, after suitable commitment and effort, to an exposed summit. Of such dreams are perfect days made – but all too rarely. It hadn't taken long to decide that the best place to find such an objective was Skye. Unfortunately, I then discovered that the recent good weather was forecast to end at some point during the weekend. A long drive for possibly only one day's climbing seemed a little rash, but nothing ventured nothing gained, so the decision was made. The chances of doing the entire traverse seemed low, so I had decided to start at Bruach na Frithe, reasoning that if the weather held until the following day, I might get as far as the Coire Lagan section, or even to the Thearlaich-Dubh Gap.

I slept well, and when I awoke the dark blue of night was retreating westwards and daylight was already spreading across the sky in its place. I was greeted by the sight of the Cuillin, a line of icy fangs in the teeth of the wind. Breakfast was not a success. There was nothing to shelter the stove, the flame guttered faintly and the chips of ice hardly melted. Eventually, I gave up, threw away the ice cubes and drank the remaining cold water as there seemed little point in adding tea. In any event, I was impatient to be off. Sunrise was at hand and I was drawn inexorably to the crest, where the sky was touched with a tinge of cream and wisps of cloud glowed with a translucent sheen.

Above, a steep slope of frozen scree led to the horizontal crest. Here the ridge narrowed and, climbing along it, I sensed a sudden transformation in the mountain environment. As I left behind the landscape of earth, grass and loose rocks and the snow cover increased, so too did an intense sense of radiance all around. The rock seemed a burnished golden brown, almost glowing with a tangible warmth and colour, the snow reflected the pale cream luminosity of the sky and I knew then that these mountains promised riches beyond the dreams of extraordinary days. I felt an intense anticipation of warm sunlight on snow crystals on the crest, the promise of lightness, air and space that one feels high on a mountain, and this drew me urgently upwards. Perfect firn snow in runnels, ramps and crests led between rocks of immaculate colour and texture to the summit.

The promise of below was more than amply fulfilled. As I reached the crest, I saw that the entire Coruisg basin was filled with a shifting mist. Where the mist thinned, it was stretched and spun into gossamer veils, vapours of transparent delicacy that were almost invisible. The winter sun was low on the mainland horizon and the countless water droplets captured its rays, diffused and diffracted them, till it shone with a golden light The effect was as if the air itself glowed with an iridescent warmth, as if each atom had absorbed the sun's light and reflected it again with a renewed intensity. A wreath of mist floated past behind me and I was greeted by my own shadow, a wraith with a halo to keep me company in this island paradise in the sky. Imperceptibly, the mists faded and the sweep of the mountain ridge was revealed, rising and falling in its great encircling curve. My senses were dazzled by the brilliance of it all, as the peaks unfolded in their serried ranks, white teeth rising from the black jaws of the corries and etched by the light reflected from countless sparkling snow crystals. Sky, rock and snow were enchanted by a spell of incandescent beauty but only for fleeting minutes that ought to have been prolonged into a contemplative eternity.

But time and tide wait for no man, and I was curious to know what other wonders lay in store. A firm, broad, snow crest led easily downwards, a pleasant high level promenade, but soon a deep narrow gap appeared with a steep black wall frowning at the far side. I approached this obstacle with some trepidation only to find that its steepness was tempered with reassuringly incut holds and beyond I found an exposed groove well supplied with lumps of ice in all the right places. Confidence boosted I pressed on up the first of the three summits of Bidein Druim nan Ramh, eager to see what difficulties lay ahead.

The next section provided some engrossing route finding. In summer the Coruisg face here consists of wet slabs strewn with loose stones. Now it was heavily carpeted with densely packed, hard frozen snow. This snow was bonded to the underlying rock more firmly than I'd ever seen, shading from white on the surface to an ever denser grey where ice met rock. I couldn't recall encountering snow conditions as good as this before. I crossed the gully which fell from the deep gap between the first of the two summits and climbed up a long ramp on its far side. At its apex was an exposed step, where a swing round the edge gained the snowed up slabs beyond. In powder this step would have been a precarious exercise requiring protection, now it was an exhilarating move with reassuring security for both hands and feet. Beyond, a series of traverses and upward moves crossed the face to gain the east ridge from Coruisg, and the summit a little way farther. Now confidence was at full pitch and I was absorbed in a steady rhythm on the steep snowy switchbacks, always with a breathtaking drop and always on the most reassuring of snow.

Of course, the ridge in winter is sensational but by the time I'd reached the first of the four summits of Sgurr a'Mhadaidh, sensational had become the norm. A short abseil off each of the first three summits made life easy and secure. As I approached the main peak the mist came in again and the summit ridge appeared ahead and above as an impossibly steep crest, falling away at an exaggerated angle on both sides and seemingly too sharp to allow anything but a precarious passage of the summit. This must have been a trick of the mist, for in fact, just beyond the highest point there was a spot just big enough to sit down with my back against a restful rock and revel in the atmosphere and the knowledge that most of the difficulties of the day should now be over.

The mist cleared again, to reveal the shadowy and snowless basin of Coruisg, embraced by the mountains but looking out to calm waters beyond. Ahead now lay Sgurr a'Ghreadaidh, a sinuous curving fin, gently scalloped along its crest. Unexpectedly, this proved to be the highlight of the day. A long and sustained section of impressive narrowness, too steep to allow passage below the crest, required progress in balance along the very apex of the ridge with no handhold for physical or moral support. There was no cornice but the sense of exposure was formidable and required continuous concentration. Truly, like tightrope walking. I was getting tired now and stopped frequently to take a deep breath and gather my resources. Despite the nervous tension there was a pronounced sensation of breathless excitement, almost weightlessness, of being more than usually detached from the solidity of the earth and closer to some other more intangible realm. When the ridge finally relented and broadened out the tension eased and was replaced by a surge of exhilaration.

Swinging round to the south I could look out across Glen Brittle towards the Minch, where a deep haze was settling on the western horizon, the softening sky bringing that air of calm contentment which marks the approaching end of a good day. The ridge was friendlier now, less steep, more of a faithful companion than a challenging adversary. I passed welcoming spots which appeared designed for contemplative relaxation, sheltering boulders and snowy hollows for luxury bivouac sites. The shadows lengthened, the light began to colour the snow and rocks again and my senses seemed both dulled and heightened at the same time by fatigue. The lower part of the western sky was turning to pastel pink and smoky blue and the horizon was smudged with soft colours as the daylight started to slip away beyond the ocean on the ebbing tide of time. I crested the summit ridge of Sgurr Dearg with a little daylight to spare and my euphoria was tempered only by an icy blast of spindrift.

The Pinnacle looked superb with all the holds coated in hard ice, but my immediate task was to find somewhere sheltered to sleep. Halfway down the base of the Pinnacle on the Coire Lagan side there was a slanting slot created by a sloping overhang. There was a snow drift in the slot and I excavated a mummy-shaped niche. The slopes below swept down into the bowl of Coire Lagan, the snow fading into a wild rocky chaos in the dying light. I felt very pleased with my efforts as the stove purred away inside the niche, well sheltered from the wind. As I got into my sleeping bag, it occurred to me that my bivouac site was somewhat coffin-shaped, though I felt reasonably safe in the assumption that it was unlikely to be my last resting place. At this point the solitude was interrupted by the arrival of three other climbers over the top, the first people I'd met all day. It turned out that their efforts rather put my adventures in the shade. They'd driven all the way from Sheffield on the Friday night, and had started from Sgurr nan Gillean that morning. They did not stop to talk for long, and plunged downwards with the last of the daylight. I could have descended too, but I felt a strong affinity with this cold high place which I was reluctant to break.

Sleep did not come easily that night. The wind had strengthened considerably, and from the security of my little niche I heard and felt the gusts buffeting the mountainside. The chances of continuing tomorrow were fading with the passing of the day. Across the coire, the twin fangs of Alasdair and Thearlaich brushed the base of a dense horizontal screen of cloud. Above me, looking round the overhang, I could see rents in the cloud cover and a few stars still shining through. The night scene carried a sense of foreboding, a threat voiced repeatedly by a cold angry wind. I turned over the possibilities in my mind. Would the weather hold till dawn and allow me to get as far as Sgurr Alasdair at first light? Would I be caught in a storm during the night? Should I make an escape now? Looking beyond the ridge I caught a glimpse of a light on the horizon, somewhere far away to the south, along the coast, far from the Cuillin, far from Skye, a reminder of the security of the other world. The wind whistled around the towers of An Stac and smacked against the wall of the Pinnacle above me. Instead of counting sheep I counted the minutes between gusts.

The decision was made when the interval between gusts could be measured in seconds rather than minutes. Despite the lack of sleep I felt well rested, visibility was adequate enough to find the way and I lost height easily on good snow. Below the bealach, the snow cover ran out, my torch failed and I found myself stranded in the middle of frozen screes in total darkness. But it was now only a case of going straight down and a few bone-jarring minutes later the tiny bowl of the upper coire appeared. The lochan, sheeted thickly with ice, formed a horizontal plane, counterposed by the sharp verticals of the surrounding huge blocks of gabbro, the whole creating a ghostly impression in the gloom. I sat down to remove my crampons and as I looked up at Sgurr Dearg, a veil of soft grey mist drew across the screes and a light rain began to fall.

On the way down the rain steadily intensified. After a while the bulk of Sgurr Dearg faded completely into the mist and the darkness, the going underfoot turned from rock to grass, then to the path, the track and finally the glistening tarmac road. Glen Brittle in the middle of a wet January night seemed eerily strange, a desolate place at the edge of the world, utterly quiet, the few dwellings shuttered and oblivious of the stranger passing through. The rain came down in sheets and a wild gale blasted the few trees by the side of the road.

It was after five in the morning when I finally regained my starting point. It must have been after midnight when I decided to descend, not a moment too soon. The timing of my return added an acute sense of satisfaction, of completeness, to my trip. I felt little sense of regret that a second day and the complete traverse had slipped from realisation with the arrival of the Atlantic front. After all, it had been the best mountaineering I had experienced in Scotland.

SCOTLAND'S MOUNTAIN NAMES: THE VIEW FROM TIMOTHY PONT

By Ian R. Mitchell

In the Pantheon of Scottish mountaineering there is, at the moment, no place for Timothy Pont, though there undoubtedly should be. Not only was he the first person to produce accurate drawings of many Scottish mountains, but he was also the first – outside of Gaelic poetry – to record the names of many of those mountains as well. In addition, he climbed – or persons associated with him climbed – Ben Lawers in the 1590s, the first recorded ascent of a Highland peak by any Lowlander. In this article I will deal with Pont's contribution to our knowledge of Scottish mountain names, and the interested reader can follow up other aspects of his mountain investigations in the sources indicated at the end.

Of Timothy Pont little is known. His father was a leading figure in the Kirk and three times Moderator of the General Assembly. Pont was born in the early 1560s and graduated from St. Andrews University in 1583. He was minister in Dunnet, Caithness for a decade or so until about 1610, and died possibly four years afterwards. Financed partly through his father's agency, Pont travelled around Scotland from 1583 until about 1596 on an extended cartographic study of the country. A project like Pont's could have been initiated with a view to extending knowledge of the country, especially the lawless Highlands, as an instrument for the imposition of central authority, governmental and/or ecclesiastical.

Though the mapping work had started with the approval of James VI, he had lost interest on his move south in 1603, and later Charles I provided a grant towards publication. One of those involved in that task was Robert Gordon of Straloch in Aberdeenshire. Gordon confirms in a letter that the map-maker's journeys were made on foot, and that he travelled extensively,

"He [Pont] travelled on foot through the whole of the Kingdom, as no-one before him had done. He visited all the islands, occupied for the most part by inhabitants hostile and uncivilised, and with a language different from our own; being often stripped, as he told me, by fierce robbers, and suffering not seldom, all the hardships of dangerous journeys, nevertheless at no time was he overcome by the difficulties, or disheartened."

That any one person could, in the social and physical conditions of the late 16th century, have undertaken such journeys is impressive. That he could, in addition, have mapped the areas visited to a good standard is almost incredible. Pont's work found fruition in 1654 in Amsterdam in *Blaeu's Atlas*. The maps printed therein, though based on Pont, are not by him, having passed through various hands before being engraved by Dutch cartographers. The mountain detail on these atlas maps is also poor, stylised peaks predominating, though the names of the mountains therein are largely based on Pont's original sketch maps. Pont is therefore the father, or step-father, of our knowledge of mountain names.

We can assume that Pont, like almost all Lowland Scots at this time, initially had, in all probability, no Gaelic. His father certainly did not speak the language, and Gordon implies that Pont was in the same position. He undoubtedly picked up some Gaelic over his decade of travelling, but the point is that there is no possibility that Pont was responsible for naming the peaks he drew. For his place and mountain names, he must have relied for information on local informants and guides. Pont took great care in his transcribing of the names, attempting to capture the phonetic sound of the Gaelic. We can thus have no hesitation in stating that Pont's mountain names are original and authentic.

Leaving aside hills outside the Gaelic speaking area, and minor hills, there are 90 names of 'significant hills' (largely Munros and Corbetts) on Pont's surviving manuscript maps. There are a further 60 names in a document generally ascribed to Pont. These names cover areas from the Southern Highlands to the North West Highlands. (See footnote for detailed explanation) Of these, 150 names, the overwhelming majority collected by Pont 400 years ago are those which, in slightly altered form, we use today. Six names on the maps and six in the document bear no relation to those currently in use, or are corrupted beyond recognition, i.e. about 8%. Given that the names in all certainty preceded Pont's investigations by some time, we can say that the mountain names of Scotland he collected have now been laid down for well over half a millennium.

Some current names occur in Pont's sources in forms little altered, e.g. Bin Nevesh for Ben Nevis, Bin Lawers for Ben Lawers, Struik Chron for Stuic a' Chroin and Month Kyin for Mount Keen. Others have worn a little more from usage, but are still easily recognisable, such as Bin Liachann, Liathach; Bin Gloin, Beinn a' Ghlo, and Karniler, Carn an Fhidhleir. However, other names have become so corrupted with the passage of time, that they have led those investigating the meaning of the names to deal with great difficulties. I would suggest that those seeking inspiration should turn to Pont, and the original and probably less corrupted forms of the mountain names, for their solutions.

One name I have always 'hid my doots aboot' is Seana Braigh in remote Ross-shire. This is given in my *SMC Munros Guidebook* (1985) as "old upper part", though I have seen it as "old slope" In his *Scottish Hill and Mountain Names,* (1992) Drummond repeats this as "old height" but is unable to provide an explanation of why the mountain gained such a strange name. Could this be because it is in fact a corruption? Or indeed, the name of something else?

In the written documents attributed to Pont, are two references to a mountain called Skormyvarr and then Scornivar. In the first instance we are told that "Coygach is at the west" of the hill and in the second that the Carron (Charroun) River "falleth out of the great hill of Scorinvar....on the south syd therof sum 2 or 3 myl from the mayn top." (p 547-8). These comments would also apply to the mountain now known as Seana Braigh. Pont himself drew a mountain called Scormyrvar after making a trip up the River Lael from Inverlael and mapping settlements in Gleann na Sguaib and the terrain at the heads of the River Lael and the Allt Gleann a' Mhadaidh. (I am indebted to Chris Fleet of the National Library of Scotland for help with identifying this drawing). From thereabouts Seana Bhraigh can be seen, and in Pont's depiction (Map 4b) Scormyrvar is shown with a prominent eastern summit, which might represent the presently-named Creag an Duine. I feel that Scornivar or Scormyvar could be an earlier form of Seana Braigh, and that the English meaning might usefully be derived from unravelling the former name and not from efforts to decipher the latter.

There is another possibility. Names of parts of mountains sometimes get transposed to the whole over time. The classic example being Lochnagar. In the *SMCJ* 23 (137), p323, E. M. Hodge states that the gamekeeper at Corriemulzie Lodge told him Seana Braigh represented the rounded and domed outlying hills to the right of the cairned summit, as seen from Corriemulzie (Probably Meall nam Bradhan and its partner), and NOT the massif presently designated by the name Seana Braigh. Additionally, according to the keeper, a Mr Mackenzie, relying on old records, the prominent subsidiary peak of the mountain, designated Creag an Duine in the guidebook, was known locally as Sgurr or An Sgurr. Craig an Duine was properly the name only of a crag on An Sgurr, recalling the attempted rescue of a sheep and thus in all probability a much later name than the one current in Pont's time. Is An Sgurr our Scornmyvarr? Dwelly's Illustrated *Gaelic Dictionary* gives an interesting possibility for barr, which would aspirate as bharr and then be anglicised as varr, as meaning topmost part. Do we therefore have Sgurr a' Bharr as the peak of the topmost part? I throw this suggestion out for consultation. At the least I feel that Seana Braigh cannot be reliably taken as the proper name of the hill in question.

Bidean nam Bian in Glencoe is a fine mountain with a fine name; but what does it mean? Can it be "peak of the mountains", as suggested in the Munros guide? Though thinking this most likely, another possibility is given by Drummond as the "peak of the hides, or pelts", or possibly as I have seen elsewhere, peak of the deer skins. I think Pont can help us out on this one, and that none of these suggestions are accurate. In Pont 12c, beside Loch Trichardan (Achtriochtan), there are two sharp twin peaks, which can only be ridges of Bidean nam Bian. Pont has named one Pittindeaun, which at first I thought was Bidean (Pittin) (nam) Bian (deaun – with d/b transposed, a common error). However, next to this is written Boddin Deaun, and two d/b transcriptions struck me as excessive. What

L: Finnauon B:
Skiry
Lariou
L: Carron
AM
Coryerback
Benn Leckderg
Achnashelach
Ry Vorachon
Edaiva-charno
L: Dowl
Ach martin
Dili...
Achnashela
ylen L: Doull
Achnanty
Imernakaig

Auo Lochay
Blairn-cleyrach
Achaintour
Inner-Lochy
Druymerban
R:
Blairmack-foylach
ylen Loch-Doun-ta-Vra
Blairmack-dreynich
Fuon Neuesh
Blair-mackaj
Blaerheuvyn
Auo Kechanish
M
Bm Neuesh

PART of LOCHAY-ABRE

we in all likelihood have here is an early name for Bidean nam Bian, of Boddin-, or Pittin-deaun, i.e. Devil's Prick, quite a common Gaelic name for such eminences, and of which the current name may be a replacement to remove the impropriety, or more likely simply a corruption. What is especially interesting is that Pont has written what seem to be two attempts at the name, as if to get it right, and these represent reasonable Gaelic pronunciation. (Pottendeun (so-spelled) appears on Map 12b as well.)

It might be argued that these eminences were, in fact, supposed to be the two Buachailles, but not so, since Pont knew those as well and drew them separately. If we look at Map 25b we have a faintish mountain in the Glencoe area, with the barely legible Bogle beside it. Is this a Pontesque Here be Dragons in good old Scots? Eye-strain revealed e.i. (?) beside it, and the nearest we can get to the proper Gaelic for Buachaille Etive Mor, is, in my amateur phonetics, Bokle Eite. (Bogle e.i. (?)). Scales fell from strained eyes and revealed a multi-peaked vista of the Buachaille, with the top of Crowberry Tower showing.

Aside from corruptions, some mountain names have actually changed over the last 400 years. A good example is Pont's Bin Chroby or Bin Chromby (it appears on two maps, 20b and 27a). From its position in both cases this is clearly the hill today designated as Carn an Righ, between Glen Shee and Glen Tilt, a name given it after James VI had used it as a hunting ground, i.e. after Pont's surveys were made. That is a simple enough explanation, but what of the following?

In the area of Strathcarron (Map 4a) Pont gives us Benn Leckderg, a name not in use today and designating a very prominent and jagged peak. After some puzzlement I identified as Fuar Tholl . Its position is exact, above Loch Dughaill and east of Fionn Abhainn river (Pont: A; Finnavon). Leckderg is shown by Pont as a three-topped hill and is in my opinion a directional aid, as many of his mountain drawings would appear to be. The three summits of Leckderg/Fuar Tholl are seen very clearly from Strathcarron, and from the foot of the Coulin Pass, (personal observation 28.4.00) which route Pont probably took to Loch Maree. At some point Leckdearg was re-named, by local Gaelic speakers, as Fuar Tholl. Possibly when transhumance took the Gael with cattle up to the 'cold hole' behind the Strathcarron slopes? Or do we have here a mountain which had one name in Strathcarron and another in Torridon, and when the OS men were doing their work they asked a Torridonian rather than someone from the mountain's southern side, for its name?

Pont did not place any mountains to the south of Strathcarron in this map, but the written sources indicate a mountain we are not familiar with: "The high hill of Bhearnish with the haughis and stank thereof…the hie hill of Bhearnais within two myl of Luir-moir," (p551-2). Those who know the area will feel that this is Bidean a'Choire Sheasgaich, between Lurg Mhor and Bearnais bothy, which had possibly yet to acquire that specific name. Again, transhumance might have provided it later.

Blair Fyffe on the third ascent of 'Trail of Tears' (VII 8) Tough-Brown Face, Lochnagar. Photo: Ed Tressider.

Pont took considerable trouble to draw a mountain beloved of all Scots mountaineers, and generally known today as the Cobbler, though it probably has more alternative names than any other hill. He shows its three peaks clearly and writes below, "a craggie hill", (Map 17a). The Cobbler in Pont's day was not a shoemaker, or even Beinn Ghobhlach, the forked hill, but Arthur's Seat, Suy Arthire. This would appear to give weight to a further variant on the hill's designation, Ben Arthur. But Pont didn't put in Suy for dramatic effect; he was told this by locals to whom the mountain had significance in Arthurian legend, and it would seem to be that Suy Arthire (i.e. Suidhe Artair) should be considered the legitimate name, confirming Drummond's speculation – *Scottish Hill and Mountain Names*, p.112. While we are hereabouts, Pont gives the name of a mountain in the exact position of Beinn an Lochain as Bin Ailt, indicating possibly another change, rather than corruption, over time.

Another change, and an extremely puzzling one, is that for the mountain we know as Schiehallion. On Map 23, Pont draws this fine hill, and clearly names it Kraich, which may be Creag or Cruach. It might be that Pont here was simply misinformed, and this seems likely when we consider that in the documents, generally thought to be by Pont – or his helpers – the mountain is referred to as Suy Challen, or Maiden's Seat, much closer to the name it now goes by. This however, would give no credence to those who argue that the mountain's name is something to do with Caledonian Fairies. Interestingly, the maiden root was carried over into Roy's mid-18th century maps, when he translated the Gaelic term as Maiden's Pap. Was the Caledonian element a Victorian Fairy Tale?

In this International Year of the Mountain we should recognise the pioneering work of Timothy Pont. And, while not arguing that we should revert to his nomenclature where locals for various reasons changed the name of a hill, I do feel that those corruptions which his work appears to highlight should be corrected in appropriate locations such as OS maps and SMC Guides.

Footnote: The Pont maps which survived were first published in *The Pont Manuscript Maps of Scotland,* Ed. Jeffrey Stone (1989), and all my references are to the maps in this source. The maps are now available digitalised, and are much more legible, in the National Library of Scotland's Pont website www.nls.uk/pont The written texts often attributed to Pont but which might be in part by his associates, are the *Noates and Observations on Dyvers Parts of the Hielands and Isles of Scotland* in MacFarlane's *Geographical Collections* Vol. 11 (1907). Page numbers quoted refer to this source. My article *Timothy Pont and Scotland's Mountains,* which has tables of the peaks identified from both sources, as well as an account of the ascent of Ben Lawers and other matters montane, is in *The Nation Survey'd,* Ed. I. C. Cunningham (2001), a collection of essays about Pont and his work, which readers of the *SMCJ* might enjoy perusing.

WHERE THE LAND MEETS THE SEA

By David Kirk

A BEAUTIFUL granite slot provided a perfect Rock 7 placement right at the start of the traverse. I couldn't see where the next gear would be and it looked thin. I could feel sea spray wetting my hair as I leaned back and pushed the tiller further out. This section would make or break things – I had to do well. The only other viable alternative was to give up now and that wasn't in my game plan.

The laser picked up speed beneath me. The sea was calmer here. If I could get up on the plane, then that would really help. The angle of the traverse ledge was increasing as I padded along it. A handhold would be nice – gear would be better. A gust of wind caught me unawares and instinct caused me to release the main sheet a little. I cursed myself as I sheeted in and made a few more tentative steps along the ledge.

The sea was altogether more bouncy now. I might still manage to plane her, but first and foremost, I needed to calm down and make sure I didn't do anything stupid. It would be a long fall from here. The wind had definitely picked up and was making balance more problematic. A small hole appeared which could possibly take a micro between granite crystals – but how strong were they? I quickly lurched my body inwards as the fluky wind suddenly backed. At least I hadn't let the sheet out this time – but I'd felt a lot closer to going over. If I could reach the buoy, at least I'd have the wind more on the quarter. Regardless of how poor it was, I felt a little better with the micro in. The corner at the end of the ramp traverse was near – surely I'd get good gear there. As I approached the buoy, I realised that the sea below it was very short and the wind was still squally – I could definitely speed up with the prevailing wind more aft, but would allowing her to plane be a good idea?

It could only be one more move to the corner – I could see a great jug handle. I wanted to be there, to be holding it. My calf muscles were screaming due to the angle of my feet. I could possibly make one quick dart. If I were lucky, I would round the buoy with inches to spare without having to sheet in and bear up. The alternative was to traverse the whole bloody ledge again and give up. I went for it. I did what was probably my steepest ever slab padding move, and suddenly, I was round the buoy. The hold was excellent. I relaxed my legs, shaking them out alternately. I pulled in the tiller to bear away from the wind and sheeted out.

Although the sea was choppy, the boat's balance felt good. I felt the speed increasing as a strong steady wind blew off the port quarter. Suddenly, I felt the hull tremble. I realised that, although the hold I had was excellent, there was no similarly excellent gear placement in the corner.

I could feel the boat starting to lift. I'd never planed in water like this before. Could I control it? My hands were sweating on the tiller. I quickly chalked up – that's normally a good confidence builder but it didn't seem to be working today. One or two little fissures in the rock might take a couple of wires. Once more I took out my small wires. Surely, I would be up at any moment. The short spell I'd had of steady wind had ended and it was gusting again. On this point of sail, I wouldn't exactly slow down much by letting out the main sheet. I would have to bring her head right round to slow down and that would really spoil my chances. Mind you, that was better than some of the other outcomes I could conjure up. Resigned to my destiny, I clipped the second of my poor wires to a rope. It would be a few tricky moves up the corner, then the angle leaned back a bit blocking my view of the rest of the cliff, but surely it would be easier. I stepped up gingerly onto a small granite ripple and made a few tentative moves up the corner.

Suddenly, I was up and on the plane. The boat's speed felt like it was tripling as it skimmed from wave crest to wave crest. It was anything but a smooth ride, but that didn't bother me in the slightest. Adrenaline coursed through my veins and I whooped with exhilaration. I no longer felt any fear. I could see that I had only a couple of moves to go and I'd be on a small ledge with good holds and a Big Solid Crack. The next buoy was approaching. I would need to bear up as I went round it and the boat would drop off the plane. Could I hold out until then? Using a tiny edge for my left hand and just the slab for my right, I pulled up.

My God, what was happening? From being on the quarter, the wind was now full abaft. Was this just a fluke, or was it changing? The cliff to my right – it was affecting the wind, causing it to back. With no warning, my foot slipped. My other foot came off too as weight distribution altered. The realisation that the wind was being backed came too late. I started to fall. The boat's stern was already through the eye and suddenly the wind had caught the sail. In a fraction of a second the boom was swinging across towards me. I felt the tendons in the fingertips of my left hand stretching as my full weight came onto them.

As it swung across, the boom caught the side of my head as I tried to duck out of the way. It continued round and slammed against the water and the main sheets, as the boat broached. The boat was on its edge now, capsizing and probably about to turn-turtle. I think I was already in the water. Pain and nausea were all I was aware of.

My tendons screamed but I succeeded in holding on. I quickly pulled myself back up into my previous position. This time my foot didn't slip. I stepped up a little higher and finally I got a good hold for my right hand. One more move and I was on the ledge. My mind buzzed with euphoria and I burst into song. The next section looked much easier, but it was time for a belay – the Big Solid Crack was exactly what it promised to be.

Once established on the ledge, I began to take in again my wider surroundings. The wind was a bit stronger here, out of the shelter of the face. There was obviously some dingy race going on down below. The dinghies were well strung out. The one nearest the cliff appeared to have capsized. Someone was next to it in the water and what appeared to be a safety boat was heading across.

ASSYNT

From the anchorage of that derelict january coire,
I argued a way with loose tongues of nomadic snow,
To enlighten my northern burden of hopeless despond
Upon a ridge of sun-lit space . . .

If time is a commodity it's in short supply,
But I make a deal and trade-in deadlines,
Shake out the prudent reef – and now can linger,
Drifting on an oscillating, rippling winter wave.

There is no upward surge to tramp the corniced crest,
To settle the point that the hugh-god called a top,
Or, poles apart, risk encounter with telescopic munroman,
Who wouldn't understand why I am here.

I have arrived at some strange natural node,
A sutherlanderish interface of colour, phase and form;
Reflecting, I measure this harmonic change of state
And roll the choral taste around my mind.

The deep blues have distilled to cloud the darkened day,
May hunt you down as you contemplate the city's separation,
A rising wind makes saxophonic threats to blow out my sail,
And now I know why I am here.

Mike Jacob.

CHILE VOLCANOES AND HIGH ANDES

By Dave Snadden

SEPTEMBER 14, 2001, 0500. Edinburgh Airport: Steel eyes and pert lip confronted me over the check in desk. "No, I cannot check you in. There are no flights to America."

"But I am going to Santiago in Chile, that is South America. I am going via Paris to Chile direct, I don't go within 3000 miles of America."

"There are no flights to America."

"I checked with the carrier last night and the flight is OK."

"I have been instructed not to check in anyone going to America."

"I am not going to America".

Stuck record repeated. Totalitarian doorman syndrome *par excellence.*

How can anyone be so imbecilic? Four of us and mountains of rucksacks and Skis – (though still way short of our amazing 70kg. per person allowance.) Even a McEnroesque tantrum merely hardened Steeleyes' resolve. I headed off for the information desk to hear someone else being sent home who was also going to Santiago. A Prozac moment was beckoning. I am not renowned for giving up easily however, so turned the big brown eye treatment (hard for someone with greenish ones) on a warm, fuzzy, motherly looking one and sweetly told my story. She at least understood geography, listened, phoned Paris and asked in her perfect French if the flight was OK – it was. This took time and we arrived back at Steeleyes as she was thinking of closing check-in, had a very terse closed body language conversation followed by boarding cards, fifty-minute transfer in Paris and only two bags missing in Santiago. Air France knew they were missing before we did. One arrived next morning via Madrid and one a few hours after that, all delivered to our door. Our plan was to piste bash and jet lag recover for the first couple of days anyway, so it was not an issue.

Our main aim was to savour Chilean ski-mountaineering. We had arranged with John Biggar to set the trip up for us (www.info.andes.com) recognising that John's local knowledge and fluent Spanish would be essential. He also sorted out logistics in terms of accommodation, transport, and food and met us at the airport with a minibus as he had been in South America for the previous week.

Stepping into the warm Santiago spring after the start of a dismal Scottish autumn is a wonderful experience. First impressions were of 25°C, us in shorts and skimpy T-shirts and the locals all running around in fleeces. It must get a bit hot in summer! Chile is a fledgling western democracy with surprisingly easy access. We needed no visas and no cash, with holes in the wall everywhere accepting our credit and Switch cards in return for copious amounts of pesos. Everything was cheap compared to Europe, but expensive for South America, or so we were told. There was fresh fruit and vegetables in abundance, plenty of supermarkets and oceans of glorious wine – it being hard to buy anything for more than a fiver and easy to find good stuff for 75p a litre. With friendly people, helpful police and a feeling of safety in Santiago the omens were good, even though the Spanish spoken by the locals bears no resemblance to that bandied around evening classes in Scotland.

Santiago is squashed between the Pacific and the Andes. The sea is far enough away (100km) that you can't see or smell it, but everywhere you go the Andes beckon. There are a number of ski resorts within a couple of hours drive of the city. These are big enough and high enough to give some really good skiing and quiet enough not to have queues, especially at the end of the season when we were there.

Our plan was to head south to the Chilean Lake District, acclimatize on some volcanoes and then head off into some bigger mountains. So we piled into our rented minibus and drove 800km south to Pucon. This is the only town in Chile that could remotely be termed a mountain town, in that it had some touristy shops and postcards and lived under the shadow of Villarica, a fume belching monster that has wiped the town out a few times over the centuries. We coaxed our soon to be abused vehicle up a cinder track to the Villarica ski resort – two tows on the flanks of the mountain that looked very closed. We scrounged a lift up by smiling sweetly at the attendant who was still recovering from some all night celebration and found ourselves shrouded in mist on an anonymous snowfield somewhere – it could have been anywhere, all we needed was the famed Andean wind to make us feel we were back in Scotland. Volcanoes are pretty easy to get to the top of in poor visibility as all you have to do is go up. Getting down can be different as a very small compass error can land you miles from where you started, a mistake easily compounded by poor maps, so we were pretty pleased when we climbed out through a temperature inversion into the most amazing scenery. Villarica is isolated and at 3000m is about 1000m above any of the surrounding hills. Snowy summit cones 20-30 km apart punctured the sea of cloud, each subtly different and each gently smoking, belching fumes or sleeping quietly depending on its mood. Villarica was the most active one we climbed and standing on the crater rim on skis with fumes and steam belching forth and having hot rocks lobbed at us was a pretty surreal experience. No wonder the locals thought we were mad. The descent was on perfect spring snow at an angle just right for skiing. It went on and on and the views were breathtaking.

Now, so as not to bore you with descriptions of the finer subtleties of volcanoes, we skied four, working north in the process. Llaima was huge and steep, Lonquimay gave an orgasmic descent and Antuco will be ever remembered for the succour of its warm rocks in the teeth of a biting wind. Everywhere there was perfect snow, the flattering sugary type that ski-mountaineers dream of. We also, at this early stage, climbed the smaller peak of Cautin and were turned back from Sierra Nevada by an approaching storm, but not before we had lunch on a windy ridge covered in monkey puzzle trees while being closely inspected by a baby condor with a 12ft. wingspan. Its spectacular mother came to check up that it was safe and, once we were deemed harmless, hurtled down the valley leaving her offspring to circle us for a magic half-hour, probably in the hope we would die from hypothermia and provide a tasty snack or two.

This was our first trip on skis in the Southern Hemisphere and it does take a bit of getting used to. On a spring-snow descent you tend to know where the non-frozen snow is because instinct tells you where the sun has been, but here it was all the wrong way round with the sun going the right way in the wrong place and northern instinct guiding you to the frozen bits. However, It doesn't take long to reset the internal compass.

Acclimatised and fit it was time to get into the remote mountains. So we stocked up at a supermarket and headed up a valley to Lago Maule, excited at the prospect of tents in the snow and total wilderness. We spent a day driving up a gravel road to a remote police post 20-30km from our goal. They politely laughed when we explained our plans.

"The road is blocked."

"How blocked?"

"Well – very blocked. You see it has been a bad winter with lots of storms and we had a landslide."

"Any chance of getting round it?"

"Oh no, we even have to get off our horses to get round it."

This doesn't sound much until you have been on a Chilean horse! So we camped in an old quarry and tried the Rio Teno valley the next day. Here we fared no better. This time water had washed roads and bridges away and we were again halted 20km from anything worthwhile. Another camp and the compensation of a Scottish-type day on the peak of Altos los Padres – a long carry, a stormy summit, a short ski and a long carry. We needed to re-think.

We then headed to Santiago and drove up the Cajun del Maipo, which is an impressive valley heading due east from the city into the heart of the high Andes. Like most roads, except the new tarmac Pan-American Highway that runs the length of the country, this was dirt track and ended at Banos Morales a small spa village surrounded by incredible peaks. Cerro San Francisco being the most spectacular with its leering South Face really looking like its nickname – the Eiger of the Andes.

Banos Morales sports an Alpine hut run by the German Andean Club, a hut straight out of the Alps, except every one speaks Spanish and it bizarrely serves up canned British beer. It seems devoid of mountaineers in the spring and is a good place to sort gear before heading into the mountains. We spied a quarry track winding up the side of the valley towards the snow line, packed the bus and were soon brought to a stop by a bulldozed pile of rocks across the track. The snow line seemed so far away and the mountain of gear huge, added to which, the attraction of actually using snow shovels for something useful was too strong. An hour of navvying and we were on our way up again till the gradient got too much by which time the snow line was only a couple of km away. We dumped the gear and started ferrying the loads while the bus was taken back to safer pastures. The road back had been re-blocked by a zealous bulldozer and only sweet smiles and pleadings of being stupid foreigners got us to the right side again. We then sledged our gear to the old spa of Banos Morales at 2500m. A spectacular approach through a steep valley flanked by rotten moraine and dizzy peaks. Banos Morales was deserted and was no more than a couple of ruined shacks. Tents were pitched on snow and we sat down to enjoy the spectacular scenery, tranquillity and birdsong. Birdsong? Up here? About 200m away a hole in the ground spewed forth a torrent of boiling sulphurous water, too hot to touch. It had carved a track through the snow to a river in the valley bottom. Under the cornices were myriads of insects, and lots of little birds obviously arriving for the summer, feasting on the insects and keeping warm by the banks of the water. So here we were in the middle of nowhere, with no maps, fantastic weather and dressed only in ski boots and Factor 30. The sunset temperature transformation was sudden, the stars incredible and the silence – oh the silence.

Dawn found us high in the valleys looking for possible routes. It took all day to explore and pin-point likely ascents. Fantastic snow and hot. What must summer be like? We found our way to the top of Cerro Catedral one day, and an unnamed peak the next. Both about 4000m. Both magnificent in terms of interesting ascent routes, amazing views and long, long descents on perfect snow.

We then made another exploration of the main valley towards Argentina under the shadow of Volcan San Jose, a 6000m monster. It would need another week to get farther into the system and another camp – for another day perhaps. Unfortunately, it was time to go. So much to do here.

There is good ski-mountaineering in the Andes. Access into the mountains is a major problem with few access roads, and those mostly dirt tracks vulnerable to winter destruction. The mountains are deserted. Transport and local knowledge do make an enormous difference to what can be achieved. We skied until the first week in October and for the high Andes this is probably getting to the end of the Ski-mountaineering season. John and David left us then and the rest of us headed north in a wild bus ride – 500km for £5, lunch and bingo included – and trekked on horse back to a 3000m camp for a night. No snow, unbelievable scenery of desert and piles of rubble masquerading as mountains, all on horses that seemed quite happy to carry you at V. Diff. over granite slabs and through wild foaming rivers. Chile is not for faint-hearted vegetarians where the options in remote valleys are large plates of slabs of steak or starvation. At least we stored up enough B12 for about a year.

We were David, Moira and Alison Snadden, Will Cadell, David Roberts and John Biggar.

NEW CLIMBS SECTION

In this introduction, ANDY NISBET summarises the new rock climbs, and SIMON RICHARDSON the new winter climbs in 2001-2002.

SUMMER

THE winter of 2001 went on for ever with the last route in the CIC hut book by Godefroy Perroux on May 7. Then started one of the poorer summers of recent times. May wasn't too bad, but each month thereafter was wetter till a dry spell in September saved us from drowning. So a very poor year for mountain rock climbing left plenty of action on the crags. Only new routes get recorded, but hopefully, the new route tally mirrors the general activity.

The weather in April was dry enough for low rock or high ice. But first in action was Pete Benson and Finlay Bennet at the Lower Crag, Poverty Point, at Neist where they climbed a couple of fine overhanging cracks. Neist continues to see more exploration, as do other nearby sea cliffs but you might have thought Polney Crag to be worked out. But Tim Rankin climbed the funky arête of Stolen Ivy (E7 6c) on Ivy Buttress, later repeated at least twice during the summer. The best weather (of the summer) was in early May when Dave MacLeod climbed another E7 in Glen Nevis (Isomorph) while Gary Latter and Mike Reed were climbing at Reiff. But most of the action was out on the Barra islands with a team of Rick Campbell, Gary Latter, Malcolm Davies, John Lyall, Ian Taylor and Glyn Stanworth on Pabbay. Towards the end of the month, Simon Harry, Pete Nugent and Bob Bowdler started the climbing on Eriskay while Kev Howett, Lucy Creamer, Steve Crowe and Karin Magog climbed some hard and impressive routes on Mingulay. With such a huge number of routes climbed since the last guide, the documentation is poor, so the list of routes this year is far from comprehensive, but a lesser level of activity continued throughout the summer.

Come June, the mountains began to dry out although hindered by the late winter. Probably slowest was the Cairngorms which managed a brief dry spell in late June and early July. Advantage was taken by Mike Reed and Pete Benson's new route on the Central Gully Wall of Creag an Dubh Loch, (The Nullfidian, E5 6b). Around this time there were two repeats of recent hard route The Origin of Species (probably E6). The islands continued to be popular with a strong team of Dave MacLeod, Niall McNair and Steve Richardson in Lewis, repeating and climbing new lines on Traigh Berie and Dalbeg.

A large number of crags in the North-west have been explored, mostly on the friendly Lewissian gneiss. Paul Tattersall has been very active around Gairloch but joined by many others to produce around 100 new routes. John Mackenzie and Sue Harper have been exploring the crags on the remote side of Loch Maree while several teams have discovered crags around Rhiconich and is as usual nowadays, worked hard at finishing them off. There must have been around 200 routes in all so the next Northern Highlands guidebook might struggle to stay in two volumes.

The weather was patchy into July, enough to tempt summer visitor Julian Lines on to the Central Slabs of the Shelter Stone Crag and success on a short route, Freya (E3 5c) with Laurence Hughes, but failure on a much more impressive one when it rained. Julian continued to climb as many days as possible throughout and continued to find more lines.

Perhaps the best set of new routes has been in Arran, starting in June but it seemed to escape the monsoon into August. Raiders John Dunne and Andy Jack climbed one of the last great problems when they managed the wall right of Abraxus on Cioch na h-Oighe. The line was repeated by Dave MacLeod a week later unaware of the original ascent and graded E8. As a major new line, there were the usual rumours of dubious tactics. In July, Julian Lines did some very bold soloing on Cir Mhor, while into August, Gary Latter, Dan Honeyman and Dave MacLeod shared the action. All in all, MacLeod and Lines had quite a summer.

The island of Great Bernera, linked to mainland Lewis by a bridge, has seen a lot of climbing during the summer around Geodha Mor Shleibhte. Andy Cunningham has been climbing here for a few years and was persuaded to reveal the information when Rab and Chris Anderson, Dave Cuthbertson, Jo George, Keith Archer and partners all climbed here without knowing the others had also been. There were a wide range of grades on several different cliffs from Severe to E6 (Mega Tsaunami, E6 6a by Cubby) and plenty of enthusiasm, so I'm sure this place will be visited next year. This was part of an amazingly enthusiastic two weeks by Rab and Chris Anderson on Lewis, when they climbed around 40 new routes, including many on the more established cliffs around Mungarstadh and Uig. Later in the year, Roger Everett and Dee Gaffney climbed on the cliffs here as well as exploring some of the obscure crags in the Uig hills and Harris.

One of the last big routes of the year was one of the best when Rick Campbell and Gary Latter climbed a line through The Bat on Carn Dearg Buttress at E6. Named The Wicked, it was finished in September and had required at least three attempts, so awaits a flash (and might wait a while). You might think it was the end of rock climbing but an Oxford University party climbed in Skye on their recently developed crags in Glen Sligachan over New Year, as well as on the sea cliffs at Neist, with new routes on both the 31st and 1st. Unpredictability, is one of the joys of Scottish climbing, and I'm glad there are still some mad folk around!

WINTER

It has been a strange winter, often wet and warm, but with amazing conditions on the few occasions when it suddenly turned cold, and culminating in a month of brilliant ice high on the Ben when everywhere else had all but finished. Global warming you might say, and you are probably right. But if global warming means more ice on the Ben, then we could do worse. This winter seems to be a strong example of predicted future weather, perhaps combined with a year of dominant westerlies. But westerlies are better than southerlies, so the increased rainfall of recent years has produced more snow on the Ben. And the warmer climate has allowed thaws even in mid-season, so instead of the prolonged powder of the Seventies, ice has been increasing throughout the winter to produce enough to survive several thaws and leave us with the best possible quality at the end of the season. The negative side has been that the lower venues have been useless and the number of days written off by rain has been quite high. And it hasn't just been the weekends!

On the climbing side, standards are continuing to rise – quite rapidly. The latest axes and crampons are fiercer weapons and definitely help, along with sharp ice screws transferred from Continental icefalls to the Ben, but there is also a confidence that all the routes done a few years ago are sensible targets for today's stronger climbers. The poor weather has meant that the number of new routes has been fewer, and the number of hard new routes has been even less. But the number of second or early ascents of hard routes has been higher than ever, with only those too low to come into condition surviving unrepeated (like Against All Odds and Guerdon Grooves which were certainly under the spotlight). So the ephemeral conditions have meant that only those on the spot (and with a bit of luck) have been able to take advantage of isolated brilliant days. Highlight of the year in this respect was Martin Moran and Paul Tattersall's ascent of The Godfather on Beinn Bhan when Roger Webb had stood below its unfrozen turf the day before. Of all the routes done this winter, this was the only one where normally reticent climbers thought: "wow!". And it doesn't need special conditions, only well-frozen turf, so maybe it will receive some attention next year. Or maybe it will need to sit a while and become more familiar before anyone will dare go near.

Of course, there were several other impressive new lines, but none up an untouched wall. Like Blair Fyffe and Es Tressidur's line up the rib right of Albatross, Guy and Pete Robertson's route right of Ice Bomb in Coire Ghranda of Beinn Dearg, Brian Davison, Dave McGimpsey and Andy Nisbet's ascent of Rampart Wall in Coire Mhic Fhearchair, Mike Pescod, Jonny Baird and Tim Riley climbing Piranha on Aonach Mor, Scott Muir and Graham Little's Planet Fear on Meall nan Tarmachan, Dave MacLeod and Gareth Hughes's ascent of MacLean's Folly on The Cobbler and for the lack of a hard one, Chris Cartwright and Simon Richardson's string of routes from the one-day-a-week men.

So now to the story of the winter. There wasn't a hint of snow until a sudden dump blocked many of the roads. It was a shock to the system fighting our way to the crags through deep powder, like Alan Mullin's six-hour approach to Coire Mhic Fhearchair and Jonathan Preston and I taking five hours to Kellett's Slab Route (VI,7) on South Trident Buttress. What a contrast to strolling up to the Ben in a T-shirt in April after breakfast with 12 hours of daylight to go. Perhaps the more accessible Stac Pollaidh was a better option for Erik Brunskill and Dafydd Morris, although their name for their route, Positive Vegetation (IV,6) makes me wonder if it wasn't. The rest of November was very flirty but gave little away, with the Northern Corries sometimes in nick and rocky routes in Coire an Lochain seeing a few ascents.

December continued along the same lines when Chris Cartwright and Simon Richardson found the only snow in Scotland in Garbh Choire Mor of Braeriach to climb Gauntless (IV,5), a short mixed climb up the left sidewall of Michaelmas Fare on the first weekend. Things looked more promising the following week when Coire Sputan Dearg came into good nick (for two days!), with James Edwards and Sam Barron making the second free ascent of Grey Slab and passing on the secret of good conditions to Dave McGimpsey, Hannah Burrows-Smith and I who struggled our way up The Chebec, rather too early in the season for good style. But the next week was back to rock climbing before snow around Christmas time. Quick off the mark were Scott Muir and Gordon Lennox who climbed a W(inter)edgewood (VII,7) before anyone else realised it had snowed. The week around Christmas was pretty snowy and a few escaped family commitments as the first good conditions arrived. The aforementioned Piranha, Scott Muir and Kevin Kelly's second ascent of Millennium Line in stormy weather and Erik Brunskill and Dafydd Morris back to Stac Pollaidh on a Rampage (V,6) all led up to the well-named Planet Fear on fragile ice. There were also a couple of hard repeats by Tim Rankin and Gordon Lennox on The Screaming (VIII,8) and Jamie Baillie and Ben Wilkinson on Punsters Crack (VII,8) on the Cobbler. Yet more names on the hard climbing scene. And Dave McGimpsey and I climbed the fine Taliballan (V,6) on our Crag X, later revealed as Stob Coire an Laoigh in the Grey Corries.

Now into January with high hopes, the weather deteriorated the day after Blair Fyffe and Es Tresidder repeated a straight version of Die Riesenwand (Coire an Fhamhair of Beinn Bhan), quoting sensational exposure along icy ledges and naming it Divine Retribution (VII,6) before realising it had been climbed before by Chris Cartwright and Robin Clothier in 1991. Also that day, Andy Forsyth and Nick Harper (more names!) tussled with one of the best routes of its type, The Nuis Chimney in Arran. The rest of January was warm and wet, stripping almost everything and even into February was poor, although Graeme Ettle and Mark Garthwaite (more names!) climbed the summer line of Poison Dwarf on Carn Etchachan at VII,8. Just as we were beginning to despair, February turned colder. Still quite stormy, thaws and freezes brought the middle to higher cliffs into icy nick and although the Ben became swamped in powder, it was the potential for the excellent late season conditions. As the cold weather arrived in mid February, the Cairngorms were first to be good, with some ice forming on Lochnagar and the Cartwright/Richardson team climbing Big Bertha (VII,7) on the Dividing Buttress of Beinn a' Bhuird. As conditions improved, Guy Robertson and Jason Currie repeated Rolling Thunder on Lochnagar in pretty icy conditions while Blair Fyffe and Es Tressidur climbed an icy Trail of Tears, neither team being stressed on routes with an epic history. Other venues around the 900m mark also became very icy and Dave McGimpsey and I made a frantic collection of routes on Stob Coire an Laoigh before its revelation online.

Now into March, the Ben was improving but the mid-height venues still held the attention. The Big Chill on Beinn Dearg and Rampart Wall in Coire Mhic Fhearchair were climbed while there was a race for Vertigo Wall on Creag an Dubh Loch. Minus One Gully on the Ben saw a couple of ascents and Royal Pardon on Aonach Beag saw the first of many ascents in the season. Now into mid-March, the expected warming towards the end of the season happened but not before Martin Moran and Paul Tattersall met the Godfather and Guy Robertson and Es Tressidur repeated the mysterious West-Central Gully. This warming really brought the Ben into perfect nick, although no-one realised just how much more perfect it was going to get the next week, and then even more perfect after that. Soon climbing the classics became climbing the face routes when Pointless saw a rare ascent and queues built up for the previously rare 'Cold Climbs tick' of Galactic Hitchhiker. The great slab between these two even built up with ice for the first time while the Shroud icicle joined up. Other ice lines formed for the first time, like the obvious gully line between Abacus and Antonine Wall (Cartwright and Richardson) and the left rib of Point Five Gully (Robin Clothier and Paul Thorburn). But the best new piece of ice was the central icefall on the Brenva Face, long watched but finally completed by Hannah Burrows-Smith and Dave McGimpsey (Super G, VI,6). And given a modest grade and write-up considering its awesome steepness was a thin and very vertical icefall right of Royal Pardon climbed by Stewart Anderson and Stuart McFarlane and named Monarch's Crown (VI,6). The story that the ice broke off under Stuart and he had to do one-arm pull-ups to regain it means that it won't see a rush for repeats!

Now into April and the most unusual ice on the Ben had gone. But the high routes were still superb while everywhere else in Scotland had disappeared. Many of the classic routes were seeing ascents every day with queues at the weekends. Lovely snow-ice and steps from so many ascents meant the routes often felt a grade easier, encouraging lots of solo ascents and giving new guide author, Simon Richardson, a grading question for the guide, due out before next winter. A few new routes were claimed on the unusually iced No. 3 Gully Buttress by McGimpsey, Nisbet and Ed Edwards and either side of Glover's Chimney by Cartwright/ Richardson but the majority were enjoying dry cold weather with an easy walk-in, comfortable route, sit in the sun on top and an amble down. Not like the rest of the winter at all And so many keen climbers – I don't feel eccentric any more.

OUTER ISLES

LEWIS, The Uig Hills, Hidden Buttress:
R. Everett was unable to locate any of the routes (except Spike Fright) and thinks the crag was written up from a distant memory. He has written up three routes, with the first two as "probably climbed before" and Hidden Treasure as definitely new.

Hidden Buttress
This fine crag starts straight from the water at its left-hand end and forms a right-rising band of rock, about 30m high, extending for over 150m up the hillside. Spike Fright (VS) traverses across the lowest part of the crag just above the water, and in 2001 this was equipped with *in situ* runners and a Tyrolean. The left-hand section of the crag is steep, but appears rather broken and of doubtful solidity. It slants up rightwards from the water for at least 50m to a large, vegetated and overhung corner system bordered on its lower right half by a band of big black overhangs. These form the left-hand limit of the best section of crag, a sea of slabs and left-slanting overlaps. Up and right of these the crag degenerates into shorter vegetated walls.

Hunting for History – 35m. H. Severe *. R. D. Everett, D. Gaffney. September 2001 (but climbed before).
Cutting through the centre of the main slabs is a left-slanting slabby ramp line that starts to the right of large blocks. Follow the line leftwards to a fine stance at 20m, then continue in the same line under overhangs, finishing up a short steep wall with care.

Where Eagles Nest – 35m HVS 4c ***. R. D. Everett, D. Gaffney. September 2001 (maybe climbed before).
This superb climb starts 10m up and right of Hunting for History below a line of overhangs that slant up and left to the top of the crag. Traverse directly beneath the roofs, with a tricky step up a short overhanging corner to a higher level after 10m. Continue directly under the roofs in a splendid position with exemplary protection. At about 20m there is an exposed step across an open corner, followed by a swing up its left arête to a very exposed ledge. Continue in the same line to the top.
Note: This best fits Eyrie in terms of description and quality, but the location is wrong and it is not E1 5b.

Hidden Treasure – 35m E2 5b **. R. D. Everett, D. Gaffney. September, 2001.
Below the line of Hunting for History is an impressive wall with an obvious narrow ledge at half-height, from which rises an easy-looking corner on its left. Below the ledge is a large plinth embedded in the ground. Start at a large spike 5m right of the plinth.
1. 20m 5b Climb a thin crack to an undercut block at 5m (runners), then step down left and follow edges and footledges quite boldly horizontally left for 5m to a short corner (RP#2). Swing left onto the ledge in the middle of the wall, then

climb the thin steep crack directly above to join Hunting for History and belay on its fine stance.

2. 15m 5a Directly above is a small overhung square-cut sentry box. Climb the gently impending wall above, first leftwards then swinging rightwards past the sentry box to join the finish of Where Eagles Nest.

Note: A direct start would be possible at a similar technical grade, but there would be no gear and the landing is awful. Even so, there is ground fall potential from the traverse.

HARRIS, Creag Mor:

Note from R. Everett: There appears to be significant potential for major routes here. There must be at least 80m width of crag between King Lear and Antipodean Exile, yet only one route, Central Grooves (E6) breaches the impressive ground. Although much is guarded by great roofs, there are certainly more entries, particularly towards the right-hand side, where a vast wall of sheer smooth rock sweeps down. Farther left, between King Lear and Herbivore, the upper part of the crag presents a substantial wall of excellent, steep, clean, quick drying and compact rock. Any route going up here would be hard, but brilliant.

King Lear: The small mossy tree mentioned in the description is to the left of the line (not right). Pitch 2 is superb, and pitch 3 is very good until you reach the vile oozing final crack. Given the spectacular positions and the general air of intimidation, most modern E1 leaders may be particularly impressed (or stressed) by this outing. Despite the technical grade being 5b on pitch 2, and only mild 5b for the roof of pitch 3, it is frequently likely to be HXS (hard extremely slimey) for the top horror crack, so a grade of E2 gives a more realistic impression of the adventure. I would give it two stars for the brilliant middle third of the climb, and the exceptional position of the second stance.

Sgurr Scaladale:

Further to A. Nisbet's comments in SMCJ 1998, closer inspection from beneath the crag suggests that the guide is probably correct, and that the gully definitions may not relate to the most obvious hideous clefts. It may even be that some of the original pioneers mixed up Central and West Gullies. In any case, anyone interested in climbing this horrendous pile of seeping blackness will no doubt remain unphased by being on the wrong piece of cliff, and would be quite happy using a description bearing no relation to reality.

SOUTH HARRIS:

Despite the vast amount of exposed rock, climbing possibilities in South Harris seem limited. The following may prove useful for a short day, or if the hills or sea cliffs are shrouded in mist or covered in spray. It is only 8 km from Tarbert ferry terminal.

Creag na Tri Piosan (Three Bit Crag) (MR122 959):

This small, but perfectly formed crag, is best seen in profile when approaching from Seilebost, which lies 6 km to the east. The crag presents a south-facing vertical wall of excellent rock. Approach in eight minutes from any suitable passing place on the A859 near the inlet to the most easterly of a line of lochans (you can't see the crag from the road at this point, so drive up and down to locate it). The foot of the crag is pleasantly flat and grassy, and the outlook encompassing both east and west coasts is superb. There is a central right-facing slim groove rising from a crack near the left end of a low band of overhangs. To its left is a higher band of overhangs, and to its right are sequentially a slim upper wall, a crack system with a small rowan, another right-facing corner high up, and the right-bounding arête. The grades of the first three routes may be a bit stiff, but they are short and well protected. The climbs are described from left to right.

Two Power Three – 11m E1 5b **. R. D. Everett, D. Gaffney. September, 2001.
Climb a flake crack leading to the middle of the band of overhangs left of the central corner line. Layback over and continue with interest to the top.

One over the Eight – 11m E1 5b **. R. D. Everett, D. Gaffney. September, 2001.
The central corner gives a fine sustained climb. Start up a steep crack near the left end of the low line of roofs.

After Eight – 11m E1 5b *. R. D. Everett, D. Gaffney. September, 2001.
Start below the widest point of the low band of overhangs. Climb straight through the roof via a small square-cut recess, then climb the wall and finishing crack between the central corner and the (unclimbed) crack system to its right.

Eight Sisters – 11m VS 4c *. D. Gaffney, R. D. Everett. September, 2001.
Climb cracks starting just right of the low band of overhangs and finish steeply up the slim right-facing corner.

EliminEight – 11m HVS 5a *. R. D. Everett, D. Gaffney. September, 2001.
The right arête of the crag. It is more interesting, but rather artificial, to keep the right hand on the arête all the way. If in doubt, place runners in the previous climb.

LEWIS, GREAT BERNERA, GEODHA MOR SHLEIBHTE (MR 133 394):
The island of Great Bernera lies between Carloway to the north east and Uig to the south-west and is linked to mainland Lewis by a bridge. The climbing is at the north west end of the island near Bostadh around Geodha Mor Shleibhte. Park at the road end at Bostadh beach and walk for 15min south-west to the crags. As usual the climbing here is on good gneiss in a wonderful situation, with grand views across Loch Roag to the sands of Bhaltos and inland over a sprinkling of small islands to the mountains of Uig and Harris.
Four parties have been climbing on sea cliffs near Geodha Mor Shleibhte and Sgeir Rebrie, each unaware of the other's activities. The following is the New Route Editor's best effort, with help from the participants. Alternative grades from subsequent parties have been included. Working from south to north:

Geodha Mor (NB 133 386):
From the road end at Tobson, walk around the coast to the Geo, about 10 minutes. The geo itself can be accessed by an easy gully to gain a handy ledge above sea level below the first routes:-
Fear Of Rejection – 15m VS 4c. P. Woodhouse, K. Archer. 28th May, 2001.

The obvious left-facing corner just right of the overhangs. Climb the corner and then the face above, good protection.

Fresh Westerly – 15m VS 5a. P. Woodhouse, K. Archer. 31st May, 2001.
Takes the crack and arête on the face just right of the previous route.

The following routes lie on the superb seaward face north of the geo. The rock is solid and well cracked with good protection. To access the routes walk a farther 100m north to drop down a gully and turn left facing out to gain the base of the routes. Good stances can be found on a ramp which descends to sea level.

Will the Real Eric Jones Please Stand Up – 18m HVS 5a **. K. Archer, P. Woodhouse. 28th May, 2001.
The obvious overlap and leftward-trending groove opposite large fallen blocks, approx. 15m to the right of the descent. Start below the ramp. Climb easy rock to the ramp and overlap. Pull over this to gain the groove. Follow this before moving slightly left on to the face to make a precarious mantel to finish. A gritstone classic!

The Stuggler – 18m HVS 5a *. P. Woodhouse, K. Archer. 28th May, 2001.
Shares a common start with Eric Jones but trends left to the base of a shallow corner.
Climb the corner to an overlap where good protection can be arranged before awkward moves gain the top of the overlap and the short finishing crack.

T'obsons Choice – 18m HVS 5a *. K. Archer, P. Woodhouse. 28th May, 2001.
Climb easy ground to the ramp then take the steep wall to the right of Eric Jones to the roof. Pass this on the left and go up to the bottom of a steep corner which is followed to the top, excellent.

Below the Salt – 18m HVS 5a *. K. Archer, A. Norton. 26th July, 2001.
Follow the descent ramp down to a small "cave"; the route starts from its right edge. Gain the wall above the cave, traverse left into a shallow corner, then around this and up to the obvious flake line which is followed to the top.

The next route starts just right beneath an overhang.
Geo-graphically Gifted – 15m HVS 5b **. K. Archer, A. Norton. 26th July, 2001.
Go up to the base of the niche, up this and a groove to beneath the overhang. Pull directly over this on surprising holds to a ledge, then to the top.

At low tide you can traverse from the end of the descent ramp along the bottom of the seaward face to where it meets the geo. From a pedestal just around and into the geo there is a micro route.
Say Aye tae a Pie – 8m VS 5a. K. Archer, A. Norton. 26th July, 2001.
From the pedestal climb the slab on the right before moving back left to pull on to the upper face by an interesting move.

Two further routes on the slab towards the south end of the seaward face. The slab can be recognised by a "dogs head" shaped quartz intrusion when viewed from

the south side of Geodha Mor. Access is by abseil down to ledges above the sea.
Living in Colour Laughing out Loud – 15m HVS 5a. K. Archer, P. Woodhouse.
31st May, 2001.
From the ledges traverse left to the arête and the base of a thin crack. Follow this
and the slab above.

Dogs Dinner – 15m VS 4b. K. Archer, P. Woodhouse. 31st May, 2001.
Climb straight up from the ledges, initially following a crack then from break to
break.

Creag Liam (MR 133 394):
Creag Liam is a small headland on the south side of Geodha Mor Shleibhte with
the climbing on the north-west through to south-west aspects. Access to the
following climbs is by an easy scramble to the left (facing out) and back right
under the crag, possible at medium to low tides. The routes are described from
right to left (facing the crag) starting with two fine corner cracks.
Conception Corner – 15m H. Severe **. A. Cunningham, B. Hogge, J.
Cunningham. 15th September, 1996 (same as Ram Raid, HVS 5a, RA/CA).
The first corner crack encountered on the access traverse.

Body and Soul - 18m VS 4c **. A. Cunningham, B. Hogge, J. Cunningham. 15th
September, 1996 (same as Battering Ram, HVS 4c, RA/CA).
The corner crack left of Conception Corner.

Interactive – 15m E1 5b **. A. Cunningham, L. Hughes. 11th May, 1998 (same as
Bernaway?, E2 5c, RA/CA and DC/JG).
Awkward cracks and shallow corners in the left arête of Body and Soul. Start near
the top of the ramp below the arête and swing right into the first crack.

The Prow – 20m E2 5b ***. A. Cunningham, L. Hughes. 11th May, 1998 (E2/3
5c, DC/JG).
An excellent strenuous climb up the overhanging crack in the front of the headland.
Start at the left corner of the prow. Climb the groove up to the roof, swing right
into the crack and follow this to the top.

The crag now turns back inland into a huge square cut blocky recess. The next
four routes are on the right-hand wall (facing).
Ticallion Stallion – 20m E3 5c ***. L. Hughes, A. Cunningham. 11th May, 1998
(same as Roag Rage, E4 5c, RA/CA, E3, DC/JG).
The first crackline round the corner from The Prow at the right-hand end of the
wall. Great climbing. Initially climb up to the left of the undercut crack and make
bold moves rightwards to the crack at a small roof - runners. Follow the strenuous
crack to the top.

Garden of Eadan – 15m E2 5c **. A. Cunningham, F. MacLeod. 18th May, 1999
(same as Bostadh del Sol, E3 5c, DC/JG).
The fine steep crack to the left of Tricallion Stallion.

Grazing Beast – 15m HVS 5b *. A. Cunningham, F. MacLeod 7th April, 1998
(same as Tobson's Choice, E1 5b, DC/JG).

Start near the back-right corner of the recess, just left of Eadan. Climb a steep black crack and take an awkward curving jam crack to finish.

Na Fir Clis – 15m VS 5a. F. MacLeod, A. Cunningham. 7th April, 1998.
The back-right corner crack of the recess.

Brigitt's Liberation – 15m Severe *. B. Hogge, J. Cunningham, A. Cunningham. 15th September 1996 (VS 4c, RA/CA)
Climb the left trending stepped black dyke starting just left of Na Fir Clis. Finish through an awkward slot in the same line.

Recess Ramp – 20m H.Severe. A. Cunningham, F. MacLeod. 18th May, 1999.
Start to the right of the back left corner of the recess (Great Northern) and climb a stepped right diagonal line to finish at the top of Na Fir Clis.

Great Northern – 15m HVS 5a **. A. Cunningham, F. MacLeod. 7th April, 1998 (same as Bostadh Nova, E1 5b, DC/JG).
The back-left wide corner crack of the recess.

The crag now runs past a second prow near which are three routes. No descriptions yet but quoting from Jo George, after Great Northern/Bostadh Nova are "The Bostadh Strangler (E3 5c ***, RA/CA), the superb looking overhung stepped corner and wide crack; The Bostadh Tea Party (E3 5b **, RA/CA, or E3 5c ***, DC/JG), the crack up the right side of the smooth wall round the edge from the last route; and finally the line of the crag - the superb ships prow to the left of the previous route to give Mega Tsaunami."

Mega Tsaunami – 30m E6 6a ***. D. Cuthbertson, J. George. 16th June, 2001.
The superb ships prow to the left of Bostadh Tea Party. Fails a four star rating as a rest is possible by going out right (and then returning) before the steep final prow is climbed. Start at the foot of The Bostadh Tea Party and traverse left along the lower of two breaks to reach a groove beneath an overhang in the arête. Climb up to and over the overhang to the base of a short steep smooth open groove. Climb this to a large hold out on the right, step back left and ascend a groove in the arête to an undercut flake. The next section kicks out to provide a strenuous finale up the thin discontinuous crack just right of the prow.

Beyond the prow, the crag turns the corner into a north-west aspect with a series of grooves and arêtes dropping into the sea. A colony of shags nest on the inland part of the cliff and in the cave at the back of the geo. Abseil down the line of the routes to the lowest convenient stance. The routes are described from right to left facing the crag from the far side of the geo.
High Pressure – 20m Mild VS 4b. A. Cunningham, F. MacLeod. 18th May, 1999.
A line up the left side of the first groove encountered round the edge. Abseil onto a small grey ramp stance. Climb a line of flake cracks and ledges.

Pillar Groove – 20m VS 4c. A. Cunningham, F. MacLeod. 18th May, 1999.
The third open groove from the right (facing) has a huge tapered block set into its left side. Abseil onto a small black ledge above the undercut base and directly

below the block. Climb up and round the right side of the block and chimney up into the crack on the right to finish.

To the south of the headland is a small bay with a short steep black wall cut by various right to left diagonal lines. (This is easily seen from the start of the descent to Creag Liam). The next route climbs the lower diagonal.

Tir nan Og – 20m E1 5b *. A. Cunningham, F. MacLeod. 24th April 1998 (same as A Different Slant, E1/2 5b, RA/CA).

Scramble down to the start of the route to the left (facing out) and move back right to the top of a black ramp. Hand traverse the diagonal break starting level with the top of the ramp.

Note: RA/CA also climbed *Little Gem* (V. Diff *) and *Right On* (E1/2 5b **) in this small geo, which they called Slanting Geo.

Sgeir Rebrie (MR 132 396):

This is the main part of glaciated domed cliffs on the north side of Geodha Mor Shleibhte. The highest point rises to 40m but is split by a slabby terrace just above half height.

The following route is found on the north side of the highest point. Descend stepped ground and a slabby ramp leftwards until able to cut back right under a short crag above high tide level.

Short Changed – 10m HVS 5a *. F. Fotheringham, S. Howie. July, 1997.

Climb a steep right-angled corner crack.

The next route lies on the glaciated rocks of the upper tier. Descend slabby ground south of the highest point until able to move right under the top tier.

Banking On It – 18m VS 4c *. F. Fotheringham, S. Howie. July, 1997.

Climb an open twisting groove/crackline bounding the right of the steep prow. Finish via an awkward crack in the steepening before the final easy slabs.

The following two routes are located at the south end of the crag, just on the change of aspect. Abseil access from a semi-buried block in a hollow of grass in the top easy angled slabs.

Bostadh Groove – 20m VS 4c **. A. Cunningham, S. Howie. 19th May, 1999 (same as One for the Flatlanders, VS 4b, KA/AN).

From the semi-buried block, abseil through a slot in the edge and down the line of the route to barnacled rock at low tide, or a ledge on the right (facing) if the sea threatens. Follow the groove direct.

To the Max – 20m HVS 5b *. A. Cunningham, S. Howie. 19th May, 1999 (same as Journey to the Edge, VS 5a, KA/AN)

Abseil to the left (looking out) of Bostadh Groove to a ledge above barnacle level. Climb stepped grooves heading for a seemingly wide crack through the top bulge. Reach over the bulge to discover there is not a crack, so pull through the bulge leftwards onto the easy slab to finish.

About 25m north of the previous routes a vague gully can be descended. This leads to a slab which is traversed leftwards (facing in) to a short corner. Reverse the corner to the top of a ramp. The start of the route is a prominent chimney/groove to the right of the black arête.

Return of the Absent Friend – 40m HVS *. A. Norton, K. Archer (alt). 24th July, 2001.
1. 20m 5a Climb the chimney/groove to a ledge at its top. Take the left hand layback crack (crux) to a large ledge.
2. 20m 4c Climb the slab using a huge undercut flake to a corner. Climb this and a short layback to finish.

Bosta'in – 40m VS *. K. Archer, A. Norton (alt). 27th July, 2001.
From the start of Return of the Absent Friend, descend another short corner to gain sea level ledges. Walk left (facing in) and the route starts in the centre of the wall just right of a rock pool.
1. 25m 4c Step on to the wall and gain a left-rising ramp. Follow this, then up a corner to a ledge beneath an overhang.
2. 15m 4b Take the chimney and corner at the back of the stance.

TRAIGH NA BERIGH (SMCJ 2000, pp328-330):
Cnippy Sweetie – 15m E7 6b ***. D. MacLeod, S. Richardson. 12th June, 2001.
This excellent wall climb takes the smooth wall between Barrier Reef and Cnip Fit. Climb Barrier Reef to its first pocket. Dyno to another pocket a long way up and right and continue rightwards to a horizontal (small cams). Climb up and left with difficulty using flanges and a pocket to reach another break (small wire). Finish directly. Technical and sparsely protected climbing. Abseil inspected, then flashed.

Rouge Traighder – 15m E5 6b **. D. MacLeod. 12th June, 2001.
Start between Tunes of Glory and Barrier Reef, below some curving overlaps. Climb direct through the bulges and move up the pocketed wall above (bold) to reach the good protection crack of Barrier Reef. Continue up with a hard move to gain a thin horizontal. Move up and left to join and finish up the last few moves of Tunes of Glory. On sight first ascent.

Note: D. MacLeod and N. McNair made on-sight repeats of other routes on the crag, noting that Tunes of Glory is E5 6b, not E6 6b. Barrier Reef is E5 6a, not E6 6a/b. Berie Berie is E4 6a, not E5 6b and S. Richardson notes that Milk Traigh is E3 5c/6a, not E2 5c/6a.
Separately, G. Latter notes that he thought Barrier Reef to be E5 6a ***; Tunes of Glory, E5 6b **; Berie-Berie, E4 6a **.

MUNGARSTADH AREA:
Painted Geo:
The following routes lie on the black wall on the south side of the geo, left of the descent, towards the back of the geo. The wall is split into two parts by an area of rockfall higher up, on the left of which is an obvious flakeline/wide crack.

Coal Mining – 40m E3 5c/6a. R. and C. Anderson. – 30th June, 2001.
The crackline up the left side of the left-hand section of the wall. A few good difficult moves up the crack leads to deteriorating rock up which one is forced to

climb to reach unpleasant ground and then a shelf. The rock on the headwall is poor; escape rightwards along the shelf.

At the Face – 30m E1 5a *. R. and C. Anderson. 30th June 2001.
The crack and ledges just left of centre on the right-hand section of the wall. Gain a ledge, move up to a spike and continue directly above past ledges and flat holds to reach a slab, finishing up this and going rightwards on the shelf.

Aurora Geo, The Cioch Wall:
Note: From R. Everett: Things are Looking Up is better at E2, rather than 'at the upper limit of E1'. In some ways it is more complex and intimidating (although technically easier) than the neighbouring E3, The Roaring Foam. This route is low in the E3 grade (obvious moves and well protected).

Magic Geo, East Face:
Note from R. Everett: *Flannan Slab Direct:*
This would seem to be far from direct. The start that most fits the description is actually from the lowest right point of the Red Wall, round to the left of the main slab, best approached by an abseil down the Red Wall. The 'hand-traverse' of the original 'Direct' description appears to be above the large slanting overhang. This is probably what confused the people who claimed 'Bubbles', which is probably a combination of a line just left of Flannan Slab, joining the upper section of the 'Direct' at half height. The following line probably starts further left than Bubbles, and is probably the most appropriate description for 'Flannan Slab Direct'. The grade was rather knarly E1 5b on the day (for the bottom 5m), and would be so whenever the lowest rocks are slimy (which is probably quite often). The 3 stars are well merited. The description fits the alternative start mentioned for F.S.D. If Flannan Slab Direct is described like this, 'Bubbles' disappears, as it must cover essentially much the same ground.

Flannan Slab Direct – 45m E1 5b ***.
Start near the left end of the wall, beneath the mid-point of a large slanting overhang 15m up the wall. Climb a shallow groove with difficulty (crux) to better holds in another groove that leads to a large ledge on the left arête below the left-hand end of the large slanting overhang. Step back down and traverse right to easier ground, then move up to the foot of a series of left-facing flakes and corners. Follow these up and left, then climb the slab just right of the final arête to the top.

Hidden Geo:
Stormin Norman – 35m E1 5b **. R. and C. Anderson. 11th July, 2001.
Slightly eliminate but very good climbing taking the arête and crackline just left of the open corner of Spiny Norman. Step on to the left arête and climb this until forced up right into the crack and continue up this until forced into the corner at the top.

ISLIVIG AREA, AIRD FENISH, Aird Point:
A small but perfect crag on the south-western tip of the Aird Fenish headland.

Tidal Rave – 20m E4 5c ***. R. and C. Anderson. 14th July, 2001.
The left-hand route. From the plinth at the left side of the wall descend a short

way to a small ledge just above the high tide mark. Step into a crackline and climb this to a break, then go steeply up right to where it fades at an obvious hold (small but awkward to place wires). Pull through the quartzy section and finish directly.

Wave Dancing – 25m E4 5c/6a ***. R. and C. Anderson, D. Cuthbertson. 17th July, 2001.
A brilliant route up the crackline and slight depression in the centre of the wall. A handrail to the right of the line enables a side runner of sorts (more to stop one rolling into the seething sea than hitting the ground) to be placed in the flake crack of Top Tackle Tips. From a jug in the middle of the wall, boulder directly up pink quartzy rock to a horizontal break (wire on right), continue to the roof, then up the same line to the top.

Top Tackle Tips – 25m E6 6a ***. D. Cuthbertson, R. Anderson. 17th July, 2001.
A very good route which packs a lot of climbing in on the final headwall. Start just right of WaveDancing where an obvious pedestal hold juts out. Hand traverse the hold, swing into a quartzy crack and follow this up, then slightly right to a good foot ledge. Move up to the overlap and downward pointing tooth of rock. Launch up the wall, then up and out left just below the top to finish. Protection is adequate above the overlap but strenuous to place.

Mini-Geo:
Immediately east of Aird Point is a small, narrow geo. When viewed from directly opposite on the platform just before the slabby descent to Aird Point the most obvious line is a long left-slanting corner-crack on greenish coloured rock.
Greenstone Cowboy – 15m E2 5b. R. and C. Anderson. 14th July, 2001.
The left-slanting corner-crack.

Greensleeves – 15m VS 4b *. R. and C. Anderson. 14th July, 2001.
The slabby, stepped rib left of the crack. There is no gear until just below the top, but the climbing is easy and the rock good.

The Biorach Wall
Three headlands project south/south-westwards into the sea on the Aird Fenish headland. Aird Point is the westernmost, this is the easternmost. Staca Biorach is the squat, crenellated sea stack just out in front of the crag. The crag is best viewed from directly opposite at Aird Point where it appears as a long black wall running the length of the promontory, from an area of cracks above a roof, past a slabby cracked section, through a recessed easier slabby section to finish at an area of cracks grooves and arêtes. The most identifiable feature at the right end is a dark V-slot.

Cracked Slabs Area:
The first routes lie on the left-hand area of slabs which are seamed with cracks
Dislocated Styles – 30m E2/3 5c. R. and C. Anderson. 20th July, 2001.
From the pedestal ledge, climb up right to the roof and pull round its left side into a crack. Move up, then out right on to the edge and finish easily.

Grunt – 30m VS 5b *. R. and C. Anderson. 20th July, 2001.
From the small ledge to the right of the pedestal ledge climb the crack through the roof and on up easier slabs.

Recessed Slabs Area:
This is the central area of recessed, easy-angled slabs. A corner bounds this area on the left and on the right.
Dry Roasted – 20m H.Severe/VS 4b **. R. and C. Anderson. 18th July, 2001.
From the base of the right-bounding slabby corner of the recessed section, step right and climb the rib to the top.

The V Area:
This is the steeper area of grooves and arêtes on the right side of the promontory. Routes are described in relation to the deep V-slot, right to left from its base, then left to right.
The Singularity – 20m VS 5a *. R. and C. Anderson. 19th July, 2001.
The deep V-slot. Bridge inside and at the junction take the left-hand exit.

Black Hole – 20m E1 5a **. R. and C. Anderson. 19th July, 2001.
Move up into the deep V-slot and climb the black seams up the left wall.

Anti Matter – 20m E1 5a ***. R. and C. Anderson. 19th July, 2001.
The crackline running up the left wall at the entrance to the deep V-slot.

Outer Limits – 20m HVS 4c ***. R. and C. Anderson. 18th July, 2001.
The left arête of the deep V-slot.

Biorach Corner – 20m HVS 5a **. R. and C. Anderson. 18th July, 2001.
The leaning corner left of the deep V-slot.

Slightly Salted – 20m E1 5b **. R. and C. Anderson. 18th July, 2001.
Around the edge and left of the leaning corner, a slanting sharp crack leads to a finish up a short corner.

Hyper Space – 20m HVS 5a *. R. and C. Anderson. 19th July, 2001.
At the entrance to the deep V-slot, bridge up, then transfer to cracks in the right arête and climb these until it is possible to swing around on to the frontal edge up which a finish is made.

Left Black – 20m E4/5 6a *. R. and C. Anderson. 19th July, 2001.
The roof and black wall right of the entrance to the deep V-slot. Climb to the centre of the roof and place wires in a thin crack (Rock#5 sideways). Move left beneath the roof and reach up to holds on the left edge (RP#1). A difficult stretch gains small holds in the horizontal break and gear. Climb the left arête to the top.

Right Black – 20m E4/5 6a **. R. and C. Anderson. 19th July, 2001.
Climb to the centre of the roof and place wires in a thin crack (Rock#5 sideways). Pull up past these to a hold at the end of the horizontal break and move up onto the right arête. Continue up this and finish more centrally. It is possible to traverse the horizontal break on to the previous route.

Atlantic Highway – 20m E1 5a **. R. and C. Anderson. 18th July, 2001.
The outer arête to the right of the deep V-slot, the first half climbed on the left side the remainder on the right.

Fulmar Loops – 20m HVS 4c **. R. and C. Anderson. 18th July, 2001.
The wide, recessed groove line with seamed rock just to the right. Climb the right
side and finish more directly.

Ebbing-out – 20m VS 5a **. R. and C. Anderson. 19th July, 2001.
The corner/groove line right of Fulmar Loops to finish directly up cracks.

Flowing-in – 20m Severe 4b **. R. and C. Anderson. 19th July, 2001.
The corner/groove line just right of Ebbing-out.

TORCASO AREA, Fiavig Tarras:
This is the fine Geo to the south of the summit cairn of Torcaso which runs virtually
south to north at right angles to Torcaso Geo. A huge flake fault runs up diagonally
right to left across the face beneath a steep wall split by a pair of thin tramline
cracks. To the right is a corner groove, the right wall of which is split by a fine,
steep crack. Then there is an edge and around this a right-angled corner before
where the wall decreases in height and continues rightwards into the sea. The
crocodile faultline mentioned in the guide is assumed to lie on the east-facing
wall on the other side of the geo where there is a feature which matches this
description.

Dobhrainn – 40m E2 5c **. R. and C. Anderson. 8th July, 2001.
Start from the lowest ledge just above the sea. The wide cornerline running up the
wall just left of the main diagonal fault. Move up and left into the corner and
follow this past a difficult section to a ledge. Move up right to gain the edge of the
fault, then continue up and leftwards to the top.

Kelpie Dancing – 40m E1 5b **. R. and C. Anderson. 9th July, 2001.
Start from the lowest ledge just above the sea. Climb the flake in the front face of
the huge flake/faultline. Move up leftwards and climb to the top of the flake.
Continue up the fault and take the corner above, just right of the finish to Dobhrainn.

The Big Easy – 40m Severe *. R. and C. Anderson. 8th July, 2001.
From the lowest ledges, climb up to the huge flake faultline and climb this to
finish out rightwards on black rock.

A Streetcar Named Desire – 25m E5 6b ***. R. and C. Anderson. 8th July, 2001.
The thin tramline cracks in the centre of the west face. Start at the base of the
fault. Climb the edge of the flake. Small wires protect the stretchy and blind
placement of a Rock#8, or 7 in the base of the right-hand crack. Pull right past
this, then step up left to the base of the left-hand crack which is climbed to the top.

Right of this steep wall are two cracklines right of a steep corner-groove, then an
edge.
Rhythm and Kelp – 30m E4/5 6a ***. R. and C. Anderson. 20th July, 2001.
A superb route up the steep left-hand crackline, in between the groove and the
edge.

Harry Houdini – 30m E2 5c. R. and C. Anderson. 8th July, 2001.
This takes the right-hand crackline to go up and around the edge and finish up a
widening crack just left of a right-angled corner.

Sandy Shaw – 35m HVS 4c *. R. and C. Anderson. 8th July, 2001.
The right-angled corner, gained from low down up a short crack leading into a V-groove and easy ground to its base.

Barnacle Bill – 35m HVS 4c *. R. and C. Anderson. 8th July, 2001.
Immediately to the right of the start of the previous route, climb a short, steep crack then easier broken ground to finish up a parallel crack just left of a corner.

The Pool Walls:
These are the walls around the lovely tidal pool mentioned in the guide, on which three routes were climbed in 1997.

The Butchers Dog – 25m VS 4c **. R. and C. Anderson. 13th July, 2001.
This is located on the northern edge of The Pool Wall. Scramble round to the northern seaward edge and belay at the foot of a chimney-fault with a prominent arête above it. Step left on to the edge and after a few moves on pink quartz swing left and climb the obvious crack to the top.

The Butcher – 25m HVS 4c **. R. and C. Anderson. 9th July, 2001.
The prominent arête above the chimney-fault. Step left on to the edge to climb pink quartz and move around on to the right-hand side in the middle. Continue up the arête to a sloping ledge. Move right and climb the right side of the upper arête to the top.

The following three routes, as with those on the right side of the wall are tightly packed together but nonetheless offer good climbing.
Northern Exposure – 25m VS 4c **. R. and C. Anderson. 13th July, 2001.
Climb a wide crack to a ledge as for Southern Comfort. Step left and climb a short crack to a sloping ledge, then climb a short corner to another sloping ledge and finish up the left-hand parallel groove.

Southern Comfort – 25m HVS 4c **. R. and C. Anderson. 9th July, 2001.
The line of the abseil, taking the left-hand side of the main, leaning central section of The Pool Wall. Climb a wide crack to a ledge then take the wide corner crack to a sloping ledge. Step right across the void and climb the right-hand groove running up the left side of the headwall.

Tomb Raider – 25m E4/5 6b **. R. and C. Anderson. 13th July, 2001.
The steep cracks running up the left side of the central leaning wall. Climb to the ledge just right of the corner of Southern Comfort and climb the thin cracks in the wall (a touch eliminate with back-stepping out left avoided, hence the grade) to pull onto a shelf. Climb tramline cracks up the wall and where these veer off right move up with difficulty and pull directly onto the shelf above. Cracks in the left side of the tombstone lead to the top.

Then the three routes climbed in 1997.

Stepping Out – 20m E2 5c/6a **. R. and C. Anderson. 13th July, 2001.
On the opposite (south) side of the pool is a tower-like feature with a diagonal

crack running up it. Further right, just beyond the easy slabs is another tower-like feature, just left of a chimney, with a series of stepped corners running up it. Climb a short crack to gain the first step, then follow the stepped corners and cracks to the top.

DALBEG:
Tweetie Pie Slalom – 40m E5 6a ***. D. MacLeod, S. Richardson. 13th June, 2001.
This stunning route climbs the obvious logical finish to Neptune a Calling. Follow Neptune a Calling to where it moves right into the shallow corner, escaping into Neptune. Step left and climb direct just left of the corner to a roof. Move left under this to join the soaring diagonal crack. Follow this with good protection and sustained interest to the top.
Note: G. Latter repeated the route and agreed with the grade.

Mercury and Solace – 40m E5 6a **. N. McNair, S. Richardson, D. MacLeod. 14th June, 2001.
This climb takes a line on the wall between Neptune and Wave Watcher, giving excellent but slightly escapable climbing. Start on the arête left of Wave Watcher. Climb to a ledge, step up into a groove and move left to a large pocket. Climb direct above this into another groove and move left to gain a crack line. Follow this (technical) to good holds below the start of a ramp. Follow the ragged diagonal crack on the left to gain the ramp and finish directly up the cracked wall above.

PABBAY, Banded Geo:
Prominent Nasty Looking Off-width Groove – 50m E2 5b **. I. Taylor, G. Stanworth. May, 2001.
The prominent off-width groove left of Blo' no Gael. Not nasty at all as it turns out.

Banded Geo, South Face:
Grey Cossack – 30m VS 4c. J. Lyall, M. Davies. 14th May, 2001.
Climb the rib just right of Silver Fox, over a roof, up a left-facing corner and up flakes to the top.

Shipping Views – 35m E1 5b/c. M. Davies, J. Lyall. 14th May, 2001.
Climb the wall 3m right of Bye-bye to the Widows to break through the right end of the grey roof. Follow a crack up the right edge and corners to the top.

Cereal Killer – 35m HVS 5a/b. J. Lyall, M. Davies. 13th May, 2001.
The first line left of the recess at the right end of the ledge system. Climb a left-facing quartzy corner, then cracks through a roof system.

Corn Choked Corner – 30m HVS 5a. J. Lyall, M. Davies. 13th May, 2001.
At the right end of the narrowing ledges is a recess. Climb the right-hand corner-crack, with a steep finish through a slot.

The Grey Wall:
The wall round the edge from the Pink Wall, running into the deep recess containing Spit in Paradise and U-ei.

Amber Nectar – 75m E5 ***. R. Campbell, G. Latter (ground-up). 15th May, 2001.

A route of considerable character, climbing the right side of the wall. Start at the base of the left-facing groove at the right side of the wall.

1. 40m 6a Go up this, moving rightwards over two ledges to large flake. Move left and up on flakes into a hanging groove (possible belay). Traverse out left and up another flake system leading to a roof in the pegmatite band. Cross this on good holds on the right and traverse left along the wide slot with interest to swing round left to the edge of the wall.

2. 35m 5a Continue straight up, then leftwards, finishing by a short corner leading to a large roof. Pull out left and scramble to finish.

Elysium – 35m E4 6a ***. G. Latter, R. Campbell (on-sight). 13th May, 2001.

An excellent pitch up the prominent left-slanting groove bounding the right edge of the Grey Wall. Start from the belay at the end of pitch 1 of Spit in Paradise. Trend left and traverse left into an open chimney. Go up this, then an overhanging wall on large flakes leading to a left-facing groove. Climb this, stepping right at the top past a birdy ledge to the thread belay, as for Spit in Paradise.

Note: Spit in Paradise was repeated, incorporating the above new pitch (missing out the original crux pitch) – E4 5c,6a,6a – not E3 as in guide. The excellent top pitch up the "slabby wall" ascends corner through roofs up two grossly overhanging walls.

Rubha Charnain, Small Bouys Geo (MR 604 868):

Spicy Mayhem – 20m E1 5b *. R. I. Jones, F. Murray. 30th May, 1999.

This takes the centre of the wall between Third Groove and Designer Rib, keeping away from the crack on the left and the rib on the right.

Lobstered Ross – 20m VS 5a. F. Murray, R. I. Jones. 30th May, 1999.

From the belay for Friends in Tibet climb up to the right of the recess to a crack in a small overhang. Follow this to the top.

Shags Geo (MR 597 869):

These routes are between Cracking Corner and a quartz patch that marks the start of Wok On The Wild Side. Five metres right of Cracking Corner is a vertical quartz line on a rib. Abseil from the triangular block as for Cracking Corner to a ledge just above sea level and below an overhang. The quartz line is directly above this.

Truly Stunning – 48m VS 4c *. R. I. Jones, M. Snook. 31st May, 1999.

From the ledge step left and climb the vertical wall and small overhang on large jugs. Climb the centre of the left-hand wall of a corner to a large ledge. Climb through the roof above to the left of the triangular overhanging block.

Quartz Waltz – 48m VS 4c. R. I. Jones, M. Snook. 31st May, 1999.

From the ledge, step up and right. Make a hard move across and up to exit to the right of the overhang at 3m to join the quartz crack. Climb this and as it becomes less distinct step right on to an arête and climb this to a large ledge. Climb through the roof above to the right of the triangular overhanging block.

Arch Wall, The Headwall (MR 592 873):

Many of the existing lines were difficult to locate. The following two lines did not appear to have been climbed:

Snipe Corner – 25m Severe. M. Snook, J. Sanders. 1st June, 1999.
Start 1.5m right of Orang-Utang Klaus. Climb the right-facing corner/crack to the ledge and the crack in the wall above.

Chilly Dick – 25m VS 4c/5a *. M. Gear, R. Benton. 2nd June, 1999.
Start at the lowest point of the Headwall, 10m right of the large flake. The crux is in the initial 3m. Continue straight up the slabby wall, avoiding steeper ground on the left, to join a ramp coming up from the right. Easy to the top. Better holds and protection than first appearances would suggest.

Rubha Greotach, The Galley:

At the top of the gully is a large boulder under a small corner left of an overhang.
Retreat Unthinkable! – 8m E2 5b. R. I. Jones, G. Stein. 1st June, 1999.
Belay beneath the large boulder in the gully. Make a difficult move from the top of the boulder on to the wall right of a right-facing corner below an overhang. Protect with microwires and step up and rightwards to the right corner of the overhang and a horizontal faultline. Pull up and finish up the corner above.

The following route has come to light which was done a few weeks prior to the one above. It has essentially the same line to the roof but the grades are very different.

A Cream of White Sauces – 45m HVS. J. Cox, D. Haige. 1999.
Takes a left to right traverse line across the left-hand side of The Galley. Start on the large boulder of Retreat Unthinkable.
1. 15m 5a Step off the boulder pull into the hanging corner, then climb the wall to the roof (bold). Traverse right around the arête to a belay ledge.
2. 15m 4c Continue in the same line across The Complete Works to a belay in the corner of The Abridged Version.
3. 15m 4c Cross Wiggley Wall, taking the upper of the two horizontal breaks to continue around the arête to a ledge. Scramble to the top.

To the left of the boulder is a featured wall with a very large block on the left-hand side, which is detached from the wall. The Hatman takes the centre of the wall.
The Hatman – 9m HVS 4c. R. I. Jones, M. Snook, A. Callum. 4th June, 1999.
From a boulder in the middle of the wall step up and left, before climbing up and rightwards on the obvious holds to a left facing ledge flake. Poorly protected. Pull up on to a sloping ledge and climb the short wall above.

Absolution – 10m E1 5b *. R. I. Jones, M. Snook. 4th June, 1999.
Start 2m left of The Hatman. Climb the right-facing hanging corner to a horizontal crack line. Climb the small crack line above to finish at the highest point on the wall.

To the left of the very big block is one of the descent routes.
Squiggle – 7m Severe. R. I. Jones. 4th June, 1999.
At the left corner of the block is a small crack line on the wall behind. Climb this.

Squidge – 7m Diff. R. I. Jones. 4th June, 1999.
Climb the crack line 2m left of Squiggle.

Rosinish Wall (MR 614 872):
This is visible on the Rosinish Peninsula across the bay from the campsite. Some of these lines may have been climbed before, but we can find no record of this. In the middle of the crag is a large dark chimney. About 6m right of this is a black slab. On the right of this is an inverted V-groove and an overhanging nose.
The Whoop Of The Aviator – 11m E1 5b *. G. Stein, A. Russell-Bolton, R.I. Jones. 3rd June, 1999.
Climb the overhang on the centre of the nose in a series of committing moves until easier ground at 3m. Continue up the easier crack above.

Ticks Too – 7m VS 4c. J. Sanders, A. Callum, M. Snook. 3rd June, 1999.
Climb the right-facing corner 2m right of The Whoop of the Aviator.

The Trouser's Last Stand – 11m Severe 4a. A. Callum, J. Sanders, M. Snook. 3rd June, 1999.
Climb the right-facing corner 3m right of Ticks Too and to the left of a clean wall. Continue up the crack and the wall above.

Oh No Not Another Tick – 7m VS 4c. J. Sanders, A. Callum, M. Snook. 3rd June, 1999.
Four metres right of the Trouser's Last Stand is a wall capped by a small overhang. Climb the centre of the wall and then climb through the overhang on the left-hand side. Poorly protected.

ERSIKAY, Rubha Basadearn (NF 802 104, MR from a GPS and the place names from the Hastwell guide to the islands):
A south-east facing crag on the east coast of Eriskay, with numerous potential routes. It could well become more popular with the building of the new causeway linking the island to the north. It is clearly visible one mile north of Acairseid Mhor (if approaching that harbour by boat). The main crag is not tidally affected. It consists of several buttresses increasing in height towards the impressive overhangs at the right-hand end. Approach northward across rough ground along the coast from Acairseid Mhor or eastward, below Ben Scrien, by Loch Crakavaig. The bottom of the crag is easily approached from the left (south) end. From the left (south) end of the crag: after several shorter walls facing south, the first seaward facing buttress is narrow and square cut with a vertical crack guarded by a big jammed block at 3m. Right again is a set back area and then, starting half way up the crag is a prominent layback groove with a reddish right wall. The only route so far takes this.
Eriskay Business – 30m HVS 5a. P. Nugent, B. Bowdler, S. Harry. 29th May, 2001.
Pleasant andwell protected climbing. Start beneath the groove, approx. 15m right (north) of the jammed block. Climb a cracked pillar and continue to a ledge beneath the groove. Climb the groove with increasing difficulty to an easier but steep exit.

From underneath the main crag a prominent undercut wall or 'snout' can be seen in profile, at sea level, on the point, 400m to the north. Beyond this is a series of short, steep walls. Numerous possibilities exist.

Odalisque – 15m HVS 5b. S. Harry, P. Nugent. 29th May, 2001.

Sheer pleasure and well protected. Approach down the south side of the snout, traverse under a short overhanging wall and another wall with an easy looking flake line. Around to the right is an obvious, black, right-angled corner with a 'stuck on' block at chest height, behind two huge sea-washed boulders. The route takes this corner. Start at the 'stuck on' block. Stepping on to the block, make a couple of steep moves and then continue more easily to the top.

Note: There is another, more tidally affected corner further right with an interesting looking, rising hand traverse in its right wall. The steep wall to the left of Odalisque will also go at a higher grade.

MINGULAY, Rubha Liath, Seal Song Wall:

The Wet Look 45m E1 5b. K. Howett, L. Creamer. 21st May, 2001.

Climb the corner to the left of Durdle Huxter. Start on the sea level ledge as for that route. Climb the rounded rib on the left to enter a thin corner with a small ledge. Up this to a foot ledge at its top. Climb past the left edge of the large roof of Durdle Huxter and into the bigger corner which leads more easily to the top.

Surfs-Up Direct Start – L. Creamer, K. Howett. 21st May, 2001.

If the swell is too great to access the Durdle Huxter starting ledge, begin from a flat ledge projecting from a small but deep cave just left of Swell-time ledges. From the ledge climb the left rib and through the roof via a large flake crack to join the second pitch at the flake.

To reach the following routes, abseil from the cairn at the top of Power of the Sea to the natural ledge halfway down the cliff face. The first route takes the crack immediately on the left (facing into the cliff).

Flying Hex – 15m VS 4c *. A. Callum, J. Sanders. 4th June, 1998.

Climb to a horizontal flake and move up into an open corner. Climb this to obvious twin cracks and follow these to the top.

The following routes are described moving right (facing in) or south-west from Power of the Sea.

Solid Dude – 18m HVS 5a **. J. Sanders, A. Callum. 4th June, 1998.

Start below an obvious right-slanting crackline and climb it to a position beneath the daunting overhang (Hex#11 required). Fist jam the roof in a wild position and pull through strenuously to the top.

An airy but easy traverse right for 20m from Solid Dude leads around a right-facing corner; the next three routes are in this bay.

Not Ali's Crack – 15m E1 5b. F. Murray, J.Sanders. 4th June, 1998.

On the left wall there is an overhanging right-slanting crack starting at half height. Begin directly beneath this and ascend the wall via ledges, then attack the crack direct.

Pumping Up – 15m VS 4c. J. Sanders, A. Callum. 4th June, 1998.
Start as for Not Ali's Crack and move into the corner-crack on the right. Climb it direct, exiting left at the top.

DoppelKratzer – 15m HVS 5a. A. Callum, J. Sanders. 4th June, 1998.
Start in the centre of the right-hand bulgy wall at a thin crackline. Ascend the delicate crack (poorly protected) and make an awkward balance move (crux) up, and left to mantelshelf on to a ledge. Step right to finish.

Far Eastern Walls (MR 553 814):
These 'Far Eastern Walls' may be the same as the area called 'Pink Wall' (see below), as they have the same Map Rerence, but the routes have not been matched:

Far Eastern Walls (MR 553 814):
200m east of the East Walls is a small red buttress on a tidal platform. The left of the buttress has a left-facing corner and roof. The routes are tidal.
Mingulay Blazers – 20m Severe. R. Jones. 7th June, 2001.
The obvious left-slanting crackline left of the roof.

High and Dry – 14m VS 5a. R. Benton, R. Jones. 5th June, 2001.
Takes the line on the left of the buttress and right arête of the corner. Move on to the arête from the left and climb to the top.

Frodo's Frenzy – 14m E1 5a **. R. Jones, R. Benton. 5th June, 2001.
Two metres right of High and Dry. Step on to the undercut wall and climb to a small bulge, taken on the left. Go straight to the top to finish just left of a block forming a small left-facing corner.

The Tide Waits for No Man – 14m E2 5b/c *. R. Jones, A. Dow. 7th June, 2001.
The undercut crackline 4m right of Frodo's Frenzy. Great climbing marred by a wet start (1 rest).

The Pink Wall (MR 553 814):
This small crag lies to the east of Gierum Walls, just east of a narrow parallel sided geo. There is a tidal platform at the bottom. The crag is gained by descending a grassy slope next to the geo, via gently sloping slabby rock.
The Corner – 10m Severe. R. Wilby, D. Wilby. May, 2001.
The corner left of the pink wall.

You Are Being Watched – 10m H. Severe. R. Wilby, D. Wilby. May, 2001.
Four metres right of the corner is a small arête. Climb this and the wall above.

Dun Mingulay, Creag Dubh, Sloc Dubh an Duine:
Blonde Highlights – 80m E3. L. Creamer, K. Howett. 20th May, 2001.
Climbs a line up the prominent vertical scooped recess that extends the height of the cliff about 50m left of Immaculate Crack. From the gulch in the large platform at the base of the crag, traverse left to gain smaller ledges leading to the recess.
1. 30m 5b Climb the white streaked corner in the right side of the recess. Step

right round the right arête into a smaller groove and a ledge. Continue directly up the steep bulge on to slabby rock. Trend left a little to a small break with an tiny overlap. Pull out rightwards across the smooth wall into a small shallow groove to gain a large ledge.
2. 40m 5a Climb directly up the wall and through bulges to gain a corner ramp leading rightwards to a ledge. Consecutive small shallow corners leads up grey rock, then step right to a belay under an obvious block forming a small roof.
3. 15m 5c Gain the block above. Stand on it and exit the bulge above rightwards with difficulty. Traverse right and finish next to a large pointed block.

Grey on Blonde – 85m E3. L. Creamer, K. Howett. 22nd May, 2001.
Climb a line between Big Momma and Blond Highlights and around the left-hand of the two large corner systems. Start below an obvious undercling flake between these two routes, but nearer Blonde Highlights.
1.40m 5b Go up to the undercling. Pull through directly and up a shallow groove to step right at its top on to a small ledge (serious). Up slabby rock to the base of a shallow left-facing groove. Go up this and exit right. Traverse right and up the easy wall to the big left side of the big block on the ledge.
2. 45m 5c Go up the large corner to the big roof. By-pass it on the right and continue to a glacis under a black roof. Pull over into a slim silver ramp. From its top gain a slim hanging groove above the bulge on the left which leads to a ledge. Climb up right to another ledge below the headwall, just left of Big Momma. From a small horizontal flake in the wall, pull steeply direct into an obvious finishing corner.

Big Momma – 85m E4. K. Howett, L. Creamer. 21st May, 2001.
Climbs a line up the right-hand of the two large corner systems between Immaculate Crack and Blond Highlights. Start at an obvious triangular corner / niche midway along the ledge from the gulch.
1. 40m 5c Go up the overhanging niche and exit left with difficulty. Climb a flake up to a ledge. Climb the broken overhanging groove just on the left leading into a conspicuous curving right-facing corner. Exit this rightwards and climb to the big block on Immaculate Crack.
2. 45m 6a Enter the large corner above. Follow it on good holds steeply to just below a capping roof. Take the slim corner on the right of the roof and at its top make desperate moves up a slim left-facing groove. Easier but steep rocks lead up and rightto a ledge under the headwall and large roof (possible belay). Pull directly through the centre of the roof and up the wall slightly right into a very shallow groove. Exit right.

Sron an Duin:
Ride the Monster – 110m E4. K. Howett, L. Creamer. 22nd May, 2001.
Climbs a line up the headwall above the roof and flying groove of Perfect Monsters. Start as for the Great Shark Hunt, below a slightly left-trending line of flakes and grooves.
1. 30m 5a Go up the flakes and discontinuous grooves to a small ledge about 5m below the big roof.
2. 25m 6a Continue to follow The Great Shark Hunt up to and through the big roof

leftwards to below the secondary roof. Instead of continuing to traverse left make hard moves right along the lip of the big roof to gain an open-book corner. Follow this toa small stance on the left arête.
3. 30m 5c Continue up the slimmer corner above for 3m, until a thin traverse line right can be taken to step on to an obvious small loose block. Step right again into the underclings under the roof. Follow these underthe roof into a slight recess, then pull directly over to a good flake crack. Take this and the easy wall to a ledge.
4. 25m 4c Go up the wall direct to take a belay on a block back from the edge.

Oceanside Expedition – 200m E4 ***. S. Crowe, K. Magog. 21st May, 2001.
A right to left girdle of the main wall, which perversely starts by trending up and right by starting up Sirens.
1. 40m 5c Climb Sirens to belay in the niche.
2. 50m 5b Follow the handrail of jugs leftwards underneath the diagonal roof. Pull over at the left end on to the slab above. Climb up and left to reach the prominent left facing corner of the Silkie. Follow good holds left to move up as for Sula to gain a traverse line of good holds about 2m below the roof system. Follow these left to belay below the roof as for Hurried Path.
3. 50m 5c Continue left for about 5m until it is possible to step down 3m to a lower break. This eventually leads to Voyage of Faith. Follow this up and left to belay on a small ledge at the point where Voyage of Faith leads back right.
4. 30m 5c Step right then climb up to beneath the top roof where a good break leads leftwards through the hanging roofs in a spectacular position. Belay in a small niche above the roof.
5. 20m 5a Continue up the final headwall on jugs.

The Lost World:
The Dark Half – 90m E1. D. Barlow, P. Donnithorne (alt). 4th August, 2000.
The area of rock in the back of the natural arch behind Lianamul. The walls are black and can be seen easily from the neck of land attaching Dun Mingulay to the mainland.
The route lies on the large cliff just north of the 'neck' and south of the arch. Abseil 90m down walls and corners starting 40m north of the railing in the 'neck' to gain a damp niche.
1. 35m 5a Climb the corner to a ledge on the right.
2. 30m 5a Move left and follow the next corner to a ledge on the right.
3. 25m 5a From the top of the ledge, climb directly to a grass terrace. Finish up a short overhung corner.

Dun Mingulay, Time Out Buttress (MR 543 819):
Unsure how the next route relates to existing ones (Ed). 200m east of the abseil point for Fifteen Fathoms of Fear are two large and rather precarious buttresses, both split by left-facing corners. They provide an alternative when wind prevents climbing on the main cliff. Time Out Buttress is the lower of the two.
De-institutionalisation – 25m HVS 5a *. R. Jones, A. Dow. 7th June, 2001.
Surprisingly solid climbing. Climb the left-facing corner which ends at mid-height with a roof. Step right and after 2-3 m traverse left above the roofed corner. Pull through on large jugs. Step right and climb the right-facing corner to the top.

Arnamul Promontory (SMCJ 2001, p594):
Keeping Wullie Busy – 75m H. Severe 4b. A. Callum, I. Hall. 3rd June, 2001.
Start 10m left of the abseil just right of a twin crack system.
1. 25m Climb up and left on good jugs to reach the right-hand of twin cracks.
Follow this for 20m to a large ledge.
2. 25m Move up to the right of a downward-pointing flake. Step delicately right
on to a slabby wall to gain a groove and good holds. Continue for 20m to a recess
on a large ledge.
3. 25m Climb directly out of the recess. Traverse right on a vegetated ledge to
avoid a fulmar colony before moving up to the abseil block.

Rapid Deterioration – 75m Severe. C. Mortimer, A. Dow. 3rd June, 2001.
Climb the nice crack about 4m right of Keeping Wullie Busy. After 15-20m the
crack deteriorates. Follow the most solid route to the top.

Puffin Patrol – 75m H. Severe 4c *. I. Hall, M. Snook. 4th June, 2001.
Start 10m right of the abseil at a shallow quartz-backed groove.
1. 25m Ascend the groove, moving left to gain a crack and small chockstone.
Move past the chockstone (crux) and continue easily to the top of a right-slanting
ledge.
2. 35m Turn a small overhang above on the left and step back right to a ledge.
Climb a steep wall on superb holds to a large ledge.
3. 15m Traverse left along the ledge until a rib of good rock can be followed to the
abseil block.

Guarsey Beag, Black Geo:
The Ebony Slipper – 60m E3 and A0. P. Donnithorne, D. Barlow (alt.). May,
2001.
An atmospheric route left of Journey to Ixtlan. Abseil down the overhanging arête
to a pink knobbly nose 15m above the sea (keep bouncing).
1. 20m 5c Traverse right on rounded lumps to a corner-crack and move up for a
few metres to a resting place. Swing wildly up and right to a stance on a slab by a
niche below the left-hand huge overhanging corner.
2. 40m 5c/A0 Follow the exposed ramp up left to a crack/groove and go up to the
left end of the roof. Go up with difficulty and aid into the slim hanging corner in
the left arête of the huge corner. Go up this thankfully to the top.

Guarsay Mor, Morning Wall:
Mourning After – 85m E1. H. Hunt, K. Howett. 13th September, 2001.
Climbs the wall directly right of Morning Glory. Start 5m down and right of that
route, just left of a shattered raised ledge.
1. 30m 5b Climb to level with the top of the shattered ledge. Step right and up a
black cracked wall to gain the centre of a horizontal cave. Struggle up the pure
jam crack issuing from the centre of the cave roof to gain another smaller cave.
Pull directly over this to a big ledge and block.
2. 55m 5a Climb past the block to a blackened wall. Climb it slightly rightwards
and into a left-facing groove. At its top, step left through a bulge to gain a ledge.
Climb the groove-ramp and step out left and up to gain the base of a curving
overlap. Pull out right onto the wall and follow a direct line to the top.

The Knight Before – 80m E1. N .Stabbs, H. Harris. 2001.
Climbs a direct line up the wall following the distinctive features of a right-facing corner in the centre of the face and a rightward leaning arching groove near the top of the wall. Start 10m down and right of Mourning After at an orange patch of rock and a projecting block at 5m.
1. 40m 5a Climb the wall direct, passing between two caves at 35m. Follow a steeper section to a good ledge below the right-facing corner.
2. 40m 5b Climb the corner and then direct up the wall, passing a pegmatite band to a steep pull into the leaning groove. Go up this, then easy rock to blocks on a broken ramp.

The following route lies on the far right of this wall:
Treading on Eggshells – 25m VS 4c. K. Martin, T. Wood. 2001.
Start at the base of an obvious right-slanting corner at the right-hand end of Morning Wall and gained by descending the obvious block-filled gully. Climb the corner.

Also near here in the back of the geo to the east of Morning Wall is the following:
Freddie Fulmars Funky Food Franchise – 60m HVS. T .Wood, K. Martin. 2001.
Start 50m left of an obvious chimney groove at the back of the geo, directly opposite a chimney high up on the other side of the geo. Abseil down to a ledge 2m below a square-cut roof.
1. 25m 5a Climb direct back up the corner and over the roof to a large belay ledge.
2. 35m 5a Climb the steep crack at the back of the ledge into a groove which leads to the top.

This is thought to be near *Pot of Gold* (A. Cave, C. Waddy, 1998)

Guarsay Mor, Cobweb Wall:
These are near Cuan a' Bochan (2000):
Salvaged – 100m VS. R. Makenzie, T. Sweeney. 2001.
Start from the pink streaked ledge.
1. 45m 5a Climb a steep left-facing corner. Trend left when the angle eases, for about 15m. Then go direct over the lip of a roof and onto a flat black wall. Continue to a grass terrace and belay at the foot of the left corner of a giant yellow flake.
2. 45m 5a Climb direct up the corner to the top of the flake. Then continue direct up feldspar to the top.

Bills Yellow Edge – 110m HVS. R. Mackenzie, T. Sweeney. 2001.
Follows the very edge of the wall to the right of the cobweb section itself. From the first ledge system take an abseil down the edge all the way to a large ledge.
1. 35m 5b Climb rounded jugs heading to the roof above and to the left. Exit the roof on the right and follow a rising left traverse to gain the foot of the yellow corners.
2. 35m 4c Up the corners and then trend left to gain a left rising crack. Follow the shoulder up to a large ledge.
3. 40m 5a Keeping on the edge, follow rounded rock past a yellow scoop. Continue on to the grass terrace.

Guarsay Mor, The Arena:
Found near the routes The Breach (2000), Cuan a' Cheo (2000) and Arch Angel (2000).
Ken, The Fire – 80m HVS. K. Martin, T. Wood. 2001.
Abseil from a boulder in front of a corner on the sloping grass terrace in the centre of The Arena, to reach a peapod-shaped groove 25m below a large roof.
1. 45m 5b Climb out of the groove, up the wall to the roof. Turn it on the left into a deep groove. Follow this to a hanging stance on a ramp 5m right of big ledges.
2. 35m 5a Exit through the roof above and trend right to a groove. Climb this and continue up the wall to finish.

Note: Three routes recorded as on West Face of Guarsay Mor (SMCJ 2001, p601), also known as The North Pillar, sound similar to the following:
Entebbe Sailing Club may be the same as No Puke Here?
The Grass is Singing may be the same as Alzheimer's Groove or be just to its right?
Hoon Bird sounds the same as Grey Rib?

Guarsay Mor, The Boulevard:
This is the name now adopted for the area of good rock of initial explorations near the end of the point (Ossian Boulevard and Lost Souls). Also Man Overboard (SMCJ 2001, p601).
The Mushroom of My Fear – 50m E3. R. Durran, C. Henderson. 2000.
Five metres right of Hill You Hoe is a left-facing corner capped by a small roof at 10m.
1. 15m 6a Climb the corner and the roof and short wall above with difficulty to gain the right end of the Ossian Boulevard ledge.
2. 35m 5b Climb up and slightly leftwards for a few metres, then slightly rightwards before continuing directly through some entertaining bulges to reach easier ground. Sustained.

The following two routes are to be found right on the tip of the headland. Abseil off the NW tip of Guarsay Mor to a large tidal ledge.
Aqualung – 45m Severe. D. Wilby, R. Wilby. 2001.
Slightly right of the abseil are two crack lines. Climb the left-hand crack.

Soggy Chalk – 45m Severe. R. Wilby, D. Wilby. 2001.
This climbs the crack and chimney left of Aqualung and then direct up the wall to the top.

Shags' Point:
From the tip of the point along its west wall (previously called Guarsay Beag, Central Promontory) into the back of a slight geo (previously called Wee Geo, but there is another Wee Geo) is all being referred to as Shags' Point.

The first four routes are such obvious lines that they may have been climbed before but don't seem to fit any descriptions (says M. Radtke). Abseil to ledges 4m above the sea and 5m right of the hole as described in the guide p139 (looking into the cliff).

The Wine Box Nomads – 35m VS 4c. I. Cooksey, M. Radtke. 29th May, 2001.
Climb the wall directly above the stance on perfect clean juggy rock. Climb
through a small roof and bridge up the obvious open book corner above.

Gobling Groove – 35m VS 4c. P. Donnithorne, D. Barlow. May, 2001.
The wall and rib between The Wine Box Nomads and Derek the Shaman.

Derek the Shaman – 35m VS 4c. M. Radtke, I. Cooksey. 29th May, 2001.
From the same stance traverse 3m right and climb direct on perfect juggy rock to
enter the yellow lichen-coloured grooves immediately right of the obvious open
book corner. (This route appears as a line of thin flakes from the opposite
promontory.)

Abseil down The Shield to reach:
Condemned to Happiness – 40m VS ***. J. Sanders, M. Snook. 1st June, 1998.
From the bottom of With a view to a Shag, make an easy sea level traverse left
(facing into the cliff) for 10m (Diff.), then move around a corner for about 5m
until there is an obvious left-facing corner capped by a large black overhang.
Belay here.
1. 20m 4c Climb the chimney beneath the overhang, and attack it direct (strenuous
and easier on the right). Continue up the crack above to an obvious small platform.
2. 20m 5a There are two clearly defined slanting grooves above. Move right and
pull up (strenuous) into the right-hand one (crux). Climb this to the top.

Pecking Order – 70m VS. J. Sanders, M. Snook. 1st June, 1998.
1. 25m 4b From the bottom of Easy Day for a Shag, make a rising traverse right
(facing in) to an obvious bird-filled cave, marked by the guano streaks issuing
from it. To the right is a prominent overhanging prow.
2. 20m 4c Attack the prow direct (crux) and continue straight up until just below
the cliff top.
3. 25m 4a Traverse back left beneath the cliff top to the top of the abseil point.

Puffin Threesome – 45m VS 4b. A. Callum, S. Gardner. 1st June, 1998.
1. 25m 4b As for pitch 1 of Pecking Order to the cave To the left is a prominent
corner.
2. 25m 4b Climb the corner to the top.

The following routes are in the much less defined geo that forms the west face of
Shags Point. It can be viewed easily by descending a slight rib midway between
the black wall on Black Geo and Shags Point itself. Looking from the south side
of the geo, the cairn and grooves below it are obvious. Equally obvious is the
huge right-to-left diagonal crack. A vertical fault line also rises from the same
source (just above sea level). The following routes all start from a large ledge 10m
above the sea (50m abseil).
Scragging Shags – 50m E1 5a. P. Donnithorne, D. Barlow. May, 2001.
Fine climbing on a strong line. From the large ledge, climb the diagonal crack
leftwards to a larger ledge with a pink vein crossing it. Continue in the same line
to an exposed rib; launch up and right into a hanging corner to finish over a small
capping roof..

Pleasurable Puffins – 50m E1 5b. P. Donnithorne, D. Barlow. May, 2001.
Follow the previous route to the pink vein ledge, then take a steep crack up right
to a roof, swing round it on the right and traverse left above it. Climb a rib and
finish over large flakes.

The Screamer – 50m HVS. E. Alsford, N. Doust (alt.). May, 2001.
1. 20m 4b From the ledge, step right into the vertical fault line and follow it for
15m to a good ledge on the right.
2. 30m 5a Climb up above the belay, then through a bulge and up to the top.

Fulminating Fulmars – 65m E2. P. Donnithorne, E. Alsford (alt.), D. Barlow.
May, 2001.
A fine varied route.
1. 25m 5b From the ledge, step right across the fault, then traverse along a faint
break to a hidden crack/groove. Go up this, then steeply up rightwards to the
centre of the ledge.
2. 40m 5a From the right end of the ledge, climb steeply up on huge holds to an
exposed groove. Trend rightwards over blocks to finish up an obvious slabby
wall.

Wee Geo, Tarmacadam Wall:
Wee Geo defines the east side of Shag's Point. Its west wall is called Tarmacadam
Wall and its east wall is called Ryan's Wall. The much less defined geo that forms
the west face of Shags Point has also in the past been called Wee Geo. Tarmacadam
Wall contains the route Bird in the Nest (1998). This route climbs the most obvious
'S'-shaped crack towards the left end of the wall. A small tidal ledge sits near its
base. Towards the right side of the wall is an obvious right-facing corner extending
the full height and containing a conspicuous protruding block near the top. Sea-
washed ledges sit at its base (uncovered at low tide). Just left of the base of the
corner and about 3m above the high tide level is a sloping glacis. The following
route starts here and the next route has the same access. Gain the glacis by an
abseil from a huge block on the top of the hillside above.
All Weather Seal 'unt – 35m HVS. K. Howett, H. Hall. 11th September, 2001.
1. 15m 5a Climb into the hanging corner in the top of the glacis past one ledge and
on to another and an impass. Gain flakes out on the steep wall on the right. Follow
them to their end and pull on to the wall above. Go up to a big ledge and large
block.
2. 20m 5a Stand on a raised ledge above the block. Gain the vertical fault in the
wall above and follow it with a tricky pull on to a sloping ledge below a final
overlap. Pull over direct and gain slabs to finish.

Ron the Seal's Quick Drying Wall Climb – 35m HVS. N. Stabbs, H. Harris. 2001.
Abseil from a large block well back on top of the promontory down the wall to the
left of the large corner to gain a glacis about 3m above high tide level. It does
exactly what it says on the tin!
1. 15m 4c From the left end of the glacis, climb the left wall of the corner to a
ledge and follow the arête and corners directly to the halfway ledge.
2. 20m 5a Follow the central crack for 2m then gain a small ledge out left. Climb
the striated wall direct to the top.

Creag Dhearg, The Right Wall:

The following routes start from the central belay ledge on Creag Dearg. It is important to keep swinging during the 40m abseil in order not to miss the central belay ledge.

A Deathly Hush – 40m E3 5c. K. Magog, S. Crowe. 25th May, 2001.

From the far left end of the ledge, follow the ramp to reach a prominent V-shaped groove. Climb the left arête of this to reach a ledge. Pull on to the ledge and tentatively traverse right along the detached flake for about 4m to pull into the base of a slim right facing corner. Bold. Follow the corner to the top. A direct start is possible at 6b but the rock is dubious.

Little Miss Sitting Pretty – 40m E5 6a. S. Crowe, K. Magog. 21st May, 2001.

From the centre of the ledge take a leftward rising line to gain the left side of a ledge below the pair of right-facing grooves. Follow the left-hand groove and continue directly with increasing difficult above the groove until below the left extremity of the final roofs. Ignoring the possibility to escape left, step right and pull over the roof and up the final headwall on jugs.

Big Chief Turning Bull – E4 6a (SMCJ 2001 p599)

Existing route following the right-hand of the pair of right-facing grooves.

Fulmar Squaw – E3 5c (SMCJ 2001 p599)

Existing route following two prominent curving flakes.

The Road to Nowhere – 40m E3 5c. K. Magog, S. Crowe. 21st May, 2001.

Climb rightwards from the ledge for about 4m to gain a vaguely scooped grey shield of rock. Follow the faint scoop to the ledge. From here climb the black scoop above to a good break. Traverse right slightly to gain a slim right facing ramp line. Follow this up and left until it reaches Fulmar Squaw. Finish as for Fulmar Squaw on increasingly good holds.

Tom a' Reithean Peninsula, Haunted Geo (MR 573 847):

After passing the top of the largest geo on the east coast of Tom a' Reithean, start to head east. A large grassy rake should soon be found; this should be followed down southwards and then back northwards until large ledges and a large high level sea cave are found about 30m above the sea. The routes lie on either side of a low-level cave. The first two routes are accessed by abseil, via an obvious groove onto a small ledge above high water mark on the right-hand side looking in of the cave. The geo is an almost perfect U-shape.

Spectre Grooves – 20m V. Diff. S. Porteus, T. Catterall. 2001.

Start at the large left-facing corner at the right end of the ledge. Climb a series of grooves passing a roof by its right-hand side at half height. Continue up the groove to the top, an excellent route.

Ghost Ship – 25m HVS 5a. T. Catterall, S. Porteus. 2001.

From the left end of the ledge, climb the undercut corner immediately right of the cave and follow small grooves to a quartz band. Follow the crack above and gain the slab, follow the crack to the top.

The next two routes are accessed by descending down sloping ledges heading south from the top of Spectre Grooves. From the ledge at the bottom of this, traverse round the corner to the right when looking in.

The Exorcist – 30m E4 6a. T. Catterall, S. Porteus. 2001.
Start from the right-hand end of the ledge. Make an airy traverse around the corner towards the cave. Climb the corner and crack above to a small square topped pillar. Hard moves lead right across the wall to the right-hand end of the roof, easier climbing above leads to the top.

The next route lies south of the descent ramp and is accessed by an excellent sea level traverse on large holds. Follow the traverse until a deep cut narrow geo is reached. 4m back the way you have come is the prominent rib of Maire Celeste.

Marie Celeste – 40m Diff. S. Porteus, T. Catterall. 2001.
Climb the prominent rib past a light coloured rock band at half height to easy ground in a superb situation.

The Crags North East of the Bay, Waterfall Geo:
This is the next geo north of Geo an Droma. Its south wall is composed of easy slabs offering a full view of the main wall which faces south. The main features are a well defined left-facing corner on the right, two vertical chimneys to its left and a steep pink feldspar wall with twin cracks left again, before the wall steepens up further into the back of the geo. There are no ledges at the base and it drops into deep water. Access is by descending the easy slabs down to the point and traversing back into the geo at sea level (Diff).

Wandering Soul – 20m V. Diff. K. Howett. 1999.
The left-facing corner.

Dressed to the Right – 20m Severe. K. Howett. 1999.
The cracks in the right wall of the corner.

Dressed to the Left – 20m Severe. K. Howett. 1999.
The wall just to the left of the corner.

Gneiss Slot – 20m V. Diff. R. Mackenzie. 2001.
The chimney crack to the left.

Flysheet Minch Crossing – 20m VS 5a. R Mackenzie. 2001.
Left of the chimney. Climb up over bulges to an offwidth slot. Struggle up this and continue direct.

Island Madness – 40m HVS 5a. R. Mackenzie. 2001.
Traverse left under all the previous routes. Once past Flysheet Minch Crossing, take a rising diagonal crack climbs over bulges to gain further juggy cracks up the feldspar wall.

Also recorded here, but as yet their relationship to the above is uncertain:
Another V. Diff! – 12m V. Diff. R. Jones. 2001.
4m right of the corner.

Not So V.Diff! – 12m H.Severe 4b. R. Jones. 2001.
2m left of the corner. Direct through the roof.

Anticipatory Diffness! – 12m V.Diff. R. Jones. 2001.
Direct up the wall 2m right of the corner.

Basking Seal Geo:
The Shag Who Spied Me – 40m E4 5c. S. Crowe, K. Magog. 26th May, 2001.
The steep wall, starting just left of the prominent groove, and then crossing the
lightning- shaped feature at the roof. Pull through the roof and up the final headwall
on jugs.

(Not Another) Northumbrian Wall – 40m E4 6a. S. Crowe, K. Magog. 26th May,
2001.
The steep wall just right of the lightning-shaped groove via a faint twin crack
system to a break at two thirds height. Step right and continue up the final groove
on good holds.

MULL, Sron Gharbh (wrongly called Creag Liath previously):
Unnamed – 15m E2 5b/c. B. Davison, C. Moody 30th August, 2001.
At the right end of the crag is a huge ivy. Climb the rib just left of it, traverse left
and continue up the rib proper.

Wull's Exam Fiasco (SMCJ 2001) was climbed by C. Moody and A. Soloist.

Balmeanach:
Baby Kissing Tour – 20m E1 5a/b. C. Moody, R. MacKechnie. 2001.
Right of Mur Sans Spit is a corner crack, start just left of it. Climb up with runners
in the corner crack, near the top finish up a thin flake crack on the left.

Ardchrishnish:
Cabin Fever – 12m E1 5b. C. Moody, C. Black. 2001.
Shallow corner right of First Route.

Fievre – 10m VS 5b. C. Moody. 2001.
The rib right of Floral Arrangement, with a thin start.

Egg Hunt – 12m HVS 5a *. C. Moody, C. Black. Easter, 2001.
Start up Honeysuckle Wall and continue up the corner above instead of going left.

Scoor, The Slab:
Note: *Thick Head* (SMCJ 2001) has a corrected description:
Climbs the thin crack left of Greased Lightning. Start left of Greased Lightning,
climb up easily then step left to gain the thin crack which is followed to the top.
Thin in the lower half, bolder in the upper half.

Scoor, Eilean Garbh:
Left of Stranded Arête is a chimney; the rib between them is HVS 5a. The crack
left of Quartz Rib is Severe. The broad rib left again is VS 4b and there is a

descent chimney left of it. Right of Black Chimney, a route climbs quartz lumps at VS 4b.

Scoor, Smelly Bay:
That Stinks – 12m E2 5b. C. Moody, C. Grindley. 2001.
Start round left of A Fetid Stench. Climb a steep flake crack, move up right to gain a rib, then traverse left and finish straight up. Low in the grade.

Ardtun, The Nuclear Cliff:
Hot Spots – 15m HVS 5a. C. Moody, C. Black. 24th September, 2001.
The crack between Half Life Dangleberry and Hot Stuff.

Ardtun, Yellow Block:
Drizzle – 10m VS 4b *. C. Moody. 15th May, 2001.
Crack left of The Edge Of Madness.

Heat – 10m VS 4b *. C. Moody. 24th May, 2001.
Crack left of Drizzle.

Unnamed – 14m VS/HVS *. C. Moody. 2001.
Corner crack left of Everything He Hates About Climbing.

White Heather Club – 10m VS 4c *. C. Moody, A. Malloy, C. Black. 31st July, 2001.
A crack right of Everything He Hates About Climbing.

Jesie Peeps – 10m HVS 5a *. C. Moody, A. Malloy, C. Black. 31st July, 2001.
Another crack to the right.

Ardtun, The Blow Hole:
100 – 13m VS 4b *. C. Moody. 13th September, 2001.
Start just right of Oot Ma Rays and follow the crack slanting up right.

Erraid, Upper Tier:
Note: The short wall just left of the prominent blunt arête at the left end of the crag (between The Goupher Hole and One Dead Puffin) was climbed at 6a (serious) – Trapezium – by J. Lines and G. Latter (on-sight) on 16th July, 2001.

Chickenhead – 10m E2 5c *. G. Latter. 16th July, 2001.
The groove and short steep crack right of the slab where the crag changes direction and left of Walls Without Balls.

RLS – 10m E2 5b **. G. Latter (on-sight). 10th June, 2001.
The rightmost of two crack systems just right of Stealth, starting up short easy right-facing groove. Starts just left of A Helping Hand.

Stonecrop Groove – 6m E3 6a **. J. Lines (on-sight solo). 16th July, 2001.
A left-facing groove up the left side of the short wall beneath the descent ramp.

Aros – 8m HVS 5a *. C. Moody, A. N. Other. 1994.
A left-facing flake, finishing up a jam crack.

The Vagabond – 8m HVS 5a *. G. Latter (on-sight solo). 17th July, 2001.
A right-facing groove, stepping up left on to a ledge to finish up a jam crack.

The Dynamiter – 12m HVS 5a *. G. Latter (on-sight solo). 17th July, 2001.
There is a short blunt arête at the far right end of the crag. Climb the cracks
immediately to its right, scrambling to finish.

Lower Tier:
Erraid Shelter – 6m E2 5b **. J. Lines, G. Latter (on-sight). 18th July, 2001.
The short arête above the upper ledge, left of the arch. Just right of Mullman.

Davie – 8m E3 6b **. J. Lines G. Latter (on-sight). 18th July, 2001.
Surprisingly independent climbing up the right arête of Weeping Corner. Place a
low runner in the groove and move right to good jug on the arête (sling). Attain a
standing position on this, then continue up the arête and crack pleasantly.

The shallow groove/arête on the right side, starting up and staying close to Flood
Warning was also climbed at E2 5c.

The Pink Wall (NM 293 195 – Altitude: 20m – Aspect: SW)
The short crack-seamed wall overlooking the small west-most beach at Traigh
Gheal.
Panther – 8m Severe.
The wide crack which slants up right.

Pink One – 8m HVS 5a *. J. Lines (on-sight solo). 17th July, 2001.
Twin cracks left of a corner.

Floyd – 8m H. Severe 4b *. G. Latter (on-sight solo). 26th August, 2000.
The corner.

Elephants – 9m VS 4c *. J. Lines (on-sight solo). 17th July, 2001.
Cracks up the left side of the front wall.

Which One's Pink? – 9m VS 5a *. J. Lines (on-sight solo). 17th July, 2001.
The next crack to the right.

Pinky – 10m E1 5b *. G. Latter (on-sight solo). 17th July, 2001.
The central crack.

Perky – 8m VS 4c *. G. Latter (on-sight solo). 17th July, 2001.
A crack up the right side of the wall.

Paradise Wall (MR NM 293 193 – Aspect: NE)
A fantastic deep-water soloing venue, on the west side of the bay, about 100m
south of the small west-most beach.

Approaches: Routes 1 and 2 are approachable at all states of the tide, 3 at mid-low tide and the start of 4 is only reachable at low tide. For routes 1-3 descend a short chimney (Severe) on the east face, about 6m south of the wall, then left along ledge to gain a flake line which allows a fine descending traverse down rightwards (5b) to the base of the routes. 4 is gained by scrambling down the easy ridge just north of the chasm forming the wall.

The Brine Shrine – 12m XS 5c S0 ***. J. Lines. 16th July, 2001.
The offset slanting offwidth at the left side. A jammed chokestone low down is helpful, as are holds on the walls on either side. From a rest in the wide horizontal near the top, finish either directly up the wall, or hand traverse out left. High in the grade.

Please Rub Salt into my Wounds! – 10m XS 5c S0 **. J. Lines. 16th July, 2001.
The flaky central crack, with the crux passing a small spike low down. Finish on a good jug and excellent jams. Low in the grade.

Dreamline – 12m XS 6b *** S1. G. Latter 17th July, 2001.
The stunning hanging finger-crack (crux), widening to hands in its upper reaches. Finish by stepping into a recess out right.

Drowning in Adrenaline – 15m XS 6a *** S1/2. J. Lines 18th July, 2001.
A fantastic rising traverse line. Start by bridging across the chasm (midgets need not apply!) to a left-facing flake a few metres right of the large schist intrusion. Move up left into the intrusion, then gain the good flake out left and follow it into Dreamline. Move up this to follow the next break out left to a reasonable rest in the next crack. Continue out left on the lower (cleaner) of two breaks, hand traversing the final wide slot of The Brine Shrine to finish. Diving/jumping from the finishing ledge is obligatory.

The Longest Yet. 18m Severe 4a *. G. Latter (on-sight solo). 18th July, 2001.
The prominent open chimney well left (south) of Paradise Wall.

Note: Some notes on bouldering were received from Andy Spink (also Tiree) and have been passed on to C. Moody as the guidebook author for Mull.

Fionnphort (MR 305237):
Mesajania – 10m E6 6b ***. M. Tweedly (unsec.). September, 2001.
This route is easily seen from the main road coming into Fionnphort and overlooks the track to Torr Mor quarry. Near the Quarry entrance are lots of perfect granite boulders and craglets. This line takes a near vertical slab, with a perfect crack going up to halfway. Climb this, then make crux moves past and above on the blank face. End with a slopey exit. Route graded for an on-sight ascent.

IONA, Raven's Crag, Main Wall:
Holy Tackle – 20m VS 4c. M. Tweedly, R. Waterton, T. Charles Edwards. September, 2001.
This is to the right of Rod Tod This is God. It climbs a groove, then a crack to a shelf.
Note: May be undergraded.

ISLAY, Creag Bealach na Caillich (MR 203 614):
This bold south-west facing crag lies above Bealach na Caillich on the rough track between Kilchiaran and Machir Bay (ten minutes from Kilchiaran). Although it dries quickly, the rock is of mixed quality and much of it is draped in shaggy lichen.

Family Values – 60m VS. G. E. Little, N. Kemp (alt.). 14th October, 1999.
This route tackles the full height of the crag via a central left to right trending fault/ramp
line. Start at the lowest point of the crag.
1. 45m 5a Follow the fault/ramp line (much lichen) to gain the top of a semi-detached pillar (not obvious from below). Step right, then move up with difficulty (crux) to enter the continuation fault. Follow this (grassy in places) to reach a grassy ledge and a juniper.
2. 15m Climb the steep but relatively easy wall above to a flake at the top.

Sons and Daughters – 70m VS. G. E. Little, N. Kemp (alt). 14th October, 1999.
The left side of the crag is flanked by a wide slab with a truncated base which forms a 20m high wall. Start near the centre of this wall at a slight grey groove.
1. 25m 4c Sustained climbing leads up and left to enter and climb the obvious corner and thence gain the slab above. Ascend the slab for 5m to a small grass ledge with a belay at a wide crack up and right.
2. 45m Climb the slab near its right edge, then vegetated ground above, to belay near the top.

Lossit Walls (MR 177 556):
A series of steep gneiss walls lie on the south side of the beautiful Lossit Bay.

Trench Wall:
This, the finest and highest of the walls forms the landward flanking side of a tidal trench and provides challenging routes on vertical to overhanging rock to a height of 35m.

La Grooveulin – 35m E1 5b *. G.E. Little, S. Muir. 22nd April, 2000.
Tackles the right-facing groove, the first distinctive feature reached when entering the trench from the landward end. Start below the groove, which starts about 5m up the wall. Move up and right until flakes allow a left traverse on to a small ledge at the foot of the groove (direct access to this point may be possible via a thin crack – 6a?). Excellent climbing up the groove leads to a plaque-like barrier. Cross this with care, then continue up increasingly easier and vegetated ground.

Geodha Cam (MR 176 562):
This narrow geo lies on the north side of Lossit Bay. Its east flank comprises a slab of immaculate rock. Two short routes have been done, the centre of the slab and the obvious slabby rib (both about Diff.).

Eilean Cam (MR 163 543):
This narrow island lies a couple of kilometres to the north-west of Portnahaven and is separated from the mainland by a narrow, part tidal, defile. There is climbing

on the slabby landward side of the defile but much better climbing on the island side. At the obvious big step in the landward face, an arête (Eilean Arête) projects into the defile. To the south of this feature, above a group of three large boulders, it is possible to scramble down into the defile. A steeper scramble descent can also be made to the north of the arête. Alternatively, abseil to the floor of the defile.

Routes on the landward side of the defile:
Harry's Route – 20m Severe. G.E. Little (solo). 23rd April, 2000.
Start just to the right of the foot of Eilean Arête and climb the steepest section of the slabby face above.

Eilean Arête – 20m Diff. *. S. Muir, A. Baird, G.E. Little. 23rd April, 2000.
Climb the arête directly.

Bar Wars – 20m Diff. S. Muir (solo). 23rd April, 2000.
Start at the most southerly of a group of boulders to the north of the Eilean Arête. Climb a left-trending fault line and the wall above.

Routes on the island side of the defile:
Darth Maureen – 15m VS 4c **. S. Muir, G.E. Little, A. Baird. 23rd April, 2000.
This route takes the distinctive corner line at a step in the wall, above the cluster of three boulders. Sustained climbing.

Mr Bridge – 20m VS 4c **. G.E. Little, S. Muir, A. Baird. 23rd April, 2000.
The other distinctive corner line to the right of Darth Maureen. Enjoyable climbing with wide bridging.

Prince of Tides – 15m E2 5b **. G.E. Little, S. Muir. 23rd April, 2000.
Start below a black wall at the northern end of the northerly cluster of boulders – the defile is quite narrow at this point. Make strenuous, committing moves up the impending wall to gain a small ledge. Continue straight up on steep but easier rock.

Sanaigmore Area:
A complex of cliff-girt headlands lie to the west of Sanaigmore. An obvious corner, with a grass ledge at half height, lies just to the north of the stone dyke (MR 222 712). The right edge of the corner forms an arête.
Slatehead Arête – 35m E2 5b. G. E. Little, S. Muir. 24th April, 2000.
Climb the groove immediately right of the arête until a move left gives access to the midway ledge. Continue up the slabby wall just left of the arête. There is some friable rock.

SKYE

GLEN SLIGACHAN CRAGS, Low Crag (MR 480 259):

Low Crag lies at 300m above sea level on the eastern slopes of Sgurr Nan Gillean, about 1km north of Glen Sligachan Buttress. It is a vast crag consisting of at least eight independent buttresses, although the unexplored upper crags appear somewhat loose and broken. The crag is approached in under 1.5 hours from Sligachan, by following the Sgurr nan Gillean tourist path as far as Coire Riabhach, and turning off to the left (east) at a small cairn halfway up the steep ascent into Coire Nan Allt Geala. A faint sheep track then brings you to the first of the buttresses, Riabhach Wall.

Riabhach Wall:

The first area reached is a short gabbro wall, reminiscent of a gritstone edge. At its right-hand end is a small rectangular slab, which holds the pleasant, though escapable:

Escapist's Daydream – 10m H. Severe *. A. Baugh, R. Welford. 4th January, 2002.
Solo, but not too committing. Climb the centre of the thin slab on edges to belay some distance back.

To the left of this is a bulging rounded arête which bounds the right hand side of Riabhach Wall itself. In the centre of the wall there is a prominent triangular groove which is taken by the original route on the face. On all of the climbs here protection can be difficult to arrange, and a selection of small camming devices will prove useful. Climbs are described from right to left.

Oxford Blue – 20m E1 5b ***. S. Broadbent, K. Wigmore. 4th January, 2002.
A beautifully technical climb linking the obvious scarce holds and requiring thoughtful protection. Head straight up the wall right of The Purple Turtle to reach a small triangular niche (crux). Move out of this more easily.

The Purple Turtle – 25m HVS 5a **. A. Ross, A. Parker, A. Baugh. 4th January, 2002.
A well protected route with a challenging crux at mid-height. Climb the prominent leftwards ramp in the centre of the wall and continue directly up the thin flake-crack above. Finish rightwards along a basalt ledge.

The Groove – 25m Mild VS 4b *. S. Broadbent, K. Wigmore. 4th January, 2002.
An interesting route taking the short groove in the centre of the face. Enter the groove from a rightwards-trending crack and make several awkward moves to gain the ledge above. From here, step right and follow more broken ground directly to the top.

Kandahar – 15m E4 5c *. S. Broadbent, K. Wigmore. 4th January, 2002.
A bold route up the steep headwall 5m left of The Groove. Short but desperate,

Slab master and granite specialist Julian Lines on 'Realm of the Senses' (E7 6c), Shelter Stone Crag, Cairngorms. Photo: Dave Cuthbertson/Cubby Images.

with awkward protection. Climb up easy slabs to excellent holds in the basalt dyke, and poor tiny wire runners high on the left. Then make difficult moves on tiny edges and sidepulls, trending rightwards up the undercut flake crack to the top.

Small Slab – 15m HVS 5b. A. Baugh, R. Welford. 4th January, 2002.
Climbs the short undercut slab immediately right of two basalt seams in the left part of the wall. Starting from the right, pull through the overlap on undercut holds, and climb the slab directly to finish up the wall above. Poorly protected above the crux.

The Seamstress – 10m V. Diff. R. Welford, K. Wigmore. 4th January, 2002.
Climb between the two basalt seams to the left of Small Slab, before finishing up easy ground above.

East Ramp – 20m Moderate. K. Wigmore. 4th January, 2002.
The easy walls and ledges close to the left hand arête provide a pleasant scramble. Or try the variation start (20m, Diff, A. Parker, 4th January, 2002.). Ascend the first crack right of the start of East Ramp and finish up a choice of easy lines above.

Descent from all climbs on this face can be made by walking down an easy slab at the left (east) side of the crag.

North Buttress:
A short distance around the corner from Riabhach Wall lies another larger and more intimidating buttress. On the east face of this huge gabbro crag are many potential lines, mostly in the upper grades and probably very committing. To date, none have been climbed, although the stunningly obvious rightwards-slanting 'Varsity Crack' has repulsed at least one strong attempt!
Panoramix Area and Spaceman's Slab can be reached from here. Instead of following the crag up to North Buttress, drop down slightly to reach the impressive Panoramix Wall and the nearby Spaceman's Slab.

Upper Tier and South Buttress:
These two buttresses lie slightly above and south of Panoramix Wall, and can be approached via the descent from those routes. The rock here is generally not as sound as the rest of the crag, and no lines have yet been climbed on either buttress.

SGURR NAN GILLEAN, The Bhasteir Face:
Doctors Gully Left – 70m III. D. Ritchie, N. MacGougan. 29th Dec 2001.
Follows the summer route, starting at the foot of Deep Chimney at a right-trending fault. Two good icy pitches early season. After heavy snowfall the route banks out and will become far easier.

BHASTEIR TOOTH, North Face:
Shadbolt's Chimney – 50m IV,5. D. Ritchie, M. Shaw. 24th February, 2002.
Follows the original summer route. Short but entertaining, the initial steepness forming a short hard crux.

'Dumby' Dave McLeod on the impressive 'Achemine' (E9 6c), Dumbarton Rock. Dave Cuthbertson/ Cubby Images.

BRUACH NA FRITHE, North Face:
North Chimney – 110m III,5. D. Ritchie, N. MacGougan. 1st January, 2002.
An atmospheric climb following the summer route.

SGURR A' MHADAIDH, North West Face:
Gauger's Gully – 75m IV,4. D. Ritchie, N. MacGougan. 2nd January, 2002.
Follow the summer route. Good rock scenery throughout.

SGURR THEARLAICH, West Face.
Gully B – 120m V,6. D. Ritchie, N. MacGougan. 31st December, 2001.
Fine climbing following the summer route. The deep chimney obvious from below
provided the crux and proved considerably harder than the summer description
would suggest.

Gully C – 90m III,4. D. Ritchie, N. MacGougan. 31st December, 2001.
Good climbing following the summer route.

Gully D – 100m V,5. D. Ritchie, N. MacGougan. 23rd February, 2002.
An excellent climb with sustained interest, following the summer route. The 'piece
de resistance' providing a memorable crux pitch.

SGURR A' GHREADAIDH, The Coir'-uisg Face.
Eag Dubh Gully – 200m III. D. Ritchie, N. MacGougan. 1st March, 2002.
Unlike the fault on the north side, this gully was found to be disappointingly
shallow, mostly banked out but with 2 or 3 interesting icy pitches over chockstones.

SRON NA CICHE, Eastern Buttress:
Clinging On – 65m E4 6a. K. Howett, S. Muir. 12th May, 2001.
Climbs the final line on the Vulcan Wall section of Eastern Buttress. Start as for
Dilemma. Superb climbing.
1. 55m 6a A long and sustained pitch. Climb the initial crack of Dilemma to its
end. Where Dilemma climbs diagonally right across the wall, make a move up
then gain the obvious vertical crack just on the left. Follow this to where it fades
into tiny cracks and gain an obvious small protruding block above. Step on to the
block and step left to a foot ledge on Uhuru. Step back right and gain a thin crack
and follow it with difficulty to gain better holds. Follow these up right into a final
crack to under the roofs. Traverse 2m left past the roofs to a vertical crack.
2. 10m 5a Climb up and left to under a projecting block. Take the hand-traverse
out left to the top.

ELGOL, Schoolhouse Buttress:
Both of these routes are on the very right of the main overhanging face, left and
round the corner of Schoolhouse buttress.
L.A.S.H.A.C – 20m VS 5a. G. Dawson, J. Heggie. 15th September, 2001.
Gain a pebble filled ledge on the right of the overhanging face. Go over the overhang
and move right under the overhanging block. Climb a wide flake crack to finish
right of some heather and left of schoolhouse buttress.

Send Me the Bill – 20m E1 5c. G. Dawson. 15th September, 2001.
Start as for L.A.S.H.A.C. and go left after the initial overhang, following the

overhanging left- trending crack before swinging out on to lichen covered wafers and go up the two cracks right of a final overhang. Finish up through the heather on a thin finger crack.

SUISNISH, Carn Dearg Buttress (Sheet 32, MR 158 600)

A large broken buttress directly above the path to Boreraig and Suisnish Pillar (SMCJ 2000). Two routes have been climbed after some cleaning (still some loose rock). They can be seen from the path, above the large blocky scree that descends from the right (east) end of the broken line of the buttress, which is marked by small rowan trees at the base. The lines take an obvious corner/chimney and the crack/groove/chimney to the left.

So, Where are the Dolphins? – 20m HVS 5a **. D. McAulay, J. Rick. 8th August, 2001.

The excellent corner with a roof at half height. Turn the roof on the right and continue up the chimney. Sustained.

Sweat on a Gibbons Brow – 20m HVS/E1 5a/b *. D. McAulay, J. Hunt. 27th June, 2001.

The route takes the steep flake-crack in the wall to the left of the corner. Hard initial moves up the crack gain a stance below the hanging slabby groove. Follow the groove with interest and finish up the chimney.

NEIST, Green Lady Area:

South-East Direct - 25m VS 4b **. D. McAulay, T. Wilsdon. 13th September, 2001.

Takes the arête in the south-east wall direct, finishing as for the previous routes described in the guide. It is better protected and considerably easier than it looks from below, also better than the routes in the guide.

Financial Sector:

Lottery Live - 35m E1 5b. D. Hollinger, S. Johnson. 7th June, 2001.

A route on the large undercut seaward face projecting from the southerly end of the Financial Sector. It begins as for Fat Cats (SMCJ 1998). The obvious groove beginning in the middle of the face is gained by exposed climbing in a superb position. Start around the corner of the arête on the left. Follow a short slab to its right edge. Step right and pull around the arête on to the face and instant exposure. Follow a flake crack rightwards to make awkward moves into the base of the groove. Continue up the groove exiting left at the top.

Note: C. Moody wonders if the groove on Lottery Live seems to be the groove on Gammy's Purse, but is not sure. D. Hollinger says the route appeared unclimbed and therefore thinks not.

The Lower Crag, Poverty Point:

Keeler – 25m – VS 4b. C. Moody, C. Grindley. 7th July, 2001.

Well left (north) of Chuggers Elbow is a right-slanting recess. Climb the rib left of it using a crack on the right of the rib most of the way.

The following two routes climb the big cracklines on the so far unclimbed wall on the right side of the obvious promontory (looking out). Both are stunning big pitches with excellent protection and very accessible (perhaps ***).

Fight Club – 25m E3 6a. P. Benson, F. Bennet. 15th April, 2001.
A jamming tussle up the left-hand crack. Start directly beneath the crack and climb directly.

American Vampire – 25m E4 6a (yo-yoed). P. Benson, F. Bennet. – 15th April, 2001.
The right-hand crack line. Sustained climbing leads to the overhanging hand crack with the crux (as it should be) the last move.

Conductor Cove Note:
To the right of the 5c problem in the guide is a short almost vertical crack, H.Severe 4b (J. Shanks, J. P. Dyble, July 2000). To the left of the 5c problem is the fine edge of Razorbill Arête, HVS 5b (J.P. Dyble, J. Shanks, July 2000).

Desmond the Slapper – 12m E1 5b. D. Cuthbertson, D. Dewar. Summer, 2001.
A short but serious corner, just left of Delux Corner. The hard moves required slapping the right arête.

Neist Upper Crag:
Several lines have been climbed by members of Oxford University Mountaineering Club in the area to the south of the car park on Neist Upper Crag. The only previous route is Nostromo (1998). Identifying lines on this cliff is particularly difficult as all approaches must be made by abseil. Most of these routes are in the area of the narrow buttress, which can be located as follows. From 'The Fin',four buttresses can be identified going back west towards the car park. The second of these is undercut at its base, and has a huge ledge on its western arête. The third lies above a grassy saddle, and has a short blank wall on its south-west face. Just to the west of this is the 'narrow buttress' with good rock anchors at its top and a prominent chimney in its west face.

The Third Buttress:
The blank wall on the west face of the Third Buttress is often wet. When it dries out, however, it holds the somewhat daring:
Atlantic Ocean Wall – 30m E2 5b. A. Baugh, R. Welford. 1st January, 2002.
A poorly protected route up the hanging slab and imposing headwall. Gain the foot of the slab by abseiling to a small grassy col, and climb the obvious groove to a ledge on the right. Step left on to a steepening ramp and follow this left to below the large flake in the headwall. Climb the flake and crack to the top, where care is required with loose rock.

The Narrow Buttress:
Across the dirty gully from the previous route lies a smaller buttress. The following route climbs the fine long arête and then heads out across the steep and blank seaward face of the buttress.
Californian Dream Holiday – 25m E1 5b **. S. Broadbent, K. Wigmore. 1st January, 2002.

A sustained and interesting route up the front of narrow buttress. Approach by abseiling to the base of a prominent detached pillar which is climbed easily on its right-hand side. From the top of the pillar, swing left up a series of well protected layback moves on the left side wall, to regain the crest of the arête at a triangular notch (possible belay). Head up and right across the superb upper wall to finishthrough the centre of the final overhang. A magnificent pitch.

On the west side of the buttress is an amazingly deep chimney:
Blizzard Chimney – 15m Severe * S. Broadbent, R. Welford, K. Wigmore. 30th December, 2001.
Abseil down the chimney to a comfortable ledge. Awkwardly re-gain the chimney and follow it to an interesting exit. An entertaining struggle!

The Split Tower – 15m Diff. S. Broadbent, K. Wigmore. 31st December, 2001.
The pillar to the right of Blizzard Chimney is climbed to a challenging finish up a right-facing corner. Approach as for the previous route.

Further west of Narrow Buttress the cliff is shorter and it is possible to walk along steep grass at its base. Baywatch and Sonamaralie further along this part of the crag, but before those two routes are reached, the following line has been climbed.
Skulldiggery – 35m Severe 4a. A. Ross, A. Parker. 31st December, 2001.
Abseil down 50m west of narrow buttress to a grassy bay with three obvious cracks in its east-facing wall. Climb the left-hand flake crack before traversing 2m left to finish up a series of heather covered shelves.

Notes: From R. EVERETT:
In the Financial Sector, many of the routes are rather over-described and over-graded, but not over-starred.
Bridging Interest is HVS 5a *** (rather than E1 5b).
Security Risk is probably E1 5b (tricky move low down), but despite what the guide says the protection is pretty good if you look for it.
Venture Capital is also low in the E1 grade.
Wall Street is worth the E2 grade for the interesting top roof, but most of it is only HVS.
Wish You Were Here was done by a different team using an entirely different grading system. It is clearly E2 5b *** - a meaty pitch.

TROTTERNISH, The Storr:
Storr Gully – 150m V ** (2000). M. Fowler, P. Ramsden. 29th December, 2000.
Takes the obvious deeply cut gully just right of Deeply Digestible Gully.
1. Start just left of the gully and climb up right into it.
2/3. Two good mixed pitches lead to beneath the final impending section.
4. Climb up into the bottom of the deep cave. Step left and climb up the very steep wall (two pegs for aid/clearing) until it is possible to traverse right to just above the cave. Easier ground leads to the top. This pitch was completely plastered with snow which made it challenging. Might be easier in leaner conditions.

STAFFIN, Sgeir Bhan (Staffin Slip North):
Note: P. Braithwaite, R. McHardy and E. Birch climbed the groove left of The Swelling, excellent and well protected (Snake Bite, E2 5c).

FLODIGARRY, North Tunnel Buttress:
The south face of the northern buttress provides some of the steepest and most technical climbing hereabouts. The following line is the only one known to have been climbed, and takes a direct line up the upper left-hand side of the face.
Hogmanay – 25m E2 5c ***. S. Broadbent, K. Wigmore. 2nd January, 2002.
A gem of a pitch, taking a direct line up the south face of North Tunnel Buttress. Technical and well protected. Start by abseiling down to a belay in a niche below a small overhang, close to the left side of the wall. After surmounting the overhang, the wall above, which is split by diagonal breaks, provides the technical crux. Trend rightwards and climb over the next overlap to a small triangular slab. Balance up this and make further hard moves to finish close to the right-hand arête.

South Tunnel Buttress:
After the first ascent of Raining Men (SMCJ 2001) there was some confusion about similarity with another route, Captain Mainwaring (SMCJ 1997). A subsequent visit to the area has verified that these two routes are independent lines, although it has been suggested that Raining Men be upgraded to VS 5a, 4b.

South Stack:
The small bay to the south of South Tunnel Buttress contains a stumpy sea stack which was first climbed via the route Rude Awakenings (SMCJ 2001). Further trips to these cliffs have revealed that this stack holds several excellent short routes which are just as enjoyable, and perhaps even more accessible than those on the main buttresses. Whilst the base of many of the routes can only be reached on foot at low tide, it is possible to reach the first route very shortly after high tide, and then climb subsequent routes by abseiling down from a (new) in-situ anchor on the summit. The stack is approached by scrambling down steep grass on the south side of the bay, from where the stack's West Ridge is seen on the left. Routes are described here in an anti-clockwise sense around the stack.
West Ridge – 20m Diff. S. Broadbent, K. Wigmore. 3rd January, 2002.
The easiest way up the stack, and the line of the abseil descent, this route can bereached from the mainland in all but the highest of tides. Step across from the large block and ascend easy walls and slabs to the summit. Descend by abseil from in-situ anchor.

Jig Saw – 15m VS 4c *. S. Broadbent, R. Welford, K. Wigmore. 5th January, 2002.
The left-hand zigzag crack on the stack's south face is short but superb! Start just right of the west ridge, and step round on to the south face to climb up a good crack to a small overlap. Swing right on horizontal jams (crux) and continue rightwards to finish up the enticing fist-jamming crack.

In the centre of the south face is the obvious direct crack line which was used on the first ascent – Rude Awakenings (SMCJ 2001). The next route lies a few metres right of this.
Black Beard – 20m HVS 5b **. S. Broadbent, R. Welford, K. Wigmore. 5th January, 2002.

An intimidating line up the overhang-capped groove right of Rude Awakenings. Start from a tiny triangular ledge in the bottom of the groove, and climb easily up to a below the roof. From here, pull awkwardly up and left using good undercuts and side-pulls. Step back right and balance up the excellent left-slanting groove directly to the summit of the stack.

The following routes all lie on the stack's seaward east face, and start from an obvious flat rock ledge just above the sea.
Breakfasting Tendencies – 15m H. Severe *. S. Broadbent, K. Wigmore. 3rd January, 2002.
Start from the left (south) end of the rock ledge at the foot of the east face. Traverse 2m left and pull through the overlap at the second crack (crux). Above this, trend leftwards to finish close to the left-hand arête.

East Face Route – 15m Diff. *. S. Broadbent, K. Wigmore. 3rd January, 2002.
A pleasant and well protected route up the middle of the slabby east face. The first move is by far the hardest of the route, with pleasant easy climbing above. Start from the obvious flat ledge at the foot of the face and climb directly to the top.

Captain Quibble – 20m Severe ***. K. Wigmore, S. Broadbent. 3rd January, 2002.
An exciting route traversing out across the top of the north face. Start at the right (north) of the rock ledge and follow the excellent stepped corner to the right of the arête by making a series of fine mantelshelf moves. Above this, place good protection andthen trend rightwards on excellent, though worrying, flake holds to finish at the top of the north face.

The Cheeseblock:
South-east of the stumpy sea stack, close the north end of a small headland, lies a short tilted block of dolerite with a tempting fist crack up its overhanging west face.
Aftershock 10m – VS 5a **. A. Baugh, R. Welford. 3rd January, 2002.
Start from the big ledge on the west side of the block and climb the very overhung hand jamming crack to an exciting exit! Descend by abseil or scramble down the easier east face of the block.

RUBHA HUNISH, Meall Tuath:
The route is on loose ground, apparently not as bad as it sounds, though protection is spaced and retreat awkward.
Bogus Journey – 75m V. Diff. P. Frampton, L. Thomas. 2nd January, 2002.
Approach via the steep mud gully to a broken wall and ramp.
1. 45m Climb the wall, heading towards a corner on the skyline. Trend right until a large ledge is visible on the left, and hand traverse to gain this ledge.
2. 10m Climb the broken rock on the left of a chimney near a vertical crack, to belay on a sloping slab below an overhang.
3. 5m Descend the slab to a good belay stance.
4. 15m Move across to the corner crack, and climb an off-width crack to the top.

NORTHERN HIGHLANDS SOUTH AND WEST
(VOLUME ONE)

DRUIM SHIONNACH, West Face:
Boxer's Buttress Right Hand – 100m IV,4. M. Moran, P. Bass. 27th January, 2002.
Two pitches of interesting and sustained mixed climbing up the right side of Boxer's Buttress starting from the base of Cave Gully.
1. 30m Go up left into a shallow weakness and climb it to belay at a huge detached block.
2. 30m Go up left then back right to surmount steep steps and bulges to join the normal route.
3. 40m Easy mixed ground then snow to the top; as for Boxer's Buttress.

A' CHRALAIG, Lochan na Cralaig:
Spiked – 80m III,4. A. and P. Lunn, A. Nisbet. 14th March, 2002.
The ridge above the S-shaped crack, but bypassing the initial steep wall on the right. Start on the left side of a bay, immediately beyond the steep wall. Climb up left on steep turf to reach the crest left of a pinnacle (30m). Pass the pinnacle on the far side, then continue up short steep walls near the crest to a final horizontal arête (30m). Finish easily along this (20m).

Kraken – 60m VI,6. A. and P. Lunn, A. Nisbet. 14th March, 2002.
A big groove, which leads from the top left corner of the bay to the end of the horizontal arête. Start from the top of the bay. Go up left and back right to join the groove, thereby missing an overhanging step. Climb the groove, step right into its continuation, go over a strenuous bulge and continue steeply to the top.

FUAR THOLL, Mainreachan Buttress:
Supersleuth – 240m VII,8. G. Robertson, P. Benson, J. Currie, 24th February, 2002.
The most direct version of Sleuth provides an excellent and sustained route.
1 and 2. 60m Climb the Sleuth Start to the First Terrace (60m).
3. 40m Above is a smooth barrier wall. Climb the very prominent thin torquing crack to a hard move below a steepening (crux). Step horizontally left and up into grooves which trend back right over an overhang.
4. 20m Step left into a short steep groove and climb this to easier ground which leads to the Great Terrace.
5. 40m Ten metres above is another steeper barrier wall, the only break in which is a groove just right of centre. Climb into and then up this with difficulty then with more ease to a ledge.
6. 80m Trend up rightwards to join and finish up Sleuth.

SGORR RUADH:
Ruayahua – 130m V,6. E. Brunskill, D. Morris. 22nd December, 2001.
This route climbs the broken buttress left of Brown Gully via the front face of the prominent tower. Start at the bottom left side of the buttress below a turfy groove just left of the first tower.

1. 30m Climb the turfy groove trending right to a chimney; climb this to the top of the first tower.
2. 30m Traverse left along the ledge on to the front face of the second tower. Climb into a black groove and traverse hard left until established in the steep cracks in the middle of the face. Climb these (crux) and continue in the same line to the top of the tower.
3 etc. 70m Climb the broken buttress above to the top (many variations possible)

MAOL CHEAN-DEARG:
Ketchil Buttress – III. D. McGimpsey, A. Nisbet. 22nd December, 2001.
Start just right of the crest by a groove which leads up left to a few tricky moves on the crest leading to an easy finish.

Ketchup Buttress – 100m II. D. McGimpsey, A. Nisbet. 22nd December, 2001.
Another buttress on the right. A long groove on its right flank leads to an easy finish on the crest.

Reraig Coastal Cliff (MR 826 363):
A steep 15m crag of bedded gneiss, reached by a 30 minute shoreline walk from Reraig Cottage (9km west of Lochcarron); non-tidal; fabulous outlook to Plockton and Skye. Explored by M. and A. Moran in September, 2001.
The Schtroumpf – 15m E3 6a. A fierce corner line at the left end of the crag.
Twinkle Toes – 18m HVS 5b. Climbs the big ramp from the left side of the crag with a short tricky section where it narrows.
Roaming the Gloaming – 16m Severe 4a. A parallel ramp line below and right of Twinkle Toes, finishing up a steep corner.

BEINN BHAN, Coire an Fhamhair:
Divine Retribution – 350m VII,6. C. Cartwright, R. Clothier. 16th February, 1991.
A more direct route up the Die Riesenwand face. Climb the first three pitches of Die Riesenwand to the obvious niche. Make the exposed right traverse to reach the start of the large snow ledge, then cut back left up an obvious rising shelf for 20m until directly above the niche. Cut back left for about 20m then go up a large right-facing corner/groove for another 20m. The right-facing corner line above develops into a groove system before easing into a shallow gully and easier ground. There is about 10m of steep climbing up this groove which develops into a shallow gully leading to easier ground. Climb the corner/groove system for 30m, then a further 150m of easier climbing to gains the top.

The Godfather – 230m VIII,8. M.E. Moran, P. Tattersall. 14th March, 2002.
A mixed adventure up the face between Gully of the Gods and Great Overhanging Gully finishing up the big left-facing corner in the upper tiers. Complex and sustained climbing with the cruxes high on the route. Start mid-way across the face right of a projecting overhang. The right-hand of two diagonal weaknesses provides the key to the lower wall.
1. 45m Climb rightwards to a terrace, move 8m right and climb a broken flaked corner to gain a narrow ledge; belay 4 metres back left along this.
2. 50m Go another 4m left, then make very steep moves to gain a right-slanting diagonal line which can spotted from below the route; this leads with continuous interest to a big balcony below the girdle ledge.

3. 50m Traverse the balcony for 30m rising slightly until a short fierce groove can
be climbed to reach the girdle ledge; traverse 10m along this to belay at a projecting
block.
4. 25m Go a further 5m along the ledge to below the big corner line then climb
straight up a series of steep mantelshelves to where the corner becomes defined.
5. 15m Go right to the smooth corner, but climb a subsidiary line just left of it
which is very steep but more helpful; belay up right at the base of the upper corner.
6. 25m Climb the corner past two overhanging sections (crux) to a ledge on the
right.
7. 20m Go more easily up the final bulge in the corner and exit up steep snow.

Note: The route recorded last year as *Impending Doom* has been climbed before
by Bruce Jardine in 1986 (when presumably it was thicker) and graded V. It has
been named *The Dwarf Icefall*. The thicker but shorter icefall to the right (IV,4),
climbed by B. Fyffe and O. Samuels seems to be new.

Coire Toll a' Bhein, Main Buttress:
Silent Witness – 270m III. A. Nisbet. 4th January, 2002.
A gully which leads to the col on the pinnacled ridge. Climb ice as direct as
possible into the gully (similar start to Threatening Behaviour). The gully leads
easily into a cave. Pass the cave by climbing the buttress to the right before making
a descending traverse back into the gully just above the cave. The next steep
section was climbed by a groove on the left of the gully bed (crux), then continue
up the gully to the col. After an awkward step, finish up the easier ridge to the
plateau.

Ardheslaig Sea Cliff (MR 777 575):
A tidal cliff of red gneiss with a fine westward outlook reached in 20 minutes
shore walk from Ardheslaig township. Routes by M. Moran and party, 2002.
High Tide, Green Grass – 20m Mild VS 4c. Climbs cracks and walls just right of
the bounding arête; can be accessed at all tides.

Shaggy Crack   20m V. Diff. The obvious chimney in the crag centre reached by
an entertaining 30m sea level traverse; not accessible at highest tides.

BEN DAMPH FOREST, Creag Dubh an t-Sall:
Despite the naming in SMCJ 2000, the name should refer to the smaller sandstone
crag passed on the way to the more impressive Creag na Speireag, the crag with
the previously recorded routes. Towards the right end of the smaller crag is an
arête with a big roof at its base.
Vespa – 10m Severe. M. Moran, A. Nisbet. 27th September, 2001.
A crackline starting 5m from the left end of the roof, passing a small tree at the
halfway horizontal break.

Apis – 10m Severe. M. Moran. 27th September, 2001.
A crackline starting where the left end of the roof meets the ground. This leads to
a finish up the right arête of a small V-groove.

Bombus – 10m E1 5b *. M. Moran, A. Nisbet. 27th September, 2001.
A steep and photogenic crackline with some strenuous moves in the wall right of
the arête, then its upper continuation.

Creag na Speireag:
Big Ears – 30m HVS 5a *. M. Moran, A. Nisbet. 27th September, 2001.
At the left end of the crag, just before it starts to decrease significantly in size, is
a big left-facing flake line. Climb the flake line (big Friends useful) to a horizontal
ledge below a capping roof. Traverse 5m left along the ledge and pull through the
roof at the first obvious break.

One Cog Missing – 30m E2 5c **. M. Moran, A. Nisbet. 27th September, 2001.
Start 3m right of the flake-line below cracks in the impending wall. Gain and
climb the crackline until it peters out, then traverse boldly right for 6m along a
break to gain a parallel crackline on the right. Climb this to the overhung shelf,
then straight over the roof and up a crack to the top.

Someone's Crack – 8m Severe. C. Moody, C. Grindley. 12th May, 2001.
Right of the previous routes is a hand crack.

Pea Soup – 10m HVS 5a *. C. Moody, C. Grindley. 12th May, 2001.
To the right are three thin cracks; climb the left hand one.

Lysfoss – 12m E2 5b/c *. C. Moody, C. Grindley. 12th May, 2001.
To the right is an obvious crack up a rib. Move left on a block to gain the bulge at
the start of the crack. Climb the bulge and continue to the top.

Unnamed – 10m HVS 5b. C. Moody, C. Grindley. 12th May, 2001.
This route is the right wall of Lysfoss which faces south. Start near the right side
of the wall, climb up to the break, then move left, then up.

BEINN DAMPH:
Note: SMCJ 2001 didn't say that *Calluna* is the first big gully right of Boundary
Gully (and Moonloop).

LIATHACH, Coire Dubh Mor:
Drumnadrookit – 220m V,6 *. E. Brunskill, A. Nisbet. 27th February, 2002.
The intended line of The Temptress, but the upper ice pitch doesn't always form.
Climb the introductory pitch and the steep groove as for The Temptress. Step
right and climb a long easier groove to bulging walls left of an impressive prow.
Ice forms through a slot about 20m left of the prow. Climb this finishing with a
short overhanging section to a terrace. Traverse the terrace rightwards until above
the prow and finish up the crest formed above it.

Meall Dearg, North Face:
North East Buttress – 200m III,4 (?). S. Archer, E. Brunskill (solo). December,
1992.
This buttress forms the left wall of Gully Obscura and provides good climbing up
the crest. Start near the foot of the gully. Details unsure.

BEINN EIGHE, Coire Mhic Fhearchair, Far East Wall:
Sidewinder – V,6. M. Moran, P. Bass. 31st January, 2002.

By the summer route. Interchangeable with Glow Worm, but the second pitch gives a good technical crux in gaining the base of the main right-slanting ramp.

Eastern Ramparts:
Rampart Wall – VII,8 ***. B. Davison, D. McGimpsey, A. Nisbet. 1st March, 2002.
A sensational line through some unlikely ground. Four pitches with belays as for summer. Start 10m left of the summer route and go up to the second of two ledge systems; this is about 10m up. Traverse right to near the summer route, ignoring tempting direct cracklines. Follow a grassy crack in a corner facing away and about 10m left of Pale Rider corner to reach the belay ledge. The traverse on pitch 2 is very thin and the technical crux. Tension was used for the delicate traverse on pitch 3 but it is short and there are possibilities for freeing it. On pitch 4, the narrow slab is smooth and a steeper groove on the left was climbed (Eastern Promise winter may have shared some of this pitch, which ices up.)

Central Buttress:
Gallus – 75m E1 5a. S. R. Scott, D. Carr. 3rd June, 2000.
Start just right of Porcine Connection at a ragged vertical crack.
1. 35m 5a Climb the crack for 20m to the bottom of the corner (touching Porcine Connection). Traverse a wide foot ledge right to a blunt rib below and right of the right-hand corner. Climb this for 5m then traverse left to a hanging stance at the foot of the right-hand corner.
2. 40m 4c Move back right to the rib, then climb diagonally up and right to a horizontal break which is followed right to a detached pillar overlooking the corner of the VS Route. Carefully climb the left-hand side of the pillar to a large grass ledge.

West Buttress:
Direct Finish to West Buttress – VI,7. A. Mullin (roped solo). 18th December, 2000.
By the summer route, sustained and well protected.

Creag Mhor (Independent Pineapple Cliff):
Milk Shake – 120m II. D. McGimpsey, A. Nisbet. 26th January, 2002.
The straight gully between the two flat-fronted ridges (Sidestep and Spog aig Giomach) has two steps which can bank out or be quite tricky when lean.

Jinx – 140m IV,5. D. McGimpsey, A. Nisbet. 28th November, 2001.
The line of least resistance up the steep face right of Midge Ridge. Start at the initial chimney of Autumn Rib (narrow and right-slanting).
1. 25m Climb the chimney, then squeeze through a slot on the left to gain a higher ledge.
2. 20m Traverse this ledge left, slightly descending and with a final crawl, to its very end.
3. 20m Step left into the base of a chimney-crack and climb it.
4. 40m Trend left up steep broken ground.
5. 35m Finish rightwards up a long groove.

Smilodon – 80m Severe 4a. A. Nisbet. 18th July, 2001.
Based on the rib between the left-hand and the huge central gully (Autumn Rib is left of the left-hand gully). Start near the base of the left wall of the central gully. Climb a short cracked wall to a ledge. Go left to the crest and back right to the base of a groove. Climb the groove to where two blocks protrude from a ledge on the left. Climb the wall on the left to step back into the groove for its last move. Go up an easy section and finish by a short bulge.

TORRIDON CRAGS, Seana Mheallan:
Dirty Dancing – 30m E2 5c. A. Cunningham, A. Fyffe. 31st May, 1999.
A route left of Left in the Lurch and right of the recess routes around Forgotten Corner. Start steeply via a crack in a prow and followed by a difficult entry into a shallow steep left-facing corner. Climb to the easing, move right, easier climbing to finish.

DIABAIG, Peninsula Crags, Twin walls:
Hot Head – 15m HVS 5a *. J. Preston, J. Lyall. 17th June, 2001.
Climbs the left side of the smaller wall left-hand wall, left of Red Crescent. Start beneath a steep juggy wall. Climb straight up to a prominent projecting block at two thirds height. Pass this on the right and finish up quartz cracks.

BEINN A' MHUINIDH, Waterfall Buttress:
Racing the Sun – 100m V,5. A. Lole, G. Stein. 31st December, 2001.
The line shares belays with the summer route Tuit, though the actual route on each pitch, the third in particular, is different. Start 20m right of the waterfall at the right hand toe of the buttress.
1. 15m Climb sloping ledges trending left to a ledge with a small pine tree growing from a crack 3m above the ledge.
2. 30m Step left from the ledge and climb a slab above trending left. After 15m climb a short chimney. Continue above this to a large ledge with a tree.
3. 35m Go up and right to gain a steep chimney. Climb this and more heathery steps to gain the base of a wide crack.
4. Traverse easily right along a ledge until able to gain easy ground above.

FURNACE CRAGS, Brown Slab Crag (MR 963 706):
This is at the west end of the ridge of crag which contains Creag Mhor at the eastern end. The crag contains a fine brown slab facing south-west. All the routes were soloed by J. R. Mackenzie on 27th June, 2001. The rock is a good horneblende schist.
Brown Slabs Direct – 30m Severe *.
Start left of the corner by a thin crack and below a shallow rib at the top. Climb the slab to and up the rib on good crinkly rock.

Brown Slabs Left – 25m V. Diff *.
Climb straight up 4m left of the Direct over an overlap and up brown rock above.

Brown Slabs Right – 30m Severe.
Start near the corner and climb straight up to near a recess. Move left up the shallow rib finishing as for the Direct.

Creag Mhor:

This is at the right end of the ridge a km or so east of Furnace, identified by the grass strip leading up to its left side. The rock is a friendly hornblende schist though not always protectable but often climbable in the wet. The routes are described from left to right.

Left Wall – 60m HVS 5a. J. R. Mackenzie, S. R. T. Harper. Summer 2001.
The wall at the base of the crag has a left-facing corner; start left of this.
1. 45m 5a Climb a vertical wall past an overlap to slabs and continue much more easily up these to a thread above a heather rake.
2. 15m Climb the easy ramp right of the heather rake to the top.
Disjointed climbing with a good start. A more balanced V.Diff can be made by starting at the left end of the crag and moving up right to join the slabs.

Creag Mhor Cracks – 60m VS 4c **. J. R. Mackenzie (solo). 27th May, 2001.
A very good route. Start at a pair of short parallel cracks which lie just left of the slanting ramp of The Mad Fencer.
1. 40m 4c Climb up these cracks and over the little overhang above. Step left and climb the thin slabs direct over a brown slab to belays near the heather rake.
2. 40m 4a Move right to a shallow groove right of the rake and climb this up, then right to the top.

The Mad Fencer, Direct Variation – 60m H. Severe 4b. J. R. Mackenzie, S. R. T. Harper. Summer, 2001.
The original route here follows an illogical line. The direct is more logical.
1. 40m 4b From the belay ledge (which has no adequate belay) above the initial pitch continue straight up past a heather ledge to belays 3m right of the heather rake.
2. 20m 4a Climb the shallow groove as for Creag Mhor Cracks to finish.

Friends in High Places – 60m E2 5b *. J. R. Mackenzie, S. R. T. Harper. Summer, 2001.
A good route with a bold crux. Start below the overhanging curl of rock which lies above a ramp right of the Mad Fencer.
1. 35m 5b Climb easily to the ramp, then move to the left end of the wall and up this via a short bulge to traverse right past a small tree below a steep brown slab of excellent rock. Climb the steepening slab, moving up left to gain a narrow ledge, crux. Continue to a break above and thread.
2. 25m 4a Climb up right past broken ribs to the vertical back wall left of the Mad Fencer's crack. Climb the wall leftwards via a groove to the top.

The crags below described in the guide are not of rough gneiss but are of good quality horneblende schist.

Caisteal Mor:

The southern frontage of this crag is a vertical wall starting above a grass crevasse, sheltered but midgy! Various deer trods lead above the track to the crag avoiding the worst of the heather.
Crevasse Wall – 145m HVS 5a. J. R. Mackenzie, S. R. T. Harper. Summer, 2001.
Start at a slim pillar/flake roughly midway along the wall.

1. 15m 4c Climb this to a ledge and belays below a flake overhang on the left, an excellent pitch.
2. 45m 5a Climb over the overhang and trend up a diagonal leftwards line on blocky rock, under another overhang and up right past it to belays below a slab.
3. Go up the easy slab to a heather terrace.
4. 45m 4c Climb a short steep slab via a crack, then up easy slabs to finish.

No.1 Buttress, Riabhach Slab:
The right-hand boundary wall of the slab is of more continuously steep rock, avoiding some of the heather of the front face.
Sidewinder – 120m VS 4c *. J. R. Mackenzie, S. R. T. Harper. Summer, 2001.
A pleasantly relaxed line with some good but mossy rock lower down. To the right of the original line is a sidewall with a flake near boundary between south and east faces. Start right of the flake at the first thin crack.
1. 35m 4c Climb this direct to a slanting crack and follow this to belays beyond the right end of a heather ledge.
2. 40m 4b Climb the pleasant slab above, then an easier slab to below a final steeper slab.
3. 40m 4b Climb the steeper slab direct to the top.

RUBHA MOR, Black Heart Crag (MR 864 985):
Five routes by J.R. Mackenzie and D. S. B. Wright on 25th September, 2000. Details on request.

STONE VALLEY CRAGS, The Valley Walls:
These are the walls and slabs that line the left side of the obvious shallow, narrow valley that forms a col on the skyline at the left-hand end of the Stone Valley Crags. The walls start at a short vertical bow-shaped wall at the entrance to the narrow valley and lead to a pleasant line of slabs running along its left side. Flowerdale Wall, the bigger wall facing the approach, lies on the right at the entrance to the valley. The first routes lie on the steeper, bow-shaped wall at the entrance to the valley.
Round the Block – 20m VS/HVS 4c. R. and C. Anderson. 18th August, 2001.
At the left end of the steeper wall is a flakeline. Climb the wall to the right of this to reach the flake, then move up this to its top and climb a short blocky crack to the top.

Flash in the Pan – 20m E4 6a/b *. R. Anderson. 18th August, 2001.
The thin crack immediately to the right of Round the Block is climbed with difficulty, protected by good but small wires. Continue up the more obvious crack in the final wall.

Off the Block – 20m E2 5b *. R. and C. Anderson. 18th August, 2001.
The central line. Climb up and step onto the obvious block then climb the crack to easier ground. The top of the flake was not pulled on.

The following route lies on the stepped slab a short way to the right, above the flat floor of the valley.

Three Stepped Slab – 25m HVS 4c *. R. and C. Anderson. 18th August, 2001.
Just right of an obvious fault is a crack with an obvious jug at its base. Climb this thin crack up the first step. Climb directly up the wall above to easy ground and traverse left to climb the third step past a block.

Flowerdale Wall:
The following routes lie on the right side of the crag where there is a prominent arête with streaks of quartz running down it.
Quartzite Bird Shite – 15m HVS 5a. P. Tattersall, J. Buchanan. 19th March, 2001.
On good rock right of Mountain Everlasting, with a white saltire intrusion.

White Lining – 25m E1 5b *. R. and C. Anderson. 18th August, 2001.
The arête has a prominent narrow streak of white quartz running down it which stops short of the base of the crag at the start of a bottomless groove and flake line. Climb up the fault to the right of the arête to a spike. Swing left into the bottomless groove at the base of the white line, then gain the flakeline and follow this up the right side of the arête to finish easily up slabby ground.
Note: WL starts about 2m to the right of QBS and they both finish almost at the same point.

Avoid the Paint – 12m VS 4c. P. Tattersall, J. Buchanan. 19th March, 2001.
Right again, the last obvious line.

Rum Doodle Crag:
Heavyweights – 10m VS 5a. A. Cunningham, B. Fyffe. 7th April, 2001.
Start up the chimney right of Go Lightly, move right and finish up the left side of the wall above the heathery ledge.

Unnamed – 10m E2 5c. B. Fyffe, A. Cunningham. 7th April, 2001.
Climbs the steep prow left of Go Lightly. Start up a capped groove and pull over the roof on to a ramp. Climb onto the front of the prow and to finish leftwards. A high runner up the ramp can be used to protect.

Note: Several easier slabby and fairly minor routes were climbed by Dundonnell MRT; details on request.

Stone Valley Crag:
No Mutton – 15m H. Severe 4a. S. Blagbrough, G. McEwan. 27th April, 2001.
Starts on the ledge to the left of No Beef. Climb to a ledge, then an open right-facing corner and crack to easy ground.

No Robins – 18m E2 5c. G. Ettle, J. Lyall. 3rd June, 2000.
Start as for No Beef, but where that route steps right, continue up a thin crackline to finish at the same point. Protection is available but difficult to place.

Open Secret Direct Start – 35m HVS 5a **. J. R. Mackenzie, S. R. Harper. April, 2001.
Very good but poorly protected climbing squeezed between the initial pitches of Open Secret and Bald Eagle. Start at the base of the shallow corner of Bald Eagle

Doré Green climbing the 'Younggrat' on the Breithorn, Central Pennine Alps, Switzerland. Photo: Simon Richardson.

The Fann Mountains of Tajickistan. Photo: Rick Allen.

and climb the steep crack on its left to reach the slab via a suspect flake. Climb the slab and overlap direct to join Open Secret.

Right-Hand Dome:
Long Walk, Short Climb – 50m Severe. J. R. Mackenzie, S. R. Harper. April, 2001.
The right-hand wall has a steep rib to the right of a pink slab. Climb the rib and step left on to the front face to reach easy ground after 10m. Pleasant scrambling to the top.

RAVEN'S CRAG AREA:
Many routes have been climbed on several crags near Raven's Crag, including Fruity Crag (MR 794 714), Sneaky Crag (MR 792 713), Druid Rock (MR 793 716) and Vegie Crag (MR 795 716). Route descriptions available by e-mail on request.

BAOSBHEINN, The Rona Face:
This is the cliff located at MR 867 657 and facing WSW.
Merlinswanda – 210m IV,5. E. Brunskill, V. Chelton, D. McGimpsey. 12th March, 2002.
This interesting route climbs the left edge of the highest section of cliff. Start at the lowest left toe of the buttress below an obvious steep groove.
1. 15m Climb the groove to belay up and left at a good thread.
2. 40m Follow the groove directly above to a terrace.
3. 20m Climb the shallow groove trending first right then back left to below an obvious deep chimney.
4. 20m Climb the fine chimney and continue up to a spike.
5. 45m Climb up and right aiming for an obvious ramp which slants left to the top of the tower. Belay halfway up the ramp.
6. 30m Continue to the top of the ramp, then climb straight up by a series of grooves to a terrace.
7. 40m Follow the easiest line to the top.

GAIRLOCH CRAGS, Creag Bhadan an Aisg (NG 826 782):
This crag stands on the west side of the main A832 from Gairloch to Poolewe, about 100m from the road. It has a slabby left-hand section, where the first described routes lie, along with a mainly overhanging right-hand wall. The rock on the slabs is good rough Lewisian Gneiss, less good on the steeper section. The old dry stonework below the steep section may be the grave of two young Mackenzie heirs horribly murdered in the 15th century; hence the name of the crag – The Crag of the Place of the Burial.

Blonde Bitch's Buttress:
This is the slabby left-hand part of the crag, about 25m high, separated from the overhanging crag by a grassy descent gully. Good steep slabs, not always well protected.
Handbagged – 20m H. Severe 4b *. C. Maclellan, R. J. F. Brown, D. S. B. Wright. 30th April, 2001.

The peaks of Batian, Nelion, Point John and Midget Peak, Mount Kenya, East Africa. Photo: Tom Prentice.

Dhaulagiri from below Dgorali, Annapurna Region, Nepal. Photo: David Ritchie.

On the left of the crag, just right of some ivy and behind a tree, is a recess. Start here, go steeply up a wall, then delicately to the top break. Go slightly left between two cracks to finish.

Blondes Don't Reverse – 23m VS 4c. C. Maclellan, R. J. F. Brown, D. S. B. Wright. 30th April, 2001.
Climb the obvious central rib, with a delicate step where the crack steepens. Good protection where it matters.

5.10 Stillettos – 22m VS 4c. C. Maclellan, R. J. F. Brown, D. S. B. Wright. 30th April, 2001.
There is an obvious flaky line to the right of the central rib. Climb this, with some delicate moves where the flakes run out. Go right, then straight up through the break to finish.

Lip Gloss – 22m H. Severe 4b. C. Maclellan, R. J. F. Brown, D. S. B. Wright. 30th April, 2001.
The rough slabs to the right of the flake line give good, though somewhat artificial climbing on excellent rough rock.

Nameless Buttress:
This is the overhanging right-hand sector of the crag.
Unnamed – 12m E3 5c *. R. A. Biggar, C. Maclellan. 11th May, 2001.
At the left-hand end of the crag is a wall of good rough rock with an overhanging headwall split by a thin crack.

Unnamed – 12m E2 5b. R. A. Biggar, C. Maclellan. 11th May, 2001.
At the far right end of the crag is an off-width crack. The climb uses the crack and the wall to its right.

LOCH TOLLAIDH, Flag Wall:
Deliver Me – 12m E1 5a. L. Johnson, F. Bennet. 20th April, 2001.
Climb to a ledge left of the left arête of the main wall. Continue up just left of the arête via shallow grooves.

Raven's Nest:
Blast Off – 20m E4 6a. P Tattersall. 2000.
Climb the steep wall between Boldered-out and Blow-out to reach the base of a short vegetated corner, place a runner and tackle the bulge on the right to finish.

The Ewe Walls:
Ewe Tree Slab – 25m VS 4c. P. Tattersall. 21st March, 2001.
The slab with no tree (right of Ewephoria). Better than it looks.

Foot in Mouth – 20m E1 5b. P. Tattersall. 21st March, 2001.
Start just right of some fallen debris. Make a steep start, then move right into a hanging scoop. Go directly up on blind but good holds, then easily to a rather rounded finish.

Dinosaur Buttress:
Chitin – 8m VS 5a. A. Cunningham, D. Gemmell. 1999.
The small buttress about 30m right and up from Dinosaur Buttress. Climb the crack in the nose direct.

The Curra Wall, Upper Tier:
Pieces of Eight – 10m V. Diff. A. Fyffe, A. Cunningham. 25th April, 1999.
Start just right of the rib of After Eight and climb up and right into a short steep left-facing corner.

Fraggle Rock, Upper Tier (on left):
Arctic Dreams 20m E2 5b *. P. Tattersall, T. Doe. 7th April, 2001.
The centre of the upper tier forms a very open corner with steep walls either side. The three routes (also Dr Beaker) are on the left-hand wall, which has a slight crest. Start well left of the crest and climb a right-slanting intermittent crackline. Where this ends, make a difficult move right to a ledge and finish direct.

Deathmarch – 20m E3 5b. P. Tattersall, T. Doe. 8th May, 2001.
Climb the crest direct.

Fraggle Roll Direct Finish (Roll Up) – E3 5c *. L. Hughes, A. Cunningham. 27th April, 2001.
Climb through the holly and up the crack above.

Barking Shark – 30m E2 5b. P. Tattersall, T. Doe. 7th April, 2001.
Start below a small roof just right of Fraggle Roll. A broken crack-line leads to easy ground which is followed leftwards to an obvious finishing flake-crack.

Hidden Crag:
Mud Wrestler – 15m HVS 5a. A. Cunningham, A. Fyffe, B. Fyffe. 23rd June, 1999.
Climbs near the right end of the shorter wall round the edge left of Water Lily. Move up to a series of left-curving cracks leading onto the big heathery ledge.

Wedgie – 15m H. Severe 4b *. A. Cunningham, S. Blagbrough, G. McEwan. 25th April, 2001.
A climb on the pink wedge shaped buttress behind and left of Hidden Crag. Climb the lower section just right of a heather fault to the ledge. Climb the middle of the wall with a steep start.

Shotgun Wedding – 25m E3 5c. P. Tattersall. 8th April, 2001.
To the right of Malpasso is an upper heather terrace with this crack-line starting from it. The finishing slab is easy but unprotected.

Shadesville:
A wall right of and at right-angles to Hidden Crag.
Bitches from Hell – 20m E3 6a. M. Garthwaite, C. Smith. 2001.
Follow the crackline left of Unrepeatable to a break. Step left and climb the short wall on good holds to the top.

Unrepeatable – 20m E2 5c. P. Tattersall, T. Doe. 11th April, 2001.
The crack-line at the right side of the wall.

Upper Tier:
Eight more routes on Fetish Crag and two on Buttock Buttress. Details from
www.wildwesttopos.com.

Inlet Wall:
Chopsticks – 25m E3 5b. P. Tattersall, T. Doe. 7th May, 2001.
Left end of the crag (no details).

For Schny Dung – 15m E2 5c. P. Tattersall, C. Meek. 1st May, 2001.
The dirty groove left of the main wall.

Fill An Der – 25m E3 5c. P. Tattersall, C. Meek. 1st May, 2001.
The orange pillar and flakes left of Lifeline.

Primrose Slab – 25m VS 4c *. K. and G. Latter. 4th April, 2002.
At the far right end of the crag, overlooking Recessed Wall is a clean slab of fine
rough rock. Gain the easy-angled slab by a steeper start and climb this more easily,
finishing up the central heather crack.

Recessed Wall:
Recessed Groove – 20m E2 5b *. A. Cunningham, L. Hughes. 4th May, 2001.
A climb up the right side of the wall with a difficult start which is sometimes wet.
Climb to the first good break near a bush, move slightly left and up into the groove.
Climb to the block on Tortured Soul and finish direct.

Wee Lochan Crag:
Several more smallish routes in this area. Details from www.wildwesttopos.com.

GRUINARD CRAGS, The Beach Wall (see SMCJ 2001):
Beach Groove Garden – 20m Mild VS 4b. A. Cunningham,L. Hughes. 19th April,
1998.
The V-groove at the left end of the crag.

Armburger: As in SMCJ 2001 but graded E2 5b.**
Dechno: As in SMCJ 2001.

The next four routes are on the right-hand buttress. The unnamed route in SMCJ
2001 is a combination.
Aorta – 20m E2 5c *. A. Cunningham, D. Neville. 30th April, 1999.
Start at an overhung groove at the right side of the big recess. Climb up the awkward
groove to pull through the bulge at a crack at about 5m and onto the wall. Move
slightly left and straight up the fine headwall to finish.

Adalat – 20m VS 4c. A. Cunningham, D. Neville. 30th April, 1999.
Start as for Aorta and climb the right slanting crack and edge round onto the front

of the buttress. Move up and follow the right trending crackline near the right edge of the crag to the top.

Capillary Wall – 20m HVS 5a *. A. Cunningham, L. Hughes, 19th April, 1998.
Start at the lowest rocks to the right of the recess. Climb the middle of the lower buttress, through the wide diagonal break, crossing Adalat and straight up the cracked buttress passing a niche near the top.

Voltarol – 20m Severe. A. Cunningham, D. Neville. 30th April, 1999.
A route up the sidewall. Start under a short groove leading to a square roof. Climb steeply into the groove, move right at the roof onto the edge and finish straight up.

Road Crag (Roadside Wall, SMCJ 2001):
An insignificant looking SW-facing brown triangular shaped crag, easily seen above the road and powerlines when heading north from the main Gruinard beach car park. Better climbing than one would imagine! Descend by scrambing to the left, facing out and into the grassy gully. From right to left;
Celtic Ray – 15m HVS 5a. P. Holmes, A. Cunningham. 25th March, 1999.
Start at the right-hand end, above and right of a rose bush. Climb delicately left across a hanging slab under a roof and follow a deep left-trending crack to the top.

Mongo – 20m E2 5c *. L. Hughes, A. Cunningham. September, 2000.
Start down left of the rose bush. Climb up to and follow the diagonal break under the bulge and break through at a steep capped groove. Swing right, crux, and up via hidden holds, moving back left finishing right of the top crack of Raglan Road.

Raglan Road – 20m E1 5b **. A. Cunningham, P. Holmes. 25th March, 1999.
Start in the middle of the crag and under an obvious crack in the headwall. Good climbing. Climb steeply up and left into the central scoop. Go up this, small wires and exit rightwards into a crack leading to the big diagonal break. Finish up the steep crack in the headwall.

Tom Jones – 15m HVS 5a. A. Cunningham, L. Hughes. September, 2000.
A route on the slabby left side of the crag. Start a few metres left of Raglan Road and gain and climb a left curving flake. Long reaches for good hidden holds lead into the wide crack to finish.

Post Crag:
Post-it – 12m HVS 5a *. G. and K. Latter. 5th April, 2002.
The prominent blunt left arête of the smooth wall. Well protected.

Bog Meadow Wall Note: G. Latter repeated Summer Breeze, E5 6b and ***
after the PR removed by another party. Very well protected – only the 0.1#Camalot required in the description.

The Bayview Wall, Lower Tier:
Below Bayview Wall is a more broken section of rock. The following route lies on the attractive buttress of gnarly rock characterised by ivy growing on its left side.

Temporary Beauty – 10m VS 5a *. A. Fyffe, A. Cunningham. 4th July, 2000.
A good climb up interesting rock. Start just left of centre and climb steeply up to gain the prominent flakes. Take the natural line up and right and step left to finish.

The Bayview Wall:
Something Completely Different – 12m E2 5c. A. Cunningham, A. Fyffe. 4th July, 2000.
A short but strenuous route up the front face of the chokestone of Chokestone Gully. Start in the shadow of the chokestone and climb out the left side of the gully. Pull into and climb the short corner on the chokestone and out left via the flake crack.

Fox's Buttress (MR 958 895):
This is the narrow buttress in the corner of the dome between Optic Wall and Dog Crag. It is characterised by a fine flat-faced pillar of good rock with some deep red grooves on the right.
Gone to Ground – 10m HVS 5a. A. Cunningham, A. Fyffe. 4th July, 2000
On the left of the narrow buttress is a crack slanting right. Climb the crack and the wall on its right to finish.

Glacier Mint – 15m E1 5b **. A. Cunningham, A. Fyffe. 16th April, 2000
Fine climbing up the front of the narrow pillar. Climb the front of the pillar using the obvious ledge and the thin diagonal crack on its left. Pull right into the scoop and finish straight up.

Foxtrot – 15m HVS 5a. J. Lyall, J. Preston. 16th June, 2001
The arête left of Vulpine Groove, finishing by a short crack.

Vulpine Groove – 15m HVS 5a. A. Fyffe, A. Cunningham. 16th April, 2000
The deep red groove on the immediate right of the pillar is gained from the right and followed steeply throughout.

Barking – 15m E1 5b. J. Lyall, J. Preston. 16th June, 2001
The steep crack just right of Vulpine Groove, slanting right to finish.

Earth Matters – 15m HVS 5a. J. Lyall, J. Preston. 16th June, 2001
The leaning corner-crack right of Barking. There is a small aspen on the right a few metres up. Well protected throughout.

Around 75m up and left of Fox's Buttress is quite a large diamond-shaped slab.
Diamond Slab – 20m VS 4c. J. Preston (unsec). 14th July, 2001
Starting at the lowest point, climb the slab direct to a heathery ledge. Finish up a short steep wall by a projecting block.

Dog Crag:
Dogged Persistence – 20m E3 5c. A. Cunningham, A. Fyffe. 4th July, 2000
Start 5m right of the wide crack of Tess. Climb into a vague pink scoop, move left and gain the short but obvious crack. Climb the crack (crux) to the easing in angle and finish up by the crack in the black rock above. P. Tattersall thinks E2 5c.

Chimney Crag:
Not in Vein – 20m Severe. J. Preston. 14th July, 2001
On a section of rock on the upper right side of the crag, reached by traversing in from the left along heather and rock ledges. The route climbs a quartz vein and slabs above.

Lochan Dubh Crag (Dome Crag):
Sunset Song – 35m. E1 5b *. A. Cunningham, A. Fyffe. 12th October, 2001.
A nice pitch between the second pitches of Ducks with Attitude and Scrabble. Walk in to the start from the right. Climb a thin crack with difficult moves into the shallow groove. From the ledge climb more or less direct to the top.

Carn Goraig:
Bootless Crow – 55m HVS *. A. Cunningham, R. Baines. 6th May, 2000.
At the right end of the second tier are two steep cracklines. This route climbs the bottomless right-hand crack and Ramadan takes the left-hand crack.
1. 25m 5a Start at a mossy groove bounding the right side of the second tier. Climb clean rock right of the moss and take an obvious left trending line joining the main crack at an 'orange hole'. Follow the cracks above on to the slabs and climb up to belay below a wide blocky Y crack in the upper tier.
2. 30m 4c Move right on to a huge block and climb the rightmost steepening crack and continuation to a heather bay. Follow the line of vague cracks above.

Note: Thunderhead (SMCJ 2001) was previously climbed by A. Cunningham and R. Baines on 6th May, 2000 with a slightly different start and called Old Goats (E2 *).

Upper Tier:
Cursing Crack – 30m E3 6a *. G. Latter. 6th April, 2002.
Left of the triple cracks of Wailing Wall/Call of the Muwazzin are a further three parallel left-slanting cracks, the right two similarly close together. Climb the rightmost crack which is viciously sharp with difficulty to better holds in a recess. Continue up easier crack above, then up wall to finish up a prominent crack at the top, a few metres left of an easier looking slightly lichenous crack. Climbed in error for the final pitch of Wailing Wall, hence the name!

The Saracens – 35m HVS 5a **. G. and K. Latter. 6th April, 2002.
The left-slanting ramp and flake system starting from just above the belay on Thunder-head. Climb easy lower ramp, then the flake and continue in the same left-trending line, with a long span left to gain a good crack at one point. Finish up a short steep crack to belay at a huge block. Scramble off.

Jetty Crag:
The following two routes have almost certainly been climbed before.
Pearl Harbour – 30m HVS 5a.**. R and C Anderson. 16th June, 2001.
Climb directly to the crack in the wall right of Crab Crack and follow this into the large alcove, step right onto the blunt crest and follow this to easy slabs. Finish up the obvious short steep crack in the headwall.

Dockers Groove – 35m VS 4c/5a *. R and C Anderson. 16th June, 2001.
Start beneath the obvious groove in the slab between Munroron and Lilly the Pink. Climb to a small roof and make an awkward entry up right into the groove which is followed to its top and a finish up the slabby edge as for Munroron.

TORR NA H'IOLAIRE, The West Face of Upper Summit Buttress:
Tiger Lily – 120m VS. A. Nisbet. 8th August, 2001.
A route designed to keep to the cleanest rock. Start about 10m right of Hieroglyphics, at the right end of the level base of the slab.
1. 45m 4b Climb the main slab trending slightly left to reach and climb a right-facing corner near the top. Continue up and slightly right to a pedestal which is at the right end of the grass ledge of Hieroglyphics.
2. 45m 4b Climb the steep wall behind the pedestal on big holds, then continue slightly right on equally big holds, keeping to the best rock, until grassy ground is found on the right.
3. 30m Climb leftwards up a vague rib to the top.

Note: Arabic (SMCJ 1995) seems to be similar to Suspension (1959) in the guide (but C. Moody disagrees).

CARNAN BAN, Maiden Buttress:
Sleeping Beauty – 115m VS *. A. Nisbet. 8th August, 2001.
Right of the prominent V-slab of Ecstasy is a recessed inverted V. This route climbs the right corner of the V, then the crackline above. Start from the first platform left of the bottom left corner of the buttress.
1. 30m 4b Climb the corner to a ledge below a vertical section with a small overhang.
2. 20m 4c Climb this vertical section leading to the top of the V, then the crackline above to a big ledge.
3. 20m 4b Climb the crack above, initially overhanging.
4. 45m 4a Continue up the crack over two steep sections.

The following is two linked routes on the crest between the slopes with Barndance Slabs and Maiden Buttress. No great quality but arrives at the top of the descent ramp leading to Maiden Buttress.
Blind Date – 100m + walking H. Severe 4b/V.Diff. A. Nisbet. 8th August, 2001.
Low down on the crest is a clean patch of slab. Start at its base where there are cracked blocks in a steep wall. Climb the wall on surprising holds to reach a slabby ramp leading up left. Go up this until a crack leads up (crux) to a higher and thinner ramp. Go up this until the wall above can be climbed right of a recess. Finish up padding slabs (40m). Walk up to the prominent rocky nose above. There are several ribs which look possible on its left side but the longest and easiest rib was chosen. Start at the lowest rib on the left. Climb this, leading into a scoop. Go up the scoop and move right to finish up a blocky rib (60m).

Ghost Slabs:
Spirit of Letterewe – 370m E3 **. J. R. Mackenzie, S. R. T. Harper. July, 2001.
A fine, but bold line, taking the centre of the left-hand slabs via the two overlaps.

There are sections where the leader (and possibly second) 'must not fall'. Start at a boulder above the loch.
1. 50m Climb the easy slab aiming for a tree below a corner up left.
2. 45m Continue in the same line up black juggy rock, moving left to belay.
3. 25m Continue up a black slab to a tree belay.
4. 40m 5b Move left to a steep rib overlooking a corner and climb this direct with poor protection to step left to a crack. Continue straight up the slab to below the left end of the first overlap.
5. 50m 5a Climb a steep groove (last protection) to step right on to the lip of the overlap. Traverse right in an exposed position, then go straight up the middle of the excellent slab to a small groove on the left.
6. 50m 4c Climb up the slab to the second overlap (often wet) and traverse left under it to a hidden chimney. Climb the steep juggy chimney to exit right on to a narrow ledge. Traverse to its right end and a diagonal crack (poor belays).
7. 40m 5a Climb above to a fine slab, unprotected and climbed centrally to a heather cornice and ledge above. Climb the final short slab to grass and trees below the funnel.
8. 50m 4c The funnel starts with wet and goat-trodden chimneys, soon steepening to an overhanging black chimney. Move left and climb a fine but bold groove to an easing, move right into a short chimney, then back left up pleasant slabs to where the funnel opens out.
9. 20m Move back right into the exit chimney climbed on huge spike holds.

NORTHERN HIGHLANDS NORTH (VOLUME TWO)

SGURR NA LAPAICH, Sgurr nan Clachan Geala:
Lap Dance (SMCJ 2001): Pitch 1 should read: A sloping ledge approx. one-third way up the face, not halfway.

GLENMARKSIE CRAG:
The Conjuror – 40m HVS 5b **. R Biggar and partner (lower pitch). Summer, 2000. Top pitch – R. Biggar, J. R. Mackenzie. 30th March, 2000.
A fine route that climbs the slabby walls below and above the big overhangs of the Juggler. It gives two contrasting pitches with the top pitch providing the meat of the climb. Start below a short wall up left of The Juggler and down from Dog Leg.
1. 22m 5a Climb the wall to easier slabs which are followed to below the big roof.
2. 18m 5b Traverse the horizontal crack rightwards and then directly up the vertical crack to a shelf. Climb the crack up left, stepping over the overhang en route to finish up the rippled slabby headwall, an excellent pitch.

SGURR NA MUICE:
Cold Litter – 130m IV,4 *. J. R. Mackenzie. 2nd March, 2002.
This is the steeper and narrower gully to the right of Piglet, which has a clutch of tiny trees in the lower groove. Climb the groove which has a steep exit near to the edge of Swine Fever. Move left to a pair of thin grooves and climb the left one to a small bay. Step up right below a jutting flake to gain the base of another narrow

groove which ends in a deep crack. Climb this to reach the snow ramp that runs below the top crags. Immediately above is a huge block and a recess in the wall above. Climb the crux, a thinly iced corner in the recess and step up left to climb more easily to the top. The line followed gave the best climbing, grade III apart from the crux, but is escapable (otherwise **).

Styless – 125m III *. D. Broadhead, J. R. Mackenzie. 16th February, 2002.
A pleasantly sustained romp up turfy grooves, chimneys and other entertainments, well protected with good belays. To the right of Sty High is a rib that has a shallow turfy chimney line. Climb this direct to an overhang (50m). Move right to a similar groove and up this to below a steepening (25m). Continue in the same line over various obstacles (25m). Continue up more fun and games to the top (25m). The route could be extended by one of the direct starts.

If Pigs Could Fly – 165m III * J. R. Mackenzie (solo). 21st March, 2002.
A fine route of sustained steepness in the next bay left of Gammon Gully. It holds snow readily and probably keeps its condition longer than any other route here, being very sheltered. Climbed under well frozen turf but sugary snow. The left recess of the bay contains the line, a fine narrow hose of ice or turf which is followed to a chimney. Turn this on the right and continue straight up to the top over turfy bulges. Occasional cornice. Belays would seem to be thin on the ground but might be more obvious in thinner conditions.

Pork Chop Grooves – 100m II. J. R. Mackenzie. 2nd March, 2002.
This lies on the broken but pleasantly steep summit buttress that lies between Gammon Gully and Pigsty Gully. It forms a good finish to Gammon Gully or can easily be reached from above by descending the snow slope (grade I) from the little col just north of the summit. The buttress lies north and adjacent to the slope. It is often in condition being high up. Left of centre is a narrow rock rib that harbours a narrow turf groove to its right. Climb this groove to its exit and then follow the continuation groove to the top. Good solid turf climbing.

STRUIE HILL CRAG:
D. Allan notes that the MR for the crag should be 657 848 (the guide is wrong).
Struie Icefall – 25m IV,4. D. Allan. 3rd January, 2002.
In the centre of the crag, a steepish icefall forms most winters. It is clearly visible from the road. Climb it and the heathery corner above.

FANNICHS, Carn na Criche:
The first two climbs are at the very left end of the steep lower band of the crag where four icefalls lie about 20m left of the crag end and about 50m left of the first of the full height routes (Blood on the Tracks).
Saboteur's Delight – 30m IV,4 **. W. Deadman, R. I. Jones. 1st March 2002.
The leftmost icefall is a left-slanting ramp; short but enjoyable.

Huntsman's Anguish – 45m IV,4. R. I. Jones, W. Deadman. 1st March 2002.
The next unclimbed icefall is 4m right of Saboteur's Delight. This route is another 4m right. Start just right of a slightly projecting block. Climb the lower icefalls

delicately on their left, then direct to the top. Easier if started on the left of the block and lower ice falls not taken direct. The fourth icefall is a large icicle about 10m further right, not fully formed.

Sgurr nan Clach Geala, Summit Buttress:
East of the summit is a high corrie ringed by cliffs. Most of these are short but the south side of the corrie is a larger buttress which separates the corrie from the south-east face.

Fusilier – 250m IV,5. D. McGimpsey, A. Nisbet. 31st January, 2002.
Climbs a big groove system in the larger buttress. Much is easy but there are short steep sections which could bank up and reduce the route to grade III. Start up the main groove to steep walls (45m). Go right up a ramp, then straight up to more steep walls (45m). Continue up a wide right-trending groove and a short steep wall (crux) to a prominent chimney (40m). The chimney is possible but it is easier to traverse right and step down on to iced slabs which are then climbed to reach an ice bulge which leads to an easier section (50m). A short steep groove leads to easier ground followed to the upper crest (45m). Finish up the crest which leads to the ridge just south of the summit (25m).

BEINN DEARG, Coire Ghranda:
Rogue Trader – 250m IV,4. J. Lyall. 18th March, 2002.
Start in a snow bay between Yon Spoot and Grotto Gully and take a left-slanting line into a chimney. Climb the chimney and broken ground to a terrace, then a short ice pitch to a second terrace. Follow the obvious fault on the upper tier, going right, then back left in the final section.

Coire Ghranda, Upper Cliff:
The Big Chill – 150m VII,7 **. G. and P. Robertson. 1st March, 2002.
Another excellent and icy mixed route taking the first natural line right of Ice Bomb. An obvious feature is the big plume of ice flowing from a groove high up (right of Damoclean icicles). Start about 20m right of the fault of Ice Bomb directly below an overhanging nose of rock.
1. 50m Climb directly up to underneath the nose then follow a right-trending fault over difficult bulges to a perch by a protruding spike.
2. 50m Pull directly over the bulge, then move left to follow the obvious line to below thinly iced grooves. Climb these direct to a poor belay at the top of a tapering ramp (junction with Cold War).
3. 50m Step down and left on to steep thin ice and pull up to a thin ramp. Move right along this to gain and climb the ice plume direct into the easier upper groove. On the first ascent (in excellent conditions) there was a nasty sting in the tale.

RHUE SEA CLIFFS, First Prow:
How Now Brown Prow – 15m E2 5b. T. Rankin, G. Lennox. 10th June, 2001.
Basically The Prow direct. Start below Halcyon Days' top corner and pull up to stand on the first break. Traverse left to a ledge below a roof. Surmount the roof and follow jugs left to the left edge of the prow. Pull up left to climb the wall, finishingout right. A wild little route, rope management being the crux.

BEN MOR COIGACH, Cona'Mheall (MR 064 053):

Achininver Pinnacle. The route is described more clearly as follows.

Achininver Pinnacle – 150m V. Diff *

A pleasant ramble improving with height. Start at the square block at the base and follow the best line to below a wide crack at about half height. Either climb this 10m pitch direct or turn it on the right and go up a groove to a level blocky section. At the end of this follow a series of short grooves with an assortment of cracks to near the top where a groove right of an easy chimney and left of a harder groove leads direct to a final good pitch up a steep cracked groove.

The North West Face:

This lies left of the Achininver Pinnacle and lies above a broken lower tier. It is composed of a series of ribs and cracks.

Vee Groove – 30m VS 4c. J. R. Mackenzie (solo). 21st May, 2001.

This is the first prominent feature moving left from the square block at the foot of the tier. Climb the rib right of the overhung start, step left into the groove and up this to a steeper finish up the right-hand crack.

Pebble-Dash Crack – 30m HVS 5a *. J. R. Mackenzie (solo). 21st May, 2001.

The roof left of Vee Groove is split by a wide crack. Either struggle up this or move in from the left from a heather ledge. Jam the crack and go up the pleasant rippled rib to a final steep juggy exit.

Cocked Hat Crack – 25m HVS 5a **. J. R. Mackenzie (solo). 21st May, 2001.

An excellent climb. Start 25m left of the large block below Vee Groove at a rib topped by a triangular block. Climb the corner on the right then move left into the crack which provides great jamming to a more delicate exit.

The West Face:

This lies more than half way up the Achininver Pinnacle to the right and is easily approached via the big scree gully. The most obvious feature low down is a short but clean slabby wall.

Two Pebble Cracks – 15m VS 4c. J. R. Mackenzie (solo). 21st May, 2001.

Climb the parallel jamming crack on the left of the wall then step right into a curving groove which leads to the top.

Two Pebble Wall – 12m HVS 5b *. J. R. Mackenzie (solo). 21st May, 2001.

A good route. Start at the centre of the smooth wall by two pebbles which are used to gain holds. Move right and climb the flake above to the top.

Middle Crag:

Juniper Wall – 75m Severe. J. R. Mackenzie (solo). 27th April, 2001. This lies just left of Patey's route. Start at the foot of the crag by a large block climbed on its left side and up past juniper to a keyhole corner. Up this and the flakes above to below the final steeper nose of the buttress. Traverse left across a juniper slope to a shallow corner beyond a gap. Climb this to the top.

Right-Hand Buttress:

This is the shorter but steeper crag split by cracks on the right of the crag. It is home of several gritstone style jamming cracks and thrutches.

Anarchist Crack – 30m HVS 5b *. J. R. Mackenzie. 1st May, 2001.
Takes the left-hand and widest crack on the south-west face overlooking the road.
Climb the lower nose via an overhanging crack, 10m 5b. Fight, struggle and protest
your way up the wide crack to the top. Excellent value.

Sgurr an Fhidhleir:
Nose Direct, Tower Finish – VII,8. G. Robertson, P. Benson. February, 2001.
By the summer line but in two pitches, the first belay taken at the top of the
groove above the cracked slab. The crux was moving right at the top of the slab to
gain the groove (same as summer?). "One of the best winter pitches and quite soft
at VII,8 for the route overall. It really should become the standard way as there's
much more turf than the normal route and it's much more spectacular and
sustained."

CUL MOR:
Balderdash – 120m IV,5. G. Robertson, A. Matheson. 2nd January, 2002.
On a low-lying buttress north-east of the main coire on the north side of Cul Mor.
The crag is reached by dropping down earlier from the same shoulder used to
approach the main coire. Its most prominent feature is an icefall on the left.
1. 50m Climb the steepening icefall to a snow ramp.
2. 30m Move right up the ramp for 10m then pull left into a groove system which
is followed into a right-trending gully, crux.
3. 60m Follow the easy gully to the top.

Main Crag:
White Rabbits – 100m IV,6. R. Webb, K. Grindrod. 1st March, 2002.
Climbs the left arête of Easy Gully. Three short hard sections (grade unsure).

Three Chimneys – 150m IV,6. R. Webb, N. Wilson. 24th February, 2002.
Start at a prominent ice chimney low down on the right-hand side of Easy Gully.
Climb this and ensuing chimneys, taking the left-hand upper one. Difficulties
increase with height.

CUL BEAG, West Face:
Cul of the Wild – 250m V,6. S.M. Richardson, C. Cartwright. 30th December,
2001.
A natural winter line up the centre of the West Face. Start 50m right of Kveldro
Ridge below an icy gully.
1 to 3. 150m Climb the gully over several steep steps to a terrace, and move up to
a prominent right-facing corner.
4 and 5. 70m Follow the corner to a prominent notch at its top. Junction with
Kveldro Ridge.
6. 30m Climb the flake-crack on the right (crux), step left and pull over a steep
wall to easier ground and the top.

STAC POLLAIDH, No.1 (West) Buttress:
Rampage – 85m V,6. E. Brunskill, D. Morris. 26th December, 2001.
This route tackles the very steep north face via a series of ramps and grooves.

About 10m up the gully from North West Corner is a large corner bounded on the left by a blocky rib. Start about 5m left from the rib at three obvious cracks leading to a blocky ledge. A very good route.

1. 30m Climb the leftmost crack to the blocky ledge. Climb the undercut blocky groove on the right (crux) and continue up and left to a large ledge and recess.
2. 40m Climb the left-trending ramp to its top, then climb up and right to a right-trending ramp. Climb this and the continuation groove above and pull through the impressively situated bulge at the top.
3. 15m Climb the open groove above to the summit.

Anniversary Cleaver – 105m IV,4. S. Frazer, J. Lyall, M. Twomey. 1st March, 2002
Start 5m right of North-West Corner and follow a right-slanting mossy fault into an alcove. Break out right and climb the rib by a vegetated groove leading to a snow bay (45m). Climb out of the left side of the bay to follow a groove, then a corner on the left to gain ledges (35m). Go up and right to finish by a groove/gully (25m).

Positive Vegetation – 100m IV,6. E. Brunskill, D. Morris. 9th November, 2001.
This route follows a series of cracks and grooves via a prominent left-facing corner in the middle of the lower tier, about 15m right of Three Day Grooves, finishing up the obvious right-trending cracks on the left side of the slabby face on the upper tier. Good technical climbing.

1. 35m. Start at a steep, turfy crack and climb up and right to below the prominent left-facing corner. Climb the corner continuing up and right to the large terrace.
2. 30m. Climb easily up the terrace to below a right-facing corner formed by a large rib.
3. 35m. Climb the groove on the left side of the rib to below two prominent grooves. Traverse right and follow right-trending turfy cracks into a corner line and to the top.

Variation Start: – 35m IV,4. D. Allan, B. Fyffe, D. McGimpsey, D. Moy. 29th December, 2001.
Start down and right of Positive Vegetation at a turfy groove directly below the upper pitch. Climb the groove and move right on to a ledge with a large pinnacle-block. Climb a strenuous short corner-crack then continue up turfy steps to the terrace. Using this start, the route overall becomes IV,5.

Treasure Hunt – 50m IV,5. S. Frazer, J. Lyall, M. Twomey. 1st March, 2002.
A variation finish to December Grooves, after starting up that route. Ten metres right ofthe final corner of December Groove, a line of turf slants up right. Follow this and an awkward chimney-crack to gain a large block. Step down and right to gain a right-slanting crack which is followed to the edge (40m). Go straight up to a short chimney with a through route (as for Party on the Patio - 10m).

REIFF, Pinnacle Area:
Kiggen Corner – 12m E4 6a. J. Read, J. Wilson. 15th July, 2001.
The corner from where Kurgan starts. Climb the corner direct to the big ledge and the short wall above to finish.

Note from T. Redfern: Velvet Scooter (SMCJ 1998) is the same route as Reiff note 3 in SMCJ 1995.

Spaced Out Rockers Cliff:
Note: *Culach:* E5 6a suggested by M. Reed on second ascent. The date for Spaced out Rockers should have been 22nd August, 2001.

The Leaning Block Cliffs:
Whispers – 15m E5 6a **. G. Latter, M. Reed. 10th May, 2001.
The thin incipient crack in the wall just right of The Screamer. Climb direct up the wall, then the thin crack with hard moves at two thirds height. Finish more easily above good break.

Otto – 12m E7 6c (F8a+) ***. G. Latter (redpointed). 19th September, 2001.
Fierce powerful climbing forging directly up the centre of the leaning wall avoided by The Quickening. Climb the good breaks as for The Quickening, then continue directly, with difficult moves to gain and leave the prominent flake, stepping left at the top break to finish at a good V-notch. Well protected by small cams.

Freedom! – 15m E4 6a *. G. Latter, D. Hollinger. 16th September, 2001.
A direct line up the wall right of Braveheart. Climb directly to bulge at mid height, cross this to good slots and continue straight up to a good holds in a recess. Finish more easily directly above.

Amphitheatre Bay, West Face:
Minjeetah – 25m E5 6b ***. M. Reed, G. Latter. 10th May, 2001.
The stunning corner and cracks through the triple roofs at the right end of the face. Cross the initial roof on good holds and climb the corner, moving out left to a large ledge. Traverse right above the second roof and up crack strenuously to a rest in a depression beneath final roof. Move out left to a good flange, pulling through final roof on good holds to finish up short easy corner.

Rubha Ploytach, West Face:
An Ros – 8m E2 6a *. G. Latter. 6th November, 2000.
Start 2m right of Lilidh. From a good edge, stretch to the sloping break. Gain the ledge above with a long reach, finishing direct past a thin crack.

POINT OF STOER:
Traligill Rising – 10m HVS 5a. S. McCabe, T. Redfern. 6th June, 2001.
A route in the bay just below the parking / picnic area at Stoer lighthouse, to the south of the road. The first obvious corner to the north of the bay, above a rock platform, climbed direct.

ALLADALE, An Socach:
The Pimp – 200m V,5 **. D. Allan, D. Mitchell. 1st March, 2002.
An icy mixed line up the rib left of The Pillar. Rock protection is limited; carrying ice screws and warthogs is recommended. Start 20m up and left of the start of The Pillar icefall under an overhang.
1. 35m Climb rightwards up an overhung turf ramp, then go straight up on turf

and climb a step on the right to a narrow ledge just left of The Pillar (same belay).
2. 50m Move left round a nose and up a ramp, then move left and surmount an overhang on ice (crux). Continue straight up on ice to easier ground.
3. 45m Continue up to a left-trending ramp. Climb it, then move right and straight up.
4. 45m Climb a right-trending snow gully to blocks.
5. 25m Continue to the top.

SCOURIE, Rubh' Aird an t-Sionnaich (SMCJ 2000):
Waiting For The Maiden – 20m HVS 5a *. R. I. Jones, M. Dent. 28th July, 2001. From 2m left of Twin Cracks, climb directly through a small roof to another pair of twin cracks. Climb steeply on big holds to a left-facing corner. Step right and pull through.

Totally Unintentional – 20m MVS 4b. C. Hodgkinson, A. Callum. 28th July, 2001. Traverse left of Waiting For The Maiden to a cleft. Climb just right of the arête and the bay with The Wee Corner.

ROCK GARDEN CRAGS (MR 248 506. W-facing. Cliff Base 50m):
Immaculate juggy gneiss, 250m from road. Ample scope for numerous short routes and bouldering on clean rough rock. Other shorter crags exist apart from those listed below.
Park in a large layby 400m to the south.

Rock Garden Slab: Closest to road, three minutes.
All routes sight soloed by J. R Mackenzie on 7th October, 2001.
Rock Garden Arête – 15m V. Diff **. Climb central arête from blocks at foot, excellent.

Rock Garden Right – 15m V. Diff *. Climb up shallow scoop just right of arête.

Rock Garden Left – 15m V. Diff. Climb up wall and slab just left of arête.

Garden of Delights Wall:
Lies a short distance left of the pink slab; more excellent rock.

Left-hand Side:
Earthly Pleasures – 20m V. Diff **. Climb the unlikely wall left of centre on good holds all the way.

Garden of Delights – 20m VS 4c **. Start centrally from block and boldly straight up to top.

Right-hand Side:
Crystal Planter – 15m H. Severe 4b *. Start below thin quartz crack and seam move up then across left and up to top. Unlikely and good.

Rockery Wall:
Lies above Rock Garden slab.

Stone Flowers – 15m H. Severe 4b **. On the left of the wall is a slab bottomed by an overlap. Climb up to the overlap centrally and move left and up on to the slab which is climbed straight up.

Archaen Perfection – 15m Mild VS 4b **. Between the slab on the left and a pillar on the right is a narrow scoop bottomed by a wall. Climb the vertical wall to the scoop and so to the top.

Old Stones – 15m V. Diff. Climb the red pillar direct.

RED CASTLE CRAG (NC 262 493):
Approach: Park at the north end of the Skerricha loop road at MR 246 508. Cross the main road and head south-east. Cross a causeway where Loch na Thuill narrows and continue south-eastwards along the east side of the loch. The crag is visible on a knoll beyond the south end of the loch. 40 minutes.

The crag is of compact red gneiss of very good quality, quick drying and in the sun in the afternoon. The crag is one wall curving round from north-facing on the left side to west-facing on the right, which is a fine slab.

Left Flank:
Left-hand Crack – 20m Severe **. D. Allan. 22nd April, 2000.
Pull over a bulge to start, then follow the crack to the top.

Northumbria Wall – 22m HVS 5b *. D. Moy, D. Allan. 29th April, 2000.
Start 2m left of the corner of the buttress and make hard moves to a thin crack at 3m. Continue to a steep wall and pull through it trending left to a spike. Climb straight up, then move right to finish up an easy groove.

Geordie Wall – 22m HVS 5a *. D. Moy, D. Allan. 29th April, 2000.
Climb steeply up the corner of the buttress, then continue up a scoop to a steep wall. Climb it trending right (crux) to finish more easily.

The Crack – 22m VS 4c **. D. Allan, D. Moy. 29th April, 2000.
Follow a prominent crack where the crag changes direction.

Cumbrian Corner – 15m E2 5c **. B. Birkett, T. Rogers, H. Lancashire. 23rd August, 2001.
An obvious large left-facing corner.

Kendall Wall – 15m E4 6a **. T. Rogers, H. Lancashire, B. Birkett. 23rd August, 2001.
The wall left of Lancashire Crack, using the crack initially for protection.

Lancashire Crack – 15m E2 5c **. H. Lancashire, T. Rogers, B. Birkett. 23rd August, 2001.
A thin vertical crack up a smooth wall.

Right Wall – 15m E1 5a **. H. Lancashire, T. Rogers, B. Birkett, D. Allan. 23rd August, 2001.
Follow hidden jugs up the right side of the wall after a reachy start.

The Groove – 25m Severe 4b **. D. Allan, D. Moy. 29th April, 2000.
A prominent roofed V-groove right of the steep red wall. Start directly below the groove and climb a short corner. Continue up the slabby groove and cross the overhang above its left end. Move left above and finish to the left.

Slab One – 25m Severe 4b **. D. Moy, D. Allan. 29th April, 2000.
Start at a block and climb up on to the slab. Climb up the left side of the slab to finish up two small steps at the left end of the steep headwall.

Slab Two – 25m Severe 4b **. D. Allan, D. Moy. 29th April, 2000.
Start at a quartzy vein and climb directly to a short thin crack at half height. Continue directly to the steep headwall, gain a ledge and go up a dog-leg crack to finish.

Slab Three – 22m Severe 4a **. D. Allan. 22nd April, 2000.
Start right of Slab Two and climb a wide crack to a niche. Finish up a broken left-facing corner.

Slab Four – 20m Severe 4a *. D. Allan. 22nd April, 2000.
Climb a curving crack and carry on directly to finish up a left-facing corner.

Slab Five – 18m Severe 4b *. D. Allan. 22nd April, 2000.
Take the right-hand end of the slab.

The Wee Slab
Some metres farther right, on the broken right-hand section, is The Wee Slab.
Right Side – 4c **. D. Allan. 22nd April, 2000.
Left Side – 4a **. D. Allan. 22nd April, 2000.

The Two Pillars – V. Diff *. D. Allan. 22nd April, 2000.
Situated farther right again. Climb into a niche between two grey pillars, then go up the left pillar to finish.

Diagonal Crack – V. Diff *. D. Allan. 22nd April, 2000.
Farther right again. Climb broken ground to the crack and follow it up right.

LAXFORD BAY (MR 225 481):
A series of low-angled gneiss slabs on the north side of Laxford Bay which face south and catch any sun. There are several bands of slabs but the routes listed are on the two bands which are centred and highest on the hillside and a third which is to the left and somewhat lower. Park off the road by the jetty where the A838 bends away from Laxford Bay towards Rhiconich. Strike diagonally up the hillside to the slabs which are about 10 minutes from the road.
What we did on our Holidays – 40m Severe 4a *. S. and K. Charlton. 17th July, 2001.
This route takes a line up the leftmost slab on the highest tier starting at a shallow groove directly below the left end of a grass ledge at 10m. Climb the groove almost to the grass and then move diagonally left over easy rock heading for a crack running to the left below the final steepening. Climb the slab straight up to the top starting to the right of the crack.

Evening Sunset – 40m V. Diff **. S. Charlton. 4th September, 2002.
5m right of the start of 'What we did on our Holidays' is another shallow groove running on to the slab. Start up this and move right below the grass and then follow the crest of the buttress.

Evening Tide – 45m Diff. **. S. Charlton. 4th September, 2002.
Takes the centre of the right-hand of the two higher slabs. Several harder variation starts can be made from a small bay about 15m above and to the left of the lowest point of the slab.

The next two routes lie on a single sweep of slabs down and to left.
Doggy Dilemma – 30m Severe 4a *. S. and K. Charlton. 17th July, 2001.
Takes the central crack starting from the left end of the grass bank. Follow the crack to the steepening and then climb the slab direct to the top.

Munroist's Meander – 30m H. Severe 4a *. S. and K. Charlton. 17th July, 2001.
From the lowest point of the slab a faint rib runs up and slightly right. Follow the rib to the top with a few delicate moves up its right side at 10m.

RHICONICH CRAG (NC 259 520):
D. Allan and N. Wilson independently think the crag is overstarred.

RHICONICH, Creag Gharbh Mhor (MR 269534 to 271536):
Three separate crags of the usual superb gneiss which are situated above the A8383 about 2+km beyond the Rhiconich Hotel towards Durness. The crags face north-west and catch the late afternoon and evening sun and are easily seen from a small belvedere on the left of the road about halfway along a straight section some 2 km beyond the Kinlochbervie junction.

The main glaciated slab lies about 300m above and to the left of the belvedere and is clearly visible. The Red Wall is lower and to the left again, only the top few metres being visible form the belvedere. The third crag (the Red Slab) lies well to the right of the glaciated slab at about the same height and is the furthest right of the rocky band running out from the slab. Again only the top can be seen from the belvedere. The easiest approach is to strike straight up the hillside from the belvedere to reach a deer track which runs below the rocky band and then follow this either left for the glaciated slab or Red Wall or right to reach the Red Slab.

The Glaciated Slab:
The slab is essentially triangular in shape inverted on one apex. Grassy ledges on both the right and left almost cut the apex. That on the left ends about 5m up from the base while the right hand ledge/bank starts about 10m up and runs out from the redcave/overhang. The overhang nearly reaches the ground below the left ledge. The first four routes start from the lowest point of the slab, while the others start from either the left or right ledges.
Chasing the Dragon – 40m HVS 5a ***. S. and K. Charlton. Summer, 2001.
After a somewhat messy start up to the right of the cave, this takes the immaculate slab direct to the top. Protection on the slab is spaced. Start up the shallow rib on the right-hand side of the cave/overhang. Climb to blocks at about 5m and move

rightover these to gain grassy rock which is crossed rightwards to gain a crack on the right at the base of the main slab. Use the crack to gain the slab and climb direct to the top.

Crouching Tiger – 40m VS 4c **. S. and K. Charlton. Summer, 2001.
Start as for Chasing the Dragon to where that route moves rightwards across the grassy rock. From this point move up slightly left to gain another obvious crack at the start of the slab. Climb directly up the slab to the large detached block. Better protection than Chasing the Dragon.

Jewel in the Crown – 40m VS 4c **. S. and K. Charlton. Summer, 2001.
Start just to the left of the red cave/overhang below a short crack which leads to the obvious ledge at about 5m. Climb the crack to the ledge (crux) and then move on to the slab and follow a line diagonally right below a shallow rib which ends at a good crack. Move up and right again to below a faint arête on the headwall. Climb the arête to reach a short crack and the trend up and right to the rocky ledge at the top of the slab.

Hidden Dragon – 40m HVS 4c **. S. and K. Charlton. Summer, 2001.
Start at the lowest point of the rocks above a small hidden pool. Climb the slight ramp rightwards to gain the left end of the ledge at 5m (about 3m left of where Jewel in the Crown gains this ledge). Move up and the left to the base of the obvious crack. Follow this on to the slab and then climb to the left end of a ledge. From here move slightly left and then straight up to cross the deep grassy crack about 5m from the top. Above the grassy crack convoluted rock leads to the top.

The Red Slab:
This consists of a red slab on the right (which cannot be seen until below the crag) below and left of which is a grey wall with an obvious 'circular crack' low down which merges into a left to right diagonal break which defines the left edge of the red slab. To the left again is an obvious hanging groove and then a left-slanting overhang above a short steep wall. On the right of the circular crack is a chimney crack running directly up onto the slab.

The Crack – 35m H. Severe or Mild VS 4a/b **. S. and K. Charlton. 30th August 2001.
Start directly below the circular crack. Gain the crack and then follow it over a ledge to a junction with the slab. Gain the slab and follow it straight up to a ledge and then take the 'crozzly' slab above.

Westering Home – 35m V. Diff **. S. and K. Charlton. 30th August 2001.
Bridge the chimney crack and move on to the slab. Follow a crack in the slab to a steepening below a ledge and then follow another crozzly slab to the top (from the ledge this crozzly slab is about 5m right of the one on *The Crack*).

SHEIGRA, First Geo:
The next three routes lie on the north wall of the geo, inland from the descent groove.
Crispy Cereal – 20m V. Diff. E. Flaherty, A. Banks. 16th June, 2001.

Climb the next prominent, deep groove inland from the descent groove. Where it splits, go either left to easy ground or better, go right up the slabby corner to finish.

Culture of Silence - 20m VS 4c. A. Banks, E. Flaherty. 16th June, 2001.
A good route with a strenuous start and a delicate finish. Start 3m right of Crispy Cereal. Climb the vertical weakness to ledges directly below the left edge of the overhung bay. Step up left around the arête with feet on the sloping ramp/break, and climb directly up the centre of the slab, stepping right to finish up an easy rib.

Critical Consciousness – 20m E4 6a. A. Banks, E. Flaherty. 16th June, 2001.
A direct and serious route taking the black slab, overhang and pink headwall to the right of two cleaned E2 grooves (existing routes). Climb straight up the black slabs passing an overlap to the widest part of the overhang before it splits into two levels. Pull over this and climb directly up the steepening headwall, passing two short parallel cracks to finish between a pink quartz vein (on the left) and a large boss of rock.

At the End of the Road – 10m E3 5c. S. Crowe, K. Magog. 18th June, 2001.
Start at a short bulging right-facing groove system in the black rock immediately right of the short steep red wall and just left of Acid Jazz (SMCJ 1995). Follow the series of grooves. Poor protection.

Daylight at Midnight – 25m E3 6a. S. Crowe, K. Magog. 18th June, 2001.
This route climbs the left hand side of a double corner that separates the Inner and Outer Walls. Scramble up to a good ledge then belay below the steep corner. Climb easily up to below the corner. Large cams #5 and #6 protect the short powerful left- hand flake system above. From the ledge above continue directly to the top.

Outer Walls:
Big U – 30m vertical and a long traverse. Diff. A. Banks, E. Flaherty. 13th June, 2001.
An enjoyable excursion. Head out towards the headland south of the First Geo until easy scrambling on large holds leads down in a broad zig-zag to the boulder choke (at the other side of the "very small inlet", guide p279). From the boulder choke, traverse out eastwards towards the bay above the high tide level until reaching a sloping ledge beneath a jutting overlap at the point where the coast turns north towards the beach. Step over the overlap and climb the flake and slab above to easy ground.

On the north wall of 'the very small inlet', two routes have been climbed:
How Much? – 20m V. Diff. A. Banks, E. Flaherty. 13th June, 2001.
Start 8m left of the highest point of the boulder choke at a short steep crack. Climb this and easier bulging slabs above.

Who? – 20m Diff. A. Banks, E. Flaherty. 13th June, 2001.
Start 4m left of How Much? Beneath a fist-sized pocket at 3m. Climb straight up to a shallow right-facing corner and follow this.

Second Geo:

The Cuckoo Conundrum – 55m E3 5c. S. Crowe, K. Magog. 17th June, 2001.
A right to left girdle of the red wall crossing above the cave. Follow the Dark Flush as far as the black streak, cross this at the weakness to gain the ramp on Bloodlust. Continue boldly up and across the smooth red shield of rock on pockets as for Bloodlust Superdirect then step left again to finish up the arête of Juggernaut.

No Porpoise – 30m E4 6a. S. Crowe, K. Magog. 17th June, 2001.
Start as for Dolphins and Whales but continue directly up the right hand side of the pocketed wall heading for the prominent steep left-facing groove. Power up this to the top.

Dolphins and Whales – 30m E4 6a. G. Latter, P.Thorburn. 16th June, 1996.
The pocket-infested wall above the slabby corner of Shark Crack. Belay higher up the slabby lower ramp of Shark Crack, beneath the centre of the wall. Follow a line of huge pockets Second diagonally leftwards to a break running across the centre of the wall. Continue up in the same line to a huge pocket just right of the arête. Move up to a good finger pocket, then head out rightwards to a good vertical slot. Directly above on better holds to a sloping finish. Many large friends useful. The final short crux wall could be avoided by escaping up the left side of the arête, giving a superb E2 5b.

DUNAN BEAG:
To the south of Dunan Beag, 3km south of Cape Wrath, is a rocky gorge which opens out into a beautiful sheltered bay and popular seal playground (NC 251 719). The first two routes lie 200m inland, up the gorge, on a buttress rising directly out of a pleasant deep pool.
Bivi Bath Buttress – 15m VS 4c. A. Banks, E. Flaherty. 17th June, 2001.
Start at the seaward end of the pool and take a diagonal line up and rightwards on good rock to a ledge. Finish up a black corner above.

Bivi Bath Traverse – 15m 5c. A. Banks. 17th June, 2001.
An excellent traverse of the buttress at pool level.

The next route lies at the northern end of the boulder beach in the bay, on a series of large overlapping slabs.
Gruntled – 55m Mild XS. A. Banks, E. Flaherty. 17th June, 2001.
In the centre of the overlapping slabs is a fist-sized corner-crack which closes at half height, then reopens as a shallow chimney. Start 4m right of this at a shallow stepped groove. Climb the groove steeply for 4m, then step left on to the open slab. Follow the right edge of this until it steepens, then step right above an overlap back into the now more slabby groove. Follow this to its top and a large blocky flake-crack to grass slopes and no belay. Much loose and unstable rock.

CRANSTACKIE, Midnight Crag (MR 343 544. W-facing. Cliff Base 300m):
A nose of gneiss overlooking Strath Dionard. Approach by the track up Strath Dionard, starting near Gualin House. The river is wide but shallow, a straightforward wade, often dry in wellies. The nose has two cracked faces separated by an arête with a prominent groove broken by a roof at half height.

Wind Sock – 55m E2 **. D. McGimpsey, A. Nisbet. 29th July, 2001
A route up the centre of the left face.
1. 45m 5c Start up a pink scooped slab to reach a shallow right-facing corner. Climb the corner to its top, then move right along a horizontal crack passing a thin crack above. Move up and back left into the thin crack, climbed to gain a ramp slanting up left to below a bulge. Pull through the bulge into a small niche and continue above trending left over awkward walls to a final wall.
2. 10m 4b Climb this leftwards to a finishing slab.

Merlin Crack – 60m HVS *. D. McGimpsey, D. Allan. July, 2001.
Up the right side of the face, including a prominent crack. Start right of the pink scooped slab.
1. 30m 5a Climb some blocky grooves, then step left round an arête on to the left face. Climb a crack until it peters out. Move right to the prominent crack, go up this and its continuation until a ledge leads right into Evening Groove (a more direct line was tried but blanks out).
2. 30m 4c Pitch 2 of Evening Groove.

Evening Groove – 55m VS. D. Allan, D. McGimpsey, J. Preston. 20th July, 2001.
The prominent groove between the two faces is the best line but not the best climbing.
1. 25m 4b Climb the groove to below the roof.
2. 30m 4c Go up left under the roof and climb the upper groove.

Midnight Express – 50m HVS *. J. Preston, D. Allan, D. McGimpsey. 20th July, 2001 (finishing left). D. Allan, A. Nisbet. 6th September, 2001 (as described)
Four consecutive cracks (the clean ones) up the right face. Start at the base of the face.
1. 25m 5a Climb a crack in the centre of the wall to a heathery ledge. Move right and climb a second crack.
2. 25m 5a Step left and go up the next crack, with a move left and back right at its top. The final crack on the right is deeper and clean, the highlight. Finish easily leftwards.

The Pink Slab – 60m VS 4c. D. Allan, D. McGimpsey. July, 2001.
A central line up the obvious pink slab at MR 337 555, following a shallow left-facing corner at mid height. Sparse protection initially and some flakey rock.

Skerray Sea Cliffs:
Several routes have been received from R.I. Jones. It is not yet known whether they are new.

SUTHERLAND NORTH COAST:
Again, many routes have been received and will be included in the new Northern Highlands North.

CAITHNESS:
Again, a number of routes which will be in the guide. Also the following, received at the last minute:

Duncansby Head:
Little Stack – 20m VS. S. M. Richardson, M. Robson. 9th June, 2001.
The smallest of the four Duncansby stacks. Approach by swimming to gain the platform on the landward side of the stack.
1. 15m 4c Climb the landward face on good holds to a prominent break. Move round this to a good ledge on the south face.
2. 5m 4a Move right and climb a corner-crack to the top.

LATHERONWHEEL, Pinnacle Area:
Far East Arête – 10m HVS 5a. M. Robson, S.M. Richardson. 10th June, 2001.
The impending arête left of Fancy Free. Climb the right side of the arête on good holds to reach a narrow ledge below a steep wall. Pull over this to the top.

Smelly Sox – 10m HVS 5a. S. M. Richardson, M. Robson. 10th June, 2001.
The crack system between Fancy Free and Sticky Fingers. Climb the crack to where it fades below a blank wall, then pull up and right to reach the finishing niche of Sticky Fingers.

Big Flat Wall:
Welzenbach – 15m HVS 5a. S. M. Richardson, D. Green. 9th July, 2001.
Start in the large niche at the left end of the wall as for Free Fall. Climb the steep crack on the left side of the niche and trend right up the wall above finishing up a crack to the right of The Grey Coast.

Cassin's Crack – 20m HVS 5a. S. M. Richardson, D. Green. 9th July, 2001.
The right-hand of the two central cracks on the wall. Start as for The Other Landscape and climb the right side of the cave to join the right-hand crack. Follow this to the upper wall where the cracked bulge of Cask Strength leads to the top. Good sustained climbing, but surely climbed before?

ORKNEY, Yesnaby:
Sink or Swim – 35m HVS. T. Rankin, S. Johnston. 18th August, 2001.
Just south of the stack is a small headland marking the north side of the deep inlet. On its seaward face is a fine pillar of rock. This route was used as an exit out after an ascent of the stack. The huge tidal platform at the base of the pillar was gained by swimming from the stack but could be gained by abseil from a strainer post (extra rope). Start at the left end of the pillar below an obvious wide crack.
1. 25m 5a Climb the crack and slot on to a ledge. Move left into the big corner.
2. 10m 4c Climb the corner. Move left to climb a steep left-hand crack on to a ledge just below the top.

Note: T. Rankin thinks the South Face route on the stack is worth E2 due to a loose exit. The abseil stake is useless and 20m of disposable rope tied to the west arête would be useful as an alternative (the current piece may deteriorate).
Disappointment – 15m E2 5b. T. Rankin, S. Johnston (on sight). 16th August, 2001.
A disappointing route for here! Start just left of the descent chimney. Climb a short crack on to a long ledge. Climb the centre of the wall above to sloping finishing holds. Serious with poor rock.

CAIRNGORMS

LOCHNAGAR: Southern Sector:
The following routes are on a right-hand flying buttress attached to Sunset Buttress.
Right of Sunset Gully is a shallow gully (I/II), then an icy bay with a prominent
steep slot above.
The Pod – 70m V,6. B. S. Findlay, R. Ross, G. S. Strange. 6th January 2002.
Start in the bay and climb directly into and up the slot. Easy ground leads to the
plateau. Rock, frozen turf and a little ice.

Mirk – 80m V,5. B. S. Findlay, R. Ross, G. S. Strange. 17th December 2000.
Takes the left-facing *Dagger*-like corner on rocks right of the icy bay, then continues
up the easier upper crest passing a steepening on the right. Powder and frozen
turf.

Central Buttress:
Footloose – 65m E2 5c **. G. Robertson, J. Currie. May, 2001.
Start up the first pitch of Mantichore (5b), then climb the second pitch of Footloose
(5c).

Shadow Buttress Group. Tough-Brown Face:
Note: Backdoor Route Variation has been named *Backdoor Edge* and the following
has been climbed as a direct and independent start:
Direct Variation – VI,6. G. Robertson, T. Wood. 5th January, 2002.
Climb the prominent grooves in the arête right of Backdoor Route to join the
second groove. Good and quite serious under thin conditions.

Black Spout Pinnacle:
Wobble – 70m III. W. Deadman, J. Barrett. 8th April, 2001.
A steep left finish to the left branch of the Black Spout, about 50m beyond Pinnacle
Gully 2 and exactly opposite the gully of Crumbling Cranny. Climb steep snow
and some ice to a cornice finish.

West Buttress:
Bell's Pillar, Direct Start – 50m V,6. C. Cartwright, S. M. Richardson. 3rd February,
2002.
An alternative start right of the left-facing corner of the original route. Start below
the centre of the buttress and climb a steep left-facing corner to a ledge. Move left
and climb a steep chimney-crack to join the original route on the ledge at the top
of the left-facing corner.

Coire Nan Eun, Whacky Buttress:
About 100m left of The Stuic is a steep buttress with a prominent beak on its left
skyline. The tallest part of the buttress lies right of a central depression and is
characterised by a narrow pillar that leads to a platform just left of the buttress
apex. The buttress faces north-east and holds snow well after a thaw. Later in the
season it is often capped by a huge cornice.

Pillar Perfect – 90m V,6. C. Cartwright, S. M. Richardson. 6th January, 2002.
A little gem based on the corner line on the right side of the narrow pillar.
1. 45m Start at the toe of the buttress and climb an easy groove to where it splits. Follow the right-hand groove to its top and pull through a steep step to a good stance.
2. 25m Make exposed moves left onto and across the front face of the buttress to gain the right facing corner right of the narrow pillar. Climb this to good platform and continue over a short wall to the buttress top.
3. 20m Easy snow leads to the plateau.

Dyke Dastardly – 90m VI,7. C. Cartwright, S. M. Richardson. 6th January, 2002.
Another good route based on the corner-line on the left side of the pillar.
1. 45m Start as for Pillar Perfect, but take the left-hand groove at the split. Pull through the roof above (crux) to gain a small stance below the left-facing corner on the left side of the narrow pillar.
2. 25m Climb the corner to its top and pull over a steep wall to the buttress top.
3. 20m Finish up easy snow.

The Stuic:
Big Block Groove – 70m IV,4. C. Cartwright, S. M. Richardson. 19th January, 2002.
The groove-line cutting into the right edge of the buttress containing the right-facing corner of Morning Has Broken.
1. 30m Climb a series of steep steps to a good ledge at the foot of a steep wall.
2. 40m Step right round the corner and continue up a deep chimney-groove passing a huge perched block on the right to reach easier ground and the top.

Broad Cairn Bluffs:
Thieves Gully – 60m III. R. Birkett, K. Neal. 10th January, 2002.
A short but distinct gully about 300m left of the section of crag with Yoo-Hoo Buttress. A short step of ice, then a 50m steeper ice pitch.

Neez R Good – 35m III,4. K. Neal, D. Richardson. 6th January, 2002.
A short icefall 200m to the right of Funeral Fall.

CREAG AN DUBH LOCH, Central Gully Wall:
The Nullfidian – 50m E5 6b *. M. Reed, P. Benson. 24th June, 2001.
This route climbs the compelling and surprisingly unclimbed, cracked and grooved arête halfway between Wicker Man and Vertigo Wall. Start roughly below the arête. Cleaned and led on sight with 2 rest points.
1. 25m 4b Climb up easily to a big grass ledge. Go right along this then up a slab to a grassy corner (possibly common with Vertigo winter). Climb the corner to a ledge, continue up passing left of a peg to below and slightly right of the overhung arête.
2. 25m 6b Gain the arête using holds on the right wall. Continue boldly up the groove and crack system in the arête to a spike below a bulging wall. Hard moves up the short wall above lead to a reachy move over a small roof, followed by another hard move to gain a standing position. Climb the slabby corner and wall

to below a disgustingly wet and loose brown corner. A fine, technical pitch. Abseil off, or swim up the corner.

North-West Buttress:
Scirroco – 200m IV,4. C. Cartwright, S. M. Richardson. 23rd December, 2001.
The prominent line of icy vegetated grooves cutting the rib 10m right of Mistral. Follow North-West Buttress to the terrace and continue up the grooves for three pitches, pulling over a roof at one-third height.

GLEN CALLATER, Coire Kander:
A deep easy angled gully descends from the col between Carn an Tuirc and Cairn of Claise (clearly marked on the 1:50000 map at MR 186 805). This gully could be used as a descent. The following routes to its right formed after a thaw when the rest of the hillside was virtually bare of snow (with the exception of the gullies described), and would be easier with more snow.

Pick Breaker – 100m II/III. S. Muir. 7th January 2002.
To the right of the descent gully (looking up), a large icefall leads into a short shallow gully which continues to the col. Climb a shallow introductory gully to below the large icefall, which was climbed on the left to reach an easy angled upper snow gully.

Kanderhar – 100m III. S. Muir. 9th January 2002.
Further right, another large icefall leads into a longer, deeper gully. A steep 25m icefall leads to the gully which is an easy snow plod.

MAYAR, Kilbo Crag (MR 239734):
This is a name suggested for small SE-facing cliffs overlooking the Mayar Burn.
High Plains Drifter – 40m HVS 5a. R. Archbold and G. S. Strange. 20th July 2001.
Climbs the right face of the largest buttress, finishing by the more prominent left-hand of two parallel cracks in the top wall. Scramble up steep vegetation to belay at base of first wall.
1. 15m 4c Climb the centre of the wall via a short crack to a grass ledge. Move right and continue, first by a thin crack, then by a wide crack to the next ledge. Belay in a corner right of a small rowan
2. 25m 5a Climb right of the belay, then step left and up into a recess. Move right again and go up to base of a crack in the steep headwall. Climb this directly to the top on surprising holds. Quick drying and well protected.

BEINN A' BHUIRD, Coire na Ciche:
Just south of Coire na Ciche is the slight Coire Buidhe, not shown on the 1:50000 map. To the left of this are three buttresses, at first sight uninteresting and easily passed on the way to Coire na Ciche. The middle buttress (MR 099 978) is the most pronounced with a zig-zag line at the bottom and a ramp high on the right.
Na Sionnaich – 105m III,5 *. R. I. Jones, W. Deadman. 2nd March, 2002.
1. 35m Zigzag up the right side of the buttress passing a possible belay at 20m, then use a short narrow chimney on the left to pull on to a large ledge and an obvious flake-crack.

2. 30m Climb the large flake-crack/short wall to its right (crux), possibly easier if it ever ices up?

3. Climb the ramp on the right of the buttress to the top.

Dividing Buttress:

Big Bertha – 250m VII,7. S. M. Richardson, C. Cartwright. 10th February, 2002.
A good line up the right edge of Dividing Buttress taking the pillar right of Sentinel Gully. A key feature is the prominent inverted V slot at the top right-hand edge of the hanging snowfield.

1. and 2. 75m Start by climbing the easy-angled rib that starts below and right of Sentinel Gully. Belay where the angle steepens below a mixed wall.

3. 40m Climb the centre of the wall to reach the hanging snow field above.

4. 40m Move easily up and right across the snowfield and belay in a niche directly below the slot.

5. 25m Climb a steep wall and enter the slot from the left. Climb the slot (strenuous), exit on the right arête and continue up a steep narrow hanging slab (crux - bold) to reach a good belay below a short deep narrow chimney on the left wall.

5. 40m Climb the slot left of the chimney, then move right to gain a terrace. Move left along this for 10m, then break up and right up a series of grooves and slabs to where the angle eases.

6. 50m Follow the crest of the arête above to reach easier ground and the plateau.

Coire nan Clach:

Summit Buttress – 150m II. C. Cartwright, S. M. Richardson. 17th November, 2001.
At the back of the right lobe of the coire is a buttress that rises up to meet the highest point of the plateau 50m south east of the summit cairn. Start at the toe of the buttress and climb a diagonal line up right then left to a central depression. Climb a steep scoop and continue more easily right of the crest to the top.

Garbh Choire:

Alchemist's Route Direct – IV,5. D. McGimpsey, A. Nisbet. 29th March, 2002
As for the normal route but climb the obvious left-slanting chimney direct when iced (on this occasion there was a thin steep section).

Note: D. McGimpsey and A. Nisbet climbed an alternative start to Pot Luck on 29th March, 2002. Start as for Alchemist to the bay below the obvious left-slanting chimney. Climb a slabby groove on the right side of the bay to reach the well-defined section of the Pot Luck icefall.

BEINN BHROTAIN, Coire Cath nan Fionn:

Fingaloofer – 150m II. S. M. Richardson. 4th May, 2001.
Low down on the left wall of Gully A is a prominent chimney. Climb this over a steep step to reach the crest of the ridge above which leads to the plateau.

Glen Geusachan:

Unnamed – 200m I. S. M. Richardson. 4th May, 2001.
Start from MR 960 934 and climb the defined shallow gully to the summit plateau.

ANGEL'S PEAK, Corrie of the Chokestone Gully:

The Opportunist – 60m III,5. D. McGimpsey, A. Nisbet. 26th March, 2002.
There is a big but short corner which is the last feature at the right end of the cliff.
Gain and climb the corner, finishing on the right. There is an overhanging barrier
wall low down. Despite a tempting icicle, this was climbed up a narrow chimney
on the right. Climbed on ice.

BRAERIACH, Garbh Choire Mor:

Gauntless – 70m IV,5. C. Cartwright, S. M. Richardson. 2nd December, 2001.
A short mixed climb up the left sidewall of Michaelmas Fare. Start 30m up
Bunting's Gully at the depression below the start of the Left Branch.
1. 40m Follow a turf seam that runs up and right towards the crest. Leave the seam
after 20m and climb a left-facing corner to belay on the summit of the buttress.
2. 30m Cross the col as for Michaelmas Fare, then move up and left into a right-
facing chimney-corner that leads to the top.

Note: D. McGimpsey and A. Nisbet climbed White Nile direct up the groove
throughout on 26th March, 2002. Probably done before. Two 50m pitches with a
fine spike belay.

Garbh Choire Dhaidh:

Wichity Way – 160m V,6. C. Cartwright, S. M. Richardson. 16th December, 2001.
The buttress between Boomerang and Twilight Gully.
1. 45m Climb the crest of the small arête to the right of Boomerang and belay
below a prominent corner capped by a left-pointing roof shaped like an inverted
L.
2. 40m Climb an easy gully left of the corner then step right onto the corner above
the roof. Continue to easier ground.
3. 40m Move up and slightly left to enter the prominent left-facing corner system
to the right of Boomerang.
4. 35m Climb the corner to the top (crux). An excellent pitch.

COIRE SPUTAN DEARG:

Unchained – 120m I. R. Benton, R. Jones. 4th February, 2002.
The gully which defines the right side of the buttress with Anchor Route. This is
the left-hand of two possible lines starting from a small bay. Take the right fork
25m from the top; this finishes with one tricky move.

The Chebec – 80m VII,8. H. Burrows-Smith, D. McGimpsey, A. Nisbet. 6th
December, 2001.
A line centred round the summer route. Start with the 'scrambling' pitch of the
summer route but continue right to a ledge. Climb a groove to a smaller ledge
underneath the bigger right-hand overhang (20m). Move up to the right corner of
the overhang, then traverse left immediately underneath it to a tiny ledge on an
arête (here joining the summer route). Climb the crack above and continue up the
crackline to a small roof. Step right and go up a small corner until a horizontal
crack leads right to flakes (25m). Go up rightwards to finish up the short deep
chimney of The Fly. With the cracks choked with ice, a rest point was used on the
tiny ledge and two more in the crack above.

CARN ETCHACHAN, Upper Tier:
Poison Dwarf – VII,8. G. Ettle, M. Garthwaite. 3rd February, 2002.
By the summer route throughout.

SHELTER STONE CRAG, Central Slabs, Lower Tier:
Freya – 50m E3 5c. J. Lines, L. Hughes. 4th July, 2001.
Climbs good clean hairline cracks in a slab to the right of an obvious grey right-facing corner, and directly below the roof on Snipers. Start at the toe of the slab, 8m right of the right-facing corner. Climb directly up the slab on reasonable holds for 15m to reach a scoopy groove on the left (just right of the corner). Make thin moves up and right, and then direct, passing a couple of overlaps, to reach ledges beneath the start of the main routes.

COIRE AN t-SNEACHDA, Mess of Pottage:
The Message – V. Diff *. S. Muir, A. Baird. May, 1999.
Follow pitch one of Pot of Gold, then The Message throughout.
Note: A. Nisbet repeated the route but with a different first pitch on 12th December, 2001, using rock boots on dry rock. The first pitch was based on the winter route except where the left-hand of two grooves (the winter route usually climbs the right-hand) was climbed, but with a strenuous pull out left from part way up (Severe).

Aladdin's Buttress:
Wedgewood – VII,7. G. Lennox, S. Muir. 16th December, 2001.
An ascent of winter (W)Edgewood. The first two pitches are probably close to the earlier (discredited) route (SMCJ 2000 and 2001).
1. 45m Climb the groove 1m right of the arête to meet Doctor Janis, then pull out right to the big ledge.
2. 20m Climb the flake crack and thin crack above, making thin moves to exit on to Genie.
3. 25m Climb the awkward Genie layback and 6m of the Genie Corner to a delicate move left below an overlap on to a small footrail joining the diagonal crack of the summer route.
4. 25m Follow the diagonal crack over the overlap and continue diagonally left to the next arête under the roofed recess. Step left around the arête in a very exposed position to a good belay.
5. 25m Follow the groove above to easy ground.

Fiacaill Buttress:
Halibut Habit – 40m V,5/6. S. Frazer, J. Lyall, M. Twomey. 5th March, 2002.
Start 10m left of White Dwarf, slightly left of the toe of the crag. This predominately icy route follows a narrow right-slanting line, breaching the upper tower by an obvious awkward groove.

LURCHERS CRAG (Creag an Leth-Choin):
The Shepherd – 100m III,4. C. Maclellan, P. Yardley. February, 2001.
The route takes a hidden right-slanting stepped gully on the buttress to the left of North Gully.

1. 25m Start directly below the left-hand edge of the buttress. Climb an initial corner to a ledge. Traverse left for 5m and continue up a second corner to easier ground and the foot of the right-slanting gully.
2. 50m Climb the gully over a series of steps exiting right at the top to a large ledge.
3. 25m At the right-hand side of the ledge, climb a steep wall (crux) to exit on to easier ground and gain a small col. From here it is possible to abseil 50m into North Gully or continue more easily to the top.

Quinn – 75m III. B. S. Findlay, R. Ross and G. S. Strange. 10th February 2002. The straight gully cum chimney defining the right edge of the buttress containing Collie's Route. It was climbed in two pitches passing the capping arch of jammed blocks on the right.

NORTH EAST OUTCROPS

No routes here as the new guide is imminent.

HIGHLAND OUTCROPS

GLEN NEVIS, Meadow Walls:
Impulse – 15m E8 6c ***. D. MacLeod. 15th July, 2001.
An awesome line climbing the pillar-like overhanging wall standing high above the Steall meadow, well left of Going for Gold. Very bold and serious climbing with a dynamic crux. Scramble in from the left past trees and start at the foot of an obvious ramp leading up the wall. Climb the ramp to some quartz holds at its top. Place an assortment of poor small cams in these. Continue directly up the leaning wall above with increasing difficulty to a desperate lunge to a good hold. Finish directly.

River Walls:
Isomorph – E7 6b *. D. MacLeod. 13th May, 2001.
This route climbs the overhanging rounded arête guarding the entrance to the gorge at the edge of the meadows. Interesting but very serious and committing climbing. Move right along the large ledge to the arête (Friend). Climb up and left to gain the obvious line of square cut flakes on the left side of the arête (skyhook runner) and climb these with difficulty to the easier top section.

GLENFINNAN, Boathouse Crag:
R.I.B. – 15m VS 4b. C. Moody, C. Grindley. 29th July, 2001.
There is another crag left (west) of the main crag. Climb the rib on the right side of the crag.

Das Boot – 15m VS 4c. C. Moody, C. Grindley. 29th July, 2001.
Start left of R.I.B. and climb the wall between two small trees; step left just before the angle eases.

MALLAIG CRAGS, Creag Mhor Bhrinicoire:
Notes from C. Cartwright: I would argue that Nobs up North, Morar Magic and
Penguin Monster are basically the same route with alternative starts. Pump and
Dump is E2 5b, not E1 5b. We also climbed what may be a new line to the right of
West Coast Boys at E3 5c. Led by Iain Small and followed by myself and Andrew
Faulk. Starts 2m right of West Coast Boys, climbs rightwards to the top of the
obvious pillar, breaks left up impending wall above (crux) before pulling right
into, and following the obvious overhanging crackline.

ARISAIG, Sidhean Mor (SMCJ 2000, p. 391):
The following routes are on the west-facing slab. Immaculate rock with a
magnificent outlook towards Eigg and Rum.
Billy Whiz – 20m Mild VS 4b *. S. Kennedy, W Muir. 10th June, 2001.
Takes a system of cracks and flakes on the slab just left of the obvious curving
crackline (One for Ewan). Climb the initial short wall by a flake. Move slightly
right and continue to a small roof. Continue up the cracked slab and finish directly
over the final steepening.

The Great Hunt – 20m M.Severe *. S. Kennedy, W Muir. 10th June, 2001.
The obvious flakeline left of Billy Whiz with which it shares a common start.
Start up the initial wall then follow cracks above to the prominent flake. Climb
the flake.

Absolute Beginners – 20m V. Diff *. S. Kennedy, W Muir. 10th June, 2001.
The slab immediately right of One for Ewan. Start at the foot of the curving
crackline and move diagonally right along a crack to reach the slab. Climb directly
up the slab.

DUNTELCHAIG:
Two routes have been reported on two small outcrops over the summit of the hill
behind the main crags and facing south. The left-hand gives boulder problems,
whilst the right-hand is a little higher. Locals have climbed here and certainly the
left-hand route has been done before.
Frothing Farmers – 10m VS 5a.
Climbs the left-hand flake crack starting up a steep pocketed wall.

Fire Burnished Night – 10m E2 6a. K. Howett, G. Ridge. 8th March, 2001.
Climbs the central crack. Thin starting moves up a hairline crack gain good holds
at half height to reach the upper crack.

TYNRICH SLABS, Frank Sinatra Walls:
R. McAllister's unnamed route is called Gorillas in the Mix.

High Green Crag:
Ole Blue Eyes was seconded by V. Chelton and R. McAllister.

INVERFARIGAIG, Monster Buttress (MR 522 226):
Monster Magic – 20m E2 5b/c. P. Mayhew, I. Innes. 31st May, 1998.

A very sustained climb but on good holds. Start at a thin rowan tree which marks the bottom of a left-facing and slightly overhanging diedre in a lower buttress, 50m from the right-hand end of Monster Buttress. Climb steeply up to a small birch. Pass this to the right and make a long reach or layback to a high hold on the right, then moving left (crux, first done with a pre-placed nut). Climb steeply with good protection to small overhang. Traverse right (thin but good friction) to bifurcating cracks for small fingers. Finish direct to a tree.

Dances with Blondes – 20m E1 5b. S. Howe, G. Lowe, Terry (?). 22nd May, 1998. The finishing slabs are very mossy and general cleaning may now be required. Start at the base of Monster Magic. Move left and up a mossy slab to reach clean rock at 6m and an obvious widening crack. Climb this crack, passing a bulge at 10m and a block above. The crack widens dramatically at 15m (Friend#4, crux). Bridge up on jams to a committing mantelshelf finish.

The Monster Mash – 70m E2. S. Long, D. (Smiler) Cuthbertson (Alt, on-sight). 24th May, 1996).
This atmospheric and serious climb accepts the challenge of the central line up the highest point of the crag. A massive open groove system just on the right of the crag centre weaves through several bands of overhangs. The climb gains the groove from the right via steep but relatively slabby rock. A good bet when weather is inclement. A row of detached blocks marks the start, directly below a mature tree 30m up the crag on the right end of the obvious ledge in the main groove.
1. 30m 5c. Step off a pinnacle block on the left and move up to a line of holds leading rightwards to a scoop under the overhang. Flakes lead up and left through the overhang (crux). Continue steeply but with less difficulty straight up to the tree. Continue left along the ledge to belay in the rose garden.
2. 25m 5a/b. Meander up the left side of the main groove, heading for the double band of overhangs. Traverse left below the overhangs until airy moves up and left allow access through the overlap. Continue left to belay at an airy crevassed stance. Spooky climbing demanding care with the rock.
3. 15m 5a/b. Rather than escaping rightwards, enter the shallow hanging groove on the left and follow it to the obvious crack at the left end of the final overhang. Pull over the overhang on good holds and continue up the delightful groove to the top. Enjoyable climbing on perfect rock.

WOLF CRAGS (MR 948 308):
A minor crag on the Dava Moor which could provide a half day or evening in the lower grades. 13 routes of 8-12m, details on request.The rock is good quality schist but the main section is mossy (could be brushed by someone keen).

CREAG DUBH, Sprawl Wall note:
The Meejies: E6 6b suggested by A. Robertson. Others have confirmed 6b (seconding).
Notes: From R. Everett: *Instant Lemon:* Pitch 2 description should read: "25m 5c. Traverse back left on huge flat holds for 5m. Move up to a line of small holds in a pale streak, then go straight up to better holds. Step back left into a groove, then follow this to the right, finishing at the left side of a corrugated roof."

Instant Lemon Direct: The peg has gone from the lower wall. This must be now at least E5 6a, possibly E6.

Desire: This is highly over-rated and probably undergraded at E2; E3 5c no stars would be better. Pitch 1 is better up the centre of the buttress, and done this way it is 5a. Pitch 2 is solid 5b and poorly protected, requiring a committing finish on doubtful holds. Pitch 3 is a bit of a horror show. Sure, the position is impressive, even spectacular, but the rock is fundamentally unsound.

PITLOCHRY, Rockdust Crags:

These mica schist crags were developed in the late 90's and early 'naughties'. The crags lie on a pleasant open hillside approximately 7 miles north-east of Pitlochry along the A924 in Glen Brerachan, by the tiny hamlet of Straloch. The name Rockdust was taken from the nearby tenant farmers who use crushed rock to increase soil fertility. Due to its southerly-facing aspect the crag can be quite a suntrap and generally stays dry for the best part of the year. With regards to access, both the landowner and the tenant farmer seem happy to have low impact climbing on the crags.

There are two crags, the better being the obvious Main (Upper) Crag. The Main Crag comprises both sport and traditional routes due to its varied nature.

On the Main Crag, the routes from left to right are as follows:

1. *No Food for the Parasites* – 40m HVS 5a. C. Miln, I. Watson. 16th May, 1999.
This line weaves up through the hanging slab with the large horizontal slot. Belay fairly far back on top of hillside at a small outcrop.

2. *Rubblesplitskin* – H. Severe 4b. B. Strachan , J. Bod. Henderson. 1999.
This route was done in the summer of 99 and may have already been reported.

3. *The Quiet American* – 40m HVS 5a. C. Miln, I. Watson. 23rd May, 1999.
This line starts a couple of metres left of the short left-hand bolted wall, trending diagonally up rightwards to meet a fault running up the left-hand side of the wall, then on up through the small overhang at the top.

3a. *Variation:* 40m E2 5c. C. Miln, I. Watson. 23rd May, 1999.
A direct start to the route, surmounting the overhang with some difficulty.

4. *Downshifting* – 12m F6c+/7a. I. Watson. 20th June, 1999.
The leftmost sport route follows the steep lower wall on crimps through to easier ground, with a final sting in the tail.

5. *Twilight Shift* – 12m F6c/+. C. Miln. 27th March, 1999.
An excellent line which takes the more featured right-hand side of the steep lower wall, having the same grand finale as the previous route.

6. *Ha Ha Tarrawingee* – 35m E2 5b. I. Watson , C. Miln. 27th March, 1999.
This pleasant line follows the faint crackline to the right of the previous route and can either be finished out left on the bolt belays of Route 5, or can be continued to top out on steep heather.

7. *21st Century Citizen* – 20m F6c. C. Miln. 21st March, 1999.
The classic of the crag weaves up through steep walls and bulges on surprising holds to the high point of the crag. Sustained but never desperate.

8. *Quiet Revolution* – 20m F6b+. I. Watson. 21st March, 1999.
After a tricky mantle the climbing eases off for a little before tackling a small roof and finishing up the top wall to join the belays of the previous route.

9. *French Onion Soup* – 14m F6a. I. Watson. 3rd May, 1999.
An excellant line on surprising holds.

10. *Tribute to Dan Osman* – 40m E3 6a. C. Miln, I. Watson. 17th April, 1999.
An excellent route which follows the right to left diagonal fault across the main face.
10a. *Variation:* 40m E4 6a. C. Miln, I. Watson. 17th April, 1999.
Instead of completing the full traverse of the main face, finish directly up through the crack system to the left of Route 7, finishing at the high point of the crag.
11. *Gimme Shelter* – 14m F6a. C. Mayland. 3rd May, 1999.
After a tough initial few moves through the roof, the climbing eases, continuing on up to the same belay as previous route.
12. *Egyptiana Jones* – 20m F6a+. I. Watson. 11th March, 2000.
This line starts up the first three bolts of Gimme Shelter, then trends up and right across the Crack of Doom , then directly upwards on to the top wall. Take care of loose rock when crossing the Crack of Doom.
13. *Wandering Minstrel* – 8m F7a. C. Mayland. 1st May, 1999.
The short steep line up the overhanging arête packs a punch.
14. *The Crack of Doom* – 40m H. Severe 4b. C. Miln, C. Mayland. 11th March, 2000.
Start up the crackline to the right of the previous route, then trend up leftwards into the large fault to the top. You are at your own peril !

Note: The belay point for the gear routes is set fairly far back from the cliff face, up the hillside at a small outcrop. Two 50m ropes should be adequate.

The Lower Crag has been partially developed to give four routes. The rock quality is less solid. From left to right:
1. *Millennium Madness* – 16m F6a. I. Watson. 3rd January, 2000.
A surprisingly pleasant route on some very positive holds. The top wall is a lot more solid than it might appear.
2. *Virtual Life* – 16m F6a+. C. Miln. 2nd January, 2000.
Another good line through surprisingly steep ground, arriving at the same belay as route 1.
3. *Sending the Wrong Signal* – 12m F6b+. C. Miln. 15th January, 2000.
The technical difficulty is of a short duration.
4. *Cat Scratch Fever* – 12m F6b+. C. Mayland. 15th January, 2000.
Wear long sleeves and trousers on this one!

WEEM CRAGS, Secret Garden Area:
The Missing Link – 20m F6c+/7a. I. Watson. 17th June, 2000.
This excellent sustained line links the bottom wall of Faithless, taking it up through the roof then trending up and leftwards to the top headwall of Forbidden Fruit via the golden hanger.

DUNKELD, Polney Crag, Ivy Buttress:
Stolen Ivy - 15m E7 6c. T. Rankin (unsec.). 25th April, 2001.
A eliminate with funky moves up the arête forming the left edge of the Hot Tips groove. Start up Hot Tips and move left to a small overlap below the arête (Small RP's). Move up the arête until a step left gains the finish of Sideline. Protection is hard to place (take a nut key). Practised on a top rope but graded for on-sight.

NEWTYLE QUARRY:
Give me Sunshine – 20m F6c+ **. I. Taylor. June, 2001.
The bolted line left of Spandau Ballet.

GLEN OGLE, The Diamond:
Cease Fire – 15m F8a+ ***. D. MacLeod. September, 2001.
This abandoned project has finally been completed to give an excellent sustained climb. Follow the line of bolts left of Spiral Tribe. From the second bolt move directly up the wall to a good hold and continue on small finger pockets (crux) to reach goodholds just below the top.

GLEN LEDNOCK, Hideaway Crag:
Unnamed – E2 5c. K. Howett, G. Nicoll. 11th July, 1999.
The corner in the middle of the crag just left of International Colouring-in Contest finishing in the slight groove above, and to the left of the finish of that route.

Hide and Sneak Direct Start – 5c. A. D. Robertson, G. Lennox (on sight). 26th May, 2001.
Climbs the obvious overhanging crackline at the toe of the crag to join the original at the end of its leftwards traverse. Possibly easier than the original but logical.

Battle of the Bulge – E5 6a. G. Lennox, C. Adam. June, 2001.
Start left of Hide and Sneak and move up left to join that route at the break. Follow this route until it moves out right to the protruding block. Instead, continue straight up to a letterbox under the roof. Pull through the roof and follow the break leftwards to an obvious fin/jug. Move up rightwards through the short groove to join the finish of Hide and Sneak.

Unnamed – VS 5a. A. Todd A. Taylor. 11th July, 1999.
The corner to the left of Hormone Imbalance (below).

Hormone Imbalance – VS 4c. A. Todd A. Taylor. 11th July, 1999.
To the right of the crag, take a right-slanting ramp above the small cave. Also claimed by C. Adam, M. Munro. June, 2001.

TROSSACHS, Stronachlachar Crags:
At the western end of Loch Katrine, above the tiny hamlet of Stronachlachar, lies a south-facing hillside strewn with many small crags and large boulders, two of which have been developed as sport crags due to their blank, unprotectable nature. The crags can be approached from the B829 from Aberfoyle to Inversnaid. Turn left at the Stronachlachar junction and park in a fairly large passing place on the left, approx. a half mile along the road.
High up on the open hillside, left of the wooded area is the High Crag at NN 388 102. This compact micaschist crag is small but perfectly formed. The High Crag is best enjoyed in spring/summer whilst the G-Spot (see below) is better in spring or autumn when the ferns are down.
From left to right the routes are as follows:
1. *Rakshasa* – 6m F7a. C. Miln. 27th September, 1997.
This extended boulder problem has spat off a few!

2. Project.
3. *Lady of the Loch* – 10m F6b. I. Watson. 16th May, 1998.
Climb the line of small hidden pockets.
4. *My Own Private Scotland* 10m – F6c+. C. Miln. 21st September, 1997.
The central line is sustained with a sting in the tail!
5. *Highland Cling* – 10m F6b. I. Watson. 22nd September, 1997.
This very pleasant line is harder than it first looks .

The second developed crag is known as the G-Spot. This is found approximately halfway up the left-hand edge of the wooded area at NN 390 101. The crag is actually a giant mica schist boulder, yielding some very tough routes and a project to go. It was originally bolted by George Ridge in 1997, then a few years later climbed by Colin Miln, Isla Watson and George.
From left to right the routes are:
1. *Rhumba al Sol* – 12m F6a. I. Watson. 13th May, 2000.
The excellent left-hand arête.
2. *Hideous Kinky* – 12m F7b. C. Miln, I. Watson. 18th August, 2001.
Climb the blank scoop, then with great difficulty teeter tenuously up the thin top wall.
3. *Venga Boys* – 12m F6c+/7a. G. Ridge. 14th May, 2000.
Climb the right to left fault.
4. *El Mundo Fanatico* – 12m F7a+. C. Miln. 7th May, 2000.
Shares a common start with Venga Boys, then trends up and right to a tough finale.
5. Project . Open to any budding boulderers.

Inversnaid Crags:
This area lies by Inversnaid which is accessed by continuing along the B829 past the Stronachlachar Crags, to the very end of the road. There are two main crags, Wild Swans Crags and Crystal Crag, which lie on the hillside above the east bank of Loch Lomond, north of the Inversnaid Hotel. The Wild Swans Crags lie at NN 334 103 and are found up off the West Highland Way trail, just under 1.5 km from the Hotel carpark. There are two small crags with completed routes and a couple of very steep project crags. All are west-facing and the rock is very compact , micro-pocketed mica schist, hence lending itself to sport routes. Both Wild Swans Crags and Crystal Crag are best visited in the spring and autumn when the ferns are down.

From south to north as you approach the crags along a narrow goat path, you will find:
Crag One:
1. *Hobble* – 10m F7a+. C. Miln. 25th October, 1997.
A bouldery route taking the right-hand side of the crag.

Crags Two and Three:
Several projects which will yield some tough grades.

Crag Four: Wild Swans Buttress:
The best of the crags contains four pleasant routes with great views up Loch Lomond. From left to right:

1. *The Ridge* – 10m F6c. C. Miln. 31st October, 1998.
Traverse out left (crux) to the arête, then move up on to easier ground.
2. *Dark Skies* – 10m F6b+. C. Miln. 2nd November, 1997.
A tough crimpy start leads into a faint groove and more positive holds.
3. *Wild Swans* – 10m F6c. I. Watson. 23rd October, 1997.
Follow the central line of immaculate rock on micro-pockets.
4. *Moonlight Sonata* – 10m F6b+. I. Watson. 15th November, 1998.
Start at the right-hand side of the face and trend up leftwards to meet the top
section of Wild Swans.

Crystal Crag lies further north at NN 336 109, roughly 2km north of the Hotel
off the West Highland Way. Shortly after crossing a bridge, you will be forced to
squeeze between two large boulders on the trail. At this point climb steeply uphill
to the crag. A fairly tough 45-minute walk-in, but worth it. The crag is easy to spot
by its unique white crystalline patina. It faces south-west and is a real suntrap and
very sheltered, without suffering from midges.
This was discovered and developed by Colin Miln and Isla Watson, with others
later adding lines.
From left to right:
1. Project.
Joins at the same belay point as Route 2.
2. *Fear and Self Loathing* – 20m F7b. C. Miln. 3rd October, 1998.
Break out left from the shared start of Route 3 and make a gnarly traverse leftwards
before moving out onto the top wall with initial difficulty followed by more positive
holds. A real outing!
3. *Age of Aquarius* – 18m F7a+. C. Miln. 22nd August, 1998.
A superb line. Sharp technical moves lead to a ramp. Trend leftwards up the ramp
and break out upwards on to the top wall on positive holds. Sustained but never
desperate.
4. *Purgatory* – 16m F7b. C. Miln. 2nd May, 1999.
From the common start of Route 3, continue directly up through the roof. Belay
shared with Route 3.
5. *Roadkill Recipes* – 14m F7a+. G. Ridge. 22nd August, 1998.
Start just to the right of the previous routes, by the small tree. Continue up and
right through the overhang to the belay.
6. *Ruby Slippers* – 14m F7a. J. Horrocks. 18th March, 2000.
Pleasant climbing up the lower wall leads to a blind crux move below the overhang.
7. *Rebel Without Applause* – 14m F7b. C. Miln. 15th March, 1998.
Climb to gain the ramp, then up again to the quartz boss. Use this to move up the
tricky headwall.
8. *Far From the Malham Crowds* – 14m F7a. I. Watson. 2nd May, 1999.
Thin technical moves up the finely featured right-hand side of the wall.

BEN NEVIS, AONACHS, CREAG MEAGHAIDH

The new guide for this area will be out soon, so no routes are published here.

GLEN COE

Routes which have already appeared in the new Glen Coe guide are not repeated here. The following may not be in the guide. Any which have been omitted from both should be re-submitted next year, so recent first ascentionists please check.

BUACHAILLE ETIVE MOR, Coire na Tulaich:
Note: R. Jones climbed The Spate (SMCJ 2000). He thinks the description for it is wrong as it suggests that it may take the line of Awong. Awong is 4m-5m to the right of the chimney. He felt the route was IV,5 not IV,6. The route is about 70m not including the traverse. He suggests the following description:
The obvious left-slanting chimney line, icy to start then more mixed. A chokestone at 45m provides the crux. leading to a large shelf. Traverse up rightwards to finish. Good early in the season.

Stob Coire Altruim:
Note: Cerberus: Following the second ascent, M. Bass suggests a better pitch 3: 1and 2. As before (SMCJ 1997).
3. 50m Go under the chockstone, then up on to it and climb the right-hand turfy groove to easy ground and the summit.

BIDEAN NAM BIAN, Lost Valley Minimus Buttress:
A suggested name for the buttress right of Lost Valley Minor Buttress.
The Nipper – 100m II/III. G. W. M. Allan, J. Thomas. 16th February, 2002.
Climbs the left edge of this buttress. Start up and right of the left-hand toe of the buttress at an obvious fault. Climb the fault for 15m, traverse across the slabby left wall and follow the obvious line just right of the edge to easy ground. Climbed with poor conditions in the lower fault but a pleasant line.

STOB COIRE NAN LOCHAIN, Central Buttress:
Note: *East Face Route*. D. Kerr and I. Sharpe climbed the left-hand gully line throughout on 26th February, 2000, followed a week later by A. Shand and C. Grant. VI,7 agreed.

North Buttress:
Dress Circle – 60m IV,4. S. Kennedy, M. Shaw. 31st December 2001.
The groove-line slanting diagonally up leftwards to the right of North Face and overlooking the upper reaches of North Gully. Start just below and left of a small rock pinnacle in the upper part of North Gully at the foot of two short, steep grooves. Climb strenuously up the right-hand groove by some chockstones. Continue up leftwards via the continuation groove to behind a small thumb of rock (30m). Traverse leftwards along a ledge to the foot of a slabby groove. Climb the groove and its continuation above to the top of North Buttress (30m).

STOB COIRE A' CHEARCAILL:
Charcoal Buttress – 120m III,4. D. McGimpsey, A. Nisbet. 1st January, 2002.
There is an east-facing crag directly belowthe summit and largely composed of one main buttress. This route climbs the crest of the buttress, starting just left of the toe and continuing on alternate sides of the crest to the top.

AONACH DUBH, North Face:

The Twarf – VI,7. S. Chinnery, M. Morton. 24th February, 2002.

Climbed in six pitches, the first as for Fall-out up a nice little icefall. The next two pitches were the meat, a excellent chimney and then fine steep climbing on the crux corner groove on superb hooks and quite good gear. Then easier climbing up the continuation fault, finishing up and left up the obvious fault/gully line to the top. An excellent little route after getting past a treacherous sloping shelf.

Note: Repeated three weeks later by P. Benson and G. Robertson who climbed two pitches of the summer line, then took the right-hand of the two 'twin grooves' (crux) which led to easier ground.

GARBH BHEINN (ARDGOUR), Leac Beag Buttress:

Centrefold – 90m IV,4. S. Kennedy, A. Nelson. 24th February, 2002.

The vegetated groove dividing the two sections of the buttress. Climb a short gully, then step right into a small bay below the main groove. A steep thin icefall leads to the deep groove which is followed to a small cave. Awkward slabby moves lead out right then continue up an easy ramp to the upper slopes.

Stonefall Gully, Right Branch – 145m III,4. P. Farr, P. Harrop, G. Jones. 24th February, 2002.

The right-hand branch of the gully defining the right side of the buttress. Climb the gully to a cave. Exit the cave by an icefall on the right wall then follow grooves up rightwards to a further small cave. Continue up rightwards by a grooveline the reach the easier upper slopes.

Too Far Left – 60m III. P.Farr, P. Harrop, G. Jones. 24th February, 2002.

The prominent icefall on the left side of the buttress immediately left of Leac Beag Buttress. Climb the icefall in two pitches.

ARDNAMURCHAN, BEINN NAN ORD, Creag Lochain Dubha (MR 441 649):

This is a hill to the west of Beinn na Seilg with a south-west facing gabbro cliff at altitude 150m.

Dubha Lochain Monster – 40m Diff. **. C. Moody. 17th March, 2002.

There are three cracks, start just right of the left crack and climb straight up with a bulge near the top.

Predator – 40m V.Diff **. C. Moody. 17th March, 2002.

Start just left of the middle crack. Move up, step right over the crack and continue to the top.

Black Mamba – 40m Severe *. C. Moody. 17th March, 2002.

Start to the right of Predator. Climb a bulge and continue up.

Mousetrap – 50m Diff. C. Moody. 17th March, 2002.

To the right the main cliff the crag is guarded by an overlap. Cross the overlap near the right end then follow the slab to a heather ledge. Climb the small slab above, then move left to finish up the main cliff.

SOUTHERN HIGHLANDS

GLEN CROE:
Fernandez – 6c/7a **. M. Tweedley. April, 2002.
On the boulder in front of Ace of Spades. Climb the snakey arête using a hold on the right, then crimp up the arête to a jug. Painful!

THE COBBLER, South Peak, South Face:
Lasting Impression – 60m E3 **. R. and C. Anderson. 13th May, 2001.
This climbs a line just left of centre on the wall left of Porcupine Wall to cross the fault and climb a groove to a finish up Cupids Groove. The result of two days cleaning.
1. 20m 5b Start at a boulder left of centre on the wall, below the left end of the belay ledge. Climb up to the left and place a sideways Rock#7 which acts as a side runner, then return to the ground. Step off the boulder and move slightly up and right to good holds then continue directly to holds just below a pointed projecting hold where the first gear is located. Continue to a horizontal break (runners). Continue straight up to quartz holds (good wires just up to the right). Move up right and climb to the left end of the belay ledge. Climb past the horizontal break and gain a thin crack then foot traverse rightwards.
2. 40m 5b Step across the fault, climb to a blocky projection and continue up a crack and ensuing groove to its top to reach the grass ledge where the worn scramblers path from the col ends. Move up right into the groove (Cupids Groove, originally gradedVS 4c, but is more like E2 5b). From the small ledge on the right at the top of the groove gain a slabby ledge and climb to the top just left of the crack in the headwall.

North-East Face:
MacLean's Folly – 85m VIII,8 ***. D. MacLeod, G. Hughes. 23rd February, 2002.
The rarely repeated summer route makes a spectacular winter line, featuring sustained and strenuous, but reasonably well protected climbing.

THE BRACK:
Hogwart's Express – 125m VI,7. A. Clarke, F. Yeoman. 4th January, 2002.
Fine mixed climbing with great exposure. Climbs the right edge of the wall, right of Great Central Groove and Resolution, finishing up the oblique tapered fault. Start at the toe of the wall.
1. 40m Climb up to an obvious line trending up and right (as for Resolution). Continue right climbing a short wall to below a steep wall on the edge.
2. 15m Climb steeply above the belay into an overhung niche, move left (bold) to a thin turf ledge, then more easily to a ledge.
3. 30m Traverse left a short distance, then tackle the wall direct, aiming for a vague crack in its upper half. Move right crossing an iced slab to reach a ledge below the oblique tapered fault of Mainline.
4. 30m Climb the fault. When it overhangs, move on to the edge and a stiff pull to easy ground below the final wall.
5. 10m The steep thinly iced wall above (as for Mainline summer).

STOB GHABHAR, NE Coire:
Alternative Groove – 80m II. G. Allan, K. Powell, I. Reynolds. March, 2000.
Takes the obvious ramp to the left of the buttress containing Hircine Rib, 150m
east of the Upper Couloir. Start at the prominent rocks below the ramp and climb
steep snow trending left (50m). Continue up for 15m before heading right to an
obvious break in the cornice.

BEINN AN DOTHAIDH, Creag Coire an Dothaidh:
Burnout – 175m IV 4. I. Clark, A. McCaig. 24th February, 2002.
Takes the right edge of the main buttress, traverses round on to the face overlooking
the col, finishing up steep icy grooves and walls. A good varied route on steep turf
and icy bulges.
1. 35m Start 20m right of Centigrade at an icy turf ramp under a short diagonal
wall. Climb the ramp, go left round a corner and up ledges to a thread.
2. 35m Continue up steep ice, go right for a few metres, then up and left to a cave
with a thread at the back.
3. 40m Climb up bulges to a long airy traverse to reach a large flake.
4. 40m Move right and climb a steep icy groove.
5. 25m Continue to the top.

BEN CRUACHAN:
To the north of the ridge running west from Cruachan's summit to the bealach
between it and the Taynuilt peak are situated some steep crags. These are split by
a wide gully which finishes as a prominent deep chimney formed by a huge fin of
rock on its right side. This was climbed over a couple of icy steps. 60m I/II. D.
Ritchie, M. Shaw. 9th February, 2002.
Noe Buttress – 100m IV,4. D. Ritchie, M. Shaw. 9th February, 2002.
This route climbs the buttress immediately right of the wide gully. Start some 30
metres above and left of the toe of the buttress.
1. 50m Move on to the left-hand edge of the buttress, climbing mixed ground
above to gain a shallow right-slanting chimney. At its top turn the rock nose on its
right side, climbing a groove then a right-trending fault to easier ground.
2. 50m Follow the buttress crest more easily to finish.

MEALL NAN TARMACHAN, Arrow Buttress:
Planet Fear – 60m VII,7 **. S. Muir, G. E. Little. 2nd January, 2002.
The obvious icefall visible from the dam (in a good winter) in the bay 100m right
of dam busters gives a steep and serious climb on fragile ice, maybe VIII,7. Gain
the main fall/pencil by traversing across a steep slab on turf and ice from the right.
In exceptional conditions, it may be possible to climb the lower free hanging
icicle direct to the main fall.
1. 30m Traverse left above the initial icicle by an obvious line of turf/ice and
climb directly to the base of the ice smears and free hanging ice pencil. Climb this
directly with extreme care to a belay on ice below the overhanging wall.
2. 30m Climb up and right to gain turf or ice drooping over the right lip of the
overhanging wall. Somehow gain the wall above and climb the next short ice
wall.

Carlin's Buttress:
Note: D. Crawford notes that the route One for the Road, climbed with S. Burns in 1997 should be grade II (originally climbed in lean conditions). Also that *Little Gully* (SMCJ 2001, p689) is the same as *One For The Road* (SMCJ 1998).

BEN CHONZIE, Carn Chois:
Sieging the Battlements – 80m IV,5. K. Howett, A. Armstrong. 20th January,2001. Climbs an obvious ice pillar in the centre of the buttress near the summit. The obvious left- diagonal and very deep gully to the left of this route was also climbed that day at 120m grade II but would probably bank-out under heavier snow.

ARRAN

BEINN NUIS, Flat Iron Tower:
Ealta Rib – 135m V. Diff *. C. Read, S. J. H. Reid (alt.). 20th May, 2001.
An excellent sustained route on sound clean rock. Start at the very foot of the long rib that drops down westward into Ealta Coirre. This is on the opposite side of the corrie to the Full Meed Tower.
1. 25m Climb a rib between two grooves via an obvious pocket to a ledge on the right side of a roof. Step right to a short grassy groove and go up to a belay.
2. 50m Climb up the right arete and then diagonally leftwards up slabs to easy ground. Scramble up to a belay just to the left of a fine rib.
3. 35m Gain the rib from the left, just above a prominent overlap and follow cracks to a huge prow. Avoid this on the right, the move back leftwards to finish up the exposed arete. A large detached block is 10m above.
4. 25m Climb on to the block and gain the wall above. Follow an obvious hand traverse leftwards and round to a platform under a short chimney. Squirm up the chimney to the top.

BEINN TARSUINN, Consolation Tor:
Consolation Arete – 60m VS. S. J. H. Reid, N. Walmsley. 19th May, 2001.
Takes the left edge of Tarsuinn No. 1 Chimney. Fine, exposed and well protected climbing, though the rock is not above suspicion in places.
1 20m (4c). Follow the rib, avoiding the prominent prow by a traverse left and move up (crux) to a detached block. Move back right to a platform and a fine stance overlooking the chimney.
2 40m (4b). Follow cracks up the wall above to a groove under a roof. Climb up to the roof and avoid it on the right. Easier ground leads to the top.
Note: S. Reid estimates that Tarsuinn No. 1 Chimney is 60m and Tarsuinn No. 2 Chimney is 50m.

CIR MHOR, South Face:
Forge – 100m E5. J. Lines (on sight solo). 28th July, 2001.
1. 50m 5c Start as for Anvil but where Anvil goes right, continue up the groove and flakes above. When it becomes blank, move right on to the slab and up to pockets. Step right and continue up into a scoop with a tiny flake. Exit the scoop on the right and move up to a shallow-angled slab. Just before a bulging section, traverse down and left to reach Hammer.

2. 25m 5b Behind the belay, a line of pockets goes up and right. Follow these until they disappear, then go straight up the slab to a horizontal flakeline. Move right to easy ground and belay below the slabby arete on the skyline.

3. 25m 5c Using a short crack/pod on the left of the arete, make a thin move to gain the arete. Climb the arete on the right for 3m (easy), then make a hard move left on to a boss/smear and further hard moves up to small holds on the slab. Stretch right to good pockets in the very crest and climb direct to join South Ridge Direct.

Incus 55m – E6 **. G. Latter. 27th August, 2001.

A series of pitches up the wall left of South Ridge Direct, the main centre of interest being the thin flange 15m left of the S-Crack. Start on the front face just round right of Anvil Recess Start, beneath a short groove.

1. 15m Climb the short undercut groove to layback on to a slab above, then more easily up this. Climb easily right across a slab, then up past a large flake to a grass clod directly beneath the flange.

1a. 30m A longer better pitch, occasionally climbed as an approach to the S-Crack. Start farther right, beneath a left-facing groove. Enter and climb the wide slot in the groove to easier ground, then continue by a steep hand crack and cracks just to its left to the grass clod.

2. 10m Move up the corner and step left across the slab to the flange. Climb this with interest (sustained and well protected), then use a one finger pocket in the wall above to hand traverse left on a micro-granite vein to superb finishing holds. Belay on the shelf above.

3. 15m Walk right along the shelf to belay at the base of the curving corner. Climb this, moving up right at its top to a huge thread. Abseil off or climb up leftwards from the top of the corner to gain the block strewn terrace on South Ridge Direct.

Rosa Pinnacle, Upper East Face:

Hardland – 30m E5 6a ***. D. Honeyman, T. De Gay. August, 2001.

A stunning short route on the beautiful pocketed slab right of Squids and Elephants. Start just right of this route and gain the intermittent crackline in the slab (good Friend protection in these). From near the top of the second crack, break out left with difficulty to gain the huge pocket. Follow a line of pockets boldly leftwards, with a final difficult move to gain the edge of the slab and the top. Abseil off or continue as for Squids and Elephants.

The Sleeping Crack – 55m E6 ***. D. MacLeod, D. Honeyman. August, 2001.

This stunning line climbs the attractive intermittent crackline in the huge pillar right of Minotour. The second pitch gives bold exposed climbing followed by difficult moves in the crack.

1. 15m 6a Gain the first crack and follow it with increasing difficulty until it is possible to escape left on to a slab. Take a hanging belay on the huge thread.

2. 40m 6b Traverse right from the belay and boldly climb a sloping shelf to regain the crackline. Follow this with hard moves (crux), but excellent protection to an undercut flake. Follow this leftwards, then up until below the final bulge. Climb rightwards up another flake, then make a difficult move up left on finger pockets to gain the finishing slab. Pad easily up this to a flake belay on the terrace (large Friends useful).

CIOCH NA H-OIGHE, The Bastion:
The Great Escape – 100m E8 ***. J. Dunne, A. Jack. 21st June, 2001.
1. 30m 6b Climb the open groove right of the 1st pitch of Abraxas, over a roof to an obvious belay ledge.
2. 40m 6c The awesome main pitch. From the belay climb directly up the stunning leftward trending groove-line to a poor in-situ thread runner. Make difficult moves diagonally leftwards to gain the left-hand pincer. Follow this in a spectacular position to a belay on the Tidemark ramp.
3. 30m 6b Above the belay climb the obvious scoop, with a hard move at roughly 5m, to a spike runner. Ascend the slab above and finish up easier ground and the top of ledge 4.
Note: The E8 grade came from D. MacLeod who made the second ascent a week later. MacLeod's description is available by e-mail.

LOWLAND OUTCROPS

GLASGOW OUTCROPS, Dumbarton Rock:
Achemine – 35m E9 6c ***. D. MacLeod. 9th October, 2001.
Excellent and desperate climbing on the smooth headwall above Chemin De Fer. This bold addition is the hardest traditional lead in the country at present. Start up Chemin De Fer and follow this to where the crack bends left. Move up on undercuts past an overlap, to a handrail. Move right along this and make a desperately thin move rightwards to a rounded side pull. In a run out position, move back left via a small pinch and continue leftwards with desperate technical moves (crux) to eventually reach better holds and the top. Very sustained, fingery and bold climbing.

Dunglas:
Drink up, for tomorrow we die! – 30m E7 6b *. D. MacLeod. 17th July 2001.
An unusual, steep and serious route with some loose rock and an unprotected crux. The first route to breach the upper of the two black overhanging walls that dominate the crag. Start near the left end of the wall, below a series of smooth, stepped overlaps. Climb to a protruding block at the start of the overlaps. Step right and make a long reach through the overlaps to a diagonal hold (crux). Use this to move rightwards to better holds and protection. Move up left to a large cracked block below a roof (Friend in block) and pull directly through the roof to stand on the shelf above. Step right and climb more easily on loose blocks, passing a small tree on the left, to the top. Low in the grade.

Craigmore, Layback Crack Area:
Inverlussa Crack – 15m E2 5c. P. Roy and partner. June, 2001.
Start just left of White Hope. Move up to a slot (Friend), then make a couple of difficult moves up to a crack. Swing round to the left and climb a slab to the top (diagram provided).

Dunoon, Miracle Wall (see www.scottishclimbs.com):
Grace – E2 5c *. M. Tweedley. April, 2002.
Climbs the start of Angels with Dirty Faces, miss the clip and head for a break,

then follow a steep juggy wall leftwards to an obvious pinch. A delicate move gains the slab and finish. Well protected.

THE GALLOWAY HILLS, The Tauchers, The Giant's Staircase:
Switchback – new 3rd pitch added by S. Reid and J. Reid, 10th Aug 2001.
3. 50m. Move further still along the terrace to the right a long easy corner which is climbed by its right rib to slabs. Follow these leftwards to a broad heather terrace. Either walk off to the left, or climb several further pitches of heathery scrambling to the top. This is better and more in keeping than the original finish. Switchback is worth a *.

Craigencallie:
The Empty Quarter repeated and a new direct start added. The route is redescribed as the new start is better than the original.
The Empty Quarter – 50m E2 **. C King, A Mawer, S Reid (direct start). 28th July, 2001.
A superb pitch, giving fine climbing up the undercut slab. Protection is good but spaced. Start directly under the centre of the overhang at a slim pillar with a square hold.
1. 30m 5b Using the pillar, make a difficult move to gain a good hold over the roof and pull up onto the slab (alternatively take the Original Start to reach the same point from the left and deduct an E-point). Climb the slab/wall until it eases, move right and then up to a ledge.
2. 20m 4a From the left end of the ledge, traverse 5m left and climb a cleaned crack and slabs to the top.

Dungeon of Buchan, Cooran Buttress:
Cooran Buttress Direct – 120m VS *. S .Reid, J. Biggar (VL), J. Reid, M. Thompson. 22nd August, 2001.
This series of variations on Cooran Buttress provides some good climbing. Start down and right of the left-hand grassy fault at a clean slab, 10m left of the start of Cooran Buttress.
1. 25m 4a Climb the slab, moving left to the arête, and mantelshelf onto a large grass ledge. Step down left and climb directly up to heather. Climb straight up the front of the pinnacle above to a pile of blocks belay.
2. 40m 4c Climb the overhanging groove on the left, passing a precarious block to a ledge. Continue up the groove to a slab. Step right and climb the slab to a leaning block belay on a heather terrace. A fine pitch.
3. 15m 4b Climb the crack 4m left of the block (as for Traitor's Gait), for 5m, until it is possible to climb diagonally into a neighbouring crack on the right. Follow this to a terrace (5b direct).
4. 35m 5a Follow the slab, then cracks, directly to under the overhang near its left hand end. Step right across a mossy streak into the crack of Cooran Buttress. Move up and then climb up left (crux) to overcome the overhang. Finish up an easy groove.
5. 5m 5a The desperate short crack on the right makes a fitting finish or walk off.

To the right of Cooran Buttress are many small and broken outcrops. High in the centre of this area is a prominent arête. This is well worth the walk and is best gained by traversing from the top of Cooran Buttress. It gives *The Arête* (20m, HVS 5a*, S. Reid, A. Gillies, 6th April, 2002) and is climbed via a crack in its left side, passing two large blocks with care.

The Lion's Head:
Three hundred metres down and to the right of Cooran Buttress the rock becomes more continuous. This area derives its name from its supposed resemblance to a lion's head and mane when viewed from a distance. Two heathery terraces split the highest part of the crag into three walls, the headwall of which is impressively smooth. To the right of the headwall the crag slopes down to the right, gradually reducing in height.

Horns of a Dilemma – 85m HVS **. I. Magill, A. Fraser (alt.). 6th April, 2002. Pitch 3: C. King, S. Reid. 11th April, 2002.
Excellent slab climbing. At the left end of the crag the lower heather terrace peters out. Start 10m left of the left end of this terrace, beneath the left end of the headwall, at the right-hand of two vertical hairline cracks.
1. 25m 5a Make a rising traverse up into the left-hand crack and pull over its first bulge to a slab. Traverse the slab rightwards and round into a niche. Move up and step right onto a sloping ledge, then continue to a belay on the heather terrace. A complex pitch.
2. 35m 5a Scramble up the terrace to a short chimney. Climb this with interest to more heather and traverse right onto the headwall. Climb up rightwards to gain two parallel, rightward trending cracks. Superb climbing up these (the dilemma and crux) gains a good stance (it is possible to walk off right here).
3. 25m 4c Step left and follow the leftward-rising ramp to a crack. Climb the crack to its top, gain overlapping slabs on the right, and finish up these.

Aslan – 105m VS. A. Fraser, I. Magill. 6th April, 2002.
A worthwhile route, much better than appearances suggest. It climbs walls to the right of the headwall, aiming for the obvious vertical clean crack which is situated 8m right of the conspicuous twin rightward-trending cracks at the foot of the headwall. Start above a steepening in the grass gully beneath the crag, 6m left of a small tree some 12m up.
1. 40m 4a Climb into a short corner and follow this to heather, left of the tree. Take the short chimney 5m left of the tree to a heather ledge, then move up left to climb the wide crack. Continue to a ledge, then traverse leftwards, then up, to gain a heathery niche.
2. 20m 4c Exit the niche by tricky moves up grooves on the left of the niche, and continue up to narrow heather ledge. Move up left onto the headwall, and continue up left to gain the vertical crack described at the start, at its mid-point. Climb this to a ledge and belay under a large roof.
3. 45m 4c Pad right across slabs to reach, then climb the crack at the right end of the roofs. From a heather ledge above, climb a short wall to finish.

In the low wall well down to the right is a very prominent short offwidth crack. Immediately left of this is a curving handjam crack. This is the superb *Jaw Jaw* (10m, HVS 5b *, S. Reid, A. Gillies, 6th April, 2002) which is hard to start, strenuous in the middle, and puzzling to finish. The offwidth itself is *War War* (10m, E1 5b, C. King, S. Reid, 11th April, 2002) - extra large Friends required.

Right again, and just right of a pinnacle, is another short crack.
The Lion's Mane – 150m H.Severe. A. Gillies, S. Reid (alt). 6th April, 2002.
A long route with some nice moves but rather too much heather and grass.
1. 45m 4b Climb the short crack past an awkward chockstone to slabs. Follow these leftwards and up to a horizontal break just below a rounded boss of rock. Avoid this by traversing leftwards and go up to a stance.
2. 55m 4a Traverse right 5m across grass to a clean slab and follow the left-facing corner which curves up leftwards to more grass and a large pinnacle (possible belay). Climb into a groove on the right of the pinnacle and follow it to a double bulge on the right. Hand traverse the upper bulge with feet on the lower until it is possible to mantelshelf onto the slab above. Move up to a large area of heather and belay on a wall on the right some 15m below a double band of overhangs.
3. 50m 4a Climb the wall on the right, then cross grass diagonally rightwards to gain a clean slab. Follow the left edge of this to a huge detached flake. Step rightwards on to the flake with care and climb the crack to the top.

Clints of Dromore, Black and White Walls:
Some 400m to the left of Central Buttress is a steeper though much shorter wall of excellent clean granite. It is quick drying and, being away from the main mountain massif, a good winter venue. It is split by the central left-facing Honeysuckle Groove. To the right of this groove is White Wall, to the left is Black Wall, the latter being sub-divided into three distinct black slabs by slim grooves. Belays are scarce, the best being a crack just right of a detached block directly above Cupid's Bow. The climbs are described from left to right.
Cupid's Arrow – 13m VS 4b. A. Hewison, S. Reid. 2nd November, 2001.
Start towards the left edge of Black Wall at a vague blocky arête just right of a short raggedy groove. Bridge up the groove to gain the arête, which leads to a rounded finish.

The Climb with No Name – 14m E2 5b. C. King, S. Reid. 9th November, 2001.
The slab to the left of Cupid's Bow just merits the grade. Start up a quartz seam, step left slightly and then straight up, finishing over a bulge.

Cupid's Bow – 15m E1 5a. S. Reid, A. Hewison. 14th February, 2001.
The pink coloured left-facing groove, just left of the centre of Black Wall is followed until it steepens at a little nose, and moves are made to a jug on its left wall. Either continue up the groove, or, more easily, move left and back right. Finish up the scoop above. Technically easy for the grade, but protection is worrying.
Right-Hand Finish: E2 5b. C. King, S. Reid. 9th November 2001.
A serious variation pulling out right below the little nose and finishing up the right arête.

Do You Feel Lucky? – 16m E2 5b. C. King, S. Reid. 2nd November, 2001.
Weigh up your chances and climb the central black slab via an obvious half-way jug. Easy for the grade.

Stupid Cupid – 16m VS 4c *. S. Reid, C. King, J. Biggar. 2nd November, 2001.
The slim flaky groove just right of centre is followed to a flake overhang which is avoided on the left.

Make My Day! – 16m E1 5a *. C. King, S. Reid. 2nd November, 2001.
The right-hand slab is excellent, low in the grade and better protected than it looks. Climb up via pockets to a short crack on the left, move up this, then traverse horizontally right and finish direct.

Sheer Cupidity – 14m Severe 4a. J. Biggar, C. King, S. Reid. 2nd November, 2001.
Follow the cracks in the left wall of the central Honeysuckle Groove and finish out leftwards.

Honeysuckle Groove – 14m VS 4c. S. Reid, C. King. 9th November, 2001.
The obvious left-facing groove in the centre of the crag is climbed via a slim groove just right of the cracks of Sheer Cupidity to just below vegetation at the top, where wild moves via a jug on the right provide a fine finish.

White Arête – 14m M.Severe 4a. S. Reid, C. King. 9th November, 2001.
The arête to the right of Honeysuckle Groove is followed to a large grass ledge. Continue up the arête above.

Sweet Heart – 16m H.Severe 4b. S. Reid, C. King, J. Biggar. 2nd November, 2001.
Mantelshelf into a niche just right of White Arête and follow stepped rock rightwards to just right of the large grass ledge. Move up and then back leftwards to finish directly up the middle of the upper wall.

White Scoop – 16m VS 4c. S. Reid, J. Biggar, C. King. 2nd November, 2001.
A rather artificial climb taking the centre of White Wall. Start 2m right of Sweet Heart and climb the wall to a break above the large white scoop. Traverse left to just right of the large grass ledge, move up, and make a rising traverse back right to finish up a rib. Can be climbed direct at 5b.

The Notch – 15m HVS 5a. S. Reid, C. King. 9th November, 2001.
Climb the right side of White Wall to a ledge. Steep rock above leads to an obvious large notch. Finish up the rib on the right.

Craigdews:

The *Lowlands Outcrops Guide* (page 151) refers to mellow goats and a savage goat warden. No problems have been encountered to date, other than goats trying to bum fags and drink from tourists. The guidebook description has, however, served a purpose, and protected this fine roadside granite crag from the depredations of the masses. The crag is bigger and less broken than appearances suggest, is of good granite, easy 10 minute approach, less midgy than hereabouts, and gives excellent climbing and puns in a pleasant spot.
Park in the main Goat Park car park. The crag is above, and can be divided into three areas:-
1. The Tree Walls. At the right is an area of short, steep tree-studded walls, bounded on the left by slabs overlooking a left sloping bracken ramp.
2. The Central Section. This is the highest section of the crag.

3. The Dark Side. Above and left are steep, dark metamorphic walls with lower granite cliffs.
Routes are described right to left.

The Tree Walls:

Cemetery Goats – 27m HVS 5a *. A. Fraser, I. Magill.. 26th July, 2000.
Enjoyable, fun climbing, particularly in the lower corner. The largest, right-hand buttress has a steep corner on its left side, distinguishable by an overhang at 7m and a holly tree above at half height. Climb the corner past the overhang, moving right on to the wall at the top, to gain the bottom of the holly tree. Move down and right for 2m to a crack. Climb this, then continue up walls to the right of the holly tree.

The buttress to the left between Cemetery Goats and the leftward-sloping bracken ramp is the steepest on the crag, with an obvious central depression leading to overhangs.
Vorsprung Goat Technique – 27m VS 4c. A Murdoch, A. Fraser. 30th August, 2000.
Some loose rock mars an otherwise good route. Start up the central depression, until it is possible to move up right on to a ledge. Follow this right past a small tree, then move slightly left and up steep flakes to the large ledge at the top of the wall. Easier climbing to finish.

Amazing Technicolour Dreamgoat – 35m E2 5c **. A. Fraser, I. Magill. 16th September, 2001.
Quality, strenuous climbing. An overhung niche lies 5m left of the central depression. Climb this using both cracks, then up the left crack, with final moves right to gain the ledge. Continue by the crack above the ledge, then further easier walls.

The Ramp Slabs:

Left of the Tree Walls is the leftward-trending, bracken covered ramp, on the right of which are slabs.

Dirty Old Raingoat – 45m VS 4b. I. Magill, A. Fraser. 16th September, 2001.
A bold climb, mossy in places, which takes the centre of the right-hand, lower slab.

Capricorn Relish – 25m VS 4b *. I. Magill, A. Fraser. 26th July, 2000.
The upper pale slab, climbed directly at its cleanest point. Steady continuous climbing with widely spaced protection.

The Central Section:

This is the central section of the crag, under the summit of Craigdews. Essentially it consists of lower tier, with a halfway terrace at 50m, above which is an upper tier consisting of interlocking walls. A useful identifying feature at the bottom of the crag is the square-cut bay withan easy slab on its left side, which marks the start of Goats of Delirium.

Das Goat – 105m V. Diff *. A. Fraser. 6th June, 2000.
This pleasant route essentially follows the easiest line up the walls and rib bounding the right side of the halfway terrace. Start in a bay beneath a steep slabby wall, with a large flat boulder at its foot (15m right of the square-cut bay). Climb just left of the steepest part of the slabby wall, to gain and climb a heathery chimney leading to a thin grass terrace. Traverse 5m right, then continue up the rib until it is possible to gain a ledge on the left at the terrace (50m). Continue more easily up the rib to the top (55m).

Goathouse of Fleet – 52m VS 4c. I. Magill, A. Fraser. 16th September, 2001.
Although the main difficulties are avoidable, this has some good moves and is a good choice to access the upper walls. A rib lies 10m right of the square cut bay, bounding another bay on the right. Climb the rib to its top, then follow slabs above on the right (without deviation into the adjacent undergrowth) to the top. Bypassing the slabs by undignified heather lowers the grade to Severe and significantly reduces the quality.

Goats of Delirium –105m HVS 5a **. A. Fraser I. Magill. 28th June, 2000.
A classic, sustained and varied with neverending interest. The left section of the Central Section is noted for a grass terrace at 45m, above which is a steep wall split by a distinctive thin crack. Start in a square cut bay, bounded by an easy slab on the left. Start up the middle of the steep wall at the back of the bay, then move left at the steepening to almost gain a grassy groove. Move up right with difficulty to gain a flake, then continue up, and then right to the top slab. Climb a groove in this with difficulty to the terrace. Belay beneath a small isolated buttress down and right of the main wall (45m, 5a). Climb the small isolated buttress leftwards to the foot of the main wall (underneath the distinctive thin crack). Follow parallel cracks on the left side of the wall to an overhang. Above, continue up and right for 7m to gain a horizontal crack. Difficult moves above lead to the final wall, stepping right on to the terrace (35m, 5a) Above is a steep wall. Climb this at its right-hand end to gain a grass ledge. Climb a crack above until possible move up right to, and then on top of a large detached block. From the top of the block, climb the headwall to the top (30m, 5a).

Astrogoat – 48m VS 4c **. A. Fraser, I. Magill 16th September, 2001.
A long, sustained and absorbing pitch which deserves to become popular. It starts at the left end of the upper tier (above the halfway terrace), to the right of the rightward-sloping heathery groove of Central Climb, and left again of a large clump of heather at 7m. Climb a clean wall for 15m until a step left leads to a grass ledge. Above, follow cracks through a bulge, then continue to a horizontal grass ledge. Climb the wall above, then a final wall of dark metamorphic rock. Easy but unprotected metamorphic slabs lead to the top.

Craignaw:
Drainpipe Gully – III,4 *. S. Reid, A. Fraser, I. Magill. 2nd January, 2002.
Follow the summer line but quit it just before easy ground and finish up icy slabs on the right.

Silver Flow, with Direct Finish – 90m IV,4 **. S. Reid, J. Fotheringham. 4th January, 2002.
The deep right-facing gully, about 50m left of Drainpipe Gully, is climbed in three fine pitches. Follow the groove to a stance on a huge chockstone, then chimney up the gully making liberal use of its ice-glazed right wall to a second stance. Continue up to a steep icefall which is climbed direct, though it can be avoided by traversing rightwards to a faultline.

Note: S. Reid notes that Dow Spout is a tremendous and classic icefall of sustained interest (which he climbed three times in 2002), requiring rain followed by a freeze of about five days to come into condition.

THE SOUTH-WEST SEA CLIFFS, Meikle Ross, The Red Slab:
Sorry, No en-suite – 30m VS 4c *. N. Crookston, C. Prowse. 23rd March, 2002.
Start 1m left of Mental block. Climb the technical slab and continue up an obvious right-facing small corner to finish. Probably climbed before in parts.

Glenfinnian Hotel – 25m H. Severe 4b *. N. Crookston, C. Prowse. 23rd March, 2002.
Start 1m right of Coffin Crack. Climb the slab to a left-facing corner. Climb the corner till forced left. Pull through an overlap and finish on easy ground.

Dinner Meat – 20m V. Diff. N. Crookston, C. Prowse. 23rd March, 2002.
Pleasant climbing up an obvious crack 1m left of Coffin Crack.

Chairman's Crack – 10m Severe. N. Crookston, C. Prowse. 23rd March, 2002.
Climb the obvious loose corner formed by a pinnacle at the right end of the crag. Arrange a hopeful belay on top of the pinnacle.

Garheugh Port, The Main Cliff, The Promontary:
Four routes are found on the tip of the promontory, immediately left (north) of the descent. Routes are described leftwards from the descent.
My Bonny Lies Over the Ocean – 23m Severe. S. Reid, T. Mosedale. 28th June, 2001.
A pleasant route. Start just right of Foot in Mouth. Climb the ledged right-leaning groove to gain an arête on the right. Follow this and the slab above to a bulge. Avoid this by traversing the wall on the right to a wide crack which leads to a slim groove and the top.

Foot in Mouth – 23m VS 4c. A. Fraser, A. Gillies. 4th April, 2001.
A traditional but worthwhile struggle. It takes the wide crack in the centre of the green lichen covered, seaward face to a ledge, then the continuation crack above.

Gooseberry in a Lift – 23m HVS 5a. T. Mosedale, S. Reid. 28th June, 2001.
Climb the direct start to Cock Inn etc. to a ledge. Climb the hairy green arête/wall above, left of Foot in Mouth, to a platform. Climb the arête just right of the finishing crack of Foot in Mouth to the top.

Cock Inn Cap'n Birdseye – 22m Severe. A. Gillies, A. Magill. 5th June, 2001.
Worthwhile, if somewhat lichenous. Start as for the previous route, but move left
after 2m into another crack. Follow this to a ledge on the left or north wall of the
promontory. Continue up left to another ledge, then finish up a leftward-sloping
crack in the final wall.

Main Cliff, North Wall:
The north facing wall is steep but split by ledges. At its left end, in a brambly bay,
is a steep chimney running the length of the crag.
Full Moon Fever – 20m E1 **. A. Fraser, I. Magill. 5th June, 2001.
Surprisingly superb, taking the steep, unrelenting chimney. Well protected, with
the odd dubious hold.

The Fat Lady Sings – 20m E1 5a *. A. Fraser, A. Gillies, I. Magill. 2001.
A good sustained climb, in places somewhat devious and contrived. Immediately
right of the previous route is a slim rib, bounded on its right by a steep corner
leading to a grass ledge. Climb the steep corner for 5m, moving left on to the rib
as soon as possible. Follow the rib up and left, to eventually stand on a ledge on
the left edge of the rib. Boldly move slightly right, then up to good holds, following
these back left to the edge to finish.

About 100m north of the main crag, at the back of a bay, is a pillar with ivy on its
right wall. Descent from this and all the following routes is by scrambling down a
chimney situated on the seaward end of Smugglers Slab.
Dr Hemlock and Mr Damocles – 22m VS 4c *. A. Fraser, A. Gillies. 4th April,
2001.
A good climb with some interesting moves. It takes the groove in the arête, finishing
to the left of the obvious rock swords. Belay on crash barrier.

An Idea of Excellence – 22m HVS 5a *. I. Magill, A. Gillies, A. Magill, A. Fraser.
5th June, 2001.
Another good route with a thin crux. The wall left of Dr Hemlock is split by a
roof. Climb up to the alcove below the roof, which is exited at its left end. Traverse
right along the lip of the roof to a thin crack. Go directly up this (crux), then
continue to top.

Smugglers Slab:
About 150m to the north of the main crag is another smaller slab of good quality
rock. Micro cams useful. Routes are described left to right.
Too EC – 10m Severe. A. Gillies, A. Fraser. 4th April, 2001.
The undercut and vegetated wall left of Smugglers Grill is better than appearances
suggest.

Bombin the L' – 10m VS 4c *. A. Fraser, A. Gillies. 4th April, 2001.
Lovely climbing, probably the best on this face. Climb the white and green speckled
slab 1.5m right of Smugglers Grill, avoiding using that route.

Stone Crop – 10m VS 4c *. S. Reid, T. Mosedale. 28th June, 2001.
Start 2m right of Bombin the L', and just left of Landmark. Climb straight up to a

very short leftward-slanting crack. Move up to a rock flange with difficulty and then finish more easily to the top.

Portobello, Primrose Inlet:
This small south-facing wall is situated immediately north of Slab Cove. Even further north are short walls, providing pleasant and safe bouldering. In the centre of the wall, at mid height, is a ledge, easily accessed from either side by flakes. The routes lie on either side of this and are described right to left
Bottom Feeders – 10m HVS 5a. A. Fraser, I. Magill.11th May, 2001.
Short but not to be underestimated. It climbs the wall to the right of the right-hand easy flake, starting 1m to the right of the foot of the flake.

Fanny Haddock – 8m Severe 4a. I. Magill, A. Fraser. 11th May, 2001.
The wall to the left of the left-hand easy flake, starting up a small corner and finishing to the right.

Axle Bay:
This is the steep, south facing and pocketed wall situated in the small bay immediately north of the Main Cliff. The rock is good, generally somewhat better than on the Main Cliff. Routes are described right to left.
The Elle Factor – 12m VS 4c. A. Gillies, A. Fraser. 22nd June, 2001.
Well positioned with some good moves. At the right edge of the face is a slab leading to roof. Climb the slab, over the roof, then straight up the hanging groove in the arête to finish.

Jack the Kipper – 12m E2 5c **. A. Fraser, I. Magill, A. Gillies. 22nd July, 2001.
Brilliantly devious and compelling climbing unlocks the wall right of Bootless. Start 2m left of the vegetated fault between Bootless and the right arête of the face. Climb to a horizontal fault, follow this left, then climb pockets till they disappear. Above the pockets move up and slightly left, then back right to gain a good ledge on the top right of the face.

The Dogs Pollacks – 15m HVS 5a *. A. Fraser, A. Gillies, I. Magill. 13th June, 2001.
Another steep, but better protected, route up the left-hand crackline. Finish to the right, avoiding the final vegetation.

Cracked Block Cove:
Tales of the Rubblebank – 13m HVS 5a. A. Fraser, A. Gillies, I. Magill. 22nd July, 2001.
Situated on the face to the right of the Cracked Block. Contrary to all the normal rules of greywacke, the honeycombed pillar 3m from the left end of the face, actually gives a reasonably sound climb.

Kiln o' the Fuffock:
Rubbledance – 10m Severe. A. Fraser, I. Magill. 18th August, 2001.
The left corner of the crag, finishing to the left. The true finish up the slot is liable to dislodge tons of loose rock.

Larbrax:
Trapdoor Fandango – 19m E2 5c ** A. Fraser, A. Gilies, I. Magill. 18th August, 2001.
Sustained and delicate climbing up the narrow slab between the Seaward and the Central Slab. Protection is good, from RP's, but is easily overlooked. Climb the left-slanting crack to its top, then traverse right for 2m to a horizontal crack on the right of the slab. Climb directly up past triangular pockets, then move left to gain a slot then the arête. Continue up the arête to its top, then move up right (holds under juniper), to gain the centre of the slab which is followed to the top. Low in the grade.

CENTRAL OUTCROPS, Cambusbarron Quarry:
Moving Shadow – 25m E6 6b ***. M. Tweedly, L. Burns. August, 2001.
This climbs the obvious V-groove on the middle of the back wall. Climb the groove to a peg, then make a series of desperate moves past it to gain a bridging position. Then climb the groove making excellent bridging moves, to gain a ledge on the right. Have a rest, then lurch leftwards to make exposed moves to gain a wee crack and headwall. Grade for on-sight. A few good climbers climbing E5 have failed, hence the E6.

Tarzan – 15m E3 5c *. M. Tweedly, L. Burns. August, 2001.
The route is to the right of Spanking the Monkey. It climbs a detached pillar, then traverses a seam in the middle of the face (crux). Climb a left-trending crack to a ledge and lower off. If you fail on the crux, you end up taking a big swing (safe, hence the name).

PSI – 18m E3 5c **. R. Welch, A. Marr, M. Tweedly. August, 2001.
A wild climb to the left of the obvious choss pillar. Climbs cracks on the face to obvious breaks, then crux moves take you above. The gear is hard to place; the alternative is to make the easier finish without it.

Cambusbarron West Quarry:
Note: *Scales of Injustice* (SMCJ 2001) is almost certainly F7c. It was climbed by M. Somerville (unsec.).
Miss Po is probably E2. It was climbed with L. Byrnes, not with Si O'Connor.
Arse on Stumps (SMCJ 2000) is probably E3; *Dark Side of the Spoon* (SMCJ 2000) is probably E2.

EDINBURGH OUTCROPS, Arthur's Seat:
Red Chimney – 20m IV,3. D. Rubens, C. Smith. 1st March, 2001.
This route lies on the Lion's Head, towards the left end of the rocks overlooking Hunter's Bog. Climbed at night to avoid attracting attention. Despite several days of lying snow and low temperatures, consolidation was poor. Where the chimney was blocked by a sapling, a move out right was made, followed by a very difficult move on turf before regaining the chimney.

FIFE, The Hawcraig:

Garlic Bread – 12m E2 5c/6a. T. Muirhead, P. Hague. April 28th, 1999
Takes the slab direct on the right of Weasel Wall.

Pizza – 12m E2 5c. P. Hague, T. Muirhead. April 28th, 1999
Climbs the overhanging arête to the right of Garlic Bread, and immediately left of Cranium Crack.

Guillemot Head Mush – 5m VS 5a. J.P. Dyble, I. Simpson. 3rd March, 2001.
The west-facing arête of the 5m flake of Flake and Wall. Staying on the arête without using the wall to the left, pull directly over the bulge making a slap for the big ledge at the top.

EAST LOTHIAN, Traprain Law:

There is a small but worthwhile crag above the main crags with the following routes climbed by D. Hunter and M. Greenwood from 10th to 12th August, 2001.
Easy Ticket – 6m Severe. An upside down diamond with a route up the left hand corner.
Black Diamond – 6m VS. The right-hand arête of the upside down diamond.
Diamond Back – 8m E1 5a. Farther round to the right of the diamond is an obvious overhang. Go up a ramp to the bottom of the overhang, climbed going from right to left on good holds. Strenuous and reachy.

D. Rubens reports:

Scotland's Last Old Man – 20m Mild VS 4c. D. Rubens, W. Jeffrey, G. Cohen. 2nd June, 2001.
As a climbing objective this pinnacle was first discovered by Willie Jeffrey. MR 967 601. It felt serious, due to the increasingly sandy and fragmentary nature of the rock as height was gained.It is not accessible at high tide.

Turn off the A1 for Burnmouth, about two miles before the Border. Park at the road end. Walk about 15 minutes towards the Border along a rocky shore. The pinnacle comes into view, resembing an approaching (or possibly retreating) battleship.

Start at the seaward side and climb fairly easily up to a ledge. From here, make a bold move (soft rock, poor protection) up and then gain the left edge of the seaward face. Exposed, but straightforward climbing gains the herring gull infested summit.

There being no obvious belay, the first ascensionist was lowered by his second down the landward face before the second climbed, communication being relayed through the strategically placed third man by the primitive method of shouting.The second was then belayed from the landward side, care being taken not to pull him over the summit as he approached it. A very large sling would render these antics unnecessary.

G. Cohen also made a solo ascent from the landward side, which was easier, with a move of about V. Diff.

MISCELLANEOUS NOTES

The W. H. Murray Literary Prize.

As a tribute to the late Bill Murray, whose mountain and environment writings have been an inspiration to many a budding mountaineer, the SMC have set up a modest writing prize, to be run through the pages of the Journal. The basic rules are set out below, and will be re-printed each year. The prize is run with a deadline, as is normal, of the end of January each year. So assuming you are reading this in early July, you have, for the next issue, six months in which to set the pencil, pen or word processor on fire.

The Rules:

1. There shall be a competition for the best entry on Scottish Mountaineering published in the *Scottish Mountaineering Club Journal*. The competition shall be called the 'W. H. Murray Literary Prize', hereafter called the 'Prize.'

2. The judging panel shall consist of, in the first instance, the following: The current Editor of the *SMC Journal;* The current President of the SMC; and two or three lay members, who may be drawn from the membership of the SMC. The lay members of the panel will sit for three years after which they will be replaced.

3. If, in the view of the panel, there is in any year no entries suitable for the Prize, then there shall be no award that year.

4. Entries shall be writing on the general theme of 'Scottish Mountaineering', and may be prose articles of up to approximately 5000 words in length, or shorter verse. Entries may be fictional.

5. Panel members may not enter for the competition during the period of their membership.

6. Entries must be of original, previously unpublished material. Entries should be submitted to the Editor of the *SMC Journal* before the end of January for consideration that year. Lengthy contributions are preferably word-processed and submitted either on 3.5" PC disk or sent via e-mail. (See Office Bearers page at end of this Journal for address etc.) Any contributor to the SMC Journal is entitled to exclude their material from consideration of the Prize and should so notify the Editor of this wish in advance.

7. The prize will be a cheque for the amount £250.

8. Contributors may make different submissions in different years.

9. The decision of the panel is final.

10. Any winning entry will be announced in the *SMC Journal* and will be published in the *SMC Journal* and on the SMC Web site. Thereafter, authors retain copyright.

The W. H. Murray Literary Prize 2002

THE winner of the 2002 W. H. Murray Prize for his article, *Climbing In The Cold,* is Londoner and Honorary Scotsman – at least between the months of November and April – Mick Fowler. Mick's weekend raids on Scottish ice are now the stuff of legend, with apocryphal tales abounding of hardship and near-death experiences, mainly, it has to be said occurring on the M1 before reaching the ice-bound cliffs of Scotland, cliffs now peppered with Fowler routes of the highest order.

Climbing In The Cold, while detailing just what is necessary to sustain the drive – "I depended on the cheapest form of transport: in those days an Austin Mini Van. I got through 13 in all," – and passion for exploratory winter climbing at this level, from a base 600 miles away from a target climb that may or may not be in condition, also covers the all important beginnings. "One of my earliest Scottish memories is of arriving in Glen Coe intent on spending a week front-pointing up crisply frozen classics. The rain poured incessantly and the water by the Clachaig Inn was ankle deep."

Terry Gifford, Director of the International Festival of Mountaineering Literature rated the winning article highly - *Climbing in the Cold* is "Rich in recent history, pacey, witty, detailed but containing the complete learning curve – an important SMC document that's fun to read."

There can be no arguing that Mick Fowler is passionate about what he does and deeply committed but his writing gives me the impression that, unlike some modern activists, enjoyment comes before competition. An impression perhaps borne out by Mick himself in his closing paragraph. "The memories bite deeply, the friendships are warm and the pleasures long lasting. These are the important things. I remain hooked."

Mick was run close by M. G. Anderson's *Reincarnation On The Ben.* Ken Crocket remembers the accident that forms the focus of the story vividly: "*Reincarnation* is the story behind an accident on Ben Nevis I recall shuddering over some years ago. It also describes quite well the society encountered then, not just the mountaineers, but the landladies, rescuers, media monkeys and all the odds and sods which go to make up our fascinating lives."

Other pieces which attracted the judges attention included Jamie Thin's *Moonlighting/The Grand Traverse,* "Lively voice, good ideas." And Adam Kassyk's *Twenty-nine Hours On The Cuillin Ridge, "* an introspective, but positive, tale of a solo winter attempt on the Cuillin Ridge. There are good cameos of the landscape, mercifully not spoiled by over-described climbing details".

Congratulations again to Mick Fowler, and for the rest and all the other budding authors out there, there's always next year. The winning article as well as appearing in this year's Journal can also be read in full on the SMC Website.

Charlie Orr

ON HILL RUNNING
By Jamie Thin

HILL-RUNNERS are often viewed with suspicion by mountaineers. The mountains are no place for a race, you may say. But if you have ever run down a steep hillside in your shorts and light-weight fell shoes, it is very hard to go back to your big boots and heavy gear.

The first recorded mountain ascent is often thought to date from 1590, when 'Mad' Colin Campbell of Glen Lyon climbed Stuchd an Lochain. But long before that, running across the hills was the only way to spread an urgent message.

Michael Brander[1] has traced the history,

"In the wild and mountainous highlands, where no roads existed, and peat bogs, boulders and scree were likely to slow down or cripple even the most sure-footed horse, by far the quickest means of communication was a man running across country. The 'Crann-tara' or fiery cross was the age-old method of raising the clansmen in time of need. It was made of two pieces of wood fastened together in the shape of a cross, traditionally with one end alight and the other end soaked in blood. Runners were despatched to all points of the compass and as they ran they shouted the war cry of the clan and the place and time to assemble."

The clan chieftains began to arrange races among the clansmen to find the fastest man to carry the Crann-tara. The story of the first Braemar gathering, is also the story of the first recorded hill-race in Scotland.

Malcolm Canmore (1057-1093) held the first gathering at Braemar. The race was from Braemar to the top of Craig Choinich and back. Honour was at stake, but also a prize of a purse of gold and a fine sword.

"All the challengers set off led by the favourites, the two elder Macgregor brothers, but at the last moment the third and youngest Macgregor brother joined the back of the field. The youngest brother caught his elder brothers at the top of the hill and asked: 'Will ye share the prize?'.

'Each man for himself,' came the reply. As they raced back down the hill he edged into second place and then dashed past his eldest brother. But as he passed, his eldest brother despairingly grabbed him by his kilt. But slipping out of his kilt, the younger brother still managed to win, if lacking his kilt."

Perhaps that is why kilts are no longer worn in today's hill races!

The Scottish hills are particularly suited for hill-running, the going is often soft under foot and light-weight shoes cut down on the amount of peat bog you have to carry around with you.

So now if I need a challenge , I turn to running on the hills.

By July 2001, I was needing a new challenge, a milestone to pass before I reached my 35th birthday and turned into a couch potato. Ten years before, I was feeling restless and cycled from Edinburgh to the Tatras in Poland and back through the Alps, but that took all winter and I ended up in Interlaken hospital with frostbite – after a three-day sojourn on the North face of the Grosshorn. Now I was looking for a family-friendly challenge I could compress into a few days.

Big 'rounds' have always been part and parcel of the Scottish mountain scene, from Naismith's walks of Victorian vigour to the rambles of Ronnie Burn. In April, 1921 Burn thought nothing of doing 32 peaks in 12 days (with Sunday as a rest day). Possibly the first big recorded Munro round.

A selective chronology of big rounds:

1892: Willie Naismith walks 41 miles over Ben Alder from Dalwhinnie to attend the SMC Easter meet at Bridge of Orchy.

1921: Ronnie Burn climbs 32 peaks in 12 days (with Sunday off).

1961: Philip Tranter runs 19 Munros in 24 hours (Lochaber).

1974: Hamish Brown walks all the Munros in 112 days.

1977: Blyth Wright runs 17 Munros in 23hr. (Kintail).

1978: Charlie Ramsay runs 24 Munros in 24hr. (Lochaber).

1986: Martin Stone runs the Scottish 4000ers in 21hr. 39min.

1988: Jon Broxap runs 28 (now 29 Munros) in 23hr. 20min. (Kintail).

1992: Andrew Johnston and Rory Gibson, run 277 Munros in 51 days in 1992 (277/51x 7, or approx. 38 Munros a week – including swimming across Loch Lomond).

2000: Charlie Campbell runs 284 Munros in 48 days and 12hr. (284/48 x7 or approx. 41 Munros a week/51 Munros in the first 11 days – including swimming to the Islands and across Loch Lomond!)

Running all the Munros in a oner was tempting, but that would mean cashing in my lifetime's baby-sitting credits. How many Munros in a day? Jon Broxap emphatically answered this question with 29 Munros in 24 hours in 1988, and no-one has found an adequate reply in 14 years. So how about asking a different question. How many Munros in a week? To my knowledge there was no formal record for the biggest round in a week.

This began to get intriguing – I pulled out a few maps – where to link the rounds? My little mind began to whirr excitedly. Seventy-two Munros summit-to-summit in seven days might be possible – 3 x 24hr. rounds back to back with some rest and cycling in between. The Holy Grail of linking all the hills in Kintail, Lochaber and the Cairngorms in a week was maybe not so far-fetched.

My wife was planning a trip back to Belfast with the kids to see her folks, so this was my window of opportunity. I had a seven-day pass.

A rough plan emerged and then changed again as I tried to sort out the logistics – should I start in the Cairngorms or in Kintail? Eventually, I picked Kintail – as the Cairngorms were too familiar. My feet were still sore from the Scottish 4000s duathlon the month before. An amazing day out and a weird feeling to be on the top of Ben Nevis and top of Ben Macdui in the same day having run and cycled between them. I was on my own, so I needed a food dump somewhere in the middle. Eventually, I picked Fersit on the basis that it was on the direct route from Kintail via Lochaber to the Cairngorms – though whether I would reach the Cairngorms was another matter.

I drove north on the Sunday evening and stayed at the bunkhouse at Tulloch Station. Next morning the logistics operation began, I drove to Fersit and left the car packed with food, then I transferred to the bike and cycled the 10 miles to Spean Bridge and on by bus to the start at Cluanie Inn. The bus trip gave me some time to gather my thoughts. My running sack was already packed, bulging with food for three days. The plan was to set off at noon, run the South Cluanie Ridge, east to west, drop down and then back along the Five Sisters and bivvy somewhere on the ridge. Then head north and bag the Affric hills before doubling back south to return to the Cluanie Inn. My optimistic estimate was anything from 36 hours to three days. But as I stared out at the low cloud and driving rain, I began to realise my route was all very well in fair weather, but what would it be like hour after hour in the mist and rain and cold on my own? Maybe there were parallels with my winter trip to Poland after all. But come off it, this was Scotland in mid-summer – sunny July! At least frostbite was unlikely.

My base at Cluanie was the Schoolhouse – a charming tumbledown cottage owned by some friends. I left my bike there and psyched myself up to head out into the mist and rain. Then I wondered if I had enough food. Just to make sure I raided the cupboards and ate a couple of extra tins of baked beans and Devonshire custard. No excuses now, I set off into the rain and mist, which turned into sheets of driven rain as I climbed higher.

In 1988, when Jon Broxap ran 29 Munros in 24 hours, he covered the nine Munros on the South Cluanie Ridge (including the Saddle) in an awesome 3 hours 20 minutes top to top. After about six hours, I was still battling along the ridge in my light-weight running kit. I was cold and my head was down. As dusk approached I hit the first steep descent and then Sgurr na Sgine reared its head above me. In the mist, I was confused. I was now faced with an awkward choice – straight up, left or right? I chose right as the ground that I could see in the half-light looked easier and I assumed I could then scramble up the back. I contoured up and right below a prow and cut up on to some steep compact slabs then chickened out and cut further round the back of a rough corrie then, frustrated at my lack of progress, I blindly climbed up the first shallow gully I found. It was loose under foot and a bit slabby but by now I was thinking ahead and on to planning the best route up the Saddle in the dark.

The ground was just beginning to steepen when my feet shot out below me and I was spat unceremoniously back down the gully. With my full-waterproofs on and the mountainside running with water it felt like being in a snow and ice gully with no ice axe. I ground to a halt just before the boulders of the scree feeling very lonely and sore. I would be missed after a week – but not before, so it was not the place to break a bone. Sgurr na Sgine would have to wait another day and I hobbled down to the road much chastened and limping on a bruised hip.

It was Day 1 of my big adventure and I already felt like packing it in. Seven Munros and I was knackered. My planned bivvy on the Five Sisters, changed to a hunt for a sheltered spot in the glen. I now regretted dumping my sleeping bag and spare clothes at Fersit in favour of some extra grub. I was soaked to the skin and as I approached the road, I tried to steel myself for an uncomfortable night bivvied in the woods in the rain.

As I stood by the side of the road in the dark considering my options a car slowed and stopped beside me. A couple of tourists on the way to Skye.

"Do you want a lift down the glen?"

The rain was bouncing up from the tarmac. Suddenly I thought of a hostel bed and a hot bath. I jumped in. They dropped me a couple of miles down the road at Shiel Bridge and I knocked up the nearest B&B. Ten minutes later I was soaking in a hot bath. I was still thinking of packing it in when I got up the next morning, but after a big cooked breakfast and with the weather brightening up, I set off again.

The detour to Shiel Bridge offered me a gentle approach to the Five Sisters, so I tested out my hip by walking down the road to Loch Duich and then round the corner and up the stalkers' path. I was stiff and sore and there was no chance of running. But now I was here and the day was fine I might as well press on and at least the wind was now on my back.

By the time I was over the first few summits, my legs had warmed up and I could mange a downhill shuffle. My initial plan had been to return to the safe haven of the Cluanie Inn, but now that I could see north to the Affric hills, I changed my plan. I could always stop at Camban bothy at the head of Glen Affric.

Ronnie Burn had known Camban bothy well, back in 1921 it was still the summer residence of Paterson the local keeper. Now an MBA bothy, it had been coincidentally renovated by the Corriemulzie Mountaineering Club in memory of another proponent of the big round, Philip Tranter. (Philip and his pal were killed in a car accident on the way home from the mountains of Turkey in 1966).

From Ciste Dubh, I dropped down to the bothy in the glen below, before leaving my sack and heading up Beinn Fhada in the warm glow of evening. Camban was empty, as I had expected it would be on a Tuesday night, but 80 years before Ronnie Burn had been bitterly disappointed to miss the occupants.

"A great disappointment awaited me at Camban. I had specially saved myself for a good swig of milk here as Kirsty had promised it, and had specially kept from water to fully enjoy it. But the house was locked and not even a window to burgle. I heard later that Kirsty and Paterson (the keeper at Camban) were much disappointed to miss me. I got home (to Alltbeithe) between seven and eight , having done fifteen miles." (Ronnie Burn, *Burn on the Hill*)

I was on the top of the broad plateau of Beinn Fhada to watch the sunset, and happy to get back to the bothy before dark. With no stove or sleeping bag, the bothy felt pretty Spartan, but after a long day I fell into a fitful sleep.

The next morning, I was greeted with more heavy rain, so it was back on with the waterproofs and I modified my route again, this time to miss the outlier of A'Ghlas Bheinn. I met three walkers on the top of Sgurr nan Ceathreamhnan and was glad of their company as we picked our way down the steep ridge to the north and it gave me renewed confidence to strike back out into the mist on my own. By now the hills were flowing into a blurr, but the odd rocky step or sudden opening in the clouds to show the glens below, sharpened my mind.

Back at the Schoolhouse in the evening, I was way behind schedule, only 20 Munros in two-and-a-half days, so I abandoned the schedule and set myself a new target of 50 Munros in a week.

I had a big feed in the Cluanie Inn and then jumped on the bike for the 50-mile cycle to Fersit. Cycling was a change, but no rest for the legs as there was still a steady pull over the hill between Loch Cluanie and Loch Garry.

I had a pit stop at Fersit and ate a few cans of fruit and re-stocked my running sack full of chocolate bars, butties and a new set of maps. Then I headed up the Easains and over to the Larig Leacach bothy. This time I made sure to take my sleeping bag in place of extra food. I was also crafty and packed a bag of noodles in the hope that I would find the bothy occupied and be able to scarf some hot water.

I was glad to reach the Larig Leacach bothy. Earlier I had half a mind to push on through the night but then the rain had returned and a friendly pair of walkers were in the bothy with spare gas so they cooked up my noodles and I had a wee feast.

I set off early the next morning into the mist up Stob Ban but, as I reached the Grey Corries' ridge proper, the wind had died down and the sun was trying to break through. So by the time I was climbing Aonach Beag I was stripped to my shorts and T-shirt and struggling to find enough water. The fine weather held to the summit of the Ben with clear views across the Aonachs and Mamores.

I was running out of my meagre rations by now so I had a slap-up meal at the Glen Nevis campsite bar and managed to fill my rucksack with the café's leftover scones. With a full stomach, I bivvied up high at the ancient ring fort on the approach to Mullach Nan Coirean. Bivvying on a historic monument always makes my imagination run riot. I began to wonder how many clansmen died fighting over this wee knoll and where their bones were buried. But I slept well and woke early to the sound of rain on my bivvy bag. At least I was relieved to find it was rain and not the midges.

The wind and rain had returned, but my luck held as the wind was again at my back and I was blown along eastwards over summit after summit. It was good to leave behind the rocks and screes of the last of the Mamores – Sgurr Eilde Mor – and reach softer ground around the head of Glen Nevis. My feet were suffering on all the sharp rocks. On Day Two, I realised my running shoes were missing their insoles and remembered that a playful puppy had chewed them to bits on my last visit to Tobermory. All in all, my kit was in a mess, my toes were now almost out of my shoes and my rucksack didn't even have a waist strap as I had pinched it to fix my daughter's bike seat a few weeks' before.

It was evening by the time I reached Luibeilt – which was ringed by campers. When Ronnie Burn came this way in 1917 he had been asked to carry the post to Staoineag and Luibeilt from Corrour and although he had found the keeper of Luibeilt up on the hill cutting peat, Ronnie had still managed to cadge a glass of milk.

Food was on my mind too, as I had only had stale scones for breakfast, lunch and tea, but there were no glasses of milk for me. Staoineag was tempting, but too soon, as I was determined to cover the easy ground to Ossian in the dark rather than waste precious hours in the morning. I was thinking of bivvying in the woods by the loch, but the lights were still on in the hostel as I passed the door at 10.30pm – so I thought I would poke my head in. It was booked for a private party by a group of friends from Edinburgh. They ignored my unwashed state, plied me with red wine and biscuits and found a bunk for me – spot on.

Forty Munros in five-and-a-half days. Ten more to hit my mark of 50. That left me with a long day out to Ben Alder and back to Fersit. I decided to knock off Beinn na Lap before breakfast and ran up it without my sack in under an hour-and-a-half. From there I nipped up a couple of hills and then dropped down to Ben Alder cottage – Ronnie had stayed there in 1917 too – and had even had the temerity to give the keeper a shout from the other side of Loch Ericht and get ferried across the loch by "McCook and his daughter Bessie". Not a service on offer today.

Beinn Bheoil and Ben Alder were a struggle, but by the time I was climbing Geal Charn it felt like I was on the home stretch and Aonach Beag and Beinn Eibhin were a breeze along an easy ridge. Now I was doubly glad that I had already been up Beinn na Lap otherwise it would have been a big loop out and back. Instead I had just two Munros left to do – Chno Dearg and Stob Coire Sgriodain. Chno Dearg was just about my undoing as I went from one map sheet to the next and managed to take the bearing on the wrong burn. It led me the long way round before I noticed my mistake, a sure sign I was getting tired. I was uneasy about finishing on Stob Coire Sgriodain in the dark. My friend Martin had died up there when he skied through the cornice in a white-out one winter – and it still felt like a menacing place – though an easy enough hill in summer. I upped the pace as I was keen to get to the top before darkness fell but it was after 10 and dark before I got there.

Fifty Munros summit-to-summit in six-and-a-half days. It felt brilliant to reach the last top but I knew I wouldn't relax until I got down and reached the first house at Fersit. I picked my way down by the light of my head torch and inevitably got lost trying to find the track through the forest, until at last I saw the glow of a light from the farm, and only had to climb one last deer fence to reach the road. My week's therapy was over, I was physically tired but mentally refreshed. Total immersion in the hills. It was an artificial challenge but a simple one. Life was more complex, with both my daughters diagnosed with an incurable bone disease, this was my escape but also my path to understanding. After 200 miles and perhaps a 100,000ft. of ascent my anger was beginning to ebb away.

Brief summary: 50 Munros summit to summit by foot and bike.

Kintail – 20 Munros. Lochaber – 30 Munros. Started at summit of Creag a' Mhaim at 14:07 on Monday, July 23, 2001.

Finished on summit of Stob Coire Sgriodain at 22:19 Sunday, 29 2001.

Total Time – 152 hours and 22 minutes Approx. a Munro every three hours for six-and-a-half days.

Rough mileage – 150 miles on foot. 50 miles on the bike (plus a lift from some friendly tourists down to Shiel bridge).

References:

[1] *Essential Guide to Highland Games,* Michael Brander, Cannongate, 1992

[2] *Burn on the Hill,* Elizabeth Allan, Bidean Books, 1995 – Diaries of Rev. Ronnie Burn who was an eccentric hunchback churchman and scholar, and would have been a hillrunner today. One summer after climbing two Munros on his way from Loch Hourn to Glen Shiel, the last mile-and-a-half to Cluanie Inn "was reeled off without the least strain at the rate of 6 miles per hour". (SMC Journal Vol. 14, p.216).

INCIDENTS ON CIR MHOR IN 1902

By Robin Campbell

THE forbidding North-east Face of Cir Mhor held a fascination for climbers in our Golden Age. Some 13 routes were recorded there in the 1890s. According to the first guidebook editor, Harry MacRobert: "Here is to be found the finest rock-climbing in the island, gullies and ridges, caves and pinnacles, of all degrees of difficulty."[1] But tastes change, and the face rapidly lost its allure. Indeed, by 1958 the editor of the first pocket guidebook, James M. Johnstone, was brave enough to claim that "It may be said at once that not one first-class route has been discovered on the entire face". He added grudgingly that "The best combination is probably B_2C Rib – Bow Window Cave – Bell's Groove". This combination is pure 1890s, the first and last parts being assembled by John H. Bell in 1894-95 and the amusing intermediate Cave by the "twa Wullies" Naismith and Douglas earlier in 1894.[2]

Activity on the face continued into the new century for a few years and 1902 saw perhaps the most interesting spasms of the final fling of the pioneers on Cir Mhor. These events are little known, and are ignored or misdescribed in current sources. So in the year of their centenary, these second-class excursions perhaps deserve this brief memorial. On February 22, an Edinburgh party consisting of Harry G. S. Lawson, A. M. 'Sandy' Mackay and Harold Raeburn visited the island in thawing weather after a long frost.[3] After an unsuccessful day on Beinn a' Chliabhinn, the party retreated to Corrie Inn. On the 23rd, Gully A on the North-east Face was explored, but although it was well-iced, "down the ice-fall came rushing quite a well-grown river of snow-water, under which the step-cutter must

Julian Lines out there on 'Origin of the Species' (E6 6b), partnered by Tim Rankin, Creag an Dubh Loch, Cairngorms. Photo: Dave Cuthbertson/Cubby Images.

stand while at work". So they turned instead to the left-hand edge of the Gully (now April Arête). Although considerable progress was made, they turned back, discouraged by rain and "fingers paralysed by cold". Undaunted, the party turned to examine B1 and B2 gullies, but rejected these too, since "they were solid cataracts of ice from top to bottom, and if possible at all, would have taken hours of step-cutting". Raeburn then continues, in masterly understatement: "We then ascended by the 'B1C rib', the buttress between B and C. This was done by a party led by Bell on July 7, 1895. It is a capital climb of decidedly over average difficulty. The passage of the cave at the top was now rendered much easier by the large amount of snow which partly filled it up. As no-one appeared to long for the 'Bell's Groove' finish, we then ascended Cir Mhor by the easy way." So, remarkably enough, the first winter ascent of B-C Rib was made in 1902![4]

The second interesting incident occurred at the end of the year. *Jeunesse dorée* in the form of Geoffrey W. Young and Sandy Mackay came to Corrie for a New Year holiday. Mackay was Young's current Alpine partner and probable fellow author of the notorious *Roof-Climber's Guide to Trinity*. Their initial goal was A Gully once again, but just as in February, its left-hand ridge was eventually preferred. Presumably, Mackay's experiences earlier in the year had persuaded him to make a fresh effort. Unfortunately, the pair ran out of daylight, food and ideas somewhere on this awkward arête. Doubtful of the descent, they elected to evacuate into A Gully. Mackay lowered Young into the gully (nice of him!), then jumped the 30ft. or so to join Young. Unfortunately, he found a slab extending into the snow-bed and broke a leg. In Young's account of this sorry incident and the subsequent rescue, he suggests that they were on B-C Rib, but examination of letters from Mackay to Young makes the location perfectly clear. Mackay's leg was badly set, and he needed several operations (six casts are mentioned) before the leg could be restored to approximate service.[5] Although Mackay returned to climbing (notably on the famous Barrel Buttress climb of Easter 1907) and to tennis, Young lamented that 'our trusted Alpine partnership was ended, and I never again found his equal as a climbing colleague'.

Footnotes:
[1] SMCJ, 1908, X, 104.
[2] Later editors have been slightly more generous. In 1970 the second editor, William M. M. Wallace conceded that his predecessor's opinion was "largely justified", but expressed optimism for the present and future development of the face. Subsequent editors have expressed enthusiasm for its winter climbing possibilities.
[3] Raeburn's account of the visit is given as a note in SMCJ, 1902, VII, 113-14. Sandy Mackay, who also figures in the second incident described here, was a young Aberdeen climber of enormous promise and a Scottish tennis champion. See my note about the Northern Pinnacles of Liathach elsewhere in this issue for more details about Mackay.
[4] The winter ascent of B-C Rib is not recorded in any Arran guidebook. The failed attempt on April Arête was attributed to Lawson, Maclay and Raeburn by Johnstone, and this substitution of Maclay for Mackay was perpetuated by subsequent editors. The current guide adjusts the date of the "futuristic attempt" to 1892! One should not, however, think too ill of these editors: they have so much to do in coping with the New, that little time is left to worry about the Old.
[5] Young's account is in *Mountains with a Difference* (Eyre & Spottiswoode, 1951), pp. 56-62. The relevant Mackay letters to Young (numbers 988, 989 and 990 in Young's letter-book) are in the Alpine Club Library Archives.

Doré Green on the first ascent of 'Prometheus Unbound', Serpentrion Spires, Coast Range, British Columbia. Photo: Simon Richardson.

THE INFORMAL DUNDONELL MEET, EASTER 1893

In SMCJ, 1968, xxix, an illustration described as showing a 'Group of Members at the Dundonell Meet of 1910' appears opposite page 33. The caption identifies the figures as G. Thomson, A. W. Russell, H. T. Munro, J. Rennie and F. S. Goggs. This is so much embarrassing nonsense.

In the first place, Munro's black beard and youthful appearance tell us that this is an early gathering: in 1910 Munro was in his 55th year. Then the figure on the right is by no means Goggs, but rather Wm. Wickham King. And between Thomson and Munro stands W. W. Naismith, not Russell, who didn't join the Club until 1897.

In fact, this is almost certainly the informal meet at Dundonell, Easter 1893, attended by – from left to right – Thomson, Naismith, Munro, Rennie and King and photographer Wm. Douglas. The informal meet is described by Thomson in *Some Early Informal Meets* SMCJ, 1927, XVIII, 1-9. The group traversed the An Teallach ridge in opposite directions on Saturday, April 1, Douglas and Rennie proceeding north and taking the outstanding photographs used to illustrate a subsequent article by King and Munro in SMCJ, 1894, III, 10-18, while King, Munro, Naismith and Thomson proceeded south.

One of the Editors in 1968 was a certain … Robin N. Campbell.

Thoughts On Ageing

By Malcolm Slesser

WHEN elderly members of the club foregather there is always a tendency to ruminate upon the effects of age. One interesting variant on this recurring theme arose at the 2002 Easter meet. In the warmth of the Naismith Hut, reeking of whisky, the proposition was put forward that mountaineers as a class live to a riper old age than the population as a whole. This hypothesis could, if sustained, have important repercussions. For example the Treasurer might wish to review the amount of the life subscription for new members or remove the benefits of reduced subs for those of us who free load on the club into our 90s.

The discussion then moved on on how to establish the facts. Average life expectancy for new members may be quite low, given the present standard of climbing and the penetration of Global Positioning Systems as an aid to navigation. If these were to be included then it might well be that the average life expectancy of the SMC member as a body might turn out to be less than the national average.

The statistical problem, then, is to separate the acolytes from the experienced, those who have escaped death by chance, skill or, as in my case, cowardice. Having attained the plateau of healthy bliss, is the elderly mountaineer, as a cohort of the mountaineering population, more likely to live on and on.? That is the question.

Fortunately, in our midst was none other than Nigel Suess. Now Nigel has retired from banking, which though an abstract activity, is nonetheless quantitative. Moreover he has taken up mathematics. He is the sort of person for whom issues like the irregularities in co-linear partition are not only meaningful but also solvable!

Who better to examine the club's statistics and come up with an answer. I trust the Editor will prevail upon him and that his researches will be reported in the next journal.

The International Festival of Mountaineering Literature – 2001

AFTER all the trouble of getting a link set up with the International Festival of Mountaineering Literature and arranging a spot to read last year's W. H. Murray prize winning entry, your Hon. Ed. forgot to go! – Well not quite 'forgot' – In mitigation it has to be said that they were re-using last year's parking permits which meant that the date shown was a week later and I didn't read as far as the 2000 bit. The first intimation that I got that all was not well was on the Monday, an e-mail from organiser Terry Gifford which simply said: "WHERE WERE YOU?" Robin Campbell's polite query about my absence followed shortly thereafter. Needless to say I bowed and scraped at the time and here it is again – in print. It must have worked because Terry showed admirable forbearance when, presented with such a tempting escape hatch, he did the noble thing and agreed to continue as a W. H. Murray prize judge for another year – a shining example to us all.

This year's festival was as well attended as ever (apart from the obvious!). It has been suggested that the number of males attending may have been boosted by the Festival theme, 'How Long Can I Keep This Up'. But anyone arriving and expecting to find a Viagra sales promotion in the foyer instead of the usual signing in desk was, sadly, disappointed. The theme was, as the more cerebral of us always knew, that of continuing our passion for climbing at, and beyond, an age when any sensible person would have gladly opted for the pleasures of garden pottering, armchair dozing and perhaps even, horror of horrors 'the big slipper'.

One of the younger hot shots Niall Grimes reflected that: "Sometimes I think it would be nice to be old and just do the easy routes." Somehow I don't think he meant V. Diff! While some of the grand old men, including Sir Christian B pondered on the possibility that the tendency to more closely address one's own mortality as the years draw on may have a levening effect on one's relationship with risk.

Our Dinner Guest Speaker of last year Jim Curran was there to read from his new book *The Middle-aged Mountaineer* (reviewed elsewhere in this Journal) which takes a wry look into a cycling trip from Shetland to Cornwall taking in old friends and classic climbs on the way. He promised his audience that he would only read boring bits from the book because if he read the best bits they'd assume the rest was less so and wouldn't buy it. The logic is in there somewhere. Jim also showed his versatility with an exhibition of drawings for the book and two oil paintings of K2. Looks like Jim is coping with middle age plus quite well.

The Boardman/Tasker Prize for 2001 went to Roger Hubank for his novel *Hazards*. Set in the English Lake District at the turn of the century (last century that is!) his fictional characters intermingle with recognisable climbing heroes (and one anti-hero) O. G. Jones, Norman Collie and Aleister Crowley. A small tip for all you budding writers out there who fancy winning the Boardman//Tasker, get club member Peter Hodgkiss and his company the Ernest Press to publish your work – It's his fifth!

What of 2002? Well, I think I can safely say that Terry Gifford is assured of a sell-out audience for this year's event as he has managed to tempt the legendary Walter Bonatti to Leeds. I am told by Derek Pyper, who heard Bonatti at the Kendal Festival some years ago, that he gives a wonderful presentation with the services of an interpreter. I'm sure tickets will go like the proverbial hot cakes so if you want to be there book early. For booking details see the Festival website www.terrygifford.co.uk I'll be there Terry – honest!

Charlie Orr.

SCOTTISH MOUNTAINEERING TRUST – 2001-2002

THE Trustees met on August 30, 2001 and May 2, 2002.

During the course of these meetings support was given to the Jonathan Conville Memorial Trust Winter Course 2001-2002; Scottish Mountain Forum, Project Officer for Scotland, for International Year of the Mountain 2002; the Scottish National Portrait Gallery for display of paintings and objects called *On Top of the World: Scottish Mountaineers at home and Abroad;* Scottish Heart of Asia Expedition 2002 visiting Tavanbogd Region of the Mongolian Altia Mountains; the Scottish Wildlife Trust for footpath known as the 'Postie Path', Ben More Coigach; and Oban Mountain Rescue Team.

After deliberation the Trustees resolved to give their support to the Publications Co. for the Corbetts CD Project.

The Trustees, after due notice, added appropriate clauses to the Objects/ Constitution of the Trust to allow publication by digital or electronic process.

The present Directors of the publications company are T. B. Fleming (Chairman), R. K. Bott, K. V. Crocket, P. W. H. Gribbon and T. Prentice (Publications Manager).

The present Trustees are T. B. Fleming (Chairman), D. C. Anderson, R. K. Bott, K. V. Crocket, G. S. Nicoll, G. E. Irvine, P. W. H. Gribbon, C. J. Orr, W. C. Runciman and M. G. D. Shaw.

R. K. Bott and P. W. H. Gribbon are Trustee/Directors and provide liaison between the Publications Co. and the Trust. J. Morton Shaw is the Trust Treasurer. The Trustees wish to record their gratitude to S. M. Richardson and B. R. Shackleton for their services to the Trust as Trustees until recent retirement by rotation.

The following grants have been committed by the Trustees:

General Grant Fund

Jonathan Conville Winter Courses 2001/2002	£1015
Scottish Mountain Forum	£1000
Scottish National Portrait Gallery	£2000
Scottish Heart of Asia Expedition	£500
Scottish Wildlife Trust	£12000 over 3/4 years
Oban Mountain Rescue Team	£5000

James D. Hotchkis Trust Secretary.

MUNRO MATTERS

By David Kirk (Clerk of the List)

In the history of the List of Compleat Munroists, there have not been many changes in the Clerk of the List. Therefore it was with both pride and apprehension that I took on the job. I expected it to be interesting, and I've not been disappointed. Over the past 10 months, I've received letters that have moved me nearly to tears, had me in knots of laughter, and sent me reminiscing on my own best days on the same mountains described. This has been especially useful, as with two children under three, I'm currently not getting on the hill as much as I used to!

The change in the Clerk, and the associated advertisement and publicity of this, has meant that a number of people have written to me to tell of past rounds that were never previously recorded. I would like to thank them all, but I feel a special mention should be made of Mr James Davidson (2615), who compleated in 1971, at a time when just more than 100 people were listed.

Since Chris Huntley's report, published in last year's Journal, 173 new names have been added to the list. For the statos, the totals for the six previous years are as follows, counting backwards: 213, 241, 153, 208, 170, 146.

The first person listed this year has been given an earlier number as the person previously allotted that number informed me that she was already listed. This year's Compleatists follow. As before, columns are number, name, then Munro, Top and Furth Completion years.

Number	Name	Munro	Top	Furth
2504	*Stan Pearson	1998		
2521	Dave Sudell	1998		
2522	Tamara Cantlay	2001		
2523	Stuart Smith	2001		
2524	Albert McDade	2001		
2525	Ann Beeching	2001	2001	
2526	Ina Morris	2001		
2527	John Morris	2001		
2528	G. John Sutherberry	2001	2000	
2529	Raye Rickard	2001		
2530	Barry Hard	2001		
2531	Katherine Heal	2000	2000	
2532	Mathew Heal	2000	2000	
3533	Roger Jameson	2001		
2534	Andrew J. Rook	2001	1995	
2535	William H. Ramsden	2001		
2536	John G. Burton	2001	2001	2002
2537	Ethel Jessett	2001		
2538	Paul Jessett	2001		
2539	Patricia M. Crole	2000		
2540	D. W. Horner	2001		
2541	Susan Douglas	2001		
2542	Ann Gow	2001		
2543	Tim Liles	2001		
2544	David D. Campbell	2000		
2545	Andrew J. Copley	2001		
2546	James A. Baillie	2000		
2547	Mary Paton	2001		
2548	Christopher Langman	2001		
2549	Victor Aitken	2000		
2550	Margaret Aitken	2000		
2551	Carole A. A. Scott	2001		
2552	Alan P. Scott	2001		
2553	Norman A. Macleod	2001		
2554	Rona Macleod	2001		
2555	Alan D. Dick	2001		
2556	Dave Liddle	2001		
2557	William Blaen	2001		
2558	Iain Currie	2001		
2559	Phillip S. Edge	2001		
2560	Philip J. Vickers	2001		
2561	Andrew Hyams	2001		
2562	Bill Hunter	2001		
2563	Tom D. Yarwood	2001		
2564	Alice Galletly	1994		
2565	David F. Hamilton	2001		
2566	Mark Ingram	2001		
2567	Graham Ingram	2001		
2568	Carol Hawley	2001		
2569	Keith Hawley	2001		
2570	John Lagoe	2001		
2571	Sandy Willox	2001		
2572	Ian Gracie	1999		
2573	Ginny Black	2001		
2574	Paul Houghton	2001		
2575	Ian McMillan	2001	2001	
2576	Alison Anderson	2001		
2577	Jim Anderson	2001		

2578	Antony Morris	1998	1998
2579	Isabel M. G. Ord	2001	
2580	Anne Bridgen	2001	
2581	Ron Roweth	2001	
2582	Colin Brook	2001	
2583	Bill McEwan	2001	
2584	Drew Ewing	2001	
2585	Keith Williams	2001	
2586	J. Ian Macnab	2001	
2587	Gordon King	2001	
2588	Rachel Tennant	2001	
2589	George Cowan	2001	
2590	Lilian James	2001	
2591	Sam James	2001	
2592	Bill Hughes	2001	
2593	William Christie	2001	
2594	Colin S. Towers	2001	
2595	Douglas Kirkwood	2001	
2596	Alan Wilson	2001	
2597	Richard Hardaker	2001	1999
2598	John Pennifold	1995	
2599	Stephen Smith	2001	
2600	Derrol P. Taylor	2001	
2601	Alex Guild	2001	
2602	Kenneth W. Collier	2001	
2603	Martin Scott	2001 2001	
2604	Gill Brooke-Taylor	2001	
2605	Robert A. Donald	2001	
2606	Colin Crawford	2001	2001
2607	James Renfrew	2001	
2608	Phil Winnard	2001	
2609	Gordon Neill	2001	
2610	Tony Smith	2001	
2611	Ann Maltman	2001	
2612	Rick Ansell	2001 2001	
2613	Andrew Philipson	2001	
2614	Mark Saunders	2001	
2615	James Davidson	1971	
2616	Stephen A. Rice	2001	
2617	Edward Sutcliffe	2001	
2618	Evelyn Main	2001	
2619	Jim Main	2001	
2620	Gerald Davison	2001	
2621	John C. Williams	2001	
2622	Jon Moore	2001	
2623	Ellis Rowe	2001	
2624	**Lisa Silver	2001	
2625	Alan Haworth	2001	
2626	Geoffrey D. Edge	2001	
2627	Ian Pinkerton	2001	
2628	Rob Pearson	2001 2001	
2629	Margaret Pearson	2001 2001	
2630	Euan Ross	2000	2001
2631	C. Fred Y. Lawson	2001	
2632	Rhona G. Dykes	2001	
2633	Mervyn French	2001	
2634	Mike J. Wigney	1999 2000 2001	

2635	John Burns	2001
2636	Janet Burns	2001
2637	Christopher J. Horton	2001 2001
2638	Alastair Gentleman	2001
2639	James McMenemy	2001
2640	Nigel Barry	2001
2641	Alan G. Duncan	2001
2642	Louisa Fraser	2001
2643	Ian Scobie	2001
2644	Douglas Robinson	2001
2645	Hamish A. Campbell	2001
2646	Ron McGraw	2001
2647	Gordon Jarvie	2001
2648	Mark A. Rawes	2001
2649	William S. Maxwell	2001 2001 2001
2650	Tom Bryce	2001
2651	Janet M. Mitchell	2001
2652	Andrew D. Martin	2001
2653	Derek I'Anson	2001
2654	Mel Owen	1999 1999
2655	Elma Bomphray	2001
2656	Dick Lerski	2001
2657	Michael G. E. Hill	2001
2658	Julia Banks	2001
2659	Daisy Stewart	2001
2660	Peter Bardsley	1997
2661	Simon Harvey	1997
2662	Chris Marden	1997
2663	FionaMarden	1997
2664	Paul F. Murray	2001
2665	Tom Campbell	1997
2666	Andrew Ogston	1993
2667	Kevin Broadbent	1999
2668	Simon Sutherland	1994
2669	Brian Mucci	2001
2670	Alison Claxton	2001
2671	Martin F. Sinclair	2001
2672	Alistair Little	2001
2673	Steve Smart	2001
2674	Noelle Webster	2001
2675	D. Bruce	2001
2676	Ursula Stubbings	2000
2677	Ian Michael Lowit	1986
2678	Lawrence Clark	2001
2679	W. Watson	2001
2680	Philip Roberts	2000
2681	David Heddon	2000
2682	Chris Thorp	2000
2683	John Carpenter	2000
2684	John Roger Sutton	2002
2685	Donald Kerr	2002
2686	Jack Kelly	2001
2687	Charlie Stephen	1999
2688	Helen J. F. Rogers	2001
2689	Katy Thompson	2002
2690	John Gansler	2001
2691	Heather Alexander	2001
2692	Donald Robert Talbot	2001 2001 2001

The last year was unusual for three reasons, each far more important than simply a change in the person receiving the letters. The first reason was, of course, the outbreak of Foot and Mouth disease. Now much has been printed about the rights and wrongs of the countryside ban that ensued, and this report is not the place to discuss such an item. The effect on people's plans for Munro Compleation was however, undeniably disrupted, with many people having to postpone their proposed last Munro parties. This can be quite a heart-wrenching thing to have to do when it's something that has been planned for up to a year with, in some cases, people jetting in from overseas.

The other two unusual events in the last year have been of a happier nature. The first was the 100th anniversary of the first compleation. This took place on Meall Dearg (Aonach Eagach) on September 28. Several rounds were compleated on this day – more anon. There was also a Centenary Dinner to elebrate the first compleation. This was held in May 2001 and Chris Huntley has an article written on the event, which follows this report.

The third important event of the last year was the formation of The Munro Society. This organisation, set up and run by Munroists for Munroists, promises to be an important and useful organisation within the Scottish hill scene. Only Compleat Munroists are eligible to join. However, they need not be on the SMC List. The welcome mat is extended to the Unknown Munroist! For more information on the society, visit their website at www.munrosociety.org.uk, or write to the society at 5 Beechgrove Place, Perth PH1 1JB.

Another point worthy of mention at this time is the Munro Hall of Fame Summit Photo Library on the SMC website. Ken Crocket has done a terrific job in developing the Munroist List on the website and now the photo library is also an impressive feature. This is going to become an excellent historic document and I would urge anyone who has compleated in the past to visit the SMC website and take a look. Hopefully, you will feel like sending Ken or myself a final summit photograph. Ken prefers photos rather than disks or e-mails. Remember to include your number, the year and date, and the hill you are on. Photographs will be returned in due course. Anyone compleating in years to come can send their photograph along with their initial letter.

Now, what tales are there from this year's compleatists? Well make yourself comfortable...

Let's start with The Day, 100 years on from the first compleation. One very remarkable compleation was made that day by Tony Smith (2610) on a very wet Ben Vorlich. Tony married his bride Lorna in the morning in Callander. The wedding party then bagged Tony's hill in very dreich conditions, and in the evening they celebrated both events. Another less-than-usual compleation on The Day was by Alan Haworth (2625) (Secretary to the Parliamentary Labour Party), on Ben More, Mull. Ben More was also the 100th Munro that Alan and his wife, Maggie, had done together, and it was Maggie's 108th overall. As this was the total that the late John Smith reached, Maggie says she has now retired. Alan indeed did 13 of his summits with John. As for Meall Dearg, Gerald Davison (2620) compleated on it, on The Day. He had started planning for this three years earlier. Jon Moore (2622) and Ellis Rowe (2623) also did what I believe was the only joint compleation on The Day.

Two more people did commemorative compleations, which didn't actually finish on The Day. One was Andrew Hyams (2561). Wanting to pay suitable historic respect to both Sir Hugh and the Rev. Robertson, he decided to finish 100 years after the first round. He compleated on Beinn Bhrotain before taking in Carn Cloich-mhuillin on the descent, thereby finishing over Sir Hugh's planned final summit. Andrew M. Fraser (73) put in a fifth round to celebrate the centenary. He finished on the same Munro and day as his first round (Schiehallion, June 9). He has promised himself and his wife that it will be his last (but watch this space). A further commemorative ascent was made of Meall Dearg on, for some reason, the day after The Day by a worthy team comprising in their number (allegedly) a Hillzine editor, an ex-SMC Clerk of the List and a writer of stories about bothies and hills. Perhaps they couldn't get the time off work on the Friday. They probably got better weather.

The most technical Munro, the Innaccessible Pinnacle is often mentioned in letters. It gets compleated last quite often, but it's not a place to have too much champagne on top. It was William Ramsden's (2535), then later Carole (2551) and Alan Scott (2552)'s last. Carole and Alan had thought initially that the Cuillin would be too daunting for them, however, participating in a John Muir Trust work-party on Blaven changed their minds. D. W. Horner (2540) from Darlington had both the finest and most embarrassing half-hour of his round on the Pinn. After the abseil descent (his finest), a jammed abseil rope resulted in "a period of piroutting on a ledge eight feet up" in order to free it. This sounds a little like 'The Affaire Tiso' during the first winter traverse. This time, however, a large audience were watching. Norman and Rona Macleod (2553 and 2554) arrived at the Pinn towards the end of their round. The East Ridge was stowed out, and their guide, knowing they had no rock-climbing experience, gave them the option of the West Ridge or an early return home. Well with so few to go, they surprised him by going for it.

One thing I've re-discovered since taking over as Clerk, is that Munroists love statistics. Andrew Rook (2534) informed me of his compleation and also that of the Furths. He was also kind enough to detail his tally of seven other British hill lists, including Wainwrights and Nuttels. John Burton (2536) compleated his last Munro and Top as part of the same walk, on Cruachan. He promptly went off to Arran and Rum to gather Corbetts and Grahams. He sent a 'Compleat' list of the dates he'd done all his Munros and Tops. Ina and John Morris (2526 and 2527) completed in 12 years. They also worked out their total hill time during their round – 1210.5 hours; their total distance covered – 1559miles; their total height climbed – 546,869ft. This then allowed them to offer data for average time, distance and height climbed per Munro and average number of hills per day. They needed a return trip to Beinn a' Choin due to the summit undergoing a "ridiculous change from a good peak to an insignificant bump on the ridge".

The first person to be registered compleat by this new Clerk was Tim Lines (2543) from Devon. John Sutherberry (2528) also travelled up from south of the Border, from Chester. He required some 30 trips in all for his compleation. Keith Edward Williams (2585) clocked more than 100 trips from Shropshire before he finished on Beinn Narnain. Christopher Langman (2548) from Solihull reckoned that the M6 was far more of a problem than the hills. Douglas Robinson (2644) got clear conditions on 70% of his Munro summits. Given that all his summits were done on short trips from London and he went out regardless of weather, I'd say he was a very lucky man. Finally, on the subject of long-distance compleations,

John Gansler (2690) compleated while living on the Isle of Wight but did a lot of his summits while based in Brussels.

It is not common for baggers to endevour from the outset to climb all Munros and Tops. Katherine and Mathew Heal (2531 and 2532) did just that. They also added all the deleted Tops. I've always thought that the deleted Tops form many a fine summit. Anyone who doubts this should just have a day out on the plateau of Beinn Avon. Mel Owen (2654) from Huntington also did all Munros and Tops, and indeed finished crossing both Beinn a' Bhuird and Ben Avon, plus all their associated Tops. This was in one long day from Invercauld Bridge – most people prefer a slightly shorter day to compleat. Rob and Margaret Pearson (2628 and 2629) also compleated Tops and Munros together, finishing on Ben Vorlich, 35 years to the day since they met.

In the year of the centenary of the first compleation, another very early compleation was definitely by Lisa Silver (2624). Confused? Well Lisa bivvied between two of the Munros of Beinn a' Ghlo, then got up in the wee small hours to wander up the last slope to the summit. There can't have been many top-outs earlier than that.

To compleat one's last Munro alone is not usual. Steve Smart (2673) failed to get his friends along for his last summit, but reckoned that being on his own was appropriate – he'd done all the others apart from the Inn Pinn on his own. There can't be many who have had such a similar solo experience on a first round.

The weather on the final summit can add a lot to the day. Christopher Horton (2637) from Aberlour set off in heavy cloud on his final Munro, Mullach na Dheirgain. He passed right through and got an excellent cloud inversion for his finale – I know, he sent me a photo. He was lucky to get to his final summit. On his penultimate summit, Beinn Cruachan, he took a 200ft. slide, finally breaking with his axe. Christopher went on to compleat the Tops only two weeks after his final Munro.

I found myself in the same situation as Prince Charles this summer – neither of us could make it to Mervyn French's (2633) last Munro party. Mervyn had bumped into, and found he was being accompanied part way up An Socach (his 200th Munro) by the Prince. Mervyn therefore invited him (plus myself) along to his final bash.

Patricia Crole (2539) from Selkirk felt her round to be a great personal achievement. In a moving letter, she told tales of her early Munros, following on to her final summit. This included babes in arms, a surprise set of bagpipes smuggled to the top, and parties at both the top and the Dunalistair Hotel. I was also touched by Stephen Smith's (2599) story. Stephen suffers from asthma and bad knees, and lives in the south of England. Due to his slow pace and inability to carry a heavy pack, he did his round practically alone, on single day trips. He achieved his final 100 in two-and-a-half months, raising money for the National Asthma Campaign. Jim Renfrew (2607) also had an uphill struggle as he battled against arthritis to compleat. He had to undergo a hip replacement with just 22 to do.

Compleat Munroists are always invited to detail any interesting anecdotes from their hill days, and most of these don't take place on the final summit. People tend to describe their *Worst, Best, Most amusing,* incidents etc. Many of these are definitely worth airing further.

Geoffrey Edge (2626) described his *Most amusing* (in retrospect) incident. He used a bike from Fishnish to get to Ben More, Mull. As it was a beautiful day, he did the full circuit, which he hadn't planned. A headwind on the return cycle saw him within sight of the last ferry of the day as it left the pier. Chris Madden (2662) made me very envious as he described a couple of his best days as his moonlit winter traverse of Aonach Eagach, and the Forcan Ridge after a high-level snowhole. Dave Liddle (2556) explained that improving his geographical knowledge of Scotland was a good reason for him being a bagger. Realising that Glas Tulaichean and Beinn a' Ghlo were quite close came as a surprise when previously he'd always thought of them as being seperated by more than 100 miles of road. In three gulps, would describe Rick Ansell's (2612) round. In 1984, he did a solo continuous traverse of all the mainland Munros. In 1999, he did a single day traverse of the main Cuillin ridge. Finally, in 2001 he did Blaven and Ben More during a Western Isles cycling/walking trip.

It's always heart warming to see family compleations taking place, and also what my predecessors called *Munroist Longius* (I think its Latin or something for having taken a good few years to 'get a round in'). Mark (2566) and his father Graham Ingram (2567) climbed all summits together, compleating on Ladhar Bheinn. They took just eight years for their round, doing the Aonach Eagach when Mark was 10, and Skye and the Inn Pinn when he was 14. At the other end of the scale, Kenneth Collier (2602) climbed Ben Lawers in 1946 (he also remembered the date), and compleated on his 70th birthday last year on Buachaille Etive Beag.

Another excellent part of my new job is hearing from people whom I'd previously lost track of, or have some common friend with. Bill Hunter (2562) and John Lagoe (2570) were both colleagues of my father-in-law at Eskdale Outward Bound in the Fifties. They provided tales of his younger-day hill exploits, which I'd never heard before.

So, I finish with the list of those people who have amended their entry in the List in the past year. As described in previous *Munro Matters,* compleat Munroists can now amend their entry by adding their year of Corbett completion if applicable. A certificate is available for this too.

AMENDMENTS

The following have added to their entries on the List. Each Munroist's record is shown in full. The columns refer to Number, Name, Munros, Tops, Furths and Corbetts.

1110	Christopher G. Butcher	1992	2001	1995	
		2001			
2092	Steve Tompkins	1999	2001		
1133	Wattie Ramage	1992			
		2001			
2029	Greg Cox	1998	2000	2000	
1924	C.W.V. Harris	1998		1998	
73	Andrew M. Fraser	1967	1980	1977	
		1980			
		1986			
		1996			
		2001			
121	Don Smithies	1973	2001	1998	Done

1729	Dennis R. Pickett	1997	2001	1998	
1730	Keith Anderson	1997	1997	1998	
1494	Judy Vallery	1995		2001	
1495	Tom Vallery	1995		2001	
944	John Starbuck	1991	1991		2001
1853	Anne J. Fletcher	1997		2000	
1854	Graham R. Bunn	1997		2000	
2075	Martin G Hinnigan	1999	2001		
2341	Ralph Henderson	2000		2001	
317	*Grahame Nicoll	1984	1993		2001
		1997			
1702	John Ferguson	1995			2000
2507	Andy McGowan	2000		2001	
685	Derek G. Sime	1989	1989	1990	1998
2345	Graham Phillips	2000	2000	2001	
860	Peter Sellers	1991	1991	1981	2001
861	Sylvia Sellers	1991	1991	1981	2001
1045	Steve Fallon	1992	1993		
		1994			
		1995			
		1996			
		1997			
		1998			
		1999			
		2000			
		2001			
808	John Barnard	1990	1991	1990	1994
		2001	2001		
2597	Richard Hardaker	2001		1999	
2448	Joyce McCraw	2000		2001	
1292	Julian P. Ridal	1994		1995	1999
234	Anne McGeachie	1980		1997	1996
235	George McGeachie	1980		1997	1996
345	John Burdin	1984		1993	
1239	Roger C. Henshaw	1993	2001		
550	Jim Montgomery	1987	1987	1994	
674	C. Andrew Scott	1988	2000	2000	2000
2536	John G. Burton	2001	2001	2002	
707	Robert F. Gibson	1989	1996		
393	Jennifer M. Irving	1985		1997	2002

People who wish to register a round and would like to receive a certificate (either for Munro or Corbett Compleation) should send a letter with a second class s.a.e. (A4 size) to me at: Greenhowe Farmhouse, Banchory Devenick, Aberdeenshire, AB12 5YJ.

Letters informing of Amendments can be sent to the above too, however in a change to previous practise, anyone wishing to inform me of an Amendment (or of a Compleation for which they don't wish a certificate), can now e-mail me. My address is: Dave.Kirk@Greenhowefarm.fsnet.co.uk.

Finally, as someone who did not record my own round for a good number of years, I can understand why some people do not wish to be on the List. I would be interested to hear from you however, from a purely statistical point of view – names would not be divulged unless permission was given.

Anyway, be sure to enjoy yourselves out there during your days on the hill – that's the most important thing. The List, Compleations, Amendments etc., they're secondary. As the first Clerk of the List, Bill Brooker recently said to me: "Don't take things too seriously."

Centenary Dinner to Celebrate the First Compleation of the Munros by the Rev. A. E. Robertson

Sometime late in the last Millennium, Robin Campbell kindly prompted me that we were close to 2001, and that the year had the special significance as the Centenary of the First Compleation. As such this would be an ideal chance to hold another dinner for Munroists. Many readers will remember a Dinner in 1991 organised by Bill Brooker to mark the centenary of the publication of the Tables and about 200 diners had attended that. However, since then, another 1600 Munroists have added their names to the List, so I was puzzled as to how many would actually want be at the Dinner. I made speculative inquiries among other Munroists and then sent letters to the outdoor Press requesting an indication of interest. The replies I got were favourable and by autumn 2000, a hotel and date had been set.

Therefore May 19, 2001 duly arrived with the Atholl Palace Hotel, Pitlochry, booked for 215 diners of which 144 were Munroists. My thanks to Robin Campbell for entertaining us with a tribute to Rev. A. E Robertson in which he reminded us that although AER is remembered for the Round of Munros, he was also an all round mountaineer prepared to try all aspects of Scottish Mountaineering. This was followed by George Barry (2311) who was given to role of describing the life of a Munroist 100 years on and the entertainment finished with a music and slide show from Chris Chapman. Thanks also to Robin Campbell who brought a video copy of Rev A. E.Robertson performing the opening of the CIC hut on Ben Nevis.

During the preceding evenings before the Dinner, I began to make a note of the facts and figures of the attendees and these include: the earliest Munroist Nan Rae (39); the latest wasTamara Cantlay (2522) who was only listed a few days before the event. The span of ages was from Adam J. Turek (2321) aged 17 to Alan Thrippleton (59) who I believe was 91 years. The earliest compleat couple, Kathleen and John Watson (41,42) attended and the current record holder for the most polymunroic (with 10 rounds) Stewart Logan (327) was present.

Hopefully, before too long there will be another suitable anniversary for another Dinner!

Chris Huntley.

SCOTTISH MOUNTAIN ACCIDENTS 2001
REGIONAL DISTRIBUTION

(Geographical Divisions are those used in SMC District Guidebooks)

| REGION | CASUALTIES (of which fatalities are bracketed) | | | | INCIDENTS | | | | | | | | Animal Rescues | Non-Mountaineering Incidents |
| | | | | | Actual Rescues | | Other Callouts | | | | | | | |
	Injuries	Exhaustion/Exposure Hypothermia, Hyperthermia	Illness	Total Casualties	Incidents with Casualties	Cragfast or weatherbound	Separated	Lost	Overdue or Benighted	False Alarms or Hoaxes	Total Incidents			
Northern Highlands	22 (5)	1 –	2 (1)	25 (6)	22	1	4	2	10	1	40		2	3
Western Highlands	8 (1)	1 –	2 (1)	11 (2)	11	2	–	1	5	–	19		–	–
Ben Nevis	32 (3)	2 –	4 (1)	38 (4)	35	2	1	3	2	1	44		–	–
Glen Coe (Inc Buachaille)	23 (4)	1 –	1 –	25 (4)	24	6	–	2	4	–	36		–	–
Other Central Highlands	14 (1)	– –	1 –	15 (1)	15	3	–	2	2	5	27		1	1
Cairngorms	30 (4)	10 –	9 (2)	49 (6)	43	4	2	14	13	6	82		–	25
Southern Highlands	26 (3)	12 –	3 –	41 (3)	32	1	1	4	3	1	42		1	9
Skye	6 –	2 –	– –	8 –	7	3	2	3	5	–	20		–	–
Islands (other than Skye	8 (1)	– –	1 –	9 (1)	9	–	–	–	2	–	11		–	–
Southern Uplands	4 (2)	– –	– –	4 (2)	4	–	–	3	4	–	11		2	27
All Regions Totals 2001	173 (24)	29 –	23 (5)	225 (29)	202	22	10	34	50	14	332		6	65
Previous year Totals 2000	178 (29)	37 (1)	29 (12)	244 (42)	222	21	6	28	50	20	347		2	34

MOUNTAIN RESCUE COMMITTEE OF SCOTLAND
SCOTTISH MOUNTAIN ACCIDENTS 2000
Compiled by John Hinde

Police have not been mentioned in all incidents, but they have been concerned in all because it is their responsibility.

One would assume, except for Southern Uplands, that incidents in Scotland would have been less affected by foot and mouth outbreaks than in England and Wales. This seems to have been the case.

One remark was that the ratio of fatalities to casualties was greater in Scotland than in the rest of the UK. I would expect this because of the greater severity and remoteness of the mountains.

In separating mountaineering from non-mountaineering incidents I think my interpretation is more embracing than most. I do not normally exclude incidents because somebody has carried a parachute to the top of the Buachaille, or canoed a Highland river, or because they live and work in the mountains, e.g. stalkers or shepherds. I have included most off-road incidents in the mountains, moorlands or sea cliffs as mountaineering.

NORTHERN HIGHLANDS

JANUARY 18-19 – Starting Ben Wyvis ascent at 11.30 casualty (54) descended SW from somewhere near the summit trig. point. Before reaching the SW Top (An Caber) he went NW down a notorious corrie; taking short cut using ice-axe as brake he was thrown into the air, breaking a lower leg on landing (glissading wearing crampons) at 17.00. A torch would have ensured an earlier find at night with the use of night vision goggles; an orange bivvy bag would have ensured an earlier find by day. Found by ground search then airlifted by RAF at 12.05. Dundonnell and Kinloss MRTs, SARDA. 121.

JANUARY 29 – Search by BraemarMRT for missing pair of climbers on Lochnagar. The pair had problems on the cliff and bivvied overnight, but alarm was caused mainly because of language difficulties. 22.

JANUARY 30-31 – A man and two women, very well equipped with clothing and sleeping bags, but with no crampons and only one map and one ice-axe between them, started at 10.30 in good conditions. They had underestimated full winter conditions above 600m and moved very slowly near the summit of Ruadh Stac Mor, Beinn Eighe. One fell a metre or so and this caused them to go even slower so they got benighted. Next morning they failed to recognise their location, although probably in sight of the famous Triple Buttresses. For 6 hours they traversed down and round the North Spur of Ruadh Stac Mor, very dangerous ground, and were then found by RAF Sea King and airlifted, cold but unhurt. Torridon and Kinloss MRTs. 240.

FEBRUARY 3-4 – Solo coastal walker (53) failed to return to Ling Hut, Torridon. He had fallen off a path on to a ledge not far from Araid Shielings, Loch Diabeg. He broke a leg, dislocated a shoulder and suffered facial injuries. Main tracks were searched at night. He was spotted waving at 08.30 by HMCG helicopter, which could not winch him direct because of turbulence. Stretcher lowered by Kinloss and Torridon MRTs down a cliff into a boat from which he was airlifted. SARDA also used in search. Weather was gales, blizzard, very cold. 248.

FEBRUARY 10 – At the tail-end of a superb spell of Scottish winter climbing a group started in good weather, but it deteriorated in the afternoon, with higher temperatures. Two roped pairs descending Poachers Fall (180m V) Coireag Dubh Mor, Liathach, were retreating due to thaw causing poor ice conditions on the climb. An avalanche, not self-triggered, came from 200m above them. The higher pair were OK tucked into the steep face of the route as they descended. The lower pair had reached the foot of the climb and were swept a further 150m by the avalanche, one of them sustaining an ankle injury. Regrouping, one went for help. Casualty managed a slow descent till stretchered by Torridon MRT. RAF R137 forced to divert. 65 (NB) Cornice avalanched here on January 5, 1995 with two injuries, one of them fatal.

FEBRUARY 15 – Assynt MRT, HMCG and helicopter assisted police search hills, coast and crags at remote Achmelvich on west coast of Sutherland. Person who abandoned car was wanted for questioning. Found safe in Inverness on 17th. 118.

FEBRUARY 22-23 Man in 30s overdue from Liathach Ridge walk. Turned up OK. Torridon MRT. 4

FEBRUARY 24-25 – East Face of Sgurr nan Clach Geala (MR 20 NH191717) crags not marked on OS map. A rope of three at the foot of Alpha Gully (240m II) was hit by an avalanche at 12.00 . One man (59) suffered an ankle injury being swept 45m to the top of the next drop. Another (29) was swept 22m without injury. The worst injured was a man (54) with chest, facial and head trauma caused by being bounced around by the avalanche while belayed at the foot of Alpha Gully. Another pair (58, 29) were crossing Apron below Alpha and Beta Gullies. The younger suffered a back injury but managed to walk off. His companion was uninjured. Alarm was raised by two of the five who walked out to Loch a' Bhraoin on A832. Dundonnell MRT attended. Worst casualty was double-strop lifted by RAF Sea King which had to land at Loch Luichart due to gearbox failure, so he went on to Raigmore by ambulance. Hospital said he would not have survived the night on the hill. Team finished at 03.30 walking out through knee deep snow. 320.

APRIL 18-20 – Experienced mountaineer (49) killed by fall on Liathach. Travelling light, although it is difficult to tell, he ran/walked solo from Coire Dubh carpark to just north of the peak of Mullach an Rathain. Wearing fell-running shoes on hard neve, he slipped and slid, receiving a fatal blow to the head on rock sticking through the snow. Searches on two days by Kinloss and Torridon MRTs, SARDA, HMCG and two RAF helicopters. The casualty, was found by MRT search. 351.

APRIL 19 – Walker (62) stumbled on Beinn Eighe Mountain Trail, in good weather. Suffering an ankle injury he tried to hobble down with the help of friends, but once Scottish Natural Heritage workers were reached, Torridon and Kinloss MRTs were alerted. He was stretchered to the Loch Maree road and taken to Raigmore Hospital. 325.

APRIL 20 – In a party of two a wheelchair-bound woman (72) fell 3m on seacliff at Scarfskerry Point (15km ENE of Thurso, Caithness) She was pronounced dead by paramedics on scene. RAF Sea King, Duncansby, Dunnet and Scrabster Coastguard Rescue Teams were deployed. HMCG assisted police with recovery of body. Dry, calm weather. 31.

MAY 8 – Walker who split from companions on Am Faochagach (Aultguish) found on road OK.

MAY 11 - With two friends on the path climb of Ben Wyvis in good weather, male (60) had a fatal heart attack. Airlifted to Raigmore by RAF Sea King. 8.

MAY 18 – Two experienced males overdue from Fisherfield Munros. They walked out. 2

MAY 27 - Male (41) separated from four companions in mist on Beinn Ghobhlach (Little Loch Broom). Descending to the main track went wrong and walked to Scoraig. HMCG helicopter and Dundonnell MRT on standby. 2.

MAY 30 – Female (52) walking with friends in good weather at bealach south of Sail Gorm, Quinag, slipped and broke her ankle. Airlift to Stornoway by HMCG helicopter. Assynt MRT on stand-by. 8.

MAY 30 – Two men (55, 32) descending from Beinn Alligin by Coire Mhic Nobuil were overdue, having to make long detours in mist, heavy rain and darkness. A normal hill day turned into a nightmare as cloud and darkness confused navigation and burns rose in spate. They got themselves down by about midnight. The second bridge at 882597 is not shown on earlier maps, but knowing it allows all burns to be avoided. Mobile phone used. Torridon MRT search. 20.

JUNE 18 – In good weather, possibly on the rock path avoiding the main difficulties, wife was with her husband on Corrag Bhuidhe Pinnacles (An Teallach). Husband heard a cry and a noise, looked around and located his wife (51) who had fallen 90m. Unable to use his wife's mobile phone, husband spotted another party on Sail Liath about 2km distant. He ran for help and found an off-duty ambulance man who phoned Aberdeen Air Ambulance Control, who passed him on to ARCC Kinloss. RAF Sea King on exercise in the Cairngorms was tasked to attend. Casualty was double-strop winched. She 'arrested' when she arrived at Raigmore at 13.40. Dundonnell MRT not involved. 8.

JUNE 28-29 – Walker (69) had turned back from Ben Loyal on 28th because of foot-and-mouth disease notices and informed campsite owner he was going some-where else. On same day he was seen with unleashed dog, still going up about 20 minutes from summit, by descending walkers near crags on Ben Klibreck. Cloud base was about 700m. Campsite owner recognised his car at Vagasty on 29th and reported it to police. His body was found in the afternoon by RAF Sea King and Kinloss MRT with the uninjured dog beside him. He seemed to have fallen about 150m. Assynt MRT assembled. 69.

JULY 16-17 – Torridon and Dundonnell MRTs worried about the welfare of a two -year-old, involved in a long, wild country expedition. Two Czech families planned to walk around either side of Meall Mheinnidh (720m) halfway along north side of Loch Maree near Fionn Loch. Separations followed a failure to rendezvous, but all got out OK so planned searches with a helicopter were abandoned. 3.

JULY 17 – Male (37) walking off Liathach by Coire Dubh Mor with two compan-ions, sustained a deep gash in the back of his leg when struck by a falling rock. Airlift by RAF. 8.

JULY 20 – Two men overdue on Beinn Alligin. They had started off looking for bridge at 874583 which was taken away around 1994, but which was still shown in the guide they were using, reprinted 1999. When they were about to descend by 'The Horns' they decided it was too much even in the perfect conditions. They retreated to bealach between 'Tom' and 'Sgurr' and descended west by detour. Torridon MRT informed. 1.

AUGUST 8 – Two young women reported their parents both had knee problems and were overdue descending steep path in darkness. Dundonnell MRT attended, strapped up the knee of the mother; then aided both down Ardessie Burn, Sail Mhor of An Teallach. 2.

Doré Green on the first ascent of 'Welzenbach' (HVS 5a), Latheronwheel, Caithness. Photo: Simon Richardson.

AUGUST 16 – Pair (f30, m28) came some way down Sail Mhor of Beinn Eighe, got lost and phoned police. Not surprisingly, signals deteriorated as they descended. Cloud cleared sufficiently to allow them to continue. Torridon MRT member awaited their safe descent at control point. 3.

AUGUST 21 – Daughter (15) separated from parents on Beinn Eighe Woodland Trail. She probably went up on to Mountain Trail. Parents went back to search in rain and strong wind. Torridon MRT informed but all returned safely within estimated time. 1.

AUGUST 21 – Man (60) descending South Ridge of Sgurr Ban, Fisherfield Forest. He was blown over by the wind, falling 8m head over heels hitting his head on rocks. One of his two companions managed to raise the alarm in less than four hours. Dundonnell MRT and RAF Sea King winchman rendered First Aid and supported casualty down to the chopper. 32.

AUGUST 21-22 – In storm force winds on Bidein Toll a' Mhuic (main ridge of Liathach) a female (54) bivouacked. Torridon MRT searched because her car was still parked and a passer-by said she told him she was unwell. She was found at 23.15 and consented to descend with the team. She was fine and well and had chosen to wait out till storm relented. She was well equipped she carried a mobile but felt no need to use it. 66.

AUGUST 25 – female (56) slipped on SSW Ridge, Ben Hope, injuring her ankle. Husband went down, contacted services, then went back up. RAF Sea King attended, by which time casualty had got down. Airlift to Raigmore. 11.

AUGUST 27 – Woman (50s) on geography field trip was walking on a glen path between caves in Gleann Dubh, Inchnadamph. She slipped and injured an ankle. Assynt MRT assisted her to walk off.

AUGUST 28 – A wife reported two men (49, 37) overdue from Liathach in mist, rain and strong wind. Torridon MRT checked but they were soon down OK. 1

AUGUST 31-September 23 – The body of a male (33) was found by MRT on September 23 in Coire a' Ghlas Thuill of An Teallach just east of the foot of Hayfork Gully. His injuries were consistent with him having fallen 280m from the ridge of Bidein a' Ghlas Thuill. He had not contacted anyone since August 31 when he had been 'on top of a hill in the Highlands'. His car was found on A832 at Corrie Hallie. Extensive searches over five days followed his failure to return to Derbyshire. Dundonnell MRT, SARDA, HMCG and RAF helicopters. Full details of search planning and execution are available in archives. 642.

SEPTEMBER 5 – Assynt MRT searched Faraid Head for person presumed missing from an abandoned tent. Possible suicide. Nothing found. 140.

SEPTEMBER 18-19 – Descending Beinn Dearg, Ullapool and missing path circling Beinn Enaiglair pair (m28, f25) came across a deep gorge in darkness. Confusion between cragfast and benighted and lost contact in mobile calls caused a full call-out of Dundonnell MRT. Evacuation was by Argocat. The man was undergoing an asthma attack and would not have been able to walk off unaided. 25.

SEPTEMBER 22 – One of eight walkers (32) near the summit of Ruadh-stac Mor, Beinn Eighe, stumbled on a loose rock. He dislocated his shoulder trying to break his fall. It was too painful to walk. Mobile phone used. Rescue by RAF Sea King to Belford Hospital, diverted to another rescue on Ben Nevis *en route* to Raigmore. Torridon MRT in communication. 9.

SEPTEMBER 30 – Man from Israel was thought to be overdue from a walk to Cape Wrath. Assynt MRT were unable to deploy because weather was too rough for the ferry to get them across Kyle of Durness. He turned up OK at ferry house. 128.

OCTOBER 3-4 – Two men who had been drinking left Toscaig to reach Uags Bothy

Stob Coire an Lochain, Glen Coe. Climber Neil MacGougan. Photo: David Ritchie.

From the forthcoming Climbers Guide to Ben Nevis. Jonathan Preston on Kellet's Slab Route (VI 7), South Trident Buttress. Photo: Andy Nisbet.

in SW Applecross Peninsula. 1Km from roadend one (41) slipped between two boulders and broke a lower leg. Friend raised alarm. Despite nearness to road it is a remote place. Stretchered to ambulance by Torridon MRT. 77.

OCTOBER 11-12 – Weather on Ben Wyvis worsened during the day to low cloud and 100km/hr gale. Two men (30, 24) the younger a novice and kidney transplant recipient, descended from the summit towards An Cabar but turned west too soon (a common error). Lost, they returned to the summit and tried again but got blown south-east, bivvying in an old stone shelter. Overnight search by Dundonnell MRT hampered by gale and mist, but night was clear earlier. Men had seen RAF helicopter but had no torch. Found by SARDA dog then the team at 11.00. Walked a bit, but younger, exhausted, was airlifted off. Kinloss MRT had searched SE Flanks. 284.

OCTOBER 23 – Couple went low-level walking in Flowerdale Forest, east of Loch Gairloch. At Loch Airig a' Phuill woman (56) slipped on wet, rocky path injuring her ankle. Airlifted to Broadford, Skye, by HMCG helicopter. Dundonnell and Torridon MRTs. 21.

OCTOBER 25-26 – Party of two on four-day backpacking trip in Fisherfield. The boots of one fell apart five miles from end. Friend walked out and returned with a spare pair but they did not regroup in darkness. Friend raised alarm. Man (39) found at 01.00 on Slioch and walked out by Torridon and Dundonnell MRTs. 66.

NOVEMBER 15-16 – Dutch woman (30) and man (28) lost on Meall nan Ceapraichean (Bein Dearg) were found on a boulder slope by Dundonnell MRT. 170.

WESTERN HIGHLANDS 2001

JANUARY 15 – Dundonnell MRT tactfully suggested a solo woman hill walker (21) should curtail her usual ambitious plan for a six-month extended stay in the mountains. With no crampons on icy paths she had travelled from Applecross to Loch an Squid, Glen Affric. Four walked out with her, as mother had suggested she wanted to come out (mobile phone conversation) but was unable to do so. Uninjured. 33.

MAY 31-June 1 – Walker (59) in rain and mist had reached Lurg Mhor by Beinn Tharsuinn and Bidein aí Choire Sheasgaich. Deciding against Meall Mor (east peak of Lurg Mhor) he returned west down to 'Cheesecake Bealach'. He thought of descending to Loch Monar for a short cut but went south from the bealach instead of north, down to Loch Calavie. He decided to skirt west of 'Cheesecake' and hug B. Tharsuinn to Bealach Bhearnais. However, he must have hugged 'Cheesecake' too closely and went down to Loch Monar, where he overnighted. Next day he made a quick retreat, collected his bike below Pollan Buidhe, and so out to Craig. He had carried compass, map and torch. Torridon MRT. RAF Sea King recalled en route. 31.

JUNE 3 – At 12.30 man (56) in a party of four ascending Bidein a' Choire Sheasgaich from a camp at Loch Monar slipped, fell 5m and broke a leg. Companion walked towards habitation but could not get mobile reception till 15.30. Direct rescue by RAF Lossiemouth Sea King. Torridon MRT stood by in case helicopter could not get in due to weather. 25.

JUNE 21 – Man (47) on Tom a' Choinich decided to ìtake in Toll Creagach, but with no compass got lost and was overdue. Found walking to Cannich. Dundonnell MRT. 4

JULY 14-15 – Kinloss MRT called out from Ballater exercise to help Lochaber MRT, RAF Sea King and SARDA in search for overdue male (57) on Beinn

Resipol. On arrival at Loch Sunart RV at 07.15 team informed he had been found safe having walked off the hill in the wrong direction. Too tired to climb back over the top he bivvied and walked off next morning. Turned up near Polloch, Loch Shiel. 498.

AUGUST 4 – Female (29) on the Saddle slipped on wet rock (pulled by dog on lead) and broke her ankle. Companion alerted services. Kintail MRT, lifted to cloudbase by RAF Rescue 137, found casualty and stretchered her down below cloud for airlift to Broadford Hospital. 40.

AUGUST 4 – Walking with her husband about 700m east of Falls of Glomach, wife (59) slipped and broke her ankle. Rescuers were alerted four hours later by a passer-by. Airlifted to Raigmore by RAF with Kintail MRT on stand-by. 11.

AUGUST 11 – Search of Gleann Lichd by Kintail MRT for experienced walker (44) reported overdue by his wife. Found next day at hostel by RAF Sea King safe and well. 16.

AUGUST 25-26 – Descending Creag nan Damh by Am Fas-allt (towards A 97) man (40) and woman (34) lost their way due to failing light. They could see traffic on the road but were unsure of descent route. Four members of Kintail MRT spotted their torch flashes. They were escorted off the hill by 01.30. 30.

AUGUST 28 – Schoolboy (15) on award expedition was extracted from Glen Elchaig by a keeper before rescue services were mobilised. Two of the lad's companions had gone to Iron Lodge when he suffered weakness and dizziness. Taken out by 4x4 he was found to have low sugar level at Broadford Hospital. Kintail MRT and HMCG helicopter stood down. 3.

SEPTEMBER 7 – Companion walker alerted emergency services to unknown German male (35) being washed away, presumed drowned, attempting to cross River Carnoch in spate 4km upstream from the outlet into Loch Nevis. Remains found and recovered by HMCG helicopter assisted by RAF Sea King, RNLI, HMCG Auxillary and Lochaber MRT. He was identified as a German national on holiday. 94.

SEPTEMBER 18-19 – Farmer (41) set off from Loch Hourn at 13.00 to gather sheep on Beinn nan Caorach 3km to NE of Arnisdale. He was last seen alive at about 550m altitude in Coire Dhruim nam Bo. Glenelg MRT, closely followed by Kintail MRT, searched when alarm was raised at 23.30. In good, but dark, weather he was found dead of a heart attack near the same place at 03.15. Airlift by Stornoway HMCG helicopter. 218.

SEPTEMBER 26-27 – Having completed Sgurr na Ciste Duuibhe and Sgurr na Carnach (Five Sisters Ridge) walker (82) knew he had to go over Sgurr Fhuaran before he could safely descend. Benighted, his torch expired on reaching the bottom so he bivvied, walking out uninjured in daylight. Kintail and Kinloss MRTs, RAF and HMCG helos, SARDA. 234.

SEPTEMBER 29 – Male (42), one of six walkers on Beinn Fhada (Ben Attow) got cragfast when ascending a steep gully of Meall a' Bhealaich, above Bealach an Sgairne. Alarm was raised by his companions. Kintail MRT assisted him to the top of the gully and then off the mountain. 50.

OCTOBER 6 – One of a pair crossing River Shiel near Achnangart Farm (5km above Shiel Bridge) slipped or stumbled with slight injury. Kintail MRT. 4.

OCTOBER 27 – Kintail MRT rescued one of a party of three from Allt Coire Amhutt (?). The person had slipped or stumbled suffering minor injury. 35.

NOVEMBER 3-4 – Traversing NE down the ridge of Beinn Tharsuinn; when male (44) reached a bealach, and though it was Bealach Bhearnais, went right and descended to Loch Monar where he spent a cold and wet night. Found by

Torridon MRT with Kintail and SARDA on stand-by. Wearing 'golfing' waterproofs with no map, compass, torch or whistle he had got separated from two friends. Barely able to talk he was lifted by RAF Sea King to Raigmore. 78.

NOVEMBER 9-10 – Separated and lost on Glenfinnan Horseshoe in mist, walker descended to Kinlochbeoraid instead of Glenfinnan. He spent a night at the bothy and was found and lifted by RAF Sea King. Search by Lochaber MRT. 80.

DECEMBER 3 – Male suffered spinal injury when a tree blew down 1km west of Lewiston, Loch Ness. Dundonnell MRT involved in communications reference the location. RAF Sea King found casualty and airlifted him to Raigmore Hospital. 14.

DECEMBER 6 - Lochaber MRT and ambulance carried out medical evacuation of one in a group of five at Invermallie Bothy, Loch Arkaig. 50.

DECEMBEr 13 – Slip at 01.46 near Kyle of Lochalsh caused slight injury. Evacuation by HMCG ground personnel and helicopter and Kintail MRT. 52.

BEN NEVIS

JANUARY 4-5 – Father (42) and son (13) descending normal route strayed into Five Finger Gully. Son slipped, causing both to fall 100m. Father broke a lower leg then alerted police by phone. RN helicopter had engine problems in area. RAF helicopter replacement could not operate near accident due to poor weather. Lochaber MRT reached victims from normal route, stretchering father to lower level for airlift, and helping son walk out by 02.00. 285.

JANUARY 23 – Male (30) was belaying for another member of his party climbing in Coire na Ciste. The moving person caused a rock to fall, which struck his leg causing bruising. Another of the party of four rescuers, then party conveyed casualty to CIC Hut where he was airlifted by RAF Sea King. Lochaber MRT. 51.

FEBRUARY 11 – Male hill walker, spectator at a canoe race in Glen Nevis, collapsed with a cerebrovascular illness. Stretchered 800m to ambulance at roadhead by Assynt MRT just completing a training exeercise. 12.

FEBRUARY 13 – With a companion descending line of Coire Leis Abseil Posts, male (45) wearing crampons, tried to turn around to go down facing in to the hill. Turning, he lost his footing and slipped 30m, hit an abseil post, then slid a farther 90m to 120m before stopping. He had arm injuries, bruising and abrasions. He was treated on site by RAF paramedic with cylimorph, oxygen and splints and airlifted by R137. Lochaber, Kinloss and other RAF MRTS, RAF and RN helicopters. 185.

FEBRUARY 15 – After completing Italian Climb and abseiling into Observatory Gully, man (46) with a companion continued walking down the gully in darkness. Casualty's crampon caught in snow causing him to roll 60m to the foot of Observatory Buttress. He was lifted with an ankle fracture from CIC Hut to Belford Hospital by RAF Sea King. 37.

FEBRUARY 18 – Rope of two on Harrison's Climb Direct. At about one-third of the height, man (45) clipped into an existing old peg. When he put weight on it, the peg snapped which caused a fall of 14m. This fractured a scapula. He managed to evacuate himself, but was picked up by Lochaber MRT transport at head of track. 12.

FEBRUARY 18 - Descending mountain track at 16.30, man (45) slipped on snow just above Halfway Lochan twisting and breaking a lower leg bone. He managed to get down part way then phoned. Lifted by Lochaber MRT and RN helicopter from HMS Gannet. 14.

FEBRUARY 24 – Rope of two attempted Waterfall Gully. Student (20) climbed 20m when he decided to go no farther. He clipped into an *in situ* nut. When abseiling from the nut it came out and he fell breaking his back and severing his spine. Subject alerted emergency services by phone. Evacuation by Lochaber MRT stretcher carry and winch by RN Sea King. 120.

FEBRUARY 24-25 – Having set out from Youth Hostel at 0645 in good weather and kitted up at 09.30 at CIC Hut, heading for Tower Ridge, two men (31, 29) were reported overdue at 21.30. Search by RN Sea King and Lochaber MRT was initiated at 09.00 on 25th. At 09.30 other climbers at base of Glover's Chimney phoned to say they had found the pair. The elder was dead. The younger survived despite very serious head and leg injuries and cold trauma. Evacuation by the helicopter from HMS Gannet. 42.

FEBRUARY 27 – Clear weather but strong winds. Descending from Abseil Point, Coire Leis, male (45) tried to turn around to face in. Doing so he slipped on snow or rock, fell 30m striking another abseil post, then fell another 270m sustaining multiple injuries. Fall was witnessed by his companion and by Leuchars and Kinloss MRT members climbing in the corrie. Treated by RAF paramedic and by Belford Hospital doctor. Stretchered down to airlift by RAF Sea King. Lochaber MRT, RN Sea King and various RAF MRTs on Winter Course. 185.

MARCH 24 – Male (39) in a party of three approaching the foot of Green Gully lost his footing and slid. He collided with a companion, then hit a passer-by. He and the passer-by fell together 75m coming to rest on snow. He suffered slight back and head injuries, cuts and bruises. The passer-by attended to the casualty and raised the alarm. Lochaber MRT and RAF Sea King airlifted party of 3. 51.

MARCH 24 – With nine companions, woman (61) practised basic snowcraft just above CIC Hut. Walking on hard neve her crampon lost grip. Unable to stop her slide she collided with rocks after 10m causing bruising to head and chest. Lochaber MRT members attended (in the area responding to the previous incident). Airlift by RAF Rescue 137. 15.

APRIL 13 – Party of two. Unroped man (54) climbing Garadh Gully. While climbing a step of wet snow it had broken clear of the rock face causing the fall and multiple rib fractures, facial lacerations, fractured wrist and ankle. A passing climber initiated rescue by using the CIC Hut radio link. RN Sea King and Lochaber MRT. 54.

APRIL 16 – Two males had finished a climb in Number 2 Gully then walked along the plateau. While descending at the top of Number 3 Gully one of them (age 38) slipped, slid over the plateau edge and fell down the length of the gully. Airlift by RAF Sea King and Lochaber MRT to Belford Hospital and later that day airlifted to Glasgow Southern General where on April 22 he died from head injuries. 35.

MAY 14 – Ascending track near Halfway Lochan man (74) could not continue due to dehydration and exhaustion. Passer-by phoned RAF Sea King and Lochaber MRT. Fluids were given and he was airlifted with his female companion. 28.

MAY 14-15 – Man (19) with a companion set off up the track at 20.00 to find a place to camp. They became separated in darkness. Companion descended to road and reported friend missing at 22.37. Lochaber MRT took no action till 08.00 as subject was well equipped. Six team members traced him to near the South Knoll of Meall an-t Suidhe. He had been unable to come down at first light because he was lost. 28.

MAY 19 – Attempting to climb Castle Ridge from CIC Hut with a companion, female (29) suffered pain in both eyes due to contaminated contact lenses. She was unable to continue or get down. Assisted down by Lochaber MRT for treatment to damaged corneas at Belford Hospital. 32.

JUNE 9 - Attempting to walk via CIC Hut up Carn Mor Dearg Arête, male (40) got cragfast. His companion alerted police. With assistance of RN Sea King, Lochaber MRT aided him off the hill in good weather. 36.

JUNE 10 – Male (38) descending track was pulled over by his dog, injuring his knee. Lifted to Belford by RAF Sea King and Lochaber MRT. 20.

JUNE 23 – Leading Tower Ridge in good weather, male (41) belayed to a large rock and started climbing. When 5m up a handhold came away and he fell on to a ledge. The rope held him but the large rock belay dislodged and hit him on the way down. A mobile phone was used. Evacuation was by Lochaber MRT and RAF Sea King. Injuries to pelvis and arm were bruising, not fractures as suspected. 28.

JUNE 30 – Female descending track from summit in sleet and snow in a party of six took cramp in her legs. Mobile phone was used. She was winched by RN Sea King to Belford Hospital and released after treatment. 12.

JULY 20 – Setting out from the bottom at 07.45 walker (36) left two compnions to descend the normal route from the summit while he went down Coire Eoghainn. Overdue he returned safe at 19.45. Lochaber MRT, RAF Sea King. 18.

JULY 21 – Lochaber MRT alerted because three schoolboys (12, 10, 8) separated from their parental group descending the track. They were reunited before being found by the team. 10.

JULY 24 - Walking with relations between Glen Nevis carpark and Steall Meadow, girl (6) slipped and fell 15m from the path, over a small cliff and down scree. She was stretchered to ambulance by Lochaber MRT. She was to be detained at Belford Hospital for two weeks having sustained fractures of pelvis and arm, together with head injury. 12.

AUGUST 3-4 Female 47) and male student (21) contacted their family. Having reached the summit they were unable to find a way down. It was raining and getting dark. Lochaber MRT leader gave them telephone directions. They made their own way down without injury. 8.

AUGUST 5 – Female (45) slipped on Mountain Track at about 900m altitude fracturing her ankle. Airlift in calm weather by RAF Sea King and Lochaber MRT. 37.

AUGUST 12 – Reaching the summit by the normal route, a group of three (f30, f21, m22) descended by Carn Mor Dearg Arête and Coire Leis. At 14.09 hours they were unsure of their route down because of mist. Leader of Lochaber MRT was contacted by phone and was able to guide the group down without incident. 4.

AUGUST 25 – Descending track with a companion, student (17) slipped and injured his ankle. He walked down a short way, but due to pain increase he stopped at about 800m and summoned assistance. Airlifted by RAF Rescue 137 and Lochaber MRT. Released from Belford Hospital after treatment. 22.

SEPTEMBER 1 – Male (30) on a charity climb slipped at 650m aggravating an old knee injury. Lochaber MRT on track for another event came upon him and called RN Sea King already in the area. Casualty airlifted to Belford Hospital for treatment. 15.

SEPTEMBER 1 – At 600m, just below Halfway Lochan, female (21) slipped badly spraining her ankle. She had separated from her group, but Lochaber MRT were on site as safety guides. RAF Rescue 138 on exercise in the area was called. She was airlifted to Belford Hospital for treatment and later discharged. 18

SEPTEMBER 4 – Man (68) got to the summit at 13.30 with his dog, but tired on descent, finding it difficult to see in failing light. At 20.00 (at about 110m) a couple also making their way down saw he was having problems. Man stayed with him. His partner went to Achintee and phoned police. One Lochaber MRT member went up and aided subject down. No injuries were sustained. 3.

SEPTEMBER 8 – Male (43) in a party of 180 attempting Nevis for a cancer charity sustained a fatal heart attack. Lochaber MRT on site at Corner Five (1050m) attempted CPR and used suction apparatus. Airlift to Belford Hospital by RN. 16.

SEPTEMBER 22 – Taking part in a sponsored event when descending, female (36) stopped for a rest. When she stood up something snapped in her leg and she could go no farther. Rescue 137 was contacted and she was airlifted along with her companion (see following incident). Kinloss MRT. 6.

SEPTEMBER 22 – (See above incident) Due to an old injury the companion's knees gave way. Both these incidents happened at the same place, the first zig-zag above Halfway House at 750m altitude. Both women were lifted by RAF Sea King to Belford Hospital for treatment. Kinloss MRT. 6.

SEPTEMBER 22 – See above two incidents. Organised charity walk involved 10 visually impaired walkers, five volunteers and 20 rescuers. Blind walker (49) had difficulty walking on the path. He had become exhausted. Lift by RAF helicopter at 19.20. 14.

SEPTEMBER 23 – Party of three males were at the foot of Tower Ridge about to start the climb. An object seen tumbling from a ridge above them turned out to be a walker (m30) clearly dead. Airlift by RAF Sea King and Lochaber MRT. He had been walking alone and slipped or tripped. His route was not identified. 129.

October 4 – One of guided party broke her ankle on Ledge Route. Carried by group to CIC Hut then airlifted by RAF Sea King and Lochaber MRT. 11.

OCTOBER 6 – Charity walker injured her back walking up Nevis. LMRT member on site called RAF Sea King for airlift. 20.

OCTOBER 6 – Member of climbing club in party of 20 slipped on path and fell 10m into Steall Gorge sustaining a serious leg injury. Sixteen Lochaber MRT evacuated casualty to Fort William. 40.

OCTOBER 13 – Slip at Windy Corner on track caused slight injury. Lochaber MRT. 51.

OCTOBER 28 – Walker injured in a fall on track evacuated by RAF Sea King and Lochaber. 9

NOVEMBER 12 – Climber fell 70m down Garadh Gully sustaining multiple injuries. His companion raised the alarm and he was rescued by LMRT and RAF helicopter. 24

NOVEMBER 14 – Female walker failed to tell friends she was down from Nevis. Team search initiated but she was found in Fort William. 6.

DECEMBER 28 – Two climbers became cragfast on Tower Ridge. Eleven of Lochaber MRT climbed Observatory Gully intending to traverse onto the ridge by the escape route from the Eastern Traverse. RAF helicopter, which had been snow-bound north of Lochaber, managed to get through a weather break, winching the climbers off, just before the team reached them. 60.

DECEMBER 29-30 – Ten people in four separate parties made serious navigation errors descending from Nevis summit into Five Finger Gully. Thirty Lochaber MRT made their way up into the gully from Glen Nevis, found and escorted the parties. Soft snow probably prevented these incidents from becoming more serious. Few of the parties carried ice-axes or crampons. Three were slightly injured and seven OK. 165.

GLENCOE

JANUARY 2 – Four (female 26, males 38, 22, 21) attempting Aonach Eagach E to W traverse got cragfast at MR 142581 when they fell through a mud basin on Sgorr nam Fiannaidh about 200m below the ridge. They phoned and were roped and escorted down by Glencoe MRT before midnight. 67.

JANUARY 11 – Paraglider (39) affected by turbulence from earlier passing jets, was unable to control his canopy which upturned. He landed at foot of The Chasm of Buachaille Etive Mor injuring back and chest. Walked to rendezvous and conveyed by ambulance. 19.

JANUARY 11 – Friend (43) of above casualty was able to make a safe landing near him. Friend removed his own canopy to go and help then slipped on frozen rock. He fell 4m and injured a foot. Glencoe MRT provided first aid. Evacuation by RAF Sea King. 19.

JANUARY 21 – A member of Glencoe MRT witnessed a slab avalanche at the head of Coire na Tulaich, Buachaille Etive Mor. Conditions were below freezing with snow falling at the time. One of three men was climbing over a cornice which collapsed, carrying the two (46, 28) below him 90m down. They sustained limb injuries, cuts and bruises. GMRT rendered immediate help and alerted RN Sea King which lifted the two casualties. Man who triggered the avalanche was escorted down. Kinloss team also involved. 95

FEBRUARY 11 – Climbing the gully between Bidean nam Bian and Stob Coire nan Lochan at the head of the Lost Valley three people were avalanched. The three (f55, m57, m54) were swept down various distances of 180m, 210m and 240m. One was buried with only a hand showing but was extricated by the other two; all three being uninjured. Making their own way down they were met by Glencoe MRT alerted by other climbers. 34.

FEBRUARY 20 – Woman (36) and male (35) traversed Aonach Eagach east to west. Descending, they got cragfast on the east side of Clachaig Gully on wet rock in mist and darkness. A third party contacted them by phone and raised the alarm. Escorted down by Glencoe MRT by 23.00 hours. 28.

MARCH 26 – Male (36) wearing crampons, descending Bidean nam Bian towards the Lost Valley, fell. Unable to ice-axe brake he slid 30m sustaining a compound tibia fibula fracture. Nearby climbers heard cries and alerted police by phone. Rescue by Glencoe MRT and RN Sea King winching. 32.

MARCH 29-30 – Man (67) ascending Curved Ridge, Buachaille Etive Mor was fitting crampons. Pulling his ice-axe out of the snow, the snow beneath his feet gave way and he fell 120m, which caused chest injuries, abrasions and bruises. He climbed back up to within 100m of the summit and tried to get off the mountain by the easy route, but he could go no farther. Glencoe MRT was alerted at 23.00. He was found by using a flashing light, and by then had some cold trauma. Airlift by HMCG helicopter. Glencoe team finished at 08.00. 114.

APRIL 2 – Female (57) broke her ankle in two places when she slipped, wearing crampons, descending from Bidean nam Bian to the Lost Valley. Carried from the hill by other members of her party of seven, she was stretchered a short distance to the road by Glencoe MRT. From Belford to be transferred to Raigmore Hospital. 23.

APRIL 5-6 – Starting Innuendo at 15.00, two males (22, 20) had not returned from Stob Coire nan Lochan by 23.25 when Glencoe MRT was called out. The climb was successful, but slower than expected due to darkness. The pair abseiled and returned to accommodation so team was not required. 10.

APRIL 11 – Man cragfast because he lost a crampon ascending Forked Gully, Stob Coire nan Lochan. Alerted other climbers. RN Sea King and Glencoe MRT. 36.

APRIL 11 – Attempting E to W traverse of Aonach Eagach, male (41) fell 30m descending Am Bodach. Uninjured he self-rescued and continued to Meall Dearg. At 16.45 he was unable to continue. Cragfast he was lifted by RAF Sea King and Glencoe MRT. 27.

APRIL 19 – Wearing crampons and with an ice-axe a male (43) was soloing Dorsal Arête. When he was 200m above the basin of Stob Coire nan Lochan he slipped and fell to the floor of the coire injuring a leg. A passer-by alerted Glencoe MRT by phone. Airlift to Belford Hospital by RN Sea King. 30.

APRIL 24 - Male (25) and female (24) got cragfast ascending scree slopes from Dalness to Stob Dubh of Buachaille Etive Beag. They phoned and 14 members of Glencoe MRT were called out. Thereafter the pair rescued themselves. Uninjured, they were descending to the roadside when they were met by the team. They could not call off the rescuers because their phone battery had gone dead. 39.

MAY 6 – Wearing crampons, but with no ice-axe or helmet, a solo climber (51) was seen falling from Summit Gully, Stob Coire nam Beith by a climber 800m distant, through binoculars. The observer phoned Glencoe MRT and RN Sea King attended. Casualty was treated with oxygen, neck splint and vacuum mattress having skull, spine, chest and leg injuries when found below Central Gully. Transferred from Belford Hospital to Glasgow for spine checks. 39.

MAY 11 – At about 13.50 in good weather, a male (31) was seen falling from rock and scree on Gearr Aonach into Lost Valley. Emergency services were alerted and his body was found and recovered by RN Sea King helicopter and Glencoe MRT. 49.

MAY 13-14 – Male (33) and female (25) got cragfast on east face of Buachaille Etive Mor in good weather. Glencoe MRT alerted at 21.18 roped them down and escorted them from the hill at 02.45. 77.

MAY 21 – Banana Rock, Clachaig Gully, Sgor nam Fiannaidh. Leader fall of 3m caused chest injury. Equipment pulled out as she hung at rest from her protection. Casualty (22) was recovered from cliff on a stretcher by Glencoe MRT. 30.

JUNE 2-3 – From a group of six, mostly under 30, traversing Aonach Eagach E to W in good weather one decided to go down at 21.15. Five continued but two got cragfast and frightened at Stob Coire Leith. Alarm was raised. 14 Glencoe MRT and RAF helicopter recovered the casualties, one of whom (f31) had slight leg injury. 43.

JUNE 17 – Wearing trainers in good weather and watched by parents from A82 boy (10) and friends walked along lower slopes of Aonach Eagach. He slipped and tumbled over a drop of 10m. Stretchered to ambulance with head and spinal injuries by GMRT. 15.

JUNE 30-July 1 – Attempting to traverse Bidean nam Bian then Stob Coire nam Beith and down to Achnambeithach from Lost Valley, a man (43) and two woman (50, 39). At 20.30 ,due to a navigation error descending Stob Coire nam Beith in mist and rain, they got cragfast and cold. They were found by Glencoe MRT and escorted down, the older woman with slight hypothermia. RN Sea King could not operate in that weather due to onboard equipment not allowing sufficient lift. 108.

JUNE 30-July 2 – Dead man (45) was found at 11.45 on July 2 having apparently fallen from the pinnacles of Aonach Eagach on the Glencoe side. Missing since June 30 it was not known if he had gone to A. Eagach or Bidean nam Bian. Two-day search involved Glencoe, Kinloss, Leuchars, Lochaber and Oban MRTs, SARDA and RAF Sea King (12 hours flying). 1512.

JULY 30 – Climbing damp grass/earth lying on rock near Curved Ridge, Buachaille Etive Mor, a male (40) slipped, falling back 10m. His leg impacted and he was catapulted further backwards, stopping head down among rocks. He sustained serious back and leg injuries and moderate head injuries. Helmets were carried. His female doctor companion phoned and attended him. Airlift by service helicopter and Glencoe MRT to Belford later transferred to Raigmore for surgery. 30.

AUGUST 18 – Descending dry scree in Coire na Tulaich, Buachaille Etive Mor, male (57) tripped and fell 3m injuring the bridge of his nose. He continued down with his companion but felt unwell and unsteady. Another climber phoned. He was helped down by Glencoe MRT. 20.

AUGUST 18 – Three men (57, 48, 24) got lost on the Blue Route tourist footpath near Glencoe Lochan above Loch Leven at 22.12. It got dark quicker than they expected and their torch was defective. They contacted emergency services and were walked off by GMRT. 8.

AUGUST 25 – In good weather a man and a woman (30) were climbing unroped, with the man ahead, on the East Face of Aonach Dubh. The climb was Eastern Promise. The woman slipped on wet rock and fell on to a grassy ledge. Fall continued and she fell 22m with injuries to head, pelvic area, a limb and abrasions. She wore a helmet and rock boots. Alarm was raised and she was treated by Glencoe MRT, then airlifted to Belford Hospital by R137 RAF helicopter. 41.

AUGUST 31 – With a companion, a female (30) was descending Sgorr nam Fiannaidh after walking Aonach Eagach in good weather. She slipped on a rock abraiding her knee and face. Police were alerted via another walker and staff at Clachaig Inn. Glencoe MRT applied dressings and escorted the pair off the mountain. 44.

SEPTEMBER 1-2 – Deceased (52) was leading three other hillwalkers along Poucher's Route on North Face of Aonach Dubh when he jumped from a rock ledge on to a steep grass slope. The weight of his rucksack pulled him backwards and he was killed by a fall of 90m. Night and day searches by Glencoe and Leuchars MRTs. Spotted by RN Sea King and cliff lowered by MRT. 236.

SEPTEMBER 4 – Girl (14) walked to Lost Valley Boulder with family and friends. Despite warnings she climbed 7m up the boulder and became cragfast. Shortly after she fell down and landed on her bottom. Glencoe MRT used neck splint and vacuum mattress. She was lifted by HMS Gannet Sea King to Belford where spine injuries were found. 36.

SEPTEMBER 9 – Starting Aonach Eagach, male (58) suffered exhaustion from a medical condition when part way up Sgorr nam Fiannaidh. Passers-by called police. RAF Sea King on exercise with Glencoe MRT was diverted and lifted him to Belford Hopital where he was detained for the medical condition. 5.

SEPTEMBER 16-17 – Three women walkers (30, 29, 29) left insufficient time to complete Lost Valley to Stob Coire nam Beith Horseshoe. In dark with no torches, they phoned police. Glencoe MRT found and rescued them by 01.00. 88.

SEPTEMBER 17-18 – Female (44) seen on summit of Aonach Dubh a' Ghlinne (NE peak of Sgurr na h-Ulaidh) heading towards the North Ridge to descend. Weather was good. Her car was still in the carpark at 22.00 hours. Glencoe MRT found her body about midnight. 68.

OCTOBER 5 – Serious injury caused by slip/stumble on Bidean nam Bian. Glencoe and Oban MRTs and RAF helicopter involved. 454.

OCTOBER 13 – Glencoe MRT involved when a person was overdue at 19.54 hours in Lost Valley. 7.

OCTOBER 21 – Serious injury was caused when one in a party of three slipped crossing Allt Coire Gabhail (river in Lost Valley) about midday. Rescue by Glencoe MRT. 20.

OCTOBER 28 – In an ascending party of four at Crowberry Tower Gap, Buachaille Etive Mor, a walker (55) was struck by a rock dislodged by a party above. He sustained an open fracture of an upper arm. He was helped to the summit by friends. Two Glencoe MRT and winchman were dropped to treat him (stretcher, fracture straps, cyclimorph and other drugs). Mist came down and he was stretchered down to Glen Etive where the RAF Sea King lifted him from near the road. 78.

DECEMBER 8 – Rock climbing unroped in good weather three males finished climbing Pinnacle Face, Aonach Dubh. At top of B Buttress one of them ripped his Achilles/fib (an old or recurring injury) and 15 members of Glencoe MRT moved him for a strop lift by RN Sea King, then they descended Dinner Time Buttress in darkness. 95.

DECEMBER 25 – Mobile call said man and woman had no torches and were in Coire nan Lochan. Torches were seen in Coire Beith and checked out. The pair were escorted down by two Glencoe MRT. 56.

DECEMBER 30 – Male (35) and female (32) thought they were in Easy Gully, Buachaille Etive Mor. In fact they were in D Gully and they got cragfast at the junction of D Gully Buttress and Curved Ridge. In blizzard conditions and darkness Glencoe MRT aided them down at 21.45. 56.

OTHER CENTRAL HIGHLANDS

JANUARY 18-19 – Climbing Centre Post, Creag Meagaidh at 16.30 climber (64) felt unable to carry on due to cold and darkness. He stayed in a cave and his companion raised alarm. Rescued by Lochaber MRT and RAF Sea King. Eight team members climbed up and lowered him to base in difficult conditions. Uninjured he was able to walk out by 07.30. 79.

JANUARY 20 – Two companions of a seriously injured climber (33) raised the alarm on a mobile phone. Ascending South Pipe Direct, Creag Meagaidh; fairly high on the climb (at it's junction with Staghorn Gully) he had been hit on his helmet by a large piece of ice. This had possibly been dislodged by other climbers higher on the crag. His helmet had been broken and he had been knocked unconscious. Receiving serious skull injury he drifted in and out of consciousness. Lochaber MRT and helicopter R177 (HMS Gannet) extricated him to Belford Hospital. He was transferred to Glasgow Southern General where his condition remained stable. 82.

JANUARY 30 – Kinloss MRT and RAF Sea King recalled *en route*. Winter hill walker in Coire Creagach of Sgairneach Mhor, Drumochter Hills had been found safe (self recovery). 4.

FEBRUARY 7 – Precautionary search of a large avalanche on Fly Paper ski-run on Meall a' Bhuiridh. Ski area was closed at the time but there had been a report of two ski-board tracks leading into the debris. Happily, it had been a spontaneous release with no-one about. Glencoe, Kinloss, Leuchars, Lochaber MRTs and SARDA involved. 156.

FEBRUARY 17 – Female (34) walking in snow and ice, with a companion, was killed by a fall of 150m on SW Ridge of Stob a' Choire Leith, Grey Corries. Another walker raised the alarm and provided grid reference. Recovered by RAF Sea King and Lochaber MRT. 22.

FEBRUARY 18 – A mobile phone call to police stated a winter hillwalker (40) had fallen through a snow cornice. He had been taken to Ben Alder Cottage, Loch Ericht, where he was unable to walk. Airlifted to Raigmore by RAF Sea King helicopter. 9.

FEBRUARY 26-27 – Glencoe and Lochaber MRTs and RAF Sea King searched from Fort William, Spean Bridge and Kinlochleven to Corrour, Rannoch Moor for a pair (male and female) of hillwalkers (20s). They turned up in another area – Strathclyde Police area. 143.

MARCH 26 – Leader (22) on South Post, Creag Meagaidh fell 10m before rope stopped him, but his ankle had been injured. Two companions assisted him for 3km down Coire Ardair. He was lifted by RN Sea King and Lochaber MRT to Belford Hospital and released after treatment. 18.

APRIL 6 – With a companion descending from Carn Mor Dearg to CIC Hut. When 700m distant from hut, man (35) tripped wearing crampons, falling 22m first on snow then on rocks. He sustained a depressed skull fracture, broken ribs and ankle, cuts to head and extensive bruising. They had decided to return to CIC rather than go round the corrie rim to Ben Nevis because of low cloud and spindrift. Lochaber MRT and RAF R137 Sea King helicopter. 24.

APRIL 15 – One of three female walkers was stranded by the River Leven, 3km above the main road bridge in Kinlochleven, after she had leapt in to rescue her dog. Alarm was raised by mobile phone. Rescued by Glencoe MRT. 6.

MAY 13 – Paraglider (34) attempting a reverse take-off on Creag Dhubh (northern spur of Meall a' Bhuiridh) lifted off momentarily. He came down awkwardly, dislocating a knee cap. Casualty has suffered from similar injury in the past. Found by a passer-by he was recovered by stretcher carry and ski area chairlift by Glencoe MRT.

JUNE 11 – On the north ridge of Sgorr Dhearg (Ballachulish Horseshoe) a male (24) who had fallen twice and bruised his knee felt he was in no condition to continue at 18.20. Glencoe MRT responded to the phone alert. Despite a wrong grid ref. by the injured man's nine companions he was found and stretchered to the road. 33.

JUNE 16 – Female (26) injured her leg in a 3m fall on Binnein Shuas, Loch Laggan, at 18.50 hours. Taken to Belford Hospital, Fort William.

JULY 10-11 – Two men (34, 25) got lost on Ben Alder. Cold and wet, they phoned when they reached shore of Loch Erict 16km SW of Dalwhinnie. Airlifted by RAF. 10.

JULY 24 – At Ba Cottage (ruin) on West Highland Way a walker (23) was removing his boots to dry his feet when a rock fell on his toe, partially severing it. Airlift to Belford Hospital by Glencoe MRT and RAF Sea King. 8.

JULY 31 – Female (29) and male (28) were walking the stalkers' path on Beinn na Caillich (764m) 4km WNW of Kinlochleven. In good weather on steep, loose scree the woman became cragfast. Her companion phoned the police. Escorted uninjured to West Highland Way by Glencoe MRT. 23.

AUGUST 11 – Mountain biker (15) descending mountain bike descent track at Nevis Range on Aonach Mor was thrown from his bike, landed on his chest and was unable to continue. Stretchered off by Lochaber MRT to Belford Hospital, he was found to have no bone injuries but bruising to chest. 16.

SEPTEMBER 6 – One of 24 participants in a Duke of Edinburgh trip suffered severe abdominal pain on the West Highland Way above Kinlochleven. It was dark with rain and strong wind. She (17) was escorted to Mamore Loge (1.4km) by Glencoe MRT and taken to Belford Hospital, Fort William by ambulance. 10.

SEPTEMBER 12 – Male (38) wrenched knee on Beinn a' Bhric, Corrour. He used radio to give his location. At 21.00 Lochaber MRT and RAF Sea King were alerted. He was airlifted to Belford Hospital from NE Ridge, Leum Uilleim. 65.

SEPTEMBER 15 – Male (35) in a group of 12 was descending scree on Stob Ban (Mamores) North Ridge. It was raining. At approximate altitude of 600m he slipped and fell a short distance, breaking his leg. Stretchered of by Lochaber MRT using a leg splint and entonox. 32.

SEPTEMBER 15-16 – Walker (47) set off to do Munro Horshoe in the Monadhliath, was overdue at midnight. Cairngorm MRT called out at 08.00 stood down when he turned up at 08.40. Without a torch he had got benighted descending Carn Dearg and restarted at first light. 20.

SEPTEMBER 19 – Incorrect dates on a route card left on his car caused an air search by RAF Sea King and Lochaber MRT. Very apologetic man (37) found on steep west slopes of Aonach Beag said he was not two days overdue as the card stated. No airlift. 19.

SEPTEMBER 19 – Air and ground searches by RAF Sea King and Lochaber MRT on Stob Ban (Mamores) revealed nothing. Cries for help had been reported on the mountain. Local inquiries established that a shepherd had been working there. It is most likely that the shepherd's calls had been misinterpreted. 95.

SEPTEMBER 24 – Couple out walking reported that their dog had fallen over Grey Mare's Tail Waterfall, Kinlochleven and was lost from view. Glencoe MRT abseiled into the falls and recovered the dog which was bagged and roped and reunited with the owners. Apparently uninjured, the dog had fallen 6m and lodged in a cave above a further 60m drop. 23.

SEPTEMBER 26-27 – Man (65) on Grey Corries, Stob Coire Claurigh headed for Stob Ban. He went down Coire Rath in mist, slipped and felt pain in ankle. Stayed out overnight. Walked down by Glen Nevis and was located in Belford Hospital. Lochaber and Kinloss MRTs, SARDA and RN Sea King from HMS Gannet spent all day searching. 425.

OCTOBER 8 – Two people overdue from Mamores, They turned up, one with a slight injury. 0

OCTOBER 14 – Climbing club and coach waited at Laggan for a member who was snug at home in Edinburgh. He had come off the hill and hitched a lift home.

OCTOBER 17 – Glen Banchor. Setting out at noon to walk the three hour Wildcat Trail (a low level route at Newtonmore) a walker (67) had not returned at 19.30. He deviated deliberately and went into the Monadhliath hills. He got lost. It got dark. He dug in. He was found by chance by a gamekeeper out spotlighting. Cairngorm MRT searched the area as told by his wife. 42.

NOVEMBER 7 – Staff member fell 1m from working platform at Nevis Range causing back injuries. Airlift to Fort William by RAF Sea King and Lochaber MRT. 10.

CAIRNGORMS

2000 Late reports: SEPTEMBER 3 – Track in Glen Tanar successfully searched by Grampian Police MRT for boy (14) who had walked off from his group. 6.

SEPTEMBER 10 – Man (74) took longer than he expected to bike to Derry Lodge and climb Angel's Peak. Walked off OK. Braemar MRT. 4.

SEPTEMBER 10 – Male overdue. He had intended to do the round of Devil's Point, Cairn Toul and Angel's Peak but he was late back to his car. Braemar MRT. 4.

NOVEMBER 15 – Walking along the south bank of the River Dee 1km east of Ballater, man (84) injured a leg climbing a stile. Ambulance Service dealt with him, but needed Grampian Police and Braemar MRTs to get him across rough ground and up a steep bank. 6.

NOVEMBER 19 – Braemar, Kinloss, Kintail, Tayside and Torridon MRT members stretchered a member of HMCG off the Northern Cairngorms. Patient was on difficult terrain suffering an ankle injury. 15.

DECEMBER 17 – Descending Glas Allt to Loch Muick a party of three Dutch walkers met slight snow conditions on the path. Male (37) slipped and sustained a spiral tibia and fibula fracture. Airlifted by RAF Sea King with Braemar and Grampian Police MRTS. 54.

DECEMBER 23 – Overdue party of three males (47, 40, 40) delayed by a party ahead in Raeburn's Gully, Lochnagar got back to carpark OK and checked in. Braemar MRT. 9.

DECEMBER 29 – Hydro Board workers reported red flares seen in Lairig Ghru. Inquiry stood down. 3

DECEMBER 31-January 1, 2001 – Pair of male walkers (31, 30) climbed Lochnagar in severe blizzard conditions forecast well in advance. Overdue from the hill they got stuck driving down Glen Muick. Grampian Police, Braemar and Kinloss MRTS were called out. RAF Sea King was unable to get to Ballater due to severe weather. Cars (see next report) dug out of 2m drifts by a council snowplough and digger and all stood down at 01.00. 109.

DECEMBER 31-January 1, 2001 – Another party (f28, males 45, 35, 33) climbed Lochnagar the same day, meeting deep snow throughout and getting stuck in their car (as in above rescue). Both cars dug out.

2001 JANUARY-JUNE 4 – Body of male previously reported missing in January was found on the side of Bennachie at the foot of a waterfall. Braemar MRT recovered his body to the roadside on June 4. 36.

JANUARY 7 – Canoeist with head injuries lifted from Randolph's Leap, River Findhorn by RAF Sea King. 8.

JANUARY 9 – Male (36) collapsed in Coire an t-Sneachda 1.6km from ski car park. He lost balance and power of his legs. A call by mobile phone brought RAF Sea King airlift to Raigmore. Discharged later with no cause established. 12.

JANUARY 14 – Two men (67, 39) and a woman (43) badly timed their climb of Raeburn's Gully, Lochnagar and were overdue. Grampian Police MRT. 9.

JANUARY 14-15 – Walker (41) alone on Mayar, and unaccompanied except by two dogs, was unequipped with navigation equipment. He got lost and used his mobile phone. Information was completely erroneous leading to a lengthy search in mist and darkness by Tayciv and Taypol MRTs and SARDA. RAF Sea King attended but was unable to descend through cloud. He was found OK and aided down by 04.00. 160.

JANUARY 18 – Man suffered knee injury when ice-axe braking with a training group at the Goat Track, Coire an-t Sneachda, Cairngorm. Stretcher from box used. Cairngorm MRT and RAF Sea King. 9.

JANUARY 21 – First of two walkers on Glas Maol went through cornice falling 100m out of sight of his companion. Second male got lost in mist. Braemar MRT found them well. 53.

JANUARY 21 – Braemar, Leuchars and Tayciv MRTs called out for two lost skiers, one with a slight hip injury. Found on Glas Maol, in closed piste area, sheltering in a hut. 62.

JANUARY 21-22 – Winter Corrie of Driesh was searched till 03.30 on 22nd when two experienced climbers (38, 36) were overdue without having left route cards. Both Tayside teams, SARDA and Leuchars MRT widened search at first light. RAF helicopter was turned back by bad weather. Both men were found dead, one buried and one partly buried in avalanche debris at the foot of B Gully in Corrie Fee of Mayar. Both had sustained injuries which would have been instantly fatal. From body positions and gear it appeared they were descending when they fell, or were avalanched. They were roped together but the rope had broken. Both wore helmets and used full winter climbing gear. Stretchered down to a 4x4. 434.

JANUARY 22 – Party of three got separated on Carn Aosda when male without map and compass went to retrieve a lost glove. A93 road and ski complex were being evacuated due to weather. Braemar MRT found him on edge of piste area lost and cold. 22.

JANUARY 26 – Other climbers reported concern for two they met in Raeburn's Gully, Lochnagar, but Braemar MRT found them safe and well in their planned bothy. 5.

FEBRUARY 3 – At 12.30 informant had seen party of six at Hutchison Hut, Coire Etchachan and reported them missing at 22.00 from Linn of Dee. They soon turned up. 2.

FEBRUARY 3 – Ten walkers attempting Bynack More retreated early. With compass, but no map, they ended up in Nethy Bridge, not Glenmore, and took a taxi. Cairngorm MRT stood down before searching. 3.

FEBRUARY 3 – Two men (33, 20) slightly injured and hypothermic from being cragfast in The Runnel in Coire an t-Sneachda. Rescue by Cairngorm MRT. 70.

FEBRUARY 3-4 – All Deeside MRTs searched bothies and tracks of Glens Clunie and Callater. A car had been left in storm conditions, but pair had camped as planned in Coire Fionn. A93 was closed for three days by the snowfall. 180.

FEBRUARY 10 – Two men and two women missed marked piste on Meall Odhar in strong winds and snow falling and used mobile phone. They were searched for by Braemar MRT member in a pister on the ridge to the north. Phoned instructions were given and they got down to A93 at foot of Coire Fionn. 3.

FEBRUARY 10 – Braemar MRT member on ski-bike searched ridge south from Meall Odhar ski area for a party of three who had strayed from the piste in poor weather. With mobile phone instructions they got down to A93 1km south of the old Devil's Elbow. 5.

FEBRUARY 10-11 – Man (35) and woman (20) completed Look C Gully in Corrie Fee of Mayar. Attempting to return to glen, without map or compass, they were unable to descend in mist, darkness and freezing conditions. They were found walking out next day having overnighted in a snow cave. Large avalanche did not contribute to incident. Tayside, Kinloss, Leuchars MRTs, Taypol SARU, SARDA, RAF Sea King. 271.

FEBRUARY 17 – Coire an t-Sneachda, Cairngorm. Leading Broken Gully Direct on first pitch with two pieces of protection. Unable to get in third, in a precarious position, pick pulled turf off rock and leader (36) fell 12m fracturing both of his left ankle malleoli. He had been held by the last piece of protection (highest ?).

He was lowered two rope lengths then met at bottom by Braemar, Cockermouth, Edale, Glenmore and Penrith MRTs. 43.

FEBRUARY 18 – Rock climbing unroped on Knock of Balmyle, near Bridge of Cally, Glenshee, male (37) fell about 4m fracturing his ankle. Airlift by RAF Sea King and Tpol MRT. 10.

FEBRUARY 22 – Man on a three-day snow-holing expedition with a companion on Braeriach, broke his leg. Braemar MRT used Kassbohrer to get into Lairig Ghru. Casualty (30) airlifted by R137 RAF Sea King. 142.

FEBRUARY 23 – Having almost completed South East Gully, Creag an Dubh-Loch unroped man (21) collapsed the cornice (snow was falling at the time) which swept him down for 200m. Unable to stop with his ice-axe; on using his feet his crampons tripped him. Suffering bruised and swollen ankle and leg cuts he was able to walk down with the help of his two friends. Carried to Glas-Allt-Shiel then evacuated by police Land-Rover. 11.

FEBRUARY 26 – Male (42) stumbled in Coire an t-Sneachda injuring his ankle. Carried off by his party of 10 and several Glenmore Lodge staff in the area. 32.

FEBRUARY 26 – Man's map blew away on the summit of Geal Charn (Water of Caiplich/Ailnach). Given a bearing by Cairngorm MRT he self-evacuated in falling snow to Forest Lodge, Abernethy. 35.

MARCH 4 – False alarm and search caused by car left by cross-country skier near Cairnwell. He had hitched a lift home. Braemar MRT. 15.

MARCH 7 – Using a mobile phone, two men (31, 27) lost in Coire Raibeirt of Cairngorm were traced by Glenmore Lodge MRT. Braemar and Cairngorm MRTs involved. 128.

APRIL 1-2 – Both Tayside teams and SARDA spent eight hours searching planta-tions etc. in Glen Clova for a man (51) who walked down the glen and had decided he wanted to die in the hills. He had been met by a number of people. Heavy rain before midnight flushed him out of hiding. RAF Sea King cancelled *en route*. He required mental assessment. 79.

APRIL 4 – False alarm caused by car left at Glenshee Complex when skier had gone home. 3.

APRIL 6 – Poor belay in Raeburn's Gully, Lochnagar contributed to a fall of 180m by a rope of two men (47, 43) one of whom suffered a broken femur, and the other serious head injuries. RAF MRT in the area called R137 which airlifted the casualties. Braemar and Grampian Police also called out. 20.

APRIL 7-8 – Pair of men (37, 30) completed Shadow Buttress A, Lochnagar at 23.30. Braemar MRT was alerted by their friend. RAF Sea King found them descending Glas Allt near Loch Muick, not their intended route, and lifted them to Ballater. 16.

APRIL 8 – Mobile call from girl (15) cragfast with ankle injury at Cullykhan Bay, Pennan. RAF Sea King scrambled with Banff and Gardenstown Coastguard. Police got on scene first and walked her off and sent her to hospital. 26.

APRIL 8 – Unroped, with a companion, ascending a snow-covered ridge at Coire Dhondail from Gleann Einich, a female (32) slipped and slid 75m into small boulders. She sustained five fractures to lower right leg. Airlifted by RAF R137. Cairngorm MRT informed. 12.

APRIL 8 – Solo climbing Raeburn's Gully, Lochnagar, man (48) was trying to get over the cornice. Part of it collapsed and he fell back a few metres. He phoned saying he was stuck just below cornice with no rope to get back down the ice pitch. RAF Sea King lifted Braemar MRT to plateau. A rope was lowered to him and he was hoisted by pulley system uninjured. 27.

APRIL 10 – Man (49) with three sons (17, 15, 9) crossed Lairig Ghru from Whitewell to Corrour Bothy where they overnighted on 9th. Returning on 10th all four, especially the youngest, got wet and cold. A tent was pitched at Pools of Dee and father went for help. Group was airlifted to Glenmore Lodge by R137 RAF Sea King. 11.

APRIL 17 – Two men (27, 25) climbed Goat Track Gully but were unable to descend the Goat Track due to severe weather and decided to go round to Coire Cas. They went adrift and reached Loch Avon. They walked out over Cairngorm and down Coire na Ciste. The two men were found by Cairngorm MRT on the Coire na Ciste Ski Road. SARDA involved. 42.

MAY 12 – Descending Mounth Road from Mount Keen to Glen Tanar in hot weather, man (52) broke his ankle. Rescue was by RAF Puma helicopter with members of Braemar and Kinloss MRTs. 26.

MAY 15-17 – Attempting solo Cairngorms crossing to Braemar, man (34) got lost (calm weather with sleet). Thinking he was in Lairig Ghru he phoned for location but said he could not walk off due to blisters. He was found by RAF Sea King on the SW slopes of Angel's Peak, 1km NNW of Loch nan Stuirteag and 4km off course, cold but uninjured. He was airlifted to Glenmore Lodge, where he decided no medical help was needed. Braemar and Kinloss MRTs. 50.

MAY 16-18 – On a two-day walk through Lairig Ghru man (80) suffered a stroke during evening of 17th. He was lifted by Air Ambulance and Braemar MRT to Raigmore Hospital on 18th. 14.

MAY 16-18 – Companion (male 82) of the above casualty walked out 6km from the location on the morning of 18th, to Robbers Copse where he met other walkers who alerted rescuers. Suffering from exhaustion and hypothermia, he in turn was airlifted, but to Braemar and attended by the local doctor. RAF and RN Sea Kings involved, Braemar and RAF St. Athan MRTs. 14.

MAY 19 – Accompanied walker (56) ascending Meall Odhar and Glas Maol track from Cairnwell ski complex suffered an angina attack. Two MR members (Grampian Police and RAF St. Athan) recovered him to the roadside in a Land-Rover. 2.

MAY 22 – Walking on cliffs at night with a friend, teenager (18) got separated. His body was found at foot of cliffs at Slough of Downie, Stonehaven, by Maritime Rescue International. HMCG and RAF Sea King involved.

MAY 26-27 – Pair of walkers (f42, m37) descended into Glen Isla with snow falling and a strong wind. They were found at Dalhally by Aberdeen MRT next morning, trying to make their way back to Braemar. 90.

MAY 26-27 – Descending Beinn Bhrotain walker (27) tripped and fractured an ankle. His companion helped him down into Glen Dee where they camped. His companion walked out next day. Braemar MRT rescued him by Land-Rover. 15.

JUNE 9 – Man (41) leading a climb at Red Craig, Glen Clova in good weather was near the top of the climb at 12m. He had two runners placed. Leader fell after pulling a rock away from the crag. Top runner failed. He fell to the bottom of the cliff striking his belayer. The leader landed on his back and broke his neck – resulting in paralysis. The dislodged rock fell and resulted in the leader also suffering a severed hand. Taypol MRT and RAF Sea King. 25.

JUNE 10 – Well overdue at 21.50 walker (68) had left Linn of Dee at 06.00 to cross the Lairig Ghru. Cairngorm MRT found him at the north end and walked him out slowly to Rothiemurchus Lodge by 00.30. Having been severely impeded by the boulder field he was OK, just tired. 75.

JUNE 15 – Walker (64) stumbled descending Craigendarroch, Ballater, fracturing an ankle. Stretchered to road by Braemar MRT. 8.

JUNE 17 – Man (66) stumbled descending path south near summit of Mither Tap, Bennachie, injuring his ankle. Companion used mobile phone. Airlift was cancelled because casualty made good progress down the mountain and was uplifted by Grampian Police MRT Land-Rover. 6.

JUNE 22 – Descending Creag Choinnich (538m) at Braemar, woman (74) slipped on scree on the path, fracturing an ankle. Only five Braemar MRT rescued her on a double-wheeled MacInnes stretcher. 5.

JUNE 23 – Female climber suffered injury to her left hand by rock fall when descending gully next to Afterthought Arete, Stag Rocks of Cairngorm, RAF MRT training in the area searched. Glenmore Lodge MRT in the area found casualty. Braemar MRT and helicopter involved. Casualty evacuated. 41.

JUNE 28 – Accompanied by her husband on a walk in Glen Quoich, Braemar, wife (64) fell because of an old injury, fracturing a femur. Recovered by Braemar and Grampian Police MRTs assisting Ambulance Service. 6.

JULY 3 – Gully walker (13) with organised group on Morrone suffered a twisted ankle. His party recovered him to the foot of the gully whence he was uplifted by Braemar MRT. 4.

JULY 3 – Male walker with heat exhaustion near Derry Lodge recovered by Braemar MRT. 5.

JULY 5-15 – Man working on path (53) camping at Hutchison Refuge, Glen Derry, failed to turn up for work. His tent and belongings were still there. Area was extensively searched by Aberdeen, Braemar, Cairngorm, Grampian Police, Kinloss, Leuchars MRTs, SARDA and RAF helicopter. Found at Corrour 10 days later, unaware of concern. 1350.

JULY 10 – Three on an award expedition were unable to complete it. Suffering mild hypothermia, tired and wet they were uplifted by Braemar MRT from Derry Lodge. 6.

JULY 16 – Intending to cross from Glen Clova to Glen Muick walker (46) must have taken Glen Doll instead of Upper Clova. Found on Jock's Road by helicopter. Aberdeen MRT.

JULY 16-17 – Walking Lairig Ghru north to south, two were reported overdue. Braemar MRT found them at midnight on the White Bridge Track tired and wet. 2.

JULY 21 – In a party of seven in Coire an Lochain of Cairn Lochan, schoolgirl (14) suffering asthma and dehydration was lifted by RAF Sea King to Raigmore Hospital and treated with oxygen *en route*. 8.

JULY 30-31 – Two youths (15) reported overdue from walk over Bennachie. Found by Braemar MRT near to Rowantree Carpark at 04.00. 18.

JULY 31 – Having completed the round from Lochnagar, woman (67) descending Broad Cairn took Ibuprofen Plus for slight back pain, unaware the tablets contained codeine. Suffering an acute allergic reaction she had to be helped down by her three companions, one of whom used a mobile phone. Met by Grampian Police MRT east of the Black Burn above Loch Muick she was conveyed to ambulance at Spittal. 2.

AUGUST 12 – Near site of the former Sinclair Refuge in Lairig Ghru, male (40) member of a climbing club with 29 companions sustained a slight knee injury. RAF Sea King on exercise at Braemar lifted him to Glenmore Lodge, but medical attention was not needed. 10.

SEPTEMBER 2 – Cragfast man (22) was lowered from 50m cliffs at Auchmithie, Arbroath uninjured. HMCG, RNLI boats and fire service involved. RAF Boulmer Sea King standby.

SEPTEMBER 2 – Pair retreated early from Ben Macdui ascent and reported their three friends, whose descent from the summit had been delayed by mist, overdue. The three men turned up OK at Linn of Dee at 22.30. Braemar MRT. 9.

SEPTEMBER 10 – Party of four (all over 50) lost on Macdui plateau admitted by mobile phone to a husband that they were somewhat frightened. In rain and mist at Lochan Bhuidhe they found the path to Cairngorm and told police they were fine. They got to a large cairn on blocks (which was spot height 1141m) but their map was a pulpy mess and they did not know how to take a bearing. They were talked down by Glenmore Lodge and Cairngorm MRTs over nearly four hours. 10.

This rescue and recent similar ones raise worrying questions. Who is to blame if the party comes to grief? Rescuers can only offer help on the information given. The choice of decision will remain with the lost persons and this should be made clear.

SEPTEMBER 10 – Braemar MRT checked Land-Rover track for overdue walkers on Ben Macdui. They were found making their way off the hill. 1.

SEPTEMBER 19 – Man phoned Cairngorm MRT at 22.00 reporting his wife and others overdue. They had left Bruar with horses and were coming over the Minigaig Pass to Glen Feshie ETA 18.00. Team leader said he would give it some thought. They turned up at 22.25. Neigh bother! 1.

OCTOBER 6 – Walker fractured an ankle descending gully to rear of Corndavon Lodge. He was given Entonox and splinted, then stretchered to Land-Rover by Braemar MRT. 33.

OCTOBER 13 – Walking with friends, walker (male 51) died after collapsing on Mullach Clach a' Bhlair, Glenfeshie. Airlifted by RAF Sea King to Raigmore Hospital. 8.

OCTOBER 14 – Braemar MRT in a Land-Rover checked from Loch Muick to Gelder Shiel. Woman poorly equipped for heavy rain had been reported. Nothing found. 6.

OCTOBER 14 – Concern for object which may have been a person in Lairig Ghru seen from shoulder of Ben Macdui. Check of carparks and bothies revealed nothing unusual. Braemar. 9.

OCTOBER 17 – Braemar MRT found overdue walkers making their way off Ben Macdui. 2.

OCTOBER 25 – Female(18) descending Morrone path in rain towards Braemar had a slight disagreement with her friend and they separated. She got lost and phoned Grampian Police MRT on her mobile. She was quickly found and walked off. 6.

OCTOBER 27 – Well equipped walker (39) in rain, mist and darkness panicked and phoned. From conversation with Cairngorm MRT leader it was decided he was at spot height 1141m, Fiacaill aíChoire Chais (see incident of September 10). He was given a bearing to descend on and was met an hour later at Coire Cas zig-zags. 18.

OCTOBER 28-29 – Lost trying to descend Ben Macdui by Sron Riach (the route of ascent) man (41) and woman (33) found themselves looking down on Loch Morlich. They went east via Loch Avon. Having known about Fords of Avon Refuge they reached it at 21.00 and spent an uncomfortable night there. They walked out south by Lairig an Laoigh. Braemar MRT and RAF Rescue 137 helicopter had searched for them. 52.

OCTOBER 30-31 – Three men working at Bynack Lodge were unable to return across a spate river they had crossed in the morning. Braemar MRT passed food and gear across for them to survive. They were extracted safe and well next morning.

NOVEMBER 4 – Two men (38, 30) without compass, torch or whistle, lost in snow and mist on Ben Macdui, alerted Braemar and Cairngorm MRTs by mobile and search started as darkness fell. RAF Sea King had been diverted to Beinn an Dothaidh but was asked to look in Cairngorms when returning to Lossiemouth. Men had got down to Loch Avon and camera flash was spotted by the helicopter. Men advised to buy a compass. 86.

DECEMBER 2 – Walker (59) had forgotten his crampons. At Ben Vrackie summit, descending, he slipped on ice and hurt his ankle. He declined help from passers-by, but someone let on and he was found by police 4x4 on lower slopes. Transported to his car he declined medical attention at the time. Later he went to his local hospital and was diagnosed with a fractured fibula.

DECEMBER 13-14 – Solo walker (67) got lost on Tolmount from Glen Clova. He spent a long time trying to find return path. Followed river down to waterfall north of Craig Maud, Glen Doll; then climbed on to cliffs of Craig Maud. His torch was not working so he stayed put. Seeing rescuers overnight he had no whistle so was unable to signal. Next day he walked to near the bothy on Jock's Road where he was met rescuers. Braemar, Leuchars, Tayciv, Taypol MRTs. RAF Sea King turned back *en route*. 321.

DECEMBER 17 – On Cairn of Barns, Glen Clova in good weather, in a party of five, man (71) collapsed after feeling unwell. He was airlifted to Ninewells, Dundee by RAF Sea King but was dead on arrival. Death thought to be due to a heart attack. Taypol MRT. 10.

DECEMBER 25-26 – Party of four spent Christmas at Shelter Stone of Loch Avon. One man had sickness and diarrhoea for more than 12 hours. Two walked to the Saddle and phoned. Braemar and Cairngorm MRTs prepared for a long carry out, but eventually, Rescue 137 lifted him to Aviemore where he refused treatment. Helicopter had many problems returning to Lossiemouth due to adverse weather; landing at Kinveachy A95, refuel at Glenmore Lodge, Slochd summit A9, and Ballater A93. 177.

DECEMBER 27-28 – Climbing Aladdin's Mirror Direct going up an unknown line higher up, in Coire an t-Sneachda, woman (32) was in the lead below the soft cornice when it gave way. She fell 30m pulling her husband (40) behind. They bounced and rolled another 150m before stopping in deep soft snow, sustaining leg and chest injuries, cuts and bruises. Snow was falling at the time. Nearby climbers helped and dug a snow shelter. Cairngorm MRT alerted at 17.30 by the woman's phone stretchered them out (snow giving considerable help for sledging stretchers) just after midnight. Kinloss MRT called out but turned back at Grantown. 286.

DECEMBER 31-JANUARY 1, 2002 – Husband and wife cragfast 60m from top of Fiacaill Couloir, Coire an t-Sneachda at 18.15 Hogmanay. CB radio message picked up by a camper. RAF helicopter used but could not transport Cairngorm MRT to plateau because of poor visibility. Couple were roped up to top of climb then walked off the hill at 03.15. Team celebrated New Year by firing a flare and singing *Hail Caledonia*. 108.

DECEMBER 31 – Man and woman were reported overdue from Coire an Lochan, Cairn Lochan at 21.00 but they turned up OK.

SOUTHERN HIGHLANDS

Date? 2001 – Girl (2) missing from home had pushed her buggy into woodland at Callander Craig 750m from home. Killin MRT searched. She was found well by a passer-by on a path (Lower Wood Walk) in good weather at 12.40 hours. 4.

JANUARY 2-3 – Without map or compass two men (36, 25) separated from nine colleagues (see following narrative) and were not seen by them again that day. They had sped off at start and climbed Ben Lomond. Descending, they had gone off east 8km into Loch Ard Forest. Cold and completely lost they met Water Authority personnel, (aware of the massive search) and were picked up by police at 10.00 having spent the night under trees. Lomond, Killin, Ochils MRTs, SARDA. 228.

JANUARY 2-3 – Party of nine (see above incident), ill-equipped (some wearing trainers and jeans on snowy hillsides, wet underfoot) set out to climb Ben Lomond by the normal route. Group of six (the middle group) went to the summit, then got lost in mist on descent following footprints. Two of this middle group took the only map and compass and returned to Rowardennan to raise the alarm at 17.45 hours. The other four, plus two independent walkers who had followed the same footprints, were found by Lomond team, all suffering hypothermia, at Ref 385003 going down Moineach path east to Loch Ard Forest. They were evacuated by RN helicopter before midnight. Group of three (the last group) had not made it to the top. They had met the middle group, but rested and decided to turn back. They had strayed from the recognised route on descent but got back to Rowardennan about 19.00. Killin and Lomond MRTs and SARDA had searched; later calling in Ochils MRT. 200.

JANUARY 2-3 – Rescuer (55) climbing Ben Lomond to act as radio link for search (previous incidents) fell through a snow bridge, causing hyper-extension of a knee. He agreed to delayed evacuation while his companion continued up to establish the link. He was evacuated by Rescue 177 (RN Sea King) after six missing persons had been airlifted. His injury required a cast for 10 weeks, a quad tendon having been detached from his patella. 6.

JANUARY 20 – Woman (49) one of 15 walkers, slipped on icy, wet path on the east slopes of Dumyat injuring her ankle. Stretchered off by Ochils MRT. 17.

JANUARY 24 – Lost in the Ochils, in rough and remote Fin Glen, man (63) and woman (50) were found by RN Sea King on the second afternoon, suffering from hypothermia. It is doubtful if they would have survived a second night out in gale, rain mist and sleet. Searches by Police, SARDA, Ochils and Leuchars MRTs. 258.

JANUARY 26 – Male (30) tripped on steep, snow/ice slope descending Grey Heights of Cruach Ardrain sustaining a leg fracture. One of his party of five phoned. RN helicopter could not reach him due to storm/snow conditions. Stretcher lowered and carried to ambulance on forest road by Killin MRT. 165.

FEBRUARY 9 – Wearing crampons, descending névé and ice on path of South Ridge, Ben Ledi, walker (67) slipped and broke his leg (tibia/fibula). Airlifted by RAF and Killin MRT. Needed surgery in hospital.

FEBRUARY 10 – Abandoning an attempt to get to the top of Ben Lui a party of 11 was descending north. At Ciochan Beinn Laoigh three slipped on hard snow and fell 3m-5m which caused back and neck injuries, none serious. All were equipped with ice-axes and crampons. Casualties airlifted by RN Sea King and others escorted by Killin MRT. 132.

FEBRUARY 24 – A hillwalker (27) suffered leg and shoulder injuries, or fractures, and bruising when she fell in the area of Central Gully, Ben Lui. Position reported by companion on mobile phone. She was airlifted by RN Sea King. Killin MRT informed but engaged in another incident on Ben More.

FEBRUARY 24 – In freezing weather, with snow falling, and mist an engineer (40) tripped on his crampons on neve close to the summit of Ben More, Crianlarich. He managed to ice-axe brake but fractured an ankle. Rescue 177 helicopter from HMS Gannet attended but could not reach casualty who was stretchered down by Killin MRT. 210.

FEBRUARY 25 – In good, freezing weather, walker (29) stumbled and hurt his ankle at the col between Ben More and Stob Binnein. Casualty evacuated by RN Sea King and two companions escorted by Killin MRT. 43.

FEBRUARY 25-28 – Rescuers were alerted at 21.00 for a woman (30) who had failed to return. She had separated from her companion at Bealach a' Mhaim (between Beinn Ime and Beinn Narnain) intending to return SE over Beinn Narnain descending via Spearhead Arête and Cruach nam Miseag to car at Succoth by 18.30. Extensive searches, extending each day, were carried out on Beinn Narnain and the Cobbler from 25th to 28th by Arrochar, Kinloss, Leuchars, Lomond, Stafford and Strathpol MRTs, SARDA, RAF and RN helicopters. On 28th a glove was found on east side of A'Chrois by a hillwalker. The teams searched there and soon found her body NE of A' Chrois summit at altitude 600m. She was 3.3km ENE of Bealach a'Mhaim. She had an ice-axe but did not appear to have worn crampons. She must have slipped down gully on hard snow. She was evacuated by Strathclyde Police helicopter. 2,340.

APRIL 1 – Walker (27) developed back pain on Cobbler summit. He managed to walk down but with pain getting worse. Companion went down and called out Arrochar and Strathpol MRTs who met him west of Allt a' Bhalachain, about 20 minutes from road, and stretchered him down. 20.

APRIL 11 – Hillwalker (27) stumbled descending from the Steeple, Lochgoilhead, fracturing his ankle. Arrochar and Strathpol MRTs actioned. Airlift by police helicopter. 53.

APRIL 21 – Walker (68) slipped on the Ben A'n footpath suffering arm fracture and head cuts. She was shocked and required stretchering off by Killin MRT. 21.

MAY 15-16 – As Arrochar and Strathpol MRTs prepared to search for three overdue Dutch male hillwalkers they returned OK from a trip to The Cobbler/Beinn Narnain. 11.

JUNE 3 – Girl (9) got separated from her family on a walk up Conic Hill, Balmaha. Lomond MRT assembled for search as she turned up safe. 11.

JUNE 3-4 – Lomond MRT, five SARDA dogs and police searched low level land to north of Campsie Fells for boy who had run away from home. He was reported as having been walking in that area, but found in Glasgow Youth Hostel. 51.

JUNE 9 – Walker (29), one of eight, scrambling down South Peak of The Cobbler slipped and fell 30m. Reached by RN Sea King and RAF Leeming MRT on exercise. Dead on arrival at Glasgow SG Hospital. 20.

JUNE 9 – Four of the party of eight involved in the above incident got cragfast on South Face of Cobbler South Peak. They were rescued using their own gear in modified abseils, then, shocked, were airlifted to Arrochar. Arrochar, Leeming and Strathclyde Police MRTs.

JUNE 13 – In a party of 24 descending the Cobbler by Allt a' Bhalachain path, a schoolboy (15) jumped down a short distance aggravating an old leg injury. He walked till pain worsened. Stretched down some way by Arrochar and Strathpol MRTs to a track, then evacuated to ambulance by Land-Rover. 18.

JUNE 16 – Walker (42) tripped descending the normal route on Ben Lomond in good weather. She sustained facial injuries and may have been unconscious for moments. Her female companion used a mobile phone. Stretchered to Land Rover by Lomond MRT. Discharged from hospital after treatment and X-rays. 37.

JUNE 25 – Deceased (m42) was walking with a friend on Beinn Ime. Short of time they decided to descend below Fan Gully to Coirriegrogan, the friend went in front. Reporter heard a noise and looked round to see deceased fall on to a ledge then roll on down the river bed. He covered him with a jacket then ran down the Hydro Road till he could get a phone signal. On returning he was not sure where the fall had happened. Strathclyde Police and Arrochar MRTs searched. Body was found by RN helicopter and airlifted to Vale of Leven Hospital. 33.

JULY 3-4 – Family picnicked at Ardleish Bay. Boat took all but two back to Ardlui at about 22.00. Boat returned but man (85) had wandered off. He was found by Strathclyde Police MRT in a bog and located by shouts, just off West Highland Way suffering exhaustion and hypothermia. He was stretchered to boat which had navigated about 2km up River Falloch from Loch Lomond. Team finished at 05.30. 65.

JULY 10 – Man (20) found by dog search distressed and suffering mild hypothermia at about 250m, crouching under whins on Myreton Hill, Menstrie. Stretchered off by Ochils MRT at 22.00 hours. He had left a suicide note and phone message of his intentions. Overflown by RN Sea King and attempting to attract helicopter crew, he had not been detected despite thermal imaging. 96.

JULY 14 – With a companion descending Ben Donich in mist and rain, towards Rest and be Thankful, a woman (61) slipped and fell 150m sustaining very extensive injuries. Found and stabilised by Arrochar and Strathpol MRTs. Airlift by RN Sea King. 72.

JULY 16 – Walking couple on Overton Muir (287m) above Alexandria consumed a picnic which consisted of a bottle of whisky. An argument ensued and husband stormed off. He reported wife (41) missing after dark when she had not come home. Lost, she was found uninjured by Strathpol MRT and police dog. 18.

AUGUST 8 – Lone, male mountain biker on rocky Bealach nam Bo (near Goblin's Cave, Loch Katrine) got into difficulties and phoned. Lomond MRT alerted and Water Authority Rescue Boat was sent from east end of Katrine. He was talked down and rescued by boat, tired but uninjured.

AUGUST 9 – Woman (84) suffered a mild stroke when walking with family at Keltie Water, a beauty spot very close to Callander. Ambulance crew attended and requested Killin MRT assistance for evacuation.

AUGUST 9 – Lomond MRT, Luss rescue boat, police and ambulance were all involved when a walker (60) fell on rockiest part of West Highland Way, near Rob Roy's Cave, 1.5km north of Inversnaid. Lagging behind four younger people, he fell and sustained serious head injuries and a broken arm. They found him and used a mobile phone. Immediate rescue was by a fisherman who used his boat to transport casualty and three of party to Inversnaid. 29.

AUGUST 24 – Wearing flat-soled fashion shoes, with soles like deck shoes, a woman (45) fell and broke her ankle on grass, shortly after leaving the path at Bealach nam Bo, Ben Venue. In good weather she was stretchered off by Killin MRT. 23.

AUGUST 26 – Woman (60) suffered probable leg fracture from a slip on the east side of Ben Venue. Evacuation by RN Sea King with Lomond MRT back-up. 26.

SEPTEMBER 11-12 – Middle-aged Canadian phoned police twice as he walked West Highland Way in darkness. Lomond MRT searched because he had angina and was making little progress. He was found by Luss rescue boat using a powerful torch. 29.

OCTOBER 7 – Descending Beinn a' Chreachain on the wrong side, two women (37, 30) were benighted too far up the Water of Tulla, and at one point stuck in a bog. They used mobile phone but could not keep in contact with Strathclyde Police MRT. Team saw their lights as they walked on the railway. Escorted to 4x4. 6.

OCTOBER 21 – In a party of two, woman (40) slipped on Meall Ghaordie in mist and rain, fracturing an ankle. Mobile phone was used. Found by Killin MRT and stretchered to airlift by RN Sea King. 128.

OCTOBER 21-22 – Benighted by faulty navigation in rainy weather over the Beinn Achalladair Munros, two women (45, 35) were found by MRT search on the SE slopes of Beinn a' Chreachain. They were walked out 6km to waiting vehicle at Gorton Bothy by 08.30. Mobile phone had been carried but there was no signal. Arrochar, Oban, Strathclyde Police MRTs and SARDA involved. 258.

OCTOBER 27 – Walker (50s) in a party of two was reported 1.5km from where she was, having turned her ankle on steep ground due east of Glenmassan (hamlet?), Cowal. Benmore Adventure Centre was called out for first response, backed up by Arrochar and Strathclyde Police MRTs. Stretchered off. 42.

OCTOBER 28 – With three companions in good weather a walker (57) fell near Ben Glas Burn on Beinn Chabhair, breaking his leg. Evacuation by RN helicopter and Killin MRT. 94.

NOVEMBER 4 – Man (55) collapsed with chest pains in Coire an Dothaidh, Bridge of Orchy. Oban called Glencoe MRT who were taken up by keeper with Argocat. Defibrillator used to monitor patient with obvious cardiac rhythm problems due to anterior wall MI. Stretchered off. RAF Sea King on exercise airlifted him to Belford Hospital. 38.

NOVEMBER 18 – In a large party, walker (65) suffering illness was stretchered off by Ochils MRT. He had been in hospital the previous day for a chest/heart check-up. 25.

NOVEMBER 20 – Light reported at 17.30 flashing for over an hour on east face of Ben Ledi. Killin MRT found forest worker repairing machinery. False alarm with good intent. 12.

SKYE

2000 Late Reports: JULY 22 – Three Kinloss MRT undertaking Main Ridge traverse came across a pair of climbers, one with a sprained ankle. Others were called and pair were lifted by HMCG helicopter in good weather. 24.

DECEMBER 27 2000 – Search by Skye and Kinloss MRTs, HMCG and RAF helicopters for two missing fishermen. One had moored his boat 7km south of his intended harbour in S. Skye. Footprints were found 3km inland and he was found by SARDA handler 6km east from last known position. Second fisherman missing from same harbour was found by a passing boat hanging to the hull of his craft, then airlifted to Broadford with core temperature of 31 degrees. 450.

2001: JANUARY 29 – Three walkers (f 20, f 19, m18) scrambled up to the base of the pinnacle, Old Man of Storr and got cragfast due to icy, slippery rock and strong wind gusts. Aided down by Skye MRT. 13.

APRIL 15 – Her husband tried to catch her, but a woman (46) who slipped on wet rock at a narrow part of the Quiraing path, fell 24m down a steep, grass gully. Passers-by and Skye MRT in the area helped till paramedics arrived. She had a dislocated shoulder, general bruising and hypothermia. Although only 200m from road, due to steepness of the hill she was lifted by HMCG helicopter to Broadford Hospital. 18.

MAY 5 – On Sgurr Thormaid a female (48) was struck on the leg by a falling rock dislodged by one of her five companions. Morphine and a leg splint were used to treat her fracture and she was winched by RAF Sea King, Kinloss and Skye MRTs. Good weather. 159.

MAY 13-14 – Having taken longer than expected to complete the Dubhs Ridge, two men (70, 69) overnighted at Coruisk Hut, returning to Elgol at first light. Due to the pair's experience and the good weather, call-out was delayed till 10.00, and they got back soon after. 8.

MAY 22 – Leading Wallwork's Route, Sron na Ciche male (20) went for a handhold which came away. The rock struck his head and face. He was slightly injured although wearing a helmet. Skye MRT on the hill at the time searched for him. Others walked him off the hill and he was airlifted to Broadford by HMCG. 48.

MAY 28-29 – Starting at 09.00 on 28th, exhausted but uninjured man (40) and woman (39) walked out to Glenbrittle at 18.00 on 29th having been delayed by navigation in mist and gale and benighted somewhere near Coir a' Ghrunnda. Search by Skye MRT and RAF Sea King had started, but no route plan had been left. 77.

MAY 29 – Four women and a man (all about 38) left Glenbrittle at 06.45 heading for Loch Coruisk. In mist and strong wind they got lost high in Coire Banachdich and used a mobile phone. Skye MRT member heard their whistle blasts and led them to safe site for airlift by RAF Sea King at 21.00. 103.

MAY 31 – Skye MRT search for uninjured man (48) at An Dorus. Walked off hill. 86.

JUNE 3-4 – Novice (37) climbing in a group of nine on Am Basteir in mist and strong wind got separated from the group and lost. Skye MRT heard his shouts when sweep searching for him and he was escorted down. 91.

JUNE 7 – Woman (55) broke her ankle when 700m east of Torvaig, Portree. Walking on Sithean Bhealaich Chumhaing she slipped on wet rock after recent hail. Skye MRT, alerted by her companion, stretchered her off the hill. 25.

JUNE 19 – At 10.00 woman (43) and man (75) crossed the bridge which is 400m SW of Sligachan Hotel and spans Allt Dearg Mor. After a walk in the Cuillin they returned and found the bridge impassable due to severe rainfall. After trying other routes they contacted emergency services and were led to safety by Skye MRT at 15.40. 4.

JULY 7-8 – On the Coir a' Ghrunnda side of Sgurr Sgumain walker (36) separated in mist, got tired and bivvied down for the night. Meantime his companion reported him missing and he was met by Skye MRT making his own way down. HMCG helicopter. 32.

JULY 19 – Boy (9) slipped descending south screes of Sgurr Dearg. He fell 1m. A dislodged rock caused ankle injury. A Skye MRT member came across father and son. Radio call brought HMCG helicopter for airlift. 20.

AUGUST 13 – Person missing near Portree was uninjured. Skye MRT and HMCG helicopter. 10.

AUGUST 16-17 – Father (36) with his mother (61) and two sons (8, 6) attempted descent of West Ridge of Sgurr Dearg in rain and mist. Due to weather and poor visibility he went off course into Coire na Banachdich. He contacted his wife to alert emergency services at 19.00. Skye MRT located the group about midnight and led them off safe by 02.30. 43.

AUGUST 18-19 – Solo walker (53) when it got dark near the top of Sgurr nan Eag, decided it was safer to bivvy than negotiate slippery rocks. Overdue he walked off unaided next day. Skye MRT searched. Kinloss Rescue Co-ordination Centre alerted. 18.

AUGUST 22 – Belgian male (23) descending Coire Lagan footpath about 200m below Lochan Coire Lagan lost his footing, fell 6m and injured an ankle. Skye MRT advised an airlift. RAF Sea King. 10.

SEPTEMBER 23 – Experienced solo man (41) rock climbing unroped in Coire Uaigneich, Blaven, misread the map and ended up in a gully, cragfast. He called the police. Walked off the hill by Skye MRT without incident, uninjured. 28.

OCTOBER 15 – Two people overdue on Blaven were OK. Skye MRT. 17.

NOVEMBER 7 – Uninjured pair were overdue between Loch Coruisk and Sligachan. Skye MRT. 17.

ISLANDS

(Other than Skye)

February 4-5 – Three well-equipped walkers were overdue from Ainshval, Rum. Man (54) had slipped on summit, pulling a muscle in his back. This delayed them but they got down by 01.00. Call out of Lochaber MRT had been put off till daybreak. 2.

April 3 – Woman (30) found dead at foot of 50m cliff at Kildonnan, in south Arran. Dutch party had been camping at top of cliff.

May 4 – Successful search by Arran MRT for man overdue in Glen Rosa suffering chorea. 1.

May 6 – Walker fell in Glen Rosa injuring his ankle. Stretchered out by Arran MRT in good weather. 8.

July 16 – Walker (75) sustained ankle injury from a fall on Goat Fell when wearing lightweight footwear. She was stretchered to hospital in good weather by Arran MRT who used Entonox and vacuum splint. 26.

July 30 – Woman with ankle injury stretchered from Goat Fell to hospital by Arran MRT. Good weather.

August 11 – Man walking with a companion on Stach Ridge in mist and rain fell and injured his ankle and shoulder. Mobile phone call alerted Arran MRT. Airlift by RN Sea King. 40.

August 12 – Arran MRT assembled for walker (m40) one of a party of two in mist and rain on Goat Fell. Mobile phone was used. He turned up uninjured. 1.

August 18-19 – Two men (23, 21) left their car to walk up Ronas Hill (450m) and to Lang Ayre, a bay to the NW, on North Mainland of Shetland. Their car was left at the masts on Collafirth Hill. They got lost in calm, foggy weather but turned up uninjured at the car at 04.00. Police, HMCG, RNLI. 26.

August 24 – Person slipped on South Uist with minor injury. Airlift by HMCG helicopter. 8.

August – Male hill walker fell in Arran sustaining ankle injury. Airlift by RN helicopter. Arran MRT on standby.8

NON -MOUNTAINEERING

Late Reports: 1943-JULY 23, 2001 – Remains of wartime Manchester aircraft wreckage. Public had reported two live rounds, a loaded Verey pistol and possible remnants of leg bones dug up from a small bog in a deep ravine in the centre of an extensive forest near Huntly. Checked by Kinloss MRT. Majority of wreckage and remains had been recovered at the time and recent finds were of little significance. 36.

2000: NOVEMBER 23 – Missing man suffering dementia wandering in freezing conditions and darkness was found well at a nearby farm. Aberdeen MRT and SARDA called but not used. 9.

NOVEMBER 23 – Woman (85) with dementia wandered from residential home near Ellon. Search by Braemar MRT and helicopter. Found OK by dog handler. 60.

DECEMBER 13, 2000-February 26, 2001 – The following organisations were involved in mountain searches for a Cessna 152 missing on a flight from Inverness to Benbecula with two businessmen (39, 37) on board: Cairngorm, Dundonnell, Glenelg, Kinloss, Kintail, Leuchars, Skye and Torridon MRTs, RAF and HMCG helicopters, SARDA, GR4 Tornadoes and Hercules aircraft using heat-seeking gear. Extensive searches continued in deteriorating weather for six days, then again on December 31.

FEBRUARY 23, 2001 – Hillwalker reported finding a liferaft in a gully of Liathach. Kinloss and Torridon MRTs probed the gully in 3m of fresh snow finding liferaft and wreckage on 24th. The same day a hillwalker reported crashed aircraft on Liathach Ridge. Teams and HMCG helo recovered bodies from west end of Am Fasarianan Pinnacles. 2125.

DECEMBER 31, 2000 – Kinloss MRT were asked by Grampian Police to help in a search at Tomnavoulin for a woman last seen visiting her husband's grave that afternoon. She walked home safe before the team deployed. 22.

2001: JANUARY 2 – SARDA search of woods and fields near Newport for female (21) missing from home. Nothing found.

JANUARY 4 – SARDA helped police search river and park in Dumfries and Galloway following the discovery of the body of an elderly man believed to be a murder victim. Nothing found.

JANUARY 4-8 – Ochils MRT searched rough ground around Falkirk and Polmont for missing woman (62). Ice on Union Canal had been broken and refrozen. Her body was recovered by police after initially being brought up by a dredger. 250.

JANUARY 6 – Successful search for distressed male (100) found safe at Cults by Braemar MRT. 76.

JANUARY 8 – Aberdeen MRT involved in search for female (32) whose body was recovered in woodland near Culter. suspected foul play. 189.

JANUARY 24-25 – SARDA searched Bo'ness for depressed male (50s) Nothing found. Last sighting Jan 19. He was found under a motorway bridge, alive but hypothermic on Jan 26.

JANUARY 25-26 – Four people (female 19; males 53, 38, 22) remarkably survived the impact without major injuries when a Cessna light aircraft crash landed on the snowfield just east of the north spur of Cairn of Claise at 980m. The aeroplane was on a private flight from Peterborough to Inverness. It was snowing at the time with a strong wind in daylight. The occupants, in whiteout conditions, managed to descend possibly 50m altitude, a distance of 400-500m to a position overlooking Corrie Kander. As a result of the impact beacon RCC scrambled two RAF rescue helicopters from Boulmer and Lossiemouth. Triangulating the VHF/ UHF beacon R137 located the four survivors in the top of the gully near Carn an Tuirc. Braemar, Kinloss, Cairngorm and Leuchars MRTs were alerted at around 15.10 hours. R137 dropped four Braemar MRT close to the casualties. The four casualties were flown by R131 to Aberdeen Royal Infirmary. They were treated for various serious, but non-life threatening, injuries. Twenty-two Braemar/ Grampian Police MRT spent the second day in the area to locate the crashed aircraft. 413.

JANUARY 26 – Climbers in Raeburn's Gully reported a pair they met as being incompetent and inexperienced, and their car was still in the car park next day. The pair were found very well in a bothy. 5.

JANUARY 27 – Braemar MRT search of wood/farmland in Insch area for missing male (51). 54.

JANUARY 29 – False alarm. SARDA called but not deployed to search rough ground near Cairnryan, Stranraer after bivvy tent and sleeping bag were found. Owner safe with family.

FEBRUARY 10 – Braemar and Grampian Police MRTs recovered body from steep, snow covered embankment at Cairnie, apparently dead from shotgun wounds. 20.

FEBRUARY 11 – Two boys (13, 11) missing from care near Closeburn were found by police in Dumfries as Moffat MRT and SARDA arrived.

FEBRUARY 12 – False alarm. Moffat MRT searched farmland near Dumfries for two boys (14, 12) missing after dark. They were found OK in the town. 16.

FEBRUARY 13-15 – SARDA, Borders SARU and Tweed Valley MRT searched Pentland Hills for man (68) thought to be suicidal. His body surfaced from deep water near Castlelaw the following weekend. Rucksack had been weighted with rocks. 204.

FEBRUARY 15 – Borders SARU and SARDA, called for man (70s) missing near Yetholm, stood down *en route* as he was found by police.

FEBRUARY 24 – SARDA called for missing young woman, depressed, near Boíness. Stood down en route as police found her.

FEBRUARY 24 – Braemar MRT searched hill refuges in South Cairngorms in concern for a male who was later found sleeping rough in Aberdeen. 64.

FEBRUARY 24-25 – Three Kinloss MRT working in Torridon went to guard a rescue helicopter which had force landed near Garve.

FEBRUARY 25 – *En route* to the Cessna incident Leuchars MRT was diverted to an alternative rendezvous at Dalwhinnie to investigate another possible beacon transmission. This proved to be a spurious transmission and team returned to base. 75.

FEBRUARY 26 – Grampian Police MRT found a woman motorist safe. She had walked from her car when it got stuck in a snow drift in a storm at Ellon. 30.

FEBRUARY 27 – Galloway MRT members and vehicles stood by in case Dumfries Police needed help in managing heavy snow conditions in Langholm area. 8.

FEBRUARY 27 - March 3 – Tweed Valley MRT involved checking isolated properties, airlifting supplies, casualty pick-ups and a search due to heavy snows and power cuts. 470.

FEBRUARY 27-28 – Moffat MRT and Sea King from HMS Gannet lifted drivers from 11 vehicles stranded in snowdrifts between Langholm and Ewesless Farm (near summit of A7). Helicopter had to land when it could get no further due to extreme weather. As wind lessened during the night snowplough and MMRT Land-Rover got through. 221.

FEBRUARY 28 – Moffat MRT lifted by Scottish Power helicopter to within 1km of isolated cottage 9km NW of Langholm. Walked in through snowdrifts and confirmed that occupant, a woman (70s) was dead. 6.

FEBRUARY 28 – Moffat MRT found forest worker 5km NE of Eskdalemuir was OK. He had not checked in for 24 hours because snow had knocked out Vodaphone network. 105.

FEBRUARY 28 – Walking in from as far as Land-Rover could get, Moffat MRT checked lady (80+) was OK in cottage at Whamphray near Moffat. 60.

MARCH 2 – Leuchars MRT and AAC Gazelle helicopter searched for missing patient from Springfield Hospital. Search aborted due to dense fog. Search teams hampered in farmlands due to Foot and Mouth scare. 10.

MARCH 6 – Braemar MRT found woman (74) had died of natural causes in her cottage at Lumphanan. They had been called by police and ambulance when access was not possible due to new snowfall. Stretchered to road. 36.

MARCH 16 – Braemar MRT searched for woman who abandoned her vehicle on a forest track near Ellon. Depressed she was found intoxicated having taken alcohol and tablets. 80.

MARCH 26 – Search for 2 USAF F15 Eagle aircraft was abandoned on 26th due to severe weather. Braemar and RAF Leeming MRTs found first aircraft and dead pilot on 27th near summit of Ben Macdui. Aberdeen, Cairngorm, Kinloss, Leuchars and Stafford MRTs, Nimrod aircraft R51, Lossiemouth and Boulmer Sea Kings, Chinook and Pave helicopters were all involved. Severe weather conditions lasted for four days and snow shoes were used to good effect. Second pilot was found on 30th. Anti pollution booms were sited in Loch Avon basin and Lairig Ghru to protect mountain environment. Aircraft debris was recovered. 9515.

APRIL 3-4 – Car of missing woman (34) had been found on the old bridge in Doune. Killin MRT and SARDA searched River Teith with Ochils MRT on standby, which ended when her body was found by RN helicopter on a sandbar about 6km downstream of the bridge. 76.

APRIL 7 – Search by Tweed Valley MRT for man (58) in Gorebridge area, Edinburgh. Body found later, well out of search area, at foot of sea cliffs. 110.

APRIL 10-11 – Ochils MRT and SARDA carried out overnight search of banks of River Avon from Linlithgow to Lathallan, roads and railway for a missing man (31). Nothing found. His body was later recovered from Linlithgow Loch. 98.

APRIL 22 – Braemar and a RAF MRT searched forest at Tillyfourie near Monymusk in case driver from a crashed car had been suicidal. He was found safe and well. 50.

MAY 17 – Man (27) apparently suffering from depression, was witnessed jumping from the crags of Kinnoull Hill, Perth. A search by Taypol MRT found his body, in the same spot that all the others are found. 9.

JUNE – Woman (80) missing on outskirts of Buckie. Search manager deployed with Grampian Police MRT on standby. She was found well. 4.

JUNE 1 – Galloway MRT and SARDA called out for elderly man missing in Minigaff area, Newton Stewart. Dog team stood down on arrival.

JUNE 6-7 – Braemar, Kinloss MRTs, SARDA and RAF Sea King searched Tomintoul to Lecht area for driver of an abandoned vehicle. He was found safe in Aberdeen. 216.

JUNE 22 – SARDA called for female missing at Castle Douglas. Found well in Dumfries.

JUNE 28 – Braemar and Grampian Police MRT found missing person 150m from his home. Suffering depression he had taken his own life. 30.

JULY 15 – Casualty (m42) seen by passers-by trying to hang himself from a tree. Taypol MRT search found nothing. Another passer-by contacted police to say she had discovered casualty hanging from a tree (8km from original sighting). Area searched and male found dead at Tullybaccart, Sidlaw Hills. 27.

JULY 16 – Man covered with blood was found by boy on rocks near Girdlestone Lighthouse, Aberdeen, winched by RAF Sea King using horizontal stretcher.

AUGUST 4-5 – Girl (15) suffering depression was missing overnight near St. Fillans. She turned up next morning shortly after Tayside teams had been informed and were to start search.

AUGUST 12 – Tweed Valley MRT and SARDA searched for a patient (51) from Huntlyburn Special Care Unit. She turned up safe, well out of the search area. 41.

AUGUST 13 – Ochils MRT and SARDA searched vainly for a manic depressive at Falkirk. Another negative search was carried out on August 22. His body was later recovered from a small loch. 114.

AUGUST 14 – Police were concerned for the safety of an escaped prisoner (23) wearing handcuffs. He had allegedly been showing them stolen goods. Moffat MRT and RNLI inshore boat helped search around River Kirtle, Gretna, but he was not found. Team had to be disinfected every time they went from one farm to the next (f and m precautions). Also see October 29. 112.

AUGUST 21 – Aberdeen, Braemar, Leuchars MRTs, divers, RAF Sea King, HMCG, RNLI inshore boat, SARDA searched harbour, hills, cliffs and coastline around Stonehaven for local woman (71). She was not found at that time. 544.

AUGUST 24 – Tweed Valley MRT mobilised for search of forest and River Tweed at Walkerburn for woman (44) who turned up safe. 3.

AUGUST 28 – Search by Cairngorm MRT found man (35) in T-shirt and jeans, semi-conscious and smelling of alcohol, in woods near Tromie Bridge, Kingussie. Missing for 12 hours there had been concern that subject had done some self-harm. 36.

SEPTEMBER 3 – Assynt MRT assembled to search near Thurso for boy (11) missing from home. He turned up well. 7.

OCTOBER 7 – Search for the body of a male (21) on Gordon Moss Wildlife Reserve, 13km NW of Kelso, by Tweed Valley MRT. This area had been searched on June 13 1999. Nothing found. 119.

OCTOBER 11 – Elderly lady wandered off from restaurant at Brig o' Turk and got lost. Found by staff so dog teams were stood down *en route*.

OCTOBER 14 – Elderly patient was missing from Stracathro Hospital overnight, but turned up as Tayside teams and SARDA were deploying for search. 23.

OCTOBER 18 – Braemar and Grampian Police MRTs searched foreshore and sea cliffs at Collieston for missing person. 40.

OCTOBER 18-19 – SARDA vainly searched farmland after tent and gear had been found near Killearn.

OCTOBER 26 – Braemar and Grampian Police MRTs searched at Urquhart, Elgin for female with learning difficulties missing overnight in wooded area. Found well the next morning by SARDA dog handler. 90.

OCTOBER 29 – Dundonnell MRT requested by police to search for car driver (34) after a crash at 06.00. It was a dangerous area of slippery paths and drops into the river at Contin. She turned up OK at Strathpeffer. 6.

OCTOBER 29 – Moffat MRT aided D and G Police search fields and woods in Gretna area for man (22) last seen running away wearing white boiler suit and handcuffs. He was not found and there was concern for his welfare. He has since turned up and returned to prison. See August 14.

OCTOBER 30 – Grampian Police MRT searched for two retired women, both dementia sufferers, missing from a nursing home at Aboyne. They were found after two hours, huddled together, wet and cold, in the corner of a field about 100m from a Land-Rover track. It is thought they had walked about 1.4km. They were taken to hospital. 10.

NOVEMBER 8 – Grampian Police MRT took three retired car occupants to safety. They were unable to extract the car from deep snow on B976 Crathie to Gairnshiel, Ballater road. There was so much snow the team was unable to check the road for further vehicles, so they used a tracked vehicle and checked the road. 16.

NOVEMBER 8-9 – Car found abandoned near the foot of Auchterhouse Hill, Sidlaw Hills, 8km north of Dundee. Searches by Leuchars, Tayciv and Taypol MRT were carried out in freezing weather. Car owner (47) was found by one of four SARDA dogs which did well to find him in dense whins at night, 400m north of his vehicle. His body was face down. There had been snowfall at the time. Having swallowed a quantity of anti-depressant tablets he had succumbed to the cold overnight. 162.

NOVEMBER 21-22 – Tweed Valley MRT and SARDA searched for a missing woman (35) near Livingston. Later in the week (November 23) after a tip off, her body was found in a shallow grave on the edge of the search area; now there is a murder inquiry. 100.

DECEMBER 5-6 – Tweed Valley MRT and SARDA searched for woman (30s) who failed to return from a public house near Livingston. Body found by police searchers. Foul play suspected.

DECEMBER 13 – Borders, Lothian and Tweed Valley teams and SARDA searched Haddington for a man (65+) missing from home in the early hours; depressed but not thought to be suicidal. He was found after seven hours OK, sheltering in outbuildings at a TV mast on top of Garleton Hills (181m) 2km north of the village. 38.

December 27 – Search for woman (36) at Kincardine oíNeil, Deeside. She was found dead by police before arrival of Braemar MRT and SARDA. 31.

SUMMIT

Perfection is unattainable but here

I can go some time without fear

Of self-betrayal. Here I can just 'be',

Enjoy the rare proximation of being the *me*

Of dreams, the *me* I haunt in the glass.

Such moments are rare; even a saint will pass

From glory hours to find the heavens brass.

Hamish M. Brown.

IN MEMORIAM

J. K. W. DUNN j. 1946

KENNETH DUNN, the eldest of four children, was educated at Fettes, where he received prizes in classics. In 1929 he joined the family law firm in Glasgow. He was a member of the Glasgow Highlanders in the Territorial Army, and during the War he rose to the rank of Major. Later, he settled with his first wife, Margaret, in Blanefield until a change of employment necessitated a move to East Linton.

He was intensely practical, servicing his own cars and personally enlarging his home to accommodate his family of five daughters. His career progressed, and eventually he became Solicitor for Scotland for the Inland Revenue. His professional skills were always available to the SMC, notably at the 1990 AGM when he lucidly explained the tax implications of the Club's relationship with the Scottish Mountaineering Trust.

He was the first Honorary Secretary of the Association of Scottish Climbing Clubs and the BMC. Scottish Committee, and he advised the SMC on *National Parks in Scotland* (SMC Journal 1947 and 1950).

He was a man of many talents, who enjoyed spirited, informed discussions on topics ranging from Ancient Greek history to mechanics; geology to poetry. Each time you spoke with him, you learned something, which was delivered in a considered and erudite fashion.

For the last 20 years, he and Ishbel, his second wife, lived happily in Perthshire, where he died on November 29, 2001. Ishbel worked tirelessly to care for him, and due to her, Kenneth was able to stay in his own home, and pass away peacefully there.

I met Kenneth Dunn when he presided at the first JMCS post-war New Year Meet (1945-46) at Kingshouse. Twelve JMCS members stayed at Kingshouse (I was one of three from Edinburgh). At the meet Bill Murray was elected Honorary President; Douglas Scot, Honorary Vice-President, and Bill Mackenzie became President.

Murray, Dunn, and Scott climbed the Crowberry Ridge (four hours). The Edinburgh trio also climbed the Crowberry Ridge, though by a different route (10 hours). The Journal records that under Dunn's Chairmanship both AGM and four-course dinner were outstandingly successful.

In October 1946, Dunn was elected to the SMC, proposed by Kenneth Hunter and Bill Mackenzie. His application begins with: "Most of the rock climbs on the Cobbler, usually leading." But surprisingly, he dated none of his long list of entries. Typical entries were: "Crowberry Ridge Direct (10 times)," "Crowberry Gully (3 times in winter)".

Bill Murray, who was Dunn's Best Man, recorded that in March 1936 he traversed the Aonach Eagach ridge "with J. K. W. Dunn, A. M. MacAlpine, and R. S. Higgins", and MacAlpine confirms the date. Dunn was one of the most active members of the JMCS Glasgow section during the years immediately preceding the War; e.g, Murray alone recorded 43 climbs with Dunn from March 1936 to December 1939 – an average of once a month – including classic climbs like the first ascent of Clachaig Gully. MacAlpine and Mackenzie were their most frequent companions. In January 1939, at Inverarnan with Mackenzie and Dunn, Murray feared it "likely that we should miss a weekend's climbing for the first time in 18 months".

After the War, Dunn and Mackenzie – like most returning pre-war climbers – had to rebuild their careers and family lives. Unlike them, Murray made a career change and needed a climbing companion while he worked on his guide to Glencoe. This gave me the good fortune to climb with Murray and Dunn in the famous winter of 1947 – perhaps the last time these two friends climbed together. I also accompanied Dunn in Skye in connection with work on the Skye guide. Murray recounted that in 1946 he "assisted Kenneth Dunn in taking some youthful Glasgow gangsters on to the Glencoe and Arrochar hills."

Having been abroad for many years, I can say little about Kenneth Dunn's climbing in later days, other than that in 1949 he attended the Alpine Club meet at Meiringen with MacKellar and MacAlpine. Among other ascents they climbed the Finsteraarhom – involving a 16-hour day. Each summer he took his daughters to Derry Lodge where, with varying degrees of enthusiasm, they explored the hills and glens.

I have often thought that Kenneth Dunn played the part of Dr. Watson to Bill Murray's Holmes. In his writings, Bill Murray brings his companions to life, but his portrait of Kenneth Dunn is the most complete of all. Here are some of Bill's 'brush strokes':

"… Dunn's broad shoulders … his fair hair tumbled over his eyes … Dunn grinned gleefully from ear to ear …"

"… we discovered that once again Dunn had forgotten his boots. Dunn is one of the most hopelessly casual but yet friendly of men. You cannot damn and blast a man whose eye is sparkling with delight at meeting you. His infectious smile and naive geniality".

"From long and painful experience we knew that for calling upon Dunn at any agreed hour of the morning we must devote the better part of an hour to hounding him out of bed and to getting him dressed, fed, and properly turned out complete with climbing boots. The boots were important. They were sometimes apt to be left behind in the mad scramble of departure – irate friends clamouring in his bedroom. Mackenzie was equal to this difficulty. 'We'll tell him that the starting hour's three. He should just be ready when we call an hour later'.

"And so it was done. On arriving at his rooms at 4 a.m. we found Dunn actually out of bed and halfway through breakfast. There was something truly great in the audacity with which he at once accused us of lateness."

"One of the best second men in Scotland … I was coached over the traverse in brilliant style by Dunn, who employed the effective, though inhuman, device of ruthlessly skewering his victim with the spike of an axe … Dunn was obliged to stand for half-an-hour under a waterfall, whose volume increases with the years. But with such men as these failure can generally be made to show profits."

"Dunn was safe and solid as rock itself … [Marskell] maintained a Dunn-like immovability."

"Dunn's exceptional strength … Dunn was too skilful a mountaineer to climb anyhow but gracefully … a triumph of mind over matter."

"Dunn's presence on the [Rannoch wall, as he climbed with studied ease above remote scree, appeared an incredible flouting of natural laws."

"Dunn, whose company is more pleasing than a first ascent."

Kenneth Dunn's name was the first to come into Bill Murray's mind when he wrote the last paragraph of the book he drafted in POW camp: "When I looked to the mountains of the future from behind barbed wire, I thought not only of ends but of the best ways of striving … Bloodshed was forgotten awhile; once again I revelled in wholesome days, when the very air I breathed, in the company of Dunn, Mackenzie, and MacAlpine, of Bell and Donaldson, was that of rollicking adventure; when our mountaineering dreams were turbulent and our hearts high … there lies the true joy of battle, in exhilarating contest with the elements, upon mountains that may be won, yet never conquered; shared by companions who may be defeated, yet whose spirit I have never seen shaken."

Kenneth Dunn is survived by his wife, Ishbel, three daughters, seven grandchildren and nine great grandchildren.

Donald McIntyre.

CHARLES LOGAN DONALDSON j. 1950

CHARLIE died on February 25 aged. I met up with him on the JMCS bus meets in the late 1940s. From that meeting we spent nearly every weekend for the next three years somewhere on the hills.

Neither of us was a brilliant rock climber but we managed most of the classic climbs in Glen Coe and on Ben Nevis, with the Cobbler and Narnain thrown in. Two winter climbs on Nevis are remembered, Gardyloo Gully and Naismith's 15-minute route on the North East Buttress, which took us some three hours to complete, and the descent of the ridge in the dark. We had two trips to France, where we managed a few snow climbs, including the Aiguille de Polset and La Grande Casse, plus some ridge traverses on fine rock. We also went to Austria but had foul weather and only traversed one ridge in rain and sleet.

Charlie moved to Banff after this, and the weekend pattern was broken. My last time on the hill with him was a weekend in June in the Sixties. It was a brilliant evening and we decided it would be a waste sleeping, so we traversed the Aonach Eagach – east to west.

Charlie got married in Banff and contact was lost until he moved to Galashiels. Latterly, our only contact was the odd phone call and exchange of Christmas cards.

Many memories of great days on the hill with Charlie.

Jimmy Russell.

As the other constituent indicates above, the Donaldson/Russell pair was an almost unavoidable accompaniment to the Edinburgh JMCS bus meets of the late 1940s and 1950s. Their partnership epitomised the post-war resurgence of popular Scottish climbing from Edinburgh. These bus meets resembled those of the various Glasgow based clubs but had their own ambience, best reproduced in a Letter to this *Journal* in 1961 (xxvii, 154-6).

I quote a few sentences simply to put Charlie (and our current selves) into perspective, in the times he possibly loved best and which proved the forcing ground of so many later SMC climbing achievements and, more importantly, club friendships. In true epic style it begins by describing the heroes waiting for the bus, *sitting on the kerb at Waterloo Place, rucksacks , axes and boots on the pavement and maybe a couple of groundsheets hung up where Cairns was changing his breeks and old* Daily Mirrors *lying about with pieces of Wally's piece in them...* Then it salutes each as they climb on to the bus . . . *including Russell, tightly packaged though the other half Donaldson wouldn't get on till his own house; he lived on the Monadhliath side of Saughtonhall and never seemed to be there anyway until it was too late, probably because he was sideways on and not easily seen; these two had a famous tent, the Slum, Slum I, it was eaten into and out of again by various animals in hard winters but served these two until well before they stopped climbing . . . Marshall was there, a wee laddie and polite; Haig, Hood, Rodgie, Scott, Millar, Tait, Bulbous and more, sundry musicians on mouthorgans, combs, jugs and alimentary tracts . . . and when all those were emptied on to a stricken landscape together they drained into the night at once, like swill down a gutter.*

As the two-dimensional structure hinted at above suggested, Charlie at that time was tall, thin and multijointed, with a gingerish moustache and pale blue eyes that could roll in satisfaction, sparkle from enthusiasm or protrude alarmingly with conviction. A keen analytical brain which harboured no illusions about – but a great understanding – humanity (he was in the Civil Service, dispensing – or dispensing with – Benefits) enabled him to hold passionate argument, laced with ingenious humour, up the longest plod; or keep his hapless companions awake during an implacable game of chess in some Alpine hut before a 3am start . . .

He was good, kind company and much missed when he left Edinburgh. I shared many adventures with him. I think it was 1947 when I saw a curiously-attired rabble on the lower snows of Cruach Adrain – gas capes (surely the most infuriating garb for steep snow, let alone a narrow gully), ropes of dubious tenuity, goggles of military opacity . . . proto-Donaldson *et al.* Thus they were introduced to the JMCS.

Subsequently he was, like myself, on the hills virtually every weekend, but two occasions with him stand out. On the first, Charlie, though determinedly anti-poetic, was moved – like all romantics caught unawares – to ecstatic gibbering on Sgairneach Mor in 1951 as the summit snowfields rippled about us, in knee-high rainbow surgings of blown drift under a low sun; we waded our own ice-halos, Charlie particularly emblematic. The second was the first ascent of the *Upper Couloir Keyhole* on Stob Gabhar in March 1952 (SMCJ xxv, 98 and 164), involving a high wall, iced chimney and "100ft. of almost pure ice" to a series of jammed boulders and a final stretch of hard snow, after which we ignored an easy rock ridge and finished from the Upper Couloir itself. This route was "more interesting and difficult than the Upper Couloir"; we had descended that the week before. Charlie led throughout, a delight to watch. He also led Hood, Maclennan and myself most of the time on expeditions from Zinal in 1952, prehensile on ice and rock. Almost my last memory of him was at a wedding up Glen Shee in 1957. While others still feasted in the shack serving as a banqueting hall Charlie (not quite recovered from the previous night's celebrations with *individual* bottles of *Queen George* whisky), cigarette clamped in teeth, polished black shoes muddied, blue suit sodden, eyes glassily fixed ahead, was halfway up a neighbouring boulder on imaginary holds, a gentle drizzledampening his few locks. Great days indeed with Charlie.

G.J.F.D.

KENNETH M. ANDREW j 1972

KEN ANDREW was brought up in Monkton and educated at Ayr Academy. When I first knew him he worked for the National Coal Board but soon after gave this up and as he was already an experienced hill man and a competent photographer doing all his own black and white processing, he decided to try his hand at free-lance writing and photography. However, progress along this line proved slow and difficult and after a few years he changed direction to undertake teacher training at Craigie College in Ayr while continuing with his writing and photography. He graduated from Craigie in 1972. After a short time at Dreghorn School, he transferred to Braehead School in Ayr where he taught until his early retiral in the mid nineties.

I first met Ken at a Club lecture at Rowans in Buchanan Street in 1961, both of us having recently joined the Glasgow JMCS. Soon after, we had our first trip together to the hills to do the round of Ben More and Stobinian and its tops, just the first of many outings over some forty years to all parts of Scotland from the Solway Firth to the north coast. Ken was most active during the 1960's before he took up teaching. He completed the Munros in October 1962 (on a dreadful day on Beinn Chalum) and then later, in 1969, he completed in the same year the Munro tops, the Corbetts and the Donalds. He later completed the Donalds for a second time becoming I believe the first to do so. He also took in the English and Welsh three thousanders.

Ken fortunately enjoyed long walks usually on his own. He did many of the classic cross-country routes such as Dalnacardoch - Kingussie by the Gaick, Blair Atholl - Aviemore, Dalwhinnie - Corrour, the Corrieyarrick and of course the West Highland and Southern Upland Ways as well as the unusual marathon of the round of Loch Morar in a day. On these outings he would make full use of buses and trains using as his base for sleeping and eating the Morris Traveller he had for many years. Ken was never an enthusiastic rock-climber but could climb to V Diff standard and as he would be out on the hills throughout the year, was fully competent on snow and ice.

Club members would know Ken best for his writing and his photography. He co-authored the first edition of the guide to the Southern Uplands with Alan Thrippleton in 1972 and was the sole author of the second edition in 1992. He wrote the first guide to the Southern Upland Way for the Countryside Commission in 1984 and published Discovering Ayrshire with Dr John Strawhorn in 1988. A co-authored book on Old Ayr was published in 2001 after Ken's death.

Ken's photographs illustrated not only his own books but many others such as several of the Trust publications including The Munros along with Classic Walks, Wild Walks, etc. In addition, his illustrated articles appeared in many publications including the Scottish Field, the old Scotland's Magazine, the National Geographic and particularly, the *Scots Magazine*. His articles covered not only the hills and mountains but a great variety of outdoor subjects such as bridges, canals, old railways, Ailsa Craig etc and quite recently the new Tiso 'Outdoor Experience' in Glasgow. His pictures were also to be seen on calendars, post-cards, on Caledonian Macbrayne brochures and of course in newspapers such as *The Herald* and *The Scotsman* as well as the local Ayrshire press including in the early days, action pictures taken at Ayr United home games at Somerset Park.

Ken was a popular lecturer to clubs and groups particularly in Ayrshire and the south-west for his knowledge of this area of Galloway was encyclopaedic. He had a huge collection of slides of superb quality with his filing system enabling him to find any slide within minutes and he spoke on all variety of subjects. He was a great supporter of the paddle steamer 'Waverley' and assisted with its publicity. He was able to be seen on board on its trips around the Clyde and on the Ailsa Craig cruise he would give commentary to the passengers over the loud-speaker system.

Ken's concern for the environment was demonstrated in the 1970's when over several years he was closely involved with the group opposing the suggested dumping of nuclear waste on Mullwharchar in the Galloway Hills. The mere possibility of this appalled him and he spoke in his usual forceful way at the Public Enquiry at Ayr in 1977 which ended successfully for the opposition with the whole concept being abandoned.

My last outing with Ken was in November 1998, a walk up Moorbroch Hill, a wee Donald behind Cairnsmore of Fleet. He seemed as fit as ever. Though a small man, he could cover the ground at an amazing rate and was possessed of immense stamina. However shortly after this he began to decline, his last outing being to Tinto in the year 2000. He continued writing and lecturing until shortly before his death in July 2001. Later that year, a small group of his friends gathered to scatter his ashes on the Merrick, which he had climbed 128 times, just to the south east of the summit looking across to Loch Evoch and Mullwharchar.

W. D. Nicol.

GODEFROY PERROUX (1957-2002)

The ice climbing world was stunned when news broke of the death of French guide Godefroy Perroux in January. He was climbing an icefall near the Bionnassay Glacier not far above his home in Les Houches near Chamonix, when it collapsed. He fell with several hundred tons of ice and died instantly. It was particularly shocking that Godefroy, the 'Father of French icefall climbing' as he was often called, could have had such a serious accident doing what he loved and knew so well.

His loss was felt deeply in Scotland. Although Godefroy was not an SMC member, he was well known to members of the Club. Every season for the past 20 years he spent two weeks staying at the CIC Hut on Ben Nevis guiding clients, and his warm open manner, Gallic charm and clear love of Scottish winter climbing, had earned him a special place in the hearts of many Scottish climbers.

On his first visit to the mountain, he climbed Observatory Ridge in terrible weather. He later described the experience in the Journal and wrote: "We had underestimated this mountain and its 1344m. This first experience showed us that Scotland is more than training. With the long approach march, bad weather and difficult descents, Scottish climbing is really taxing."

Rather than putting him off, the challenging nature of the Scottish winter added an extra element to Godefroy's climbing that he did not often find elsewhere.

In the early 1990s, at a time when few world-class overseas climbers had visited Scotland, his perspective was invaluable. He looked at the Ben through a fresh set of eyes and added 15 new routes and several important variations. In particular, he focused on steep ice pitches, and routes such as the Upper Cascade (V,5) and

Le Panthere Rose (VI,6) on Raeburn's Wall are typical Perroux routes – bold and steep. To my mind however, Godefroy's finest addition to the mountain was Gremlins (VI,6), the vertical ice smear to the right of Thompson's Route on No. 3 Gully Buttress. This compelling line rarely forms and is likely to be a highly sought-after route for decades to come.

The finest tribute he paid to Scotland however, was writing a French language selected guidebook to Ben Nevis. Beautifully illustrated with a superb series of photographs, it reads like a diary of Godefroy's 100 or so ascents on the mountain. It was published just before his death and will undoubtedly encourage many more Continental climbers to visit Scotland.

High on Ben Nevis, Godefroy's spirit will live on for many years to come.

Simon Richardson.

J. RUSSELL MARSHALL j. 1945

RUSSELL MARSHALL was one of our oldest members when he died last year at the age of 91. He trained as a quantity surveyor in Glasgow, entered the building industry and, later in life, took over a building business in Largs and settled there with his sister, Betty.

He took up climbing in his twenties, became an active member of the Glasgow JMCS and by the time he joined the SMC in 1945 had done a good number of what are now known as the classic routes, both winter and summer, as well as some climbs in North Wales. He attended the Alpine Meet in Kleine Scheidegg in 1948 and the JMCS meet in Val d'Isere in 1950. He was a regular attender at SMC meets and dinners for the rest of his life and made his contribution to running the Club as custodian of the CIC Hut from 1948 until 1952.

Russell was very deaf in later life but, although it was a severe handicap, he never allowed it to keep him away from the hills or stop him from enjoying the social side of mountaineering. I counted it a privilege to be his regular chauffeur to Easter meets and dinners and to enjoy his never failing good humour on these occasions.

He was also a member of the Scottish Rights of Way Society and the Largs Stravaigers. He took part in the Stravaigers' meets almost to the end of his life and several of the Stravaigers gave him tremendous help and support in his final years.

Bryan Fleming.

Notice has also reached us of the death of Oliver Turnbull.

PROCEEDINGS OF THE CLUB

The following new members were admitted and welcomed to the Club in the year 2001-2002.

Robert Aitken (53), Research Consultant, Edinburgh.
Richard J. Bale, (30), Royal Air Force, Burghead, Morayshire.
Peter J. Biggar, (52), Open University Tutor, North Kessock, Inverness.
Michael F. Boyle, (44), General Practitioner, Linlithgow.
Hannah Burrows-Smith, (27), Outdoor Instructor, Feshiebridge, Kingussie.
George Denholm, (41), Police Office, Balerno, Midlothian.
Thomas Denholm, (47), Police Officer, Port Seton.
Robert W. Durran, (38), Teacher, Kinross, Fife.
Steven A. Elliot, (31), General Practitioner, Perth.
Rosie Goolden, (33), Freelance Instructor, Aviemore.
Richard Harrison, (37), Computer Consultant, Dringhouses, York.
Steven Hazlett, (43), Welder, Clydebank.
Ross Hewitt, (26), Mechanical Engineer, Aberdeen.
William Hood, (45), Teacher, Houston, Renfrewshire.
Brian Hume, (36), Reprographics Operator, Dundee.
Terence E. Kenny, (54), Medical Practitioner, Bickerstaffe, Lancashire.
Bruce Kerr, (40), Teacher, Edinburgh.
Andrew J. Lole, (24), Software Developer, Didsbury, Manchester.
Fergus S. J. McCallum, (35), Rope-Access Technician, Taynuilt, Argyll.
John R. McCallum, (54), Marine Engineer, Dunblane, Perthshire.
David MacLeod, (23), Student, Bearsden, Glasgow.
Heather Morning, (37), Bunkhouse Manager, Pitlochry.
Mark Shaw, (36), Salmon Farmer, Oban.
Christopher J. Upson, (38), Consultant Engineer, Glasgow.
Euan I. Whittaker, (24), Outdoor Instructor, Edinburgh.
Peter Wilson, (51), Chartered Engineer, Invergowrie, Dundee.

Easter Meet – Elphin

LAST year the Meet, which was to be held at Elphin, was cancelled due to the Foot and Mouth restrictions. In its place an informal meet was arranged by Robin Campbell at Altguish Inn where restrictions were less limiting. Robin Campbell, Dick Allen, Brian Fleming, Malcolm Slesser, Iain Smart, Oliver Turnbull, and Bill Wallace attended the meet.

In 1996, when Oliver Turnbull took on the role of Meets Secretary (this is possibly the first Easter Meet he has missed in more than 20 years) it was noted that the numbers attending increased and the weather improved. This year, on the way north under cloudless skies the forecast was for poor weather. This early promise of low cloud and showers was replaced by hazy almost dry days. There was very little snow and the ground was dry. The conditions improved every day and as usual the best day was the last – when we left for home.

The meet was well attended; the party being split between Tom Strang's and the Naismith hut. Tom was able to serve dinner on Saturday night for the whole group – a very pleasant evening. One of the notable achievements was Douglas and Audrey Scott's ascent of Stac Pollaidh. The President Ken Crocket and Peter Macdonald climbed Acheninver Pinnacle. Malcolm Slesser and Bill Wallace followed their example the next day.

Hills ascended included: Stac Pollaidh, Suilven, Cul Mor, Cul Beag, Sgurr an Fhidhleir, Conival, Ben More Assynt, Ben Klibreck, Quinag and Canisp.

Those present included the President Ken Crocket, Robin Campbell, Brian Fleming, Malcolm Slesser, Iain Smart, Bill Wallace, Dick Allen, Mike Fleming, John Gillespie, Phil Gribbon, John Hay, Peter MacDonald, Peter Madden, Douglas Scott and Nigel Suess. The guests were Ian Cumming, Richard Madden and Audrey Scott. It is suggested that the Easter Meet in 2003 will be at Loch Maree. When we hope to be able to repeat the crossing to Letterewe.

Dick Allen.

The One-Hundreth-and-Twelfth AGM and Dinner

HAVING agreed that we really should go somewhere else in 2001, the Club's annual function limped meekly a mile up Fort William's North Road to the Milton, not perhaps the grandest of hostelries, but certainly more spacious in all respects than our old friend in The Parade.

It was so good to have the afternoon pictures in comfortable surroundings and being adjacent to the bar was just sublime. Rob Milne spoke on his new-routing trip to Karstenz Pyramid in Irianjaya and Chris Ravey reviewed the latest Club outing to the Staunings. One hopes that the clink of glasses will become a regular feature.

The AGM was, by recent standards, an entertaining affair with some rousing debates on the issues of the day. The Treasurer was closely questioned on his new presentation of the accounts and the long-awaited discussion on the future of the windmill on the Ben following the two-year trial melted like the snows of winter with many of the original objectors acknowledging that the only people who seemed bothered by the thing were members of the Club itself.

The usual discussion on the best vehicle for publication of new routes was again inconclusive but then we got on to the real issue. Should the recorders of new routes be permitted to award the stars? Arguments waxed and waned. Speakers rose and fell. One member malevolently suggested asterisks for new routes in the Journal to be replaced by stars in the guides only once a full quality assessment had taken place – and a lot of members agreed. It was all tremendous stuff and put the company in good humour as they headed off to dine – walking past a large display of champagne cocktails provided by the hotel for their consumption without their knowledge.

In the dining room, the Dinner Secretary, as you would expect of a civil engineer, had devised a seating plan so cunning that not only could you be guaranteed to sit with your friends but you could also shun your enemies on request. And there was more. Clever table positioning meant that even those at adjacent tables were guaranteed to be acceptable to you. Somewhat predictably however, this was all beyond the comprehension and skills of the hotel and only some desperate last-minute furniture shifting by himself achieved the approximate aim.

Your Secretary also had his moments. Having purchased the traditional dram for the piper, he was dismayed to discover that the incumbent was approximately half the legal age. But the meal when it came was excellent. The Campbell/Wallace combo struggled manfully with the Club song while Jim Curran was a jovial and entertaining principal guest. This year, let's forget Fort William. Re-set George and head for Pitlochry on November 30.

J. R. R. Fowler.

Ski-mountaineerng Meet 2002

The lack of snow cover prevented the intended ski traverse from Cairngorm to Mar Lodge via Ben Macdui on the afternoon of Friday 15. Instead Jones and MacDonald drove over to Royal Deeside and ventured into the corrie of Lochnagar. The forecast was poor and so was the weather. The increasing north-easterly wind finally forced a retreat from the exposed second pitch of central buttress leaving the final outcome of the day as a very nice walk!

Gratefully retiring to 'The Base camp' they found a few SMC members and guests already in residence in the tastefully renovated stable block of Mar Lodge near Braemar. The quality of the accommodation was excellent and the remaining members and guests arrived as the evening progressed.

Next day Jones and MacDonald once again ventured into the corrie of Lochnagar, this time in the company of Bill Shaw. The weather was little better than the day before. After dire warnings from the avalanche forecast team digging a snow pit in the area and an audible avalanche coming down the Black Spout, they contoured the corrie, and the avalanche debris, finally reaching the summit via the north-east arête. Blizzard conditions on top dictated a descent down the Glas Allt, which might have allowed a pleasant ski descent, if they had elected to take their skis. However, the final outcome of the day was a very nice walk!

Angel, Ballance, Bickerdike, Forbes, Shackleton and Walmsley went skiing up Carn a'Gheoidh enjoying a cloudy day out and returning via the Glenshee ski slopes. Back at Mar Lodge, which is now open to the fee-paying public, a quick tour of the renovated building and furnishings was a fine end to the day. Equally impressive but far more disturbing is the ballroom which has a ceiling covered with red deer skulls and antlers. There can be few darker spectacles than this necrophilic shrine to such efficient slaughter and death.

A typical evening of culinary/victual delights and a review of recent SMC alpine ski mountaineering by slide show followed.

Sunday dawned bright and after a quick pilgrimage to pay homage to an ancient Scots Pine in the area we forced a mass ascent of Carn an Tuirc leaving the skis in the wagon. Despite, or perhaps because of, the warm windy day, we all enjoyed a very nice walk!

Members present: I. Angel, D. Ballance, J. Bickerdike, W. Forbes, C. Jones, A. MacDonald, C. Ravey, B. Shackleton and J. M. Taylor. Guests: S. Angell, W. Shaw and N. Walmsley.

C. M. Jones.

JMCS REPORTS

London Section: The section has had a strange year. We started with our usual round of drunken parties at Glanafon, a President's Meet at the same venue, and from then on the whole thing went seriously downhill, which is what we prefer anyway, going downhill that is. A meet was held in Glencoe, ill-attended because the weather forecast was bad and it's a long way from the South for a wet and windy weekend – and then it got worse.

Our week-long Winter Meet for the geriatrics was called off at 36 hours' notice because of Foot and Mouth and nasty rumours on the Net and so Jock's Spot had to do without us. The Lakes was shut, and although we could go to our cottage in

North Wales – since it is readily accessed from the main road – it was impossible to do anything but look at the hills, which in late winter/early spring were in great condition, and out of bounds. The youth chafed and went abroad, the elderly reminisced about the last out-break in the 1960s and spent their energies on good works at Glanafon, which now sports a new roof on the rear extension, newly-painted external walls and, after almost 40 years, a drying room. So good does come out of bad, sometimes.

There was a splendid meet at Black Rock in June, enlivened by the presence of two ladies from the LSCC who probably brought a little sanity to the normal proceedings. After that it was the Alps, and further, and details are sparse. Hard routes were done in the Ecrins and ex-President Jordan went to Nepal, again. This is one of the problems of a Section without a central meeting place. Midweek meets for chat are impossible and we must depend on our somewhat erratic circular. Steps have now been taken to produce this vital organ at least every two months and this seems to be happening. It is our intent to send the circular out by e-mail so if anyone outwith the London Section would like to participate please let us know. Our website will shortly be up and seriously running, and we shall post meets lists and circulars on it.

Our annual works meet fitted the normal biennial pattern. Either lots of people turn up, the weather is good, and most of them go on the hill – or, the weather is bad, few arrive, and they all get fed up and go to the pub. In either case little gets done because October is a silly month for fixing the hut. This will change. And so without a deal of effort we are back to the AGM, held once again at the Giler Arms. It was conducted in indecent haste and all over in 20 minutes. This has caused some comment so next year we must make an effort to allow the audience to speak! After an excellent dinner Andy Walker conducted an auction of mountaineering books donated by Ted Zenthon, one of our founding members, with such panache and enthusiasm that he persuaded more than £750 out of a group of members who are not known for parting with their hard-earned cash – thank you Andy. The hut fund flourishes as a result. A new year awaits – we trust it is better.

Web site – www.jmcs.freewire.co.uk

Officials elected: President, Roy Hibbert; Vice-President, Marcus Harvey; Secretary and Membership, Chris Bashforth; Treasurer, David Hughes, 9 St Anthony's Road, Leeds LS11 8DP; Hut Custodian, Rod Kleckham.

Glasgow section:– The club has continued with another active and successful year considering the many weeks curtailed by the outbreak of Foot and Mouth disease. We currently have 105 members of which 11 are female. There are 28 Life Members.

Club activity centred round weekend meets, weekly climbing wall visits and fortnightly pub meets. There were 17 outdoor meets, seven less than the previous year. Meets in the second half of the year to Elphin, Speyside, Rum, Braemar and Glencoe were very well attended; as was the AGM and Annual Dinner in the Kingshouse, Glencoe.

The JMCS meeting for the whole club took place on May 5. It was quorate with representatives from Lochaber, Glasgow and Perth. The overall feeling was that the traditions of the JMCS should not be lost even if it does not have any present day function. The consensus was to avoid the organising of an AGM and replace it with an open meet to be set up in 2002 by the Glasgow Section. However, it was later discovered that according to the constitution, an AGM must still take place. One hopes that the end result of this debate is fresh incentive to participate in one joint meet every year.

Foreign trips included an Easter trip by Colwyn Jones, Ann MacDonald, Donald Ballance and John Bickerdike who were ski-mountaineering in the Pennine Alps in Switzerland. They climbed the Allalinhorn, Strahlhorn, Breithorn, Castor and Pollux. The onset of bad weather kept them from adding to their total. Colwyn Jones also led an expedition to the Staunings Alps in East Greenland where they climbed five new peaks and made a second ascent of Sussex. (For full reports see SMC/JMCS Abroad).

Spain tempted David MacDonald, Neil Marshall, Ann MacDonald and Colwyn Jones for some warm and dry rock-climbing.

Tim Pettifer, David Lawson and John Goldie were part of an expedition to Spitsbergen climbing five peaks in four separate areas of mainland Svalbard. Skiing was the main means of ascent although some stretches involved axe and crampon work.

At home the main notable climbing achievement was Donald and Colwyn's ascent of the Old Man of Hoy in less than ideal conditions. Despite a wet summer and a warm winter, many members have been active, climbing regularly in areas throughout Scotland.

Our club hut in Coruisk, Skye continues to be a popular destination and more so in the winter now that we have a new stove for heating. Structural changes and insulation within the hut have also added to the overall amenity.

Office elected: President, Dave Eaton; Vice-President, Alex Haddow; Honorary Vice-President, David Lawson; Honorary President, Andrew Sommerville; Treasurer,Andrew Sommerville; Secretary, Vicky Stewart; Meets Secretary, David Lawson; Coruisk Hut Bookings, Alan Dunn; Coruisk Hut Custodian, Alex Haddow.

Perth Mountaineering Club, (JMCS), Perth Section):– The Club continued to have a diverse active and social schedule in 2000/20001. The membership increased during the year, breaking the 100 barrier when Elaine Cameron joined on February 3.

There were 16 weekend meets during the year and seven day meets. With no meets planned south of the Border, the effects of the Foot and Mouth crisis were not too severe. However, a planned day meet to Balquidder in March was substituted with a local bike ride, and a weekend meet in April was relocated from Glen Trool in Galloway to Roy Bridge.

A good turnout of 19 enjoyed a weekend of fabulous winter weather in Glen Coe for the Blackrock Cottage meet. A full range of winter activities took place including a very sociable Burns Supper back at the cottage.

The year's good winter weather was enjoyed by many although heavy snow did lead to a day meet to Creag Meagaidh being cancelled, or at least reconvened in Birnam. The New Year's Day walk to Ben Vrackie was also affected by snow which kept the meet convener at home digging his car out and had two other members skid off the road *en route* – fortunately without injury.

The CIC meet was held later than usual in early April, but climbing conditions were good. Alex Runciman and guest completed Slav Route – Alex's 70th route on the mountain.

In a rare reversal of fortune, an August meet at the Glen Brittle Hut enjoyed good weather while the rest of Scotland suffered torrential rain. The Cuillin was eerily quiet and several members climbed the Inaccessible Pinnacle for the first time.

Wednesday evenings have continued to offer climbing opportunities – at Hadrian's Wall at Falkirk over the winter months and at various local crags over the summer.

In July, the Club held its inaugural family meet, based in Onich. Deemed a success, this is likely to become a regular fixture.

In September, Grahame Nicoll completed his Corbetts and later in the same month Rachel Tilling climbed her final Munro.

The Annual Dinner was held at the Moulin Hotel in Pitlochry in November.

Officials elected: President, Des Bassett; Vice-president, Phil Taylor; Secretary, Sue Adams – Seven Acres Cottage, Methven, Perth PH1 3SU. Tel: 01738 840980; Treasurer, Tom Rix; Newsletter Editor, Des Bassett; Meets Convener, Alan Bailey. Committee: Carolann Petrie, Mike Aldridge, Pam Dutton, Dave Prentice and Peter Hemmings.

Lochaber Section:– The section enjoyed a promising start to 2001 with a well-attended meet to Dundonell and with the mountains covered in snow and some settled weather, the section was looking forward to a decent winter season. Unfortunately, the grim spectre of Foot and Mouth made an appearance and like the rest of the country, the section's activities were drastically curtailed. Thankfully, the mountaineering fraternity in general acted responsibly and respected the landowners wishes to refrain from going to the hills and so by May, most areas around Lochaber and farther afield had the restrictions lifted.

During the summer months several members travelled to various climbing venues both home and abroad, and latterly, meets were held in Glen Clova, Braemar, and Elphin, which were all successful and well attended.

In November, the annual dinner was held at the Tomich Hotel near Cannich, where nearly 40 members and guests enjoyed an excellent weekend. This was the section's third visit to Tomich and once again the hospitality was excellent.

In 2002, in conjunction with the 'International Year of the Mountains', the section is helping out with the preparation for a visit to Scotland by a group of Iranian mountaineers. The visit is due to take place in late summer and a reciprocal trip is being organised soon after.

Steall Cottage in Glen Nevis continues to be the main source of income for the section and 2001 brought an increase in bookings compared to recent years.

Officials elected were: *President,* Sam MacPherson; *Vice-President,* George Archibald: *Treasurer,* George Bruce: *Secretary,* Kenny Foggo, 4 Parkan Dubh, Inverlochy, Fort William, PH33 6NH. Tel: 01397 706299. *Hut Custodian,* John Mathieson, 43 Drumfada Terrace, Corpach, Fort William, PH33 7JN. Tel: 01397 772599 *Honorary Members –* D. Scott and H. MacInnes.

Kenny Foggo.

SMC AND JMCS ABROAD

Europe

SMC/JMCS members Donald Ballance, John Bickerdike, Colwyn Jones and Ann MacDonald, assembled at a bustling Glasgow Airport on Saturday, April 7, 2001 for a flight to Geneva via the then popular airline hub, Brussels.

The Sabena flight was delayed and the subsequent train trip around Lake Geneva and up the Rhone Valley deposited us in Visp close to midnight. The guest house was a short walk from the station and we finally raised the old matron from her bed to open the door.

We enjoyed a comfortable night followed by a short bus trip up the Saastal to Saas Grund. The Hohsaas ski lifts soon got us up to 3098m where the heavy snowfall had closed some slopes owing to the avalanche risk. Consulting the local pisteurs produced little useful information, but we discovered that despite the piste being closed, it had been pisted. Therefore, we soon carved our way down to the Weissmeishutte and having earlier collected a key, we were soon established in the winterrahm. The snow continued overnight and the tentative party skinning up the Triftgletscher early next morning in thick mist found the going slow and worrying and therefore turned back at 3420m.

Lunch back at the hut resulted in a decision to abandon the peak, descend to the valley floor and ascend, via the lift system and the short traverse to the Britanniahutte. This excellent hut was the base for the next two days. The first day saw an attempt on the Alphubel via the Feegetscher which was again abandoned because of deep snow and deteriorating visibility. By now the Saastal was becoming increasing unpopular and in the pre-dawn of the next morning, using the eerie glow from LED headtorches, we followed quietly in the tracks of 14 aspirant guides up the Allalingletscher. By now we had no delusions about our fitness and acclimatisation but were surprised to catch up with the big team ahead at 3630m. We creamed on ahead with 'Big Donald' leading the charge to the top of the Adlerpass. I must report we were overtaken before reaching the Col but we felt we had 'done our bit' and reached the summit of the Strahlhorn in short order behind the local professional team. Our first summit in good weather with excellent views as far as Mont Blanc and the Gran Paridiso.

The local team warned us that the descent to the Adlergletscher was steep and set off the way they had come, carving perfect 'esses' back down to the Britanniahutte. Our descent was initially steep and deep, but we enjoyed a superb ski down to the Findelgletscher, then on to Zermatt. The dependable Hotel Bahnhof had been booked, supposedly, but was out of rooms when we got there. We made do with the last dortoir accommodation and after a resplendent meal spent another comfortable night.

The queue to get up the Klein Matterhorn next morning was a severe test of patience and sanity. Later, we skied up the Breithorn and shared a near-death experience with a paraglider on the summit. However, third time lucky he finally launched himself up into the clear blue sky leaving the envious earthbound to gaze after him. The Ayas Hut on the Italian side of the ridge had just opened for the season and passing a huge serac fall *en route* we arrived late afternoon to enjoy the relaxed ambience of an Italian hut. The ambience was excellent but the hut had only been dug out by the warden from the winter snows on his arrival that morning. Damp blankets and the defrosting process made for an uncomfortable night and it was with relief that we got up for frustock at 5am. Later that morning we ascended the South West route on Pollux and Castor was later climbed by the West face. Time waits for no man, and we decided to attempt the sheer Zwillingsjoch to get down to the Monte Rosa hut. One member skied, three went on foot and two fell into the bergschrund. One got out unassisted, the other had to be quickly but efficiently rescued. Just another typical day on a JMCS trip! After the 'fun' on the Zwillingsjoch the ski track across the crevassed Grenzgletscher was clearly crazy, but had to be done. Sitting in the sun we enjoyed the sunset and took the chance to dry off various bits of kit. Next minute a helicopter flew in delivering supplies so gloves, skins and other extraneous bits of clothing spun off down the glacier.

Frustock at 4.30am next morning saw a mass migration from the hut south to the summits of Nordend and Dufourspitze. We were close to the back of the pack on leaving the hut but soon scalped the rest of the summiteers and by late morning were in front. Shortly afterwards at 4480m, the wind was so strong it was impossible to stand and we reluctantly turned back to find, nothing, everyone else had already deserted the cause. Who could blame them. Just another typical day on a JMCS trip.

Back down at the hut we found the forecast uninspiring and next day, in worsening weather we skied down the long flat, but enjoyable, Gornergletscher. Easter weekend is no time to be in Zermatt so we caught the train back to Saas Grund as the snow continued to fall. The next day was spent piste skiing above Saas Fee in perfect spring powder as the avalanche risk had closed most of the off-piste areas.

On the final day we skinned up the Allalinhorn then skied the 2200m from the summit back to Saas Fee in perfect spring powder snow under an azure sky in bright sunshine. A fine way to end the trip – superb.

SIMON RICHARDSON reports: I made two visits to the Alps last year. In January the Groupe de Haute Montagne invited me to sit on the jury of the Piolet d'Or, an annual award given to the best mountaineering achievement in the world the previous year. The award is presented at the International Ice Climbing meet at Argentiere le Bessee in the Ecrins. The six short-listed nominations included British climbers Jules Cartwright and Ian Parnell's new route on the North Buttress of Mount Hunter in Alaska, and Valeri Babanov's solo first ascent of the North Face of Kangtega in Nepal. The Golden Ice Axe (yes there really is one!) was awarded to Thomas Huber and Iwan Wolf for their ascent of Shiva's Line, the vertical north prow of Shivling in the Indian Himalaya. Although the Hunter ascent was thought to be a finer technical achievement (the judges were impressed when I explained what Scottish Grade VII mixed climbing involved), Huber and Wolf scooped the prize because they went to the summit. In an era when technical difficulty is king, it was heartening to see the award decided on traditional values.

The weather had been poor for ice climbing throughout the meet, but a sharp frost on the last night brought the higher crags into condition. I teamed up with US climber Christian Beckwith for a couple of routes at Cerviere. Christian led me up Aux Lames Citoyenes (WI5), a free-hanging ice pillar, and then it was my turn. I was keen to try a mixed route, but the bolt-protected M-routes looked too contrived. Instead I left a Scottish calling card with the first ascent of a steep thinly-iced chimney left of the established climbs.

The second visit was two weeks in July with Dore Green. Conditions were snowy on the high peaks, so we drove around searching for good conditions. This resulted in ascents of the Younggrat (D) on the Breithorn, the South Pillar of the Barre des Ecrins (TD) and the West Pillar Direct of the Scheidegg Wetterhorn (ED1). The last route, which dominates the head of the Grindelwald valley, gave a particularly fine adventure up a steep 1000m. pillar of mountain limestone, with a long and difficult glacial descent to give it some alpine spice.

JOHN HIGHAM reports: In the last two weeks of July and first week of August, my son Richard, my wife Alison and I joined the LSCC meet in Saas Grund. As we arrived a couple of days ahead of the main party and the sun was shining Richard, Alison and I had an enjoyable training day climbing the Fletschhorn (NW Ridge PD). As we finished, and the rest of the party started arriving including Jon Hutchison and Chris Gilmore (both SMC), the rain and snow fell and I began to have nightmares that this was going to be a repeat of 2000. That year's holiday had started with a week of some of the worst weather I had seen in the Alps and ruined long-laid plans. This time was not as bad although a planned ascent soon after of the Grand Cornier with Chris and Richard degenerated into a deep snow slog terminated on the conveniently nearer and lower peak the Bouquetins as exhaustion took its toll. The weather stabilised soon after and Richard, Alison and I accompanied by Chris and Eve Gilmore and probably a hundred other people made an ascent of the Weismeiss via the SW ridge (PD) on a bitterly cold but crystal clear day.

High pressure had now settled itself over the Alps and I was keen to take as much advantage of it as possible and Richard and I started the campaign with a traverse of the Nordend and Dufourspitz via the North Flank (AD). Instead of being rock the latter was still plastered with snow and ice from the recent storms and provided an exciting ascent at about Scottish IV, it also meant no crowds. Chris had been unable to join us because of a persistent knee problem but joined us when Richard and I decided to do the Northern Nadelgrat (AD), Kate Ross and Mary Lothian of the LSCC made up a second team on the day. We traversed the Nadelgrat from the north starting at the Durrenhorn and gaining the ridge via the Durrenjoch couloir, a long day followed with no technical problems but considerable exposure and commitment.

As the two weeks of the LSCC meet came to an end, lots of peaks had been done and people began to slowly go home or move to a different area. Jon and Chris decided that it was time for some hot-rocking and headed for Locarno where they reported excellent rock and plenty of sun. Richard had time for one more route before he had to return separately to the UK so we headed for the Weisshorn a mountain I had wanted to do for a long time. I had tried it in the debacle of 2000 tempted during a short spell of good weather but turned back in the face of deep snow. The conditions were much better this time although there was more snow on the East ridge (AD) than normal and Richard and I had an uneventful and fast ascent but with no views as the cloud rolled in at midday.

The end of the holiday was fast approaching but the weather was still just holding and we had time for one more route before returning home and decided to move across to Chamonix for this. Alison had had enough of the big mountains and went for a tour while I teamed up with Kate Ross to tackle the Jardin Ridge (D-) and continued to the Aiguille Verte over the Grand Rocheuse. A very early start ensured it was still dark when we reached the bergschrund and we stumbled around for quite a while looking for a way up the seemingly impassable wall of ice. We found the narrowest point and in the absence of any ice tools soon cut our way up the ice (some dim memories of the Sixties returned) and continued quickly up the gully above. A difficult chimney, loose and overhanging, led us onto the ridge proper. The ridge although narrow and intimidating was not too difficult and provided exciting positions on icy rock or corniced snow arêtes. We made good time to the Verte but the weather had deteriorated through the day and as the wind picked up we decided it was time to make our way down the Whymper couloir. The descent was slow and frightening as the abseiling on one rope took forever and occasional massive rockfalls down the opposite side of the couloir showed us this was not the best place to be in this warm weather. Unfortunately, the light ran out just above the seracs that run across the base of the couloir and we could not find a way through, as it stayed warm a relatively comfortable night was spent on some rocks at the edge of the couloir. Some free abseils over the seracs the next morning saw us safely down to join the others and to head back home.

Scottish Mountaineering Club East Greenland Expedition 2001

This expedition consisted of three SMC members, Colwyn Jones (Leader and Medical Officer), Chris Ravey and Brian Shackleton, plus three Lake District climbers, Jim Fairey, Colin Read and Nick Walmsley. They went to the Staunings Alps in the North-east Greenland National Park from 22nd July to 17th August 2001.

Scheduled flights from Glasgow to Keflavik, transferring to Reykjavik and onward to Akureyri in a Fokker 50 later the same day, were used to get to the North Coast of Iceland. At 09.30 on July 23 they flew in a small, chartered turboprop (Fairchild Metroliner 23) from Akureyri to Mestersvig, a gravel airstrip in Greenland (1hr. 55min. flight).

Later that afternoon after sorting gear and taking refuge from the mosquitoes, two members were flown by helicopter (Bell Jet Ranger) to base camp. However, as the helicopter pilot had exceeded his daily flying quota, the other four had to wait until next morning (July 24) for the final leg of the approach from Mestersvig to basecamp on the Great Cumbrae glacier (71° 57' 15.8" North 25 07' 04" West) This glacier had previously been explored and named on the 1998 SMC Greenland expedition.

The expedition objectives were a first ascent of the unclimbed South Face of Sussex (an impressive wall of golden granite), and first ascents of other peaks in the area.

The first morning was spent at base camp preparing the site, avalanche transceiver practice, rifle practice and familiarisation with the first aid kit and radio gear. Later, they all reconnoitred the South Face of Sussex confirming it was a huge wall with a problematic bergschrund.

On the 25th they explored the Great Cumbrae glacier on skis. Read and Jones tested the first pitch of a huge spur of granite provisionally entitled the Wa*ker Spur and found excellent quality rock. Next day on July 26 all six members made

Kenneth Dunn.

Charlie Donaldson.

a lemming-like first ascent of Keswicktinde by the north-west ridge. The route was graded AD and followed a Grade 2 couloir up to a col where a long exposed snow ridge led to the summit block. The barometric altitude recorded was 2430m.

After a rest day Read and Shackleton made the second recorded ascent of Sussex (2390m) on July 28 via a new route on the south-east face. It was 650m long and graded D and was used to look at a possible descent route if the south face was attempted. Sharing a couloir approach Ravey and Walmsley attempted a new route on the north-east ridge of the adjacent Sydney (2300m) and got to within a frustrating 60m of the summit, but reached an impasse of dangerous snow.

Fairey and Jones decided to attempt the huge ridge which dominated the south-east end of the glacier basin. This was the south-west spur of the western outlier of Sefstromsgipfel. The route was started at 0830 and they climbed continuously through the day and thankfully, mild night taking 28 hours to reach the summit. The route was 555m. long and graded ED with more than two-thirds of the route being Grade 6 rock-climbing and two of the 25 pitches requiring simple aid. Retreat was by multiple abseils into a long gully on the eastern flank of the spur, which took a further eight hours. As Fairey and Jones had been out of contact with base camp for more than 36 hours the other four team members had come out to look for them. While descending the gully, and in full view of the others, Fairey was caught when the deep 20cm granular surface layer avalanched and he was swept 300m down the gully and 20m into the bergschrund at the foot of the gully. The four at the foot of the gully started an immediate crevasse rescue and he was quickly hoisted out completely unhurt. Checks for a head injury during the following 24 hours revealed no (new) abnormalities.

The ridge, of excellent granite, was named the Jones-Fairey Spur (2570m) and the descent gully named Jim's Gully. Mild frostbite in one team member attributed to wearing only rock boots while climbing through the night was diagnosed.

Mild conditions between July 28 and August 8 had made snow slopes and couloirs unreliable and the avalanche may have heightened awareness of this objective danger! A number of ski tours were made up neighbouring glaciers, some previously unexplored, confirming the enormous climbing potential of the area.

By August 3 most rock ledges were now clear of snow and attention focused on the South Face of Sussex. The team first took the opportunity to ferry equipment to the foot of the face but by noon on the 4th mist had begun to form around the summits and in the afternoon there was a light snowfall. The following day was sunny and clear so an attempt was made on the intimidating face. After negotiating the awkward bergschrund, the technical difficulties were harder than expected and the team retreated after three short, hard-won pitches. They were estimated to be UK technical grade 5b/c and required a lot of cleaning. It was clear that this big wall would require big-wall tactics due to the difficulty of the climbing and the absence of water to drink on the face.

On August 6-7, Fairey and Jones attempted to climb Emmanuel by the unclimbed west ridge. After 12 pitches with technical climbing up to ED and A2, but less than halfway up the ridge, they reached a steep wall which barred their way. Early in the morning they retreated by abseil into an adjacent couloir which they then wisely pitched in descent.

Further days were spent ski touring and on August 10 Ravey, Read, Shackleton

Ken Andrew.
Russell Marshall.

and Walmsley made the first ascent of the southwest ridge of Mears Fjeld (2100m) graded PD. They first attempted an adjacent peak to Mears Fjeld but failed to achieve the summit due to dangerously unstable rock. Fairey and Jones made the first ascent of the delightful 200m south-west ridge of the pint sized Pap of Cumbrae (1885m) graded AD, a shapely minor peak at the junction of the Little Cumbrae and Cantebrae glaciers.

The following day a ski tour down on to the Sefstroms glacier proved to be very wet with deep melt streams impeding progress.

Over August 13/14, Fairey and Jones snatched the first ascent of Tandlaegetinde (tooth doctors or dentists peak) by the south face. The recorded barometric altitude was 2350m, the route took 13 hours to climb, was 500m long and graded TD. Descent took a further seven hours and was by multiple abseil back down the excellent granite face using every spare piece of tat.

August 15 was the scheduled day to return with a spare night in Mestersvig before flying out the following day. However, the weather on the 15th was poor with low cloud. The helicopter had attempted to reach base camp but been turned back by a snowstorm. The group packed for departure leaving the tents standing which was just as well as they would have to spend one more night on the glacier.

The following morning saw clear weather and the rude intrusion of the 20th century. The helicopter arrived early and flew them back to Mestersvig in two loads of three climbers, gear and all rubbish.

From Mestersvig they flew south late in the evening over the Staunings Alps giving magnificent views in the evening sun. Flying direct to Reykjavik they spent a very short night in a local hotel before leaving early for Keflavik on August 16 arriving in Glasgow by mid-morning at the end of a very successful trip.

The weather was excellent and stable during the expedition. With 23 days on the glacier, there were two days when there was light snowfall (less than a centimetre) and five other cloudy days when they went skiing. Because of the 24-hour daylight, only shadow and a clear sky ensured that snow softened by the sun would freeze to give safe conditions in couloirs and on snow slopes. The minimum recorded temperature was –8°C, but there were several occasions when no overnight freeze took place resulting in the snowpack remaining soft. A number of avalanches were observed in south and east-facing couloirs and a major powder avalanche was triggered by a serac collapse on a north-facing slope. This was in marked contrast to observations during the May 1998 expedition when there was minimum avalanche activity until a heavy snowfall at the end.

Daylight (and the need for sunglasses) was continuous throughout allowing uninterrupted climbing and obviating the need to carry bivouac gear. The Arctic sunrises and sunsets were stunning, especially when seen from a summit. The first sunset at 72°N is on the August 8.

The expedition wishes to acknowledge the financial support of the Mountaineering Council of Scotland; the Mount Everest Foundation; the Scott Polar Institute, and the technical support of Needlesports of Keswick.

REVIEWS

Dougal Haston: The Philosophy of Risk:– Jeff Connor (Canongate Books 2002, £16.99, ISBN 1-84195-215).

I met Dougal Haston on a good number of occasions, in huts, in pubs and on the hills; I climbed with him on two or three routes, always with Robin Smith – I didn't like him. He was arrogant, self-obsessed and ill-mannered. But I was in awe of him, the archetypal hard man with a hundred mile stare as though Herman Buhl had been cloned in Currie. A day spent bouldering with him and Robin on Salisbury Crags put paid to any illusions I had about my ability. I was definitely second rank beside these two. But, whereas Robin showed interest in me, encouraged me and later got in touch to climb, to Dougal, I didn't really exist. He wasn't nasty, he just didn't register my presence. And apart from a chosen few, that seems, from the evidence of Jeff Connor's interesting biography, to be how he went through his life.

Some man, but what a mountaineer! From his first rock climb in Glencoe in 1954 to his fatal ski run in Leysin in 1977, Haston immersed himself in the sport and turned it within himself into a way of life of extraordinary intensity and accomplishment. The title of Connor's book is apposite. An early devotee of Buhl – "Nanga Parbat Pilgrimage . . . was like a Bible to him" – Haston found in the risks of mountaineering a reason for living, but not one feels, for joy. When you place Haston alongside his contemporaries, Marshall, Patey, Smith, Stenhouse, Brooker, Nicol and MacInnes, for example, what set him apart was his aggressive single-minded approach, fuelled perhaps by his dabblings in Nietzche. It wasn't just the Germanic influence – the Aberdeen group managed largely to sublimate that in good humour – it was his conviction that he was indeed 'ubermensch'.

One of the fascinating areas of Connor's book comes through his access to the diaries that Haston kept throughout his life, every entry of which is signed off with "Thus spake DH". Some of the entries are chilling. Here is Haston after the Eiger ascent and Harlin's death: "I am becoming more complete. A great hardness is setting in, and I am becoming increasingly able to treat the petty and mundane with utter contempt. I have a few friends in the true sense of the word, but no one will complete this path with me . . . One as an individual must think of self – I do not mean that one must hurt others – but the ones who get hurt are usually the purveyors of the petty . . . I will do many things for people I respect, and for fools nothing. They deserve to be trampled on."

Connor has been thorough in his gathering of the evidence of the life. He draws on many personal reminiscences, from Moriarty and Marshall on the earlier years, from Joy Heron his early girlfriend, and from many companions on expeditions – he creates a rich picture. None of them pull any punches and the picture which emerges is not flattering when it deals with his emotional and social life. However, towards the end of his life, Haston began to show traces of a maturity. Recognition as one of the top mountaineers of his generation following Everest, a Currie lad being piped into the Usher Hall, seemed to be bringing him at last a sense of peace. Maude Tiso recalls a visit shortly before his death and a changed Haston which she partly attributes to the influence of Ariane Giobellina his partner. She tells Connor: "He stopped seeming to be such a driven, troubled person, and you were able to actually enjoy his company." Perhaps his death robbed us of a more likeable Haston as well as one of the most accomplished mountaineers of the century.

Connor has done a good job, though the book provides few answers to the question of why Haston developed the introverted cold personality that most knew. An index would have made revisiting the book easier and there is the odd inaccuracy which leaps out. He has Haston and Stenhouse battling their way up North East Buttress of the Buachaille, "finishing in a howling blizzard and then narrowly missing being avalanched out of NC Gully on Stob Coire nan Lochan on the way back down to Lagangarbh". *The Philosophy of Risk* is not the last word on the Haston enigma – the quality of the writing doesn't approach Robin Campbell's obituary in the 1976 Journal – but it's a very readable start.

Robin Shaw.

A Passage to Himalaya:– Edited by Harish Kapadia. (Oxford University Press/ Himalayan Club, 2001. ISBN 01-95657-74-8)

The Himalayan Club celebrated the advent of the Third Millennium by assembling and publishing a collection of the best of the articles that have appeared in its journal during the 72 years of its existence. The editor of the current journal has collated pieces reflecting the wide spectrum of interests of its members, from high mountain climbing to exploration, geography and sociology.

A brief look down the list of contributors reveals the breadth of Himalayan experience reflected here, from Kenneth Mason and Francis Younghusband through Bill Murray and Wilfred Noyce to Voytek Kurtyka and Stephen Venables. The editor should be forgiven for starting this volume with a self-indulgent section on the founding of the club itself and the course of its history. The beautifully literate, but slightly archaic, prose of the Indian contributors is striking and already the book reeks of the sub-continent and its turbulent history. The founders possessed the strong military traditions of the imperial service and their successors appear to have retained the same penchant for the martial, having obtained a foreword from the current chief of the army staff and quoted Hemmingway on the frontispiece: "The world is a fine place and worth fighting for."

There are pieces here which will really only interest those intricately acquainted with the remoter valleys of the Garhwal and Kumaun but they are liberally supplemented by well-known accounts of major expeditions by international authors. Among the classics are Diemburger's last days with Buhl, Noyce with Whillans on Trivor, and Saunders's witty recounting of Venables's epic on Panch Chuli V.

Vivid glimpses of personalities come through in some of the book reviews and among the obituaries. Tilman's piece on Shipton reveals more about the author than his subject: "It would need a readier pen than mine and someone with more discernment to assess his character." All those bivouacs must have been very silent.

One of the finest articles is not by a mountaineer or about mountains. It is Maggie Body's account of cajoling and persuading the literary luminaries of the climbing world to deliver against publisher's deadlines. If you have ever fallen under the spell of the world's greatest mountain range and the people who live there but the 55 volumes of the HJ are a little too inaccessible, buy the abridged version and sample.

Rick Allen.

K2 One Woman's quest for the summit:– Heidi Howkins, (National Geographic Adventure Press, 2000.)

Not really a book about climbing, although this does provide the backdrop to an honest, personal account of being a woman and a mother in a boys' world of commercial Himalayan climbing expeditions.

The autobiography moves, through a long drive over America in a snowstorm, from domestic abuse in a failing marriage, to adultery, violence and then divorce. The backdrop moves from K2 to Gasherbrum, to Kanchenjunga to Everest and back again to K2 and it's elusive summit.

It expanded my knowledge of the techniques of modern expedition planning and the tensions caused by live media. I also learned more about the physiological changes that occur to the body at Himalayan altitude and the sheer hard work involved in merely surviving at such extremes. The fragility of life and ease of death at high altitude hit home at several points in the book where survival is seen as, "maintaining an acceptable level of risk".

I found the book very American in both phraseology and outlook. By quickly skipping over the few esoteric/spiritual experiences described, which weren't really my cup of tea, the book held my attention – it enabled a 10-hour flight delay when returning from holiday via Geneva airport to pass virtually unnoticed! I recommend reading it.

A book just of interest to women? I asked my partner to read it to get a male perspective – his view was: "A bit off the wall at times – produced for commercial reasons, but a good read."

Ann McDonald.

Touching My Father's Soul:– Jamling Tenzing Norgay (Ebury Press London, 2001, £16.99. ISBN 0712 605819).

The old saying goes: "Never judge a book by its cover," but the publishers are taking no chances with this one. Jamling Tenzing Norgay may not be a familiar name but dust-jacket endorsements from Reinhold Messner, Galen Rowell and David Breashears cannot fail to attract the curious browser.

Inside, His Holiness, the Dalai Lama contributes a foreword with a reminder that the author is no mere Sherpa. Subtitled: "In the Footsteps of Sherpa Tenzing," this is more than just the moving story of the insecure son of a famous father taking the opportunity to emulate his success.

When the producers of the IMAX film documentary of an Everest climb had the bright idea of including Sherpa Tenzing's son in their multinational team of stars, no one had an inkling of the dramatic events that were to unfold on the mountain in the spring of 1996, except possibly lama Chatral Rimpoche. Before Jamling's wife, a devout Buddhist, would agree to support the project, she insisted on a divination from a reputable lama. Although the omens did not look good, he went anyway, with a few sacred relics, a protective amulet and a few well-chosen mantras.

The tragedy that ensued attracted almost as much interest and attention as Tenzing and Hillary's first ascent in 1953. Jon Krakauer, a journalist whose climbing skills saw him safely down from the summit on that fateful day, went on to write the definitive best-selling account *Into Thin Air* (reviewed in SMCJ 189). He now contributes an introduction and notes that this is the 17th book on the subject. After so many years and so many words in print, can there be anything more to add? The climb, of course, forms the central theme of the book, but what makes it particularly interesting is the complex character of the author. Jon Krakauer reminds us how little most people actually know about the Sherpas or indeed any of the indigenous Himalayan people who have played a vital role in helping us Westerners to explore, climb and appreciate these magnificent mountains. Thanks to his father's success, Jamling received a Western education, including some years at an American college. With a foot on each side of the cultural divide he is in a unique position to explain the Sherpa perspective, which is clearly very different on many issues. The book has a strong spiritual content, with the author describing how his own personal doubts and dilemmas concerning his Buddhist faith were finally dispelled by the tragic events on the mountain.

Enterprising and versatile, the Sherpa people quickly grasped the opportunities offered by visiting mountaineers. Such work has always been dangerous, and with disaster and death seldom far away, it is not surprising that they put great faith in routines and rituals which might be dismissed as primitive superstition. However, as the story unfolds, we come to marvel at the prospect of Kathmandu's Boudhanath Stupa illuminated by 25,000 butter lamps, to respect Miyolangsangma, the Everest goddess, and learn of an old prophesy that a Himalayan Buddhist would be the first person to climb the mountain. Immediately after the tragedy of May 10 there was time for reflection by the survivors, and difficult decisions for the IMAX team who had not yet made their summit attempt. Jamling describes his own thoughts and feelings and the satellite telephone discussions with his anxious wife, culminating in a more propitious divination from the family lama and finally success.

The other main thread of the story concerns Jamling's relationship with his famous father. Born 13 years after his historic ascent, the author clearly regrets the long absences from home that Tenzing's duties demanded and his own absence at the age of 20, studying in America, when his father died suddenly. The title page of the book acknowledges the help of co-writer Broughton Coburn who has made an excellent job of weaving a potted history of Everest into the story along with a lot of biographical information about Tenzing. Looking back almost 50 years, we can now appreciate that the challenges and difficulties he and Hillary overcame in climbing the mountain were in some ways easier to cope with than the pressures they faced on their return. It is a tribute to both men that they were able to handle their success so well, to the benefit of so many other people and not just themselves.

This book should appeal to a wide readership, even those with no background knowledge of mountaineering. Anyone with an interest in the 1996 tragedy in particular or Everest climbs in general will need no further encouragement and will appreciate the rare insight Jamling Tenzing Norgay gives into Sherpa culture and their unique way of life.

David Broadhead.

Killing Dragons:– Fergus Fleming. (Granta Publications 2000, 398 pp, 16 pages of black and white plates. £9.99, ISBN 1-86207-453-4).

During the 19th century, when Europeans were exploring every corner of the globe from the tropics to the poles, there was still a vast unexplored wilderness in the heart of Europe the 700-mile long chain of the Alps. This thesis forms the basis of Fergus Fleming's book, in which he chronicles the explorers who killed off the myth of dragons living among the high peaks. The chapters run through a roll call of the famous names of early alpinism – de Saussure, Paccard and Balmat, Agassiz, Forbes the Scottish geologist "whose topics ranged from the study of a single boulder in the Pentlands to the entire mountain chain of the Alps", and the big names of the Golden Age. Interestingly, Fleming spends nearly as much time on the great popularisers, who rarely climbed the peaks or even the high passes, but instead spent their considerable energies bringing the mountains into the consciousness of a vast public audience – Bourrit, Albert Smith the Victorian showman who invented the mountaineering lecture tour, John Ruskin, and later, of course, the travel entrepreneurs Thomas Cook and Lunn.

Fleming observes and analyses in a wealth of detail not only the activities of these explorers, but more importantly their motivations, their social circumstances, their idiosyncrasies, and most often it seem their acrimonious disputes with their contemporaries. Many of the individuals portrayed come across as driven, arrogant, abrasive and dogmatic.

The book is a well-researched social history which draws on both primary and secondary sources. It is no coincidence that the Golden Age followed directly on the opening of the railway system, permitting travel from London to Chamonix in 24 hours. Nor were many of the early pioneers gentlemen, in the strict sense of the word, rather they were principally middle-class professionals, or those who aspired to this social position and who enjoyed a six-week summer holiday. Many of the principal traits of Victorian culture – national duty, physical exercise, self improvement, spiritual reward – found a ready outlet in mountain exploration. The enduring fascination with the Matterhorn disaster is explained in terms of the Victorian penchant for melodrama, a damn good story involving "competition, betrayal, hardship, defeat at the moment of victory, and . . . the death of a nobleman". Apparently, it spawned a publishing phenomenon in a genre of 'cut-rope penny dreadfuls'. The enduring impact of this is quite remarkable. Fully 30 years after the event 50,000 people attended a lecture tour given by Whymper. One can't imagine anything like this scale of attendance for any of our contemporary figures.

The linear development of mountaineering is well documented, from scientific discovery, through the search for beauty and spiritual experience, to the pursuit of technical difficulty for its own sake. However, Fleming's approach strongly emphasizes the second of these stages, through references going back as far as Conrad Gesner in the 15th century, and through Turner, Ruskin, Wordsworth, Alfred Wills and many others. These references will provide a source of inspiration for any follower of Bill Murray. Although much of the well-known ground at least – Mont Blanc, the Golden Age, the Matterhorn – has been extensively covered by other authors, there is more than enough less well explored territory here, together with an often novel slant on the old favourites.

Adam Kassyk

The Flame of Adventure:– Simon Yates. (Jonathan Cape, 220pp, £16.99, ISBN 0-224-06045-7).

If the excerpts on the rear dust-jacket of *The Flame of Adventure* are accurate reflections of the actual reviews, Simon Yates's first book *Against the Wall* was quite well received. "A welcome antidote to a cliché-ridden genre", said one. Your reviewer was cheered, as he has read (and to be fair, repeated) enough clichés to last him a lifetime. "Elegiac, intensely readable", said another. Well, that has to be better than intensely unreadable. "It is the best account I have ever read of the process of emotions ebbing and flowing" (etc. etc.), said a third, though granted this by Geoff Birtles and therefore perhaps not to be confused with something to be taken too seriously. All in all, though, the omens were good.

Unfortunately, from the opening words of the first paragraph hope floundered, sinking along with Yates's ski poles into the wet Khan Tengri snow, in a rather uninspired account of climbing and falling in Kazakhstan. Expectations thus lowered, what follows is not without interest, but suffers from a somewhat stilted writing style that in trying hard to be interesting frequently jars and intrudes upon the reading experience. On the positive side, it is usually the introductory paragraphs of a chapter or section that suffer the most and the rest of the book reads easily enough, though it may be rather dry for some tastes.

The book describes how Yates, disillusioned or unable to cope with a more conventional lifestyle, became a full-time mountaineer, and his experiences, from a first alpine season that included the North-east Spur of Les Droites and the Walker Spur, to objectives farther afield. Since Yates does not attempt to hide what he (or his companions) did wrong as he served his high mountain apprenticeship, those willing to learn may find information on how to avoid repeating his mistakes, which is not actually something that can be said of too many mountaineering books. Should it be necessary, they will also be reminded of the risks. When he has forgotten most of the rest of the book, this reviewer will remember Yates's account of how a following Japanese party on the Croz Spur crossed that fine and invisible line between challenge and disaster.

The book contains revealing insights into some well-known names, such as Sean Smith, Mark Miller and, of course, Joe Simpson. There is also a rather touching failed love affair that echoes those of many other obsessive mountaineers and which sheds a little light on the character traits that have contributed to Yates's mountaineering success, but may have been of less help in trying to cope with everyday life.

Yates comes across as uncomplicated, without obvious malice and with a somewhat ingenuous approach to life. He seems rather likeable, not perhaps much inclined to deep thought about his motivations and not obviously suffering greatly from inner conflict. As such, he has much to be envied. However, while it may be unfair to compare him with Joe Simpson, nonetheless their history makes it almost inevitable. Though *The Flame of Adventure* is not without merit, on its evidence many people may consider that Simon Yates's greatest contribution to climbing literature was when he cut the rope on Siula Grande.

Bob Duncan.

The Book of The Bivvy:– Ronald Turnbull (Cicerone Press 2001. 139pp. £9 ISBN 1 85284 342 X).

This, the author tells us, is a book "about misery that's mixed in with pleasure, rather than taken straight: about self indulgence rather than mere survival" but, rightly, goes on to point out that modern bivibags also double as survival aids, it being a somewhat self-evident truism "that you can't have much of either fun or suffering if you died the previous winter".

Ronald Turnbull in this humorous pocket-size book deals with a subject which is obviously close to his heart, tracing the art of bivvying, from the improvised cloak, plaid or sheepskin of old through the very questionable advantages of the Tiso Orange Poly Bag, up to the five-star Gore-Tex wonders of the present day.

This is not simply a 'How To' book, although there is plenty of that, it also includes travel, geography, history, and much laughter, with a handful of philosophy and existential ponderings thrown in for good measure.

I suspect that the climbing/walking fraternity are fairly solidly divided on this issue in much the same way as the general population is on the delights or otherwise of gardening. This is a book for both, an insight for the agins and an introduction for the curious, as well as a wonderful overnight companion for the committed.

Charlie Orr.

The Way to the Cold Mountain – a Scottish mountaineering anthology:– Edited by Alex Finlay. Photographs by David Paterson. (Morning Star Publications, soft back Polygon, 2001, £7.99, 210pp, ISBN 0 7486 6288 X).

Except for its contents this is a little book. It consists of a series of prose contributions, some specially commissioned, interspersed with short poems and rather dramatic black and white photographs surprisingly effective in spite of the small format.

The contributions from about a dozen authors are all interesting with a trend towards the metaphysical. I particularly liked Andrew Greig's sympathetic account of sharing a last few drams of Glenmorangie with Norman McCaig.

Also Dutton's 'anthology within an anthology', a series of excerpts from what I would call the 'genuine' writers, chosen with Dutton's usual care and sensitivity for the genuine. Worth buying for that alone.

Iain Smart.

OFFICE BEARERS 2001-2002

Honorary President: W. D. Brooker

Honorary Vice-President: Douglas Scott

President: Kenneth V. Crocket

Vice-Presidents: R. Gordon Ross, S. M. Richardson

Honorary Secretary: John R. R. Fowler, 4 Doune Terrace, Edinburgh, EH3 6DY. **Honorary Treasurer:** John A. Wood, Spout Close, Millbeck, Underskiddaw, Keswick, Cumbria CA12 4PS. **Honorary Editor:** Charles J. Orr, 28 Chesters View, Bonnyrigg, Midlothian EH19 3PU. **Convener of the Publications Sub-Committee:** Douglas. C. Anderson, Hillfoot House, Hillfoot, Dollar, SK14 7PL. **Honorary Librarian:** Ian R. Angell, The Old Manse, 3 New Street, Largs, Ayrshire, KA30 9LL. **Honorary Custodian of Slides:** Graeme N. Hunter, Netheraird, Woodlands Road, Rosemount, Blairgowrie, Perthshire, PH10 6JX. **Convener of the Huts Sub-Committee:** William H. Duncan, Kirktoun, East End, Lochwinnoch, Renfrewshire, PA12 4ER. **Custodian of the CIC Hut:** Robin Clothier, 35 Broompark Drive, Newton Mearns, Glasgow G77 5DZ. **Custodian of Lagangarbh Hut:** Bernard M. Swan, Top Flat, 8G Swallow Road, Faifley, Clydebank, Dunbartonshire, G81 5BW. **Custodian of the Ling Hut:** William Skidmore, 1 Kirkton Drive, Lochcarron, Wester Ross, IV54 8UD. **Custodian of the Raeburn Hut:** Gerry Peet, 6 Roman Way, Dunblane, Perthshire, FK15 9DQ. **Custodian of the Naismith Hut:** William S. McKerrow, Scotsburn House, Drummond Road, Inverness, IV2 4NA. **Committee:** Chris M. Huntley; Colwyn M. Jones; David N. Macdonald; John F. Ashbridge; Jonathon A. Baird; Bernard M. Swan Rick Allen; Neil Marshall; Alastair P. Matthewson.

SMC Internet Address – http://www.smc.org.uk SMC e-mail: smc@smc.org.uk

Journal Information

Editor:	Charles J. Orr, 28 Chesters View, Bonnyrigg, Midlothian EH19 3PU. (e-mail: charliejorr@hotmail.com).
New Routes Editor:	A. D. Nisbet, 20 Craigie Avenue, Boat of Garten, Inverness-shire PH24 3BL. (e-mail: anisbe@globalnet.co.uk).
Editor of Photographs:	Niall Ritchie, 18 Meadowlands Drive, Westhill, Skene, Aberdeen AB32 6EJ. (e-mail: niallritchie@aol.com).
Advertisements:	D. G. Pyper, 3 Keir Circle, Westhill, Skene, Aberdeen AB32 6RE. (e-mail: derek@pyper.fsbusiness.co.uk).
Distribution:	D. F. Lang, Hillfoot Hey, 580 Perth Road, Dundee DD2 1PZ.

INSTRUCTIONS TO CONTRIBUTORS

Articles for the Journal should be submitted before the end of January for consideration for the following issue. Lengthy contributions are preferably typed, double-spaced, on one side only, and with ample margins (minimum 30mm). Articles may be accepted on floppy disk, IBM compatible (contact Editor beforehand), or by e-mail. The Editor welcomes material from both members and non-members, with priority being given to articles of Scottish Mountaineering content. Photographs are also welcome, and should be good quality colour slides. All textual material should be sent to the Editor, address and e-mail as above. Photographic material should be sent direct to the Editor of Photographs, address as above.

Copyright.Textual matter appearing in the Miscellaneous section of the Journal, including New Climbs, is copyright of the publishers. Copyright of articles in the main section of the Journal is retained by individual authors.

i

v

GO FOR A VIRTUAL WALK ON OUR MUNROS CD

WITH the SMC Munros CD you can: Record your real walks. Relive great days on the hills. Read about the history of hillwalking, avoid an avalanche, hear a stag roar. Plan tomorrow's trip and print out the route and map.

Strap yourself into the armchair and take a fast flight over the Bens and Glens. This updated CD maintains its position as the best on the market.

Available in all good shops, mail order (Tel. 01389 756994), or through our website – www.smc.org.uk/cdrom.htm

Minimum specs. (PC-only) are a P166, Win 95,98 or NT, 32Mb RAM, 20Mb hard disk space, 4-speed or better CD-ROM drive.

The best is yours for £40.

Howse Peak (3290m), Rockies, Alberta, Canada. Photo: Alan Kerr.

Doré Green at the second bivouac on the first ascent of South Pillar, Mount Tiedemann, Coast Range, British Columbia. Photo: Simon Richardson.